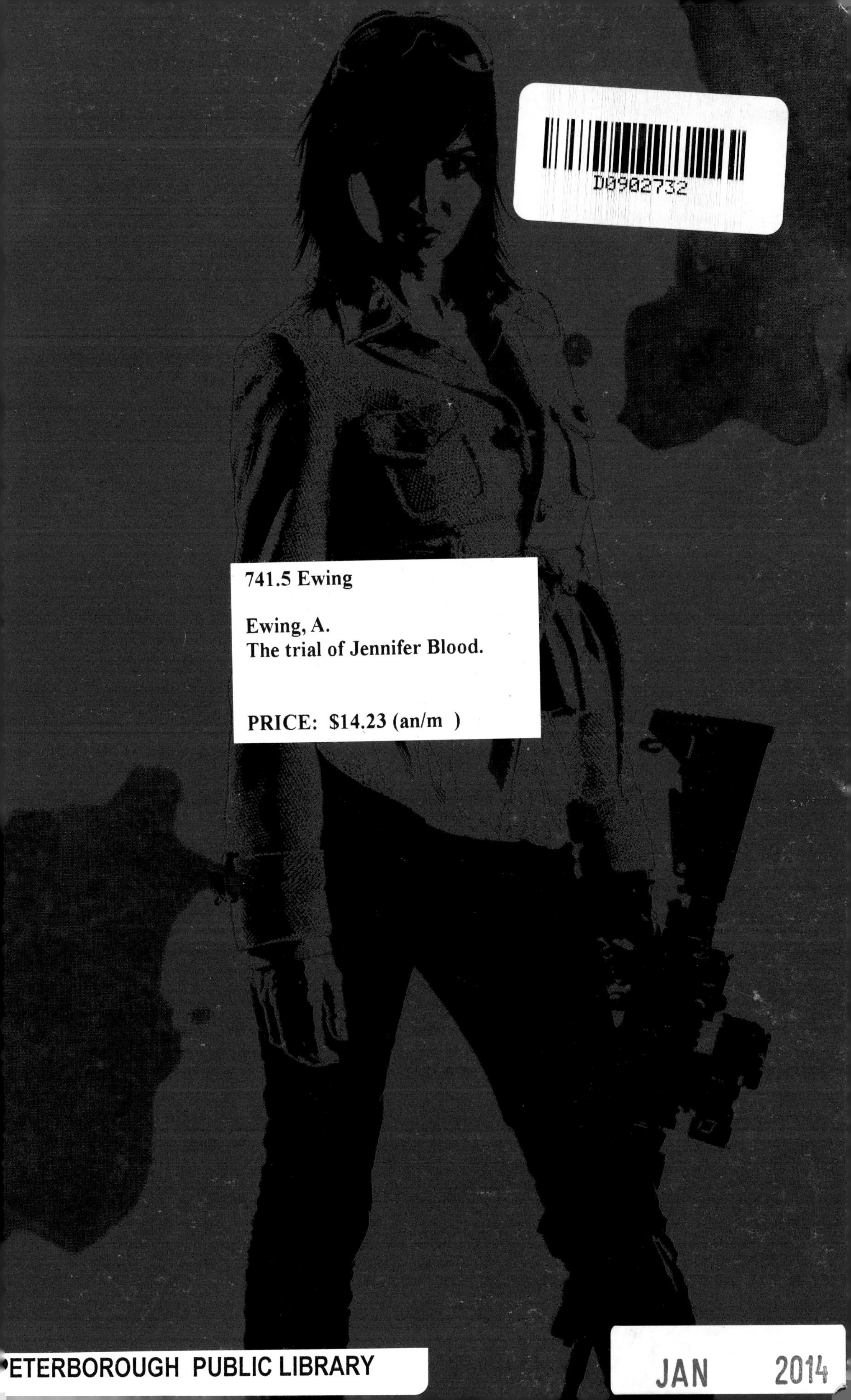

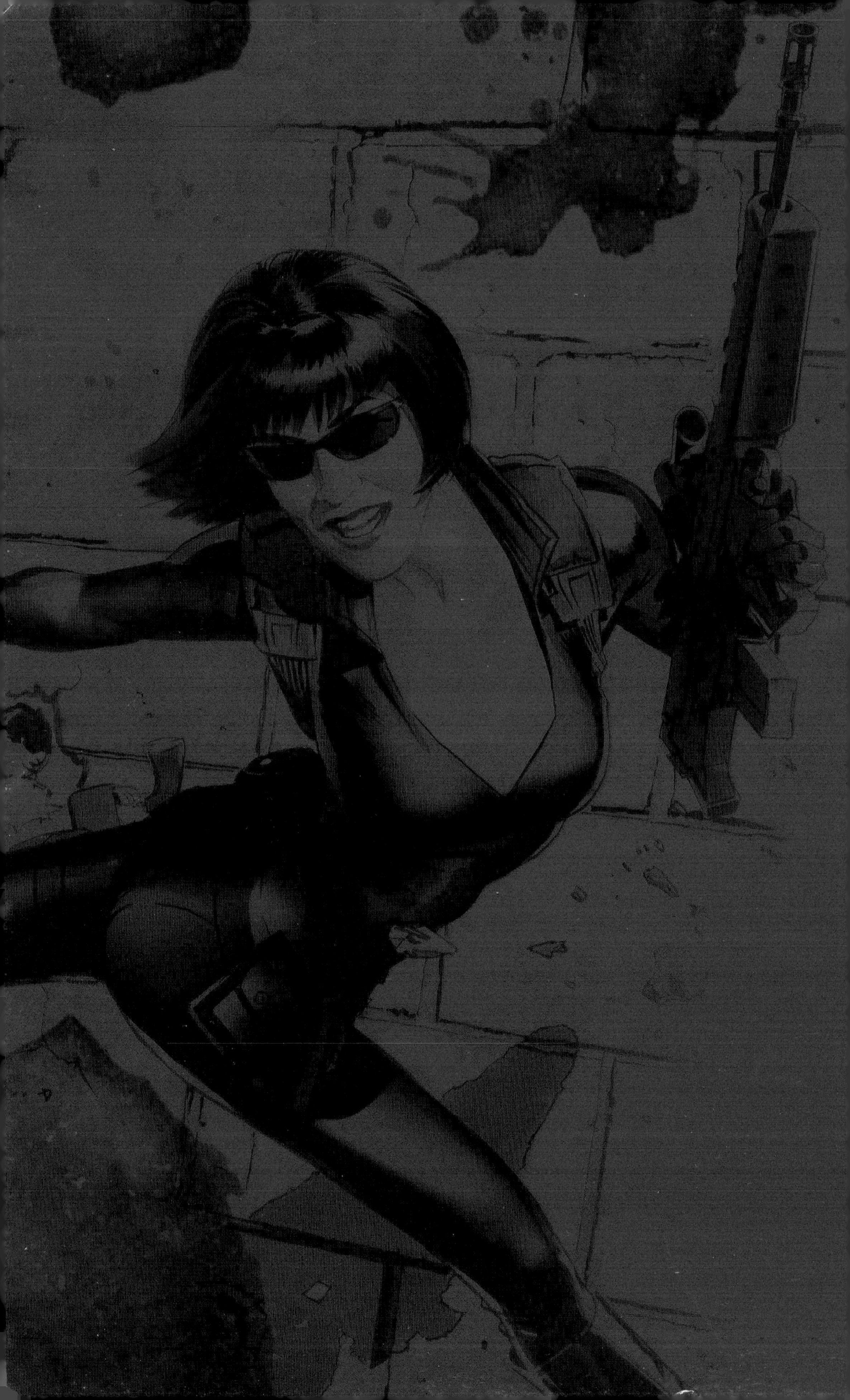

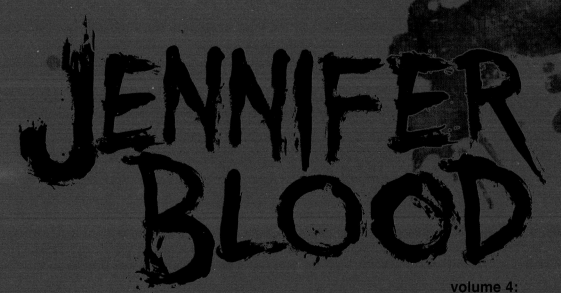

JENNIFER BLOOD

volume 4:

THE TRIAL OF JENNIFER BLOOD

written by
AL EWING

illustrated by
EMAN CASALLOS (issues 18, 20, 22, 24)
KEWBER BAAL (issues 19, 21, 23)

colored by
INLIGHT STUDIOS

lettered by
ROB STEEN

collection cover by
TIM BRADSTREET

collection design by
JASON ULLMEYER

This volume collects issues nineteen through twenty-four
of the Dynamite Entertainment series, Jennifer Blood.

DYNAMITE®

Nick Barrucci, CEO / Publisher
Juan Collado, President / COO
Rich Young, Director Business Development
Keith Davidsen, Marketing Manager

Joe Rybandt, Senior Editor
Josh Green, Traffic Coordinator
Molly Mahan, Assistant Editor

Josh Johnson, Art Director
Jason Ullmeyer, Senior Graphic Designer
Katie Hidalgo, Graphic Designer
Chris Caniano, Production Assistant

ISBN-10: 1-60690-455-8
ISBN-13: 978-1-60690-455-8
First Printing
10 9 8 7 6 5 4 3 2 1

 Visit us online at **www.DYNAMITE.com**
Follow us on Twitter @dynamitecomics
Like us on Facebook /Dynamitecomics
Watch us on YouTube /Dynamitecomics

PREVIOUSLY IN
JENNIFER BLOOD:

In 1987, Sam Blute, head of the Blute crime family, was murdered by his five brothers. His wife Jennifer committed suicide, leaving behind their only daughter Jesse.

It's 2011. Jesse – now calling herself Jen Fellows – went on a calculated, rational and extremely bloody campaign of revenge against her five uncles, as the vigilante Jennifer Blood. Over the course of a week, she killed them all one by one, finally avenging her parents' deaths.

The second week was spent cleaning up some of the fallout from the first. Some of the people she'd killed had families of their own, who naturally wanted revenge against her. More deaths were required. Gradually, things got bloodier. Less calculated. But still very rational.

According to Jen.

Even when Jen decided to burn her husband Andrew's ex-lover to death, it all seemed rational.

Perfectly rational.

So, when Andrew found out, Jen had a perfectly rational choice to make. Andrew wasn't being rational. Andrew was threatening to involve the police. Which would have meant Jen losing her children.

So Andrew had to go.

Except the police were already involved, in the shape of the decidedly non-rational Detective Pruitt, driven by the ghosts of the dead and the god of her visions to bring the Jennifer Blood Killer to justice. In the process, she revealed Jen's secrets to the world, blowing her cover as an ordinary housewife for good.

In the face of that, Jennifer Blood made the supremely rational decision to kidnap her children and go on the run, with Detective Pruitt and a trio of unbalanced hitwomen calling themselves the Ninjettes – more of that revenge from week two – following after her.

And here we are.

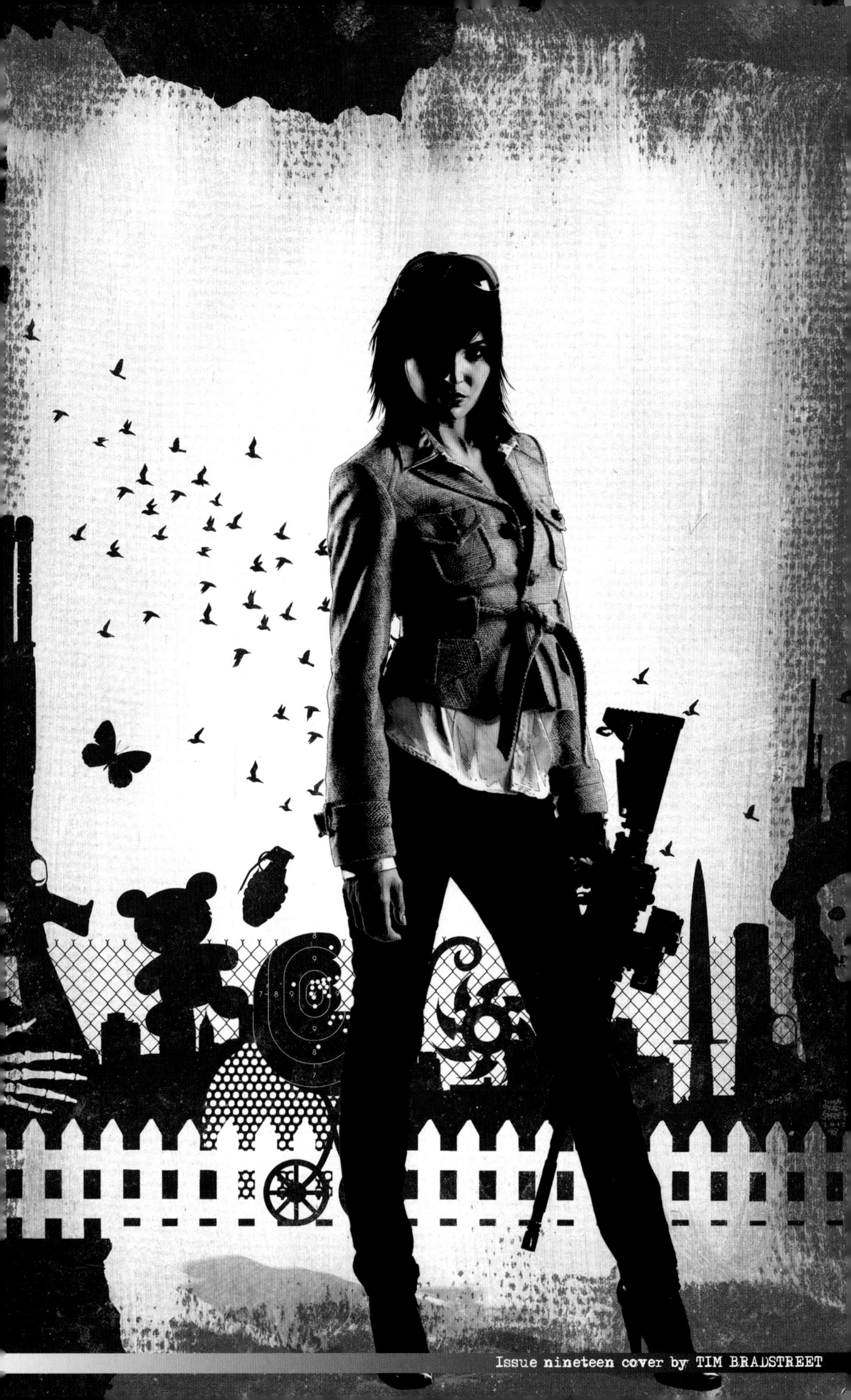

Issue nineteen cover by TIM BRADSTREET

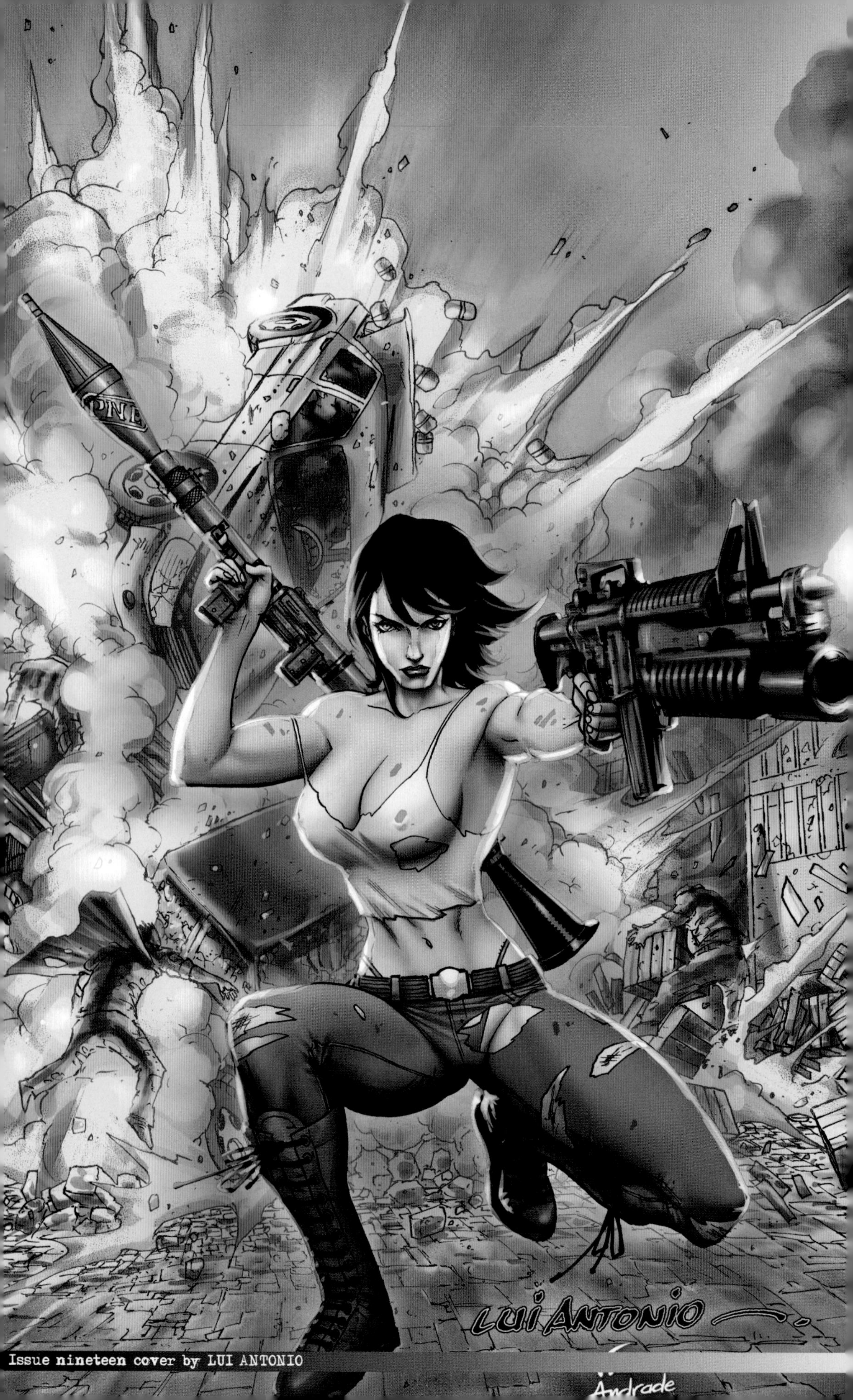
PNE
LUI ANTONIO
Andrade

Issue nineteen cover by LUI ANTONIO

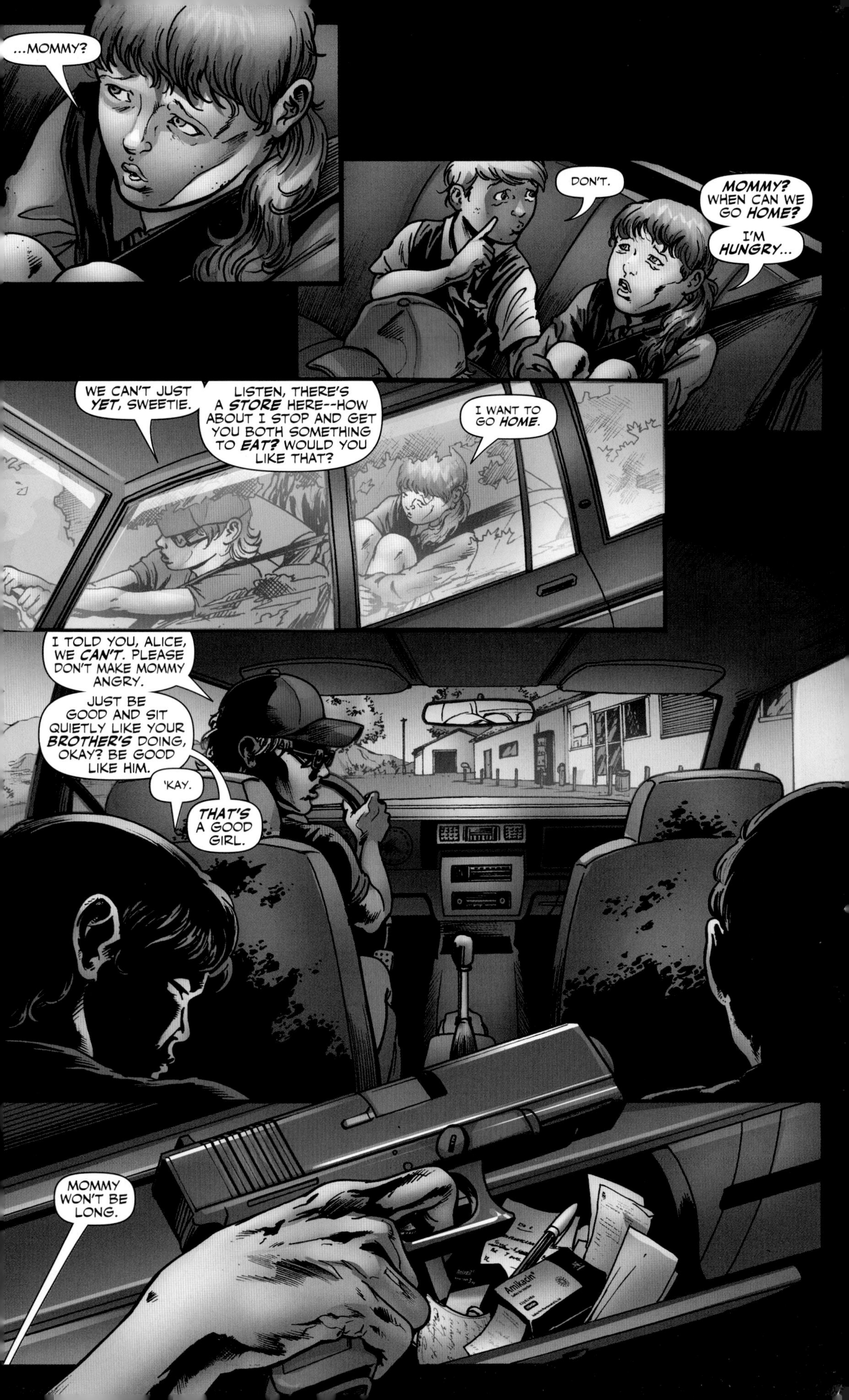
...MOMMY?
DON'T.
MOMMY? WHEN CAN WE GO HOME?
I'M HUNGRY...
WE CAN'T JUST YET, SWEETIE.
LISTEN, THERE'S A STORE HERE--HOW ABOUT I STOP AND GET YOU BOTH SOMETHING TO EAT? WOULD YOU LIKE THAT?
I WANT TO GO HOME.
I TOLD YOU, ALICE, WE CAN'T. PLEASE DON'T MAKE MOMMY ANGRY.
JUST BE GOOD AND SIT QUIETLY LIKE YOUR BROTHER'S DOING, OKAY? BE GOOD LIKE HIM.
'KAY.
THAT'S A GOOD GIRL.
MOMMY WON'T BE LONG.

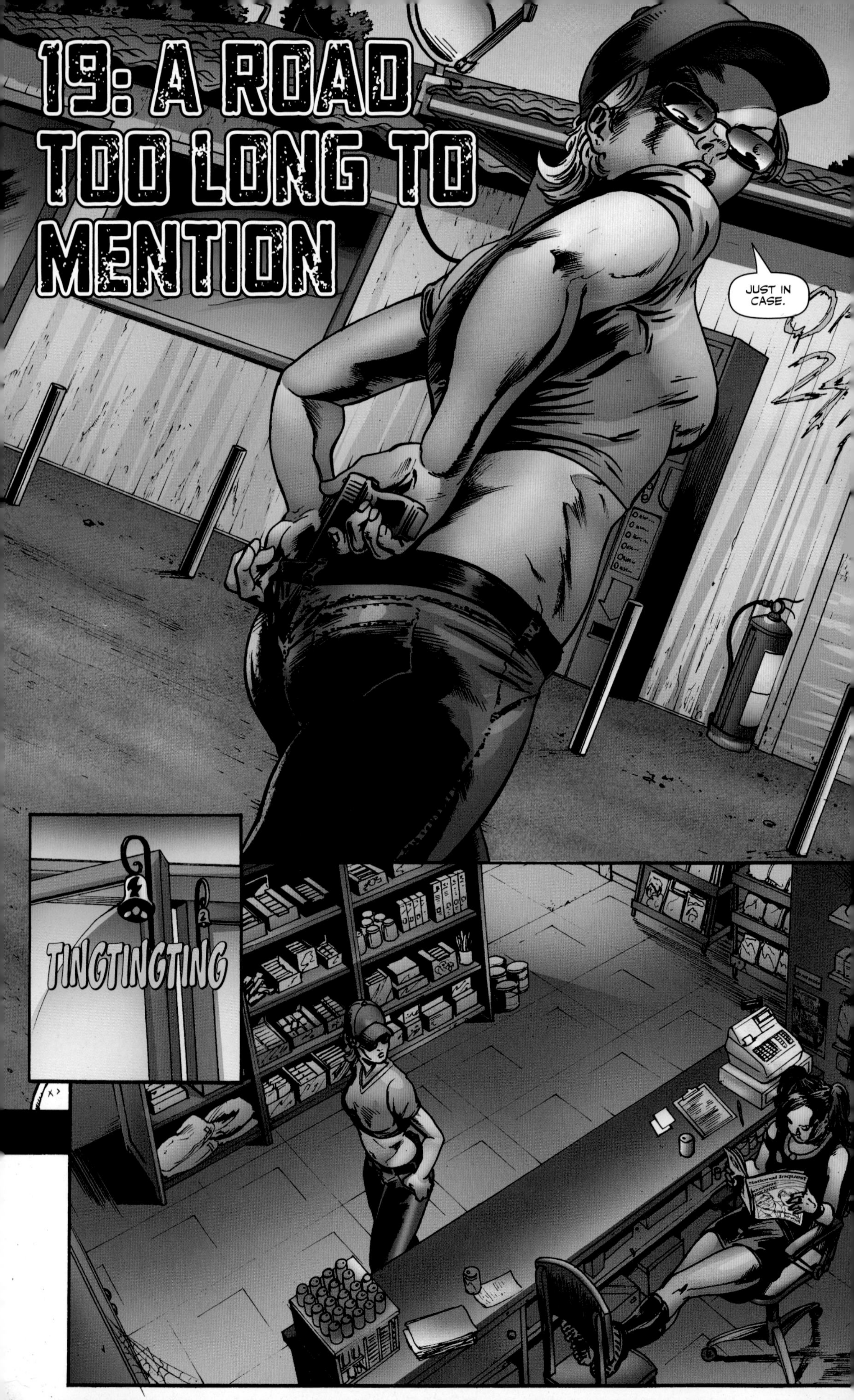
19: A ROAD TOO LONG TO MENTION
JUST IN CASE.
TINGTINGTING

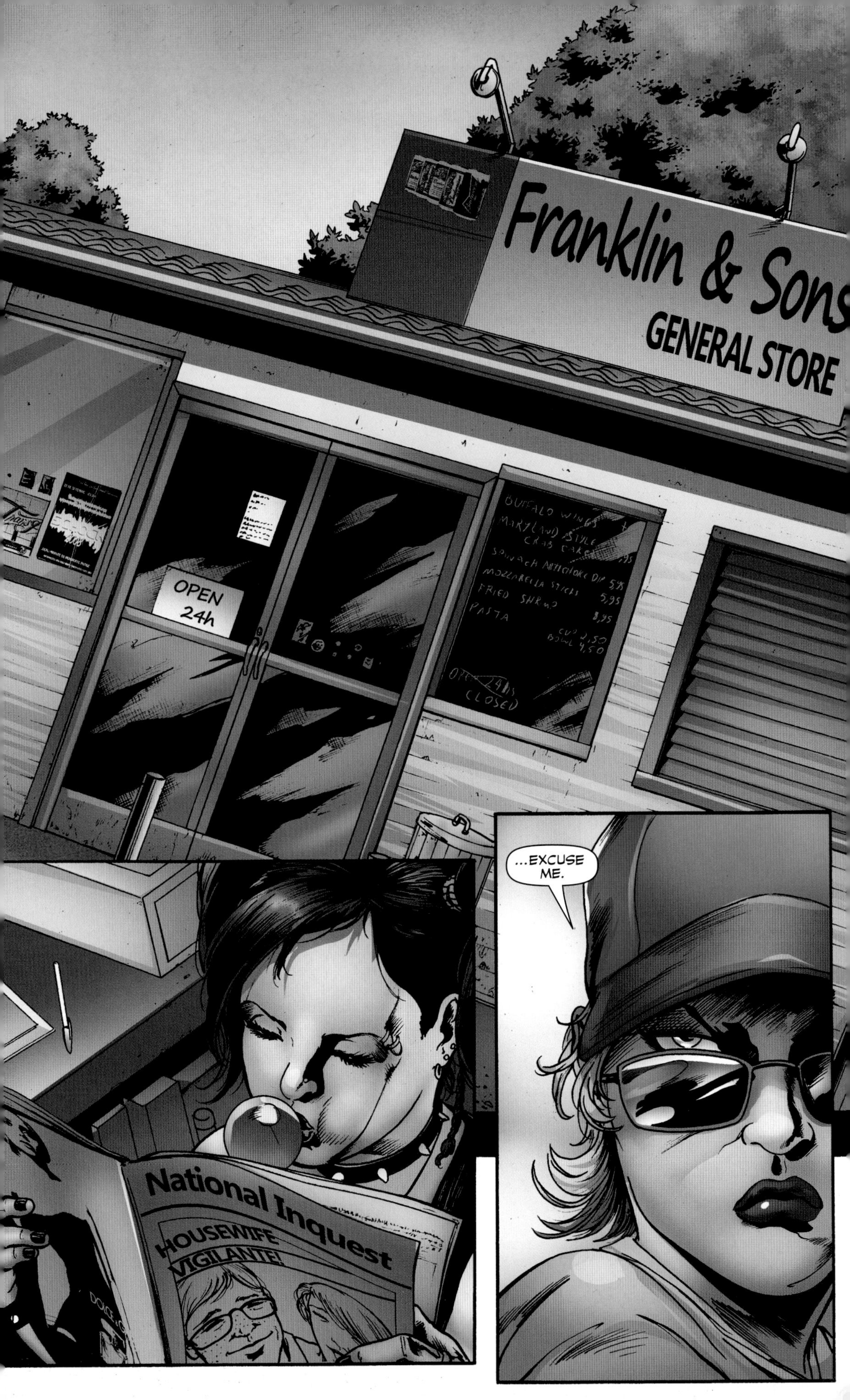
Franklin & Sons
GENERAL STORE
OPEN 24h
...EXCUSE ME.
National Inquest
HOUSEWIFE VIGILANTE!

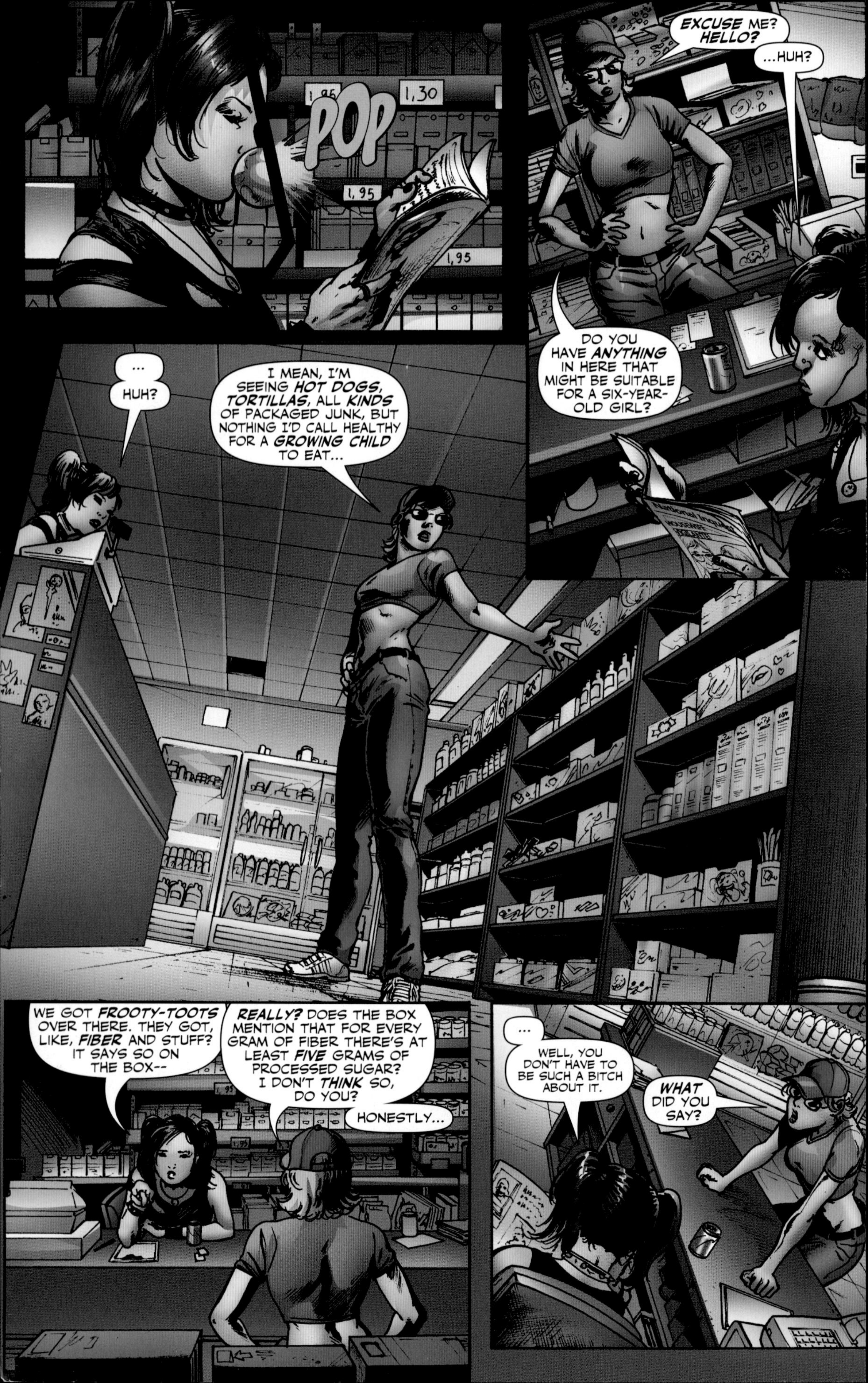

1,95
1,30
POP
1,95
1,95
EXCUSE ME? HELLO?
...HUH?
DO YOU HAVE ANYTHING IN HERE THAT MIGHT BE SUITABLE FOR A SIX-YEAR-OLD GIRL?
...
HUH?
I MEAN, I'M SEEING HOT DOGS, TORTILLAS, ALL KINDS OF PACKAGED JUNK, BUT NOTHING I'D CALL HEALTHY FOR A GROWING CHILD TO EAT...
WE GOT FROOTY-TOOTS OVER THERE. THEY GOT, LIKE, FIBER AND STUFF? IT SAYS SO ON THE BOX--
REALLY? DOES THE BOX MENTION THAT FOR EVERY GRAM OF FIBER THERE'S AT LEAST FIVE GRAMS OF PROCESSED SUGAR? I DON'T THINK SO, DO YOU?
HONESTLY...
...
WELL, YOU DON'T HAVE TO BE SUCH A BITCH ABOUT IT.
WHAT DID YOU SAY?

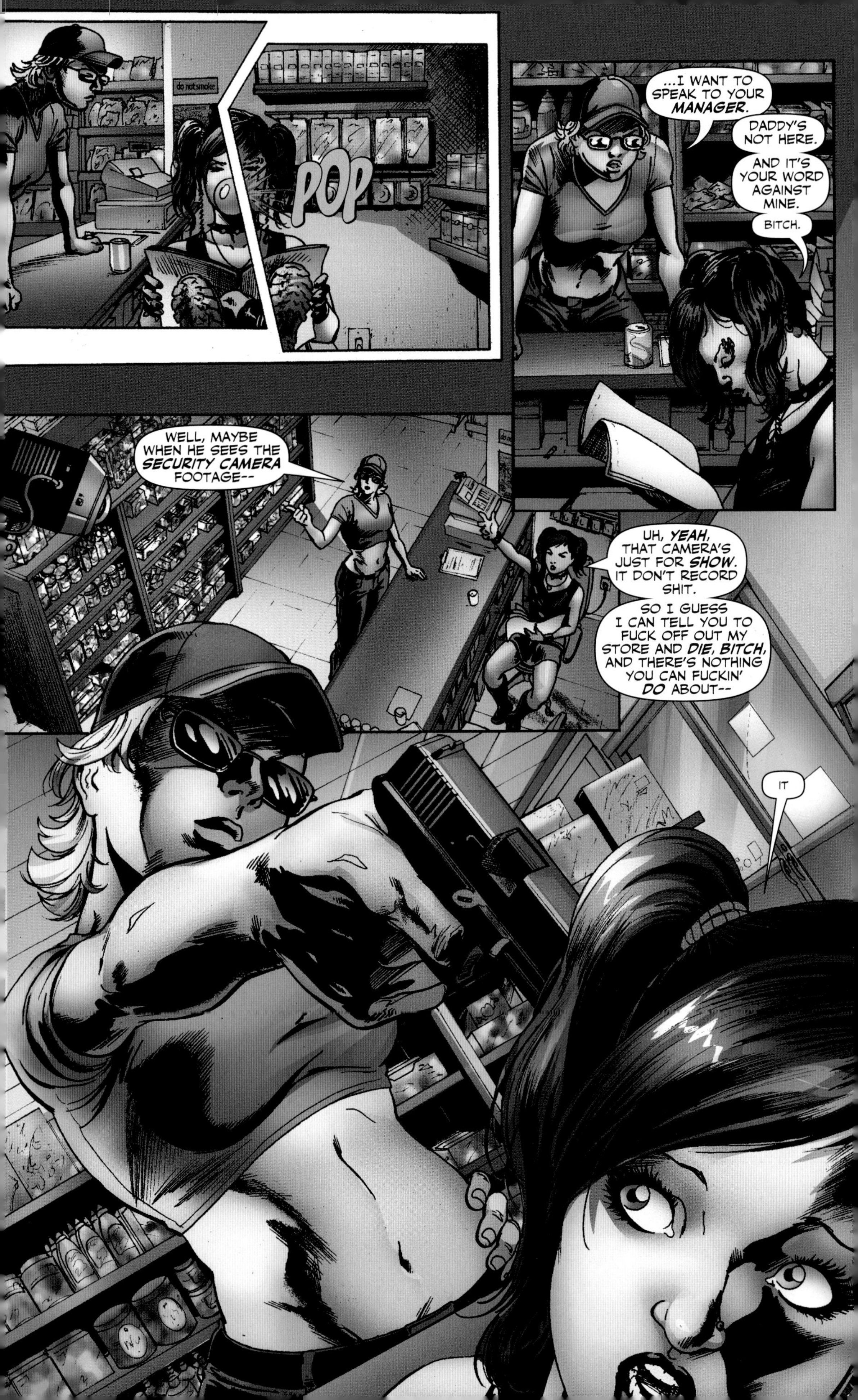
do not smoke
POP
...I WANT TO SPEAK TO YOUR MANAGER.
DADDY'S NOT HERE.
AND IT'S YOUR WORD AGAINST MINE.
BITCH.
WELL, MAYBE WHEN HE SEES THE SECURITY CAMERA FOOTAGE--
UH, YEAH, THAT CAMERA'S JUST FOR SHOW. IT DON'T RECORD SHIT.
SO I GUESS I CAN TELL YOU TO FUCK OFF OUT MY STORE AND DIE, BITCH, AND THERE'S NOTHING YOU CAN FUCKIN' DO ABOUT--
IT

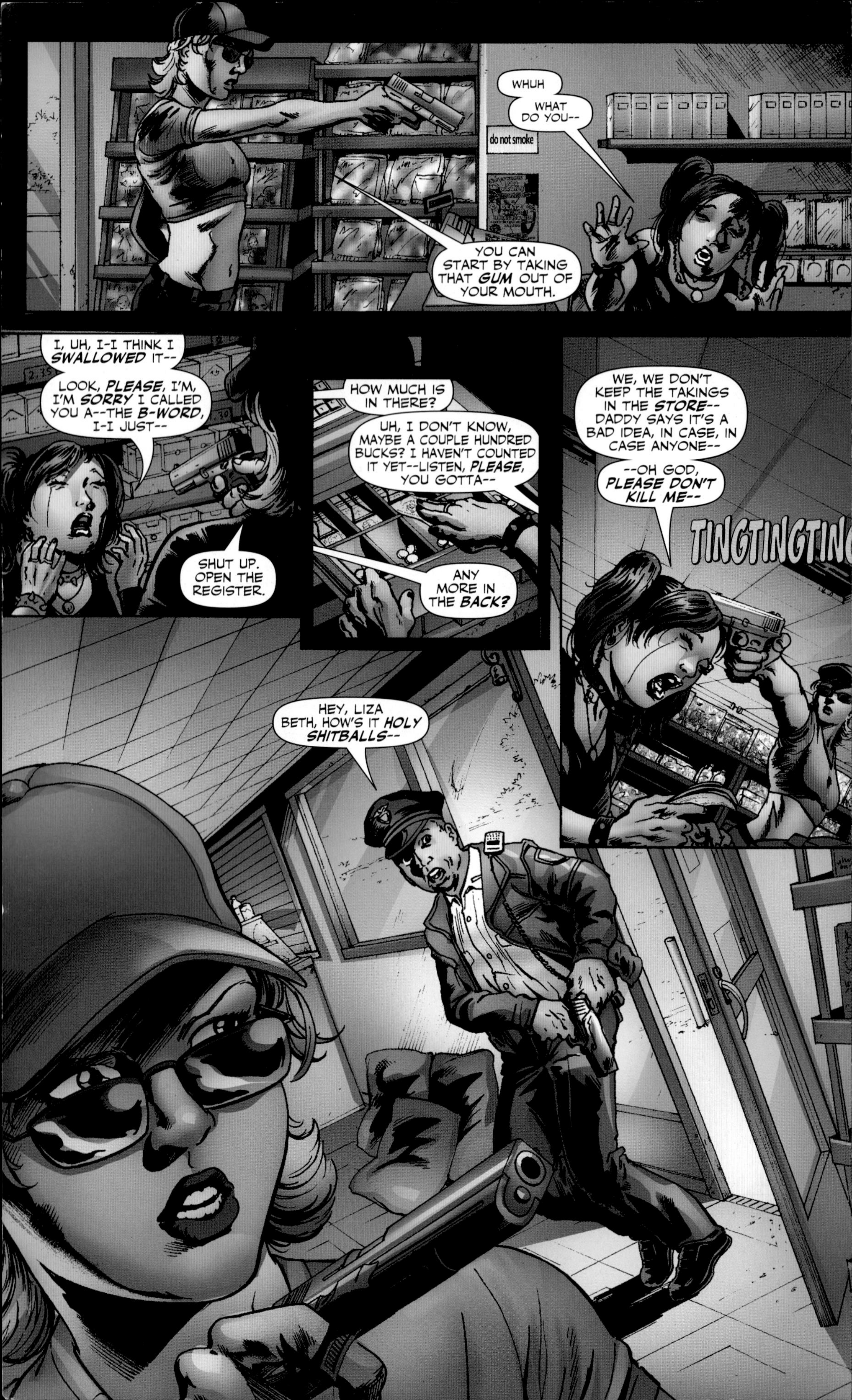

do not smoke
WHUH
WHAT DO YOU--
YOU CAN START BY TAKING THAT GUM OUT OF YOUR MOUTH.
I, UH, I-I THINK I SWALLOWED IT--
LOOK, PLEASE, I'M, I'M SORRY I CALLED YOU A--THE B-WORD, I-I JUST--
SHUT UP. OPEN THE REGISTER.
HOW MUCH IS IN THERE?
UH, I DON'T KNOW, MAYBE A COUPLE HUNDRED BUCKS? I HAVEN'T COUNTED IT YET--LISTEN, PLEASE, YOU GOTTA--
ANY MORE IN THE BACK?
WE, WE DON'T KEEP THE TAKINGS IN THE STORE-- DADDY SAYS IT'S A BAD IDEA, IN CASE, IN CASE ANYONE--
--OH GOD, PLEASE DON'T KILL ME--
TINGTINGTING
HEY, LIZA BETH, HOW'S IT HOLY SHITBALLS--

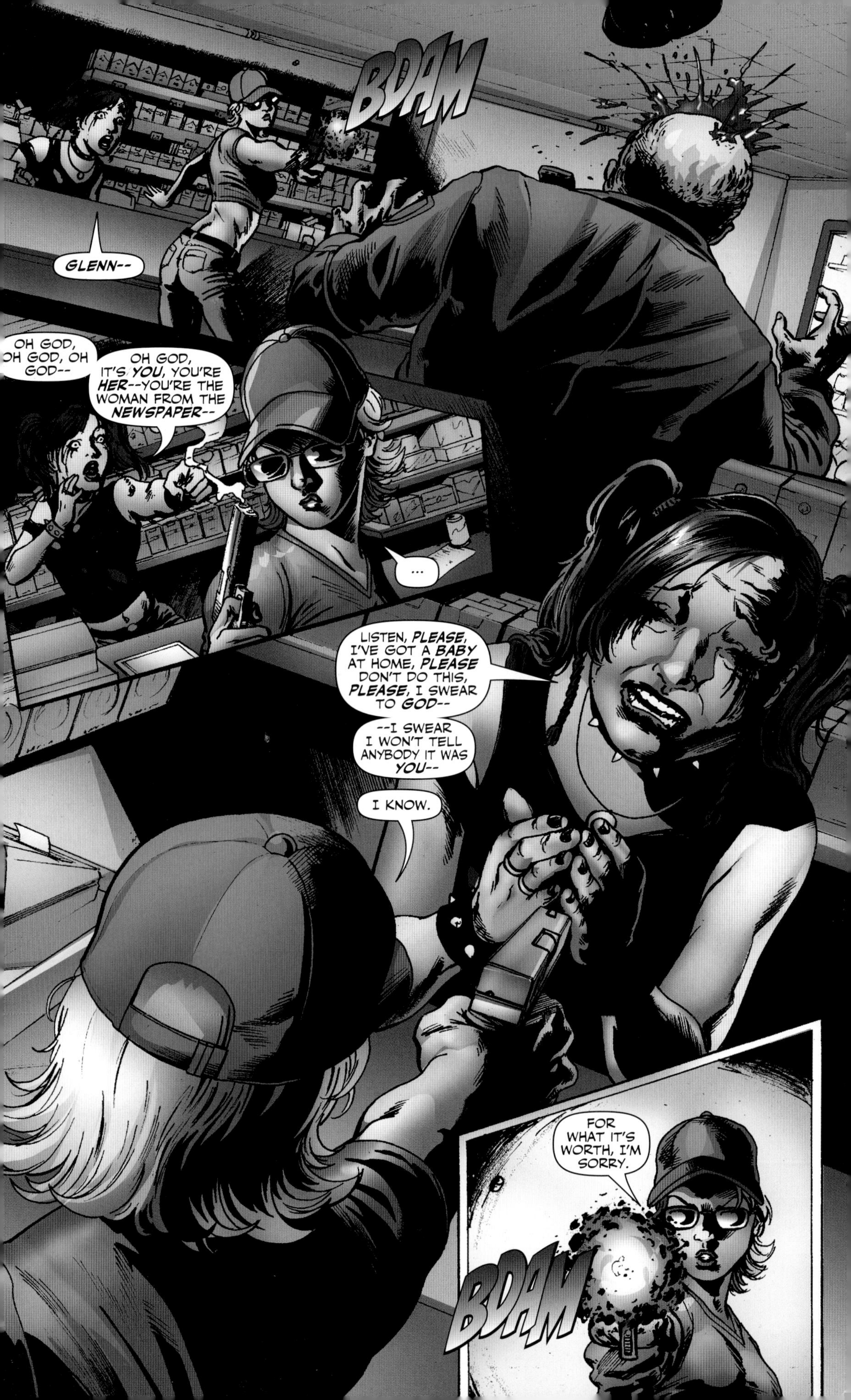
BDAM
GLENN--
OH GOD, OH GOD, OH GOD--
OH GOD, IT'S *YOU*, YOU'RE *HER*--YOU'RE THE WOMAN FROM THE *NEWSPAPER*--
...
LISTEN, *PLEASE*, I'VE GOT A *BABY* AT HOME, *PLEASE* DON'T DO THIS, *PLEASE*, I SWEAR TO *GOD*--
--I SWEAR I WON'T TELL ANYBODY IT WAS *YOU*--
I KNOW.
FOR WHAT IT'S WORTH, I'M SORRY.
BDAM

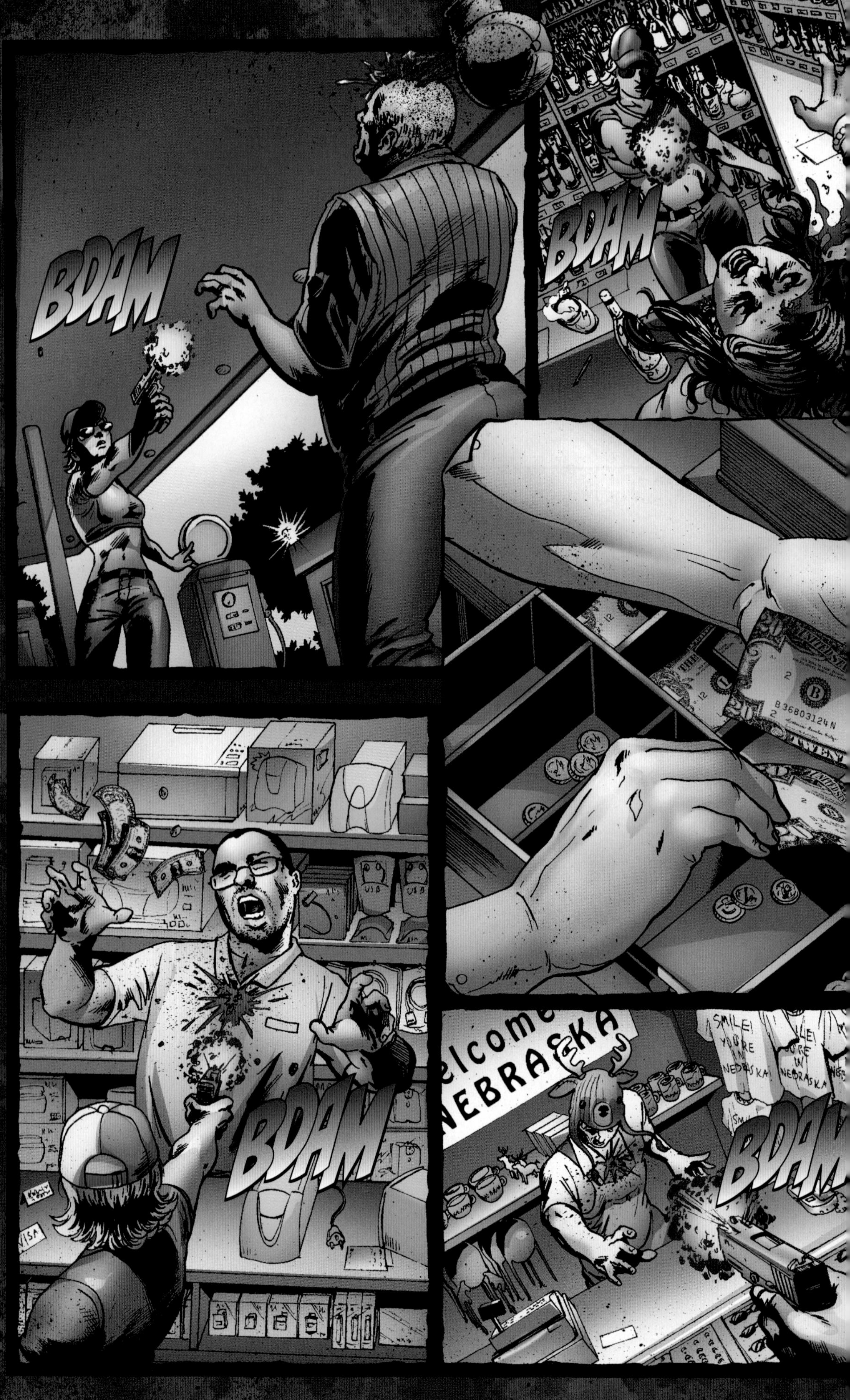

BDAM
BDAM
BDAM
Welcome
NEBRASKA
SMILE! YOU'RE IN NEBRASKA

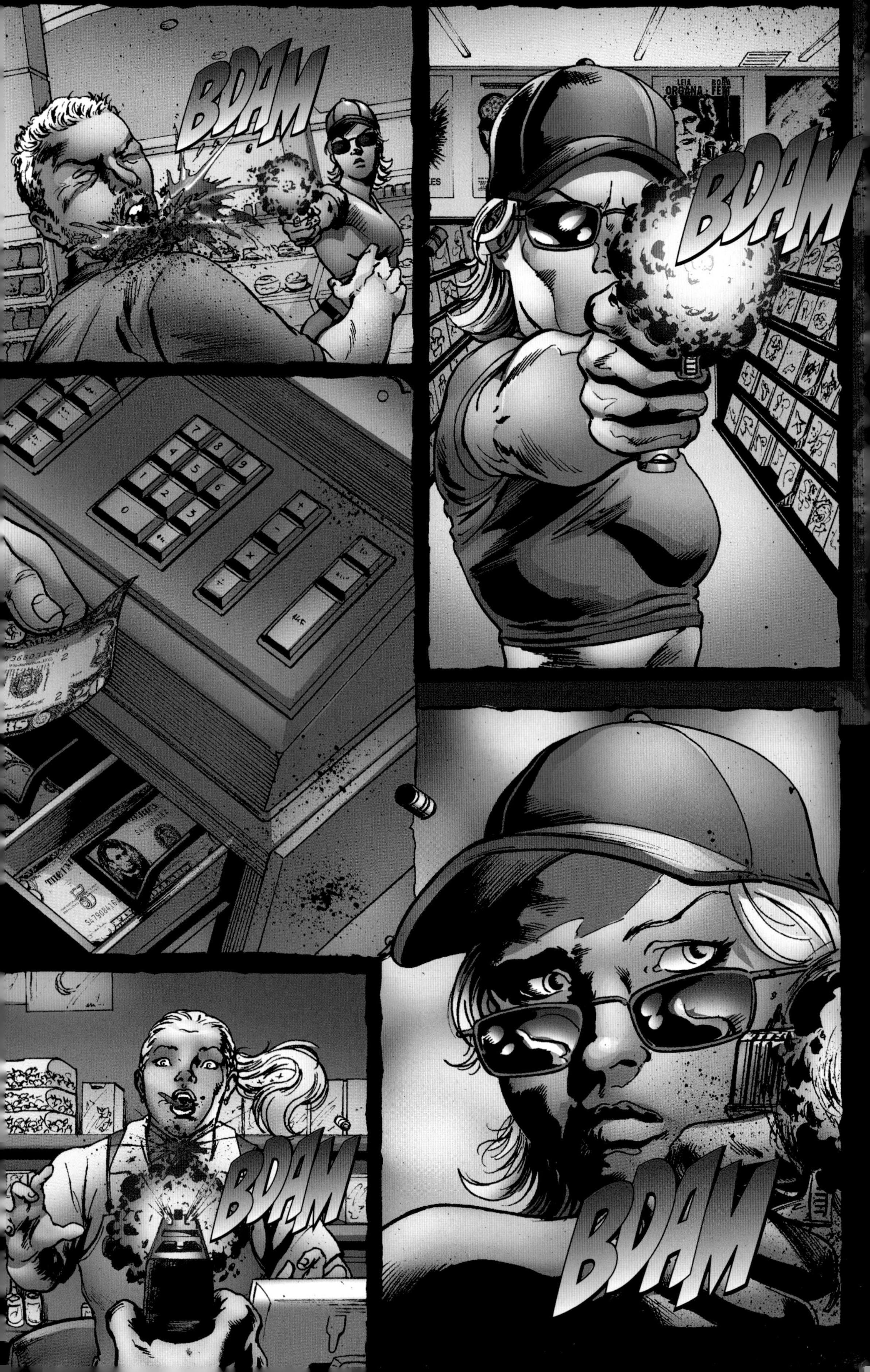
BDAM
BDAM
BDAM
BDAM

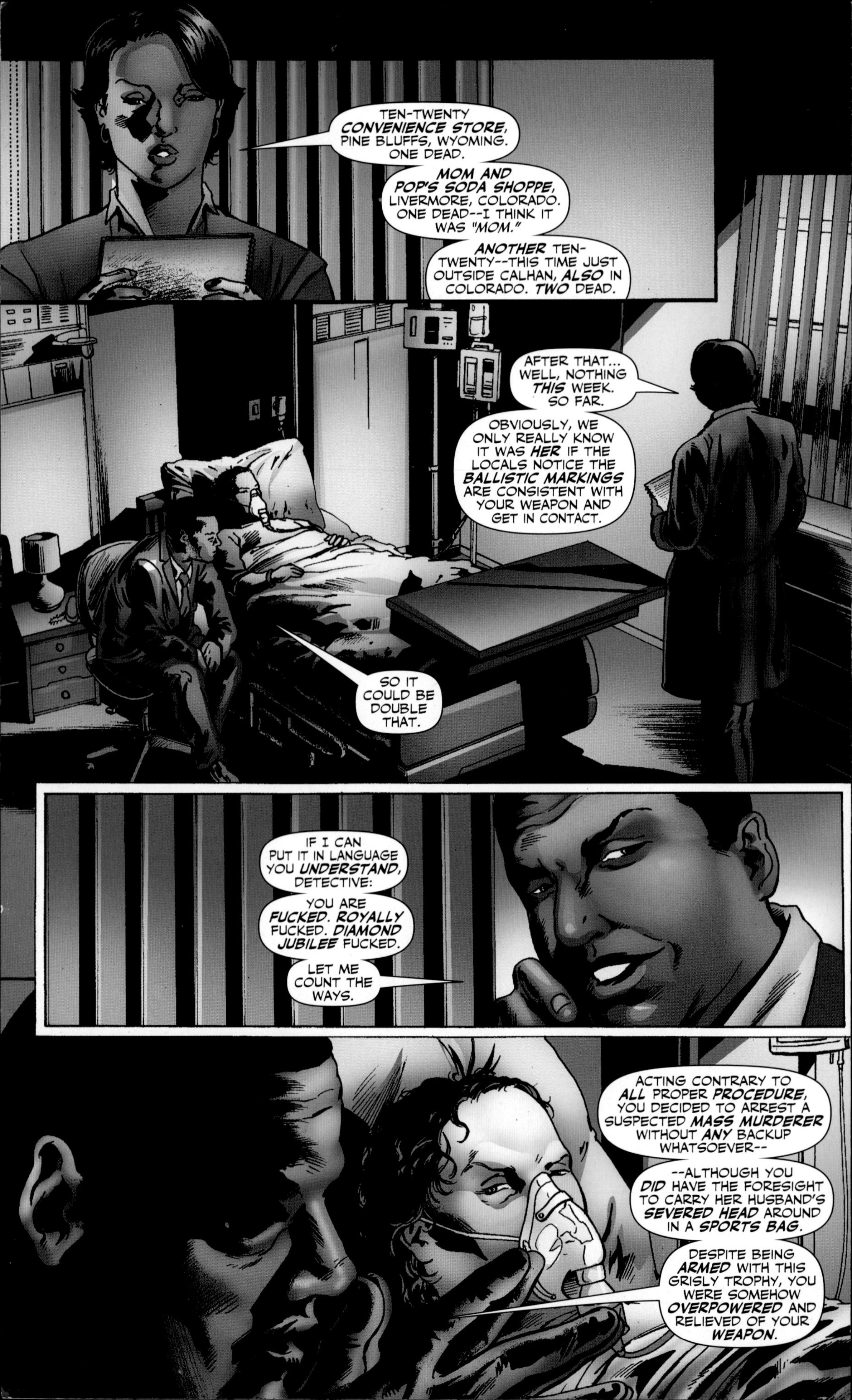
TEN-TWENTY CONVENIENCE STORE, PINE BLUFFS, WYOMING. ONE DEAD.
MOM AND POP'S SODA SHOPPE, LIVERMORE, COLORADO. ONE DEAD--I THINK IT WAS "MOM."
ANOTHER TEN-TWENTY--THIS TIME JUST OUTSIDE CALHAN, ALSO IN COLORADO. TWO DEAD.
AFTER THAT... WELL, NOTHING THIS WEEK. SO FAR.
OBVIOUSLY, WE ONLY REALLY KNOW IT WAS HER IF THE LOCALS NOTICE THE BALLISTIC MARKINGS ARE CONSISTENT WITH YOUR WEAPON AND GET IN CONTACT.
SO IT COULD BE DOUBLE THAT.
IF I CAN PUT IT IN LANGUAGE YOU UNDERSTAND, DETECTIVE:
YOU ARE FUCKED. ROYALLY FUCKED. DIAMOND JUBILEE FUCKED.
LET ME COUNT THE WAYS.
ACTING CONTRARY TO ALL PROPER PROCEDURE, YOU DECIDED TO ARREST A SUSPECTED MASS MURDERER WITHOUT ANY BACKUP WHATSOEVER--
--ALTHOUGH YOU DID HAVE THE FORESIGHT TO CARRY HER HUSBAND'S SEVERED HEAD AROUND IN A SPORTS BAG.
DESPITE BEING ARMED WITH THIS GRISLY TROPHY, YOU WERE SOMEHOW OVERPOWERED AND RELIEVED OF YOUR WEAPON.

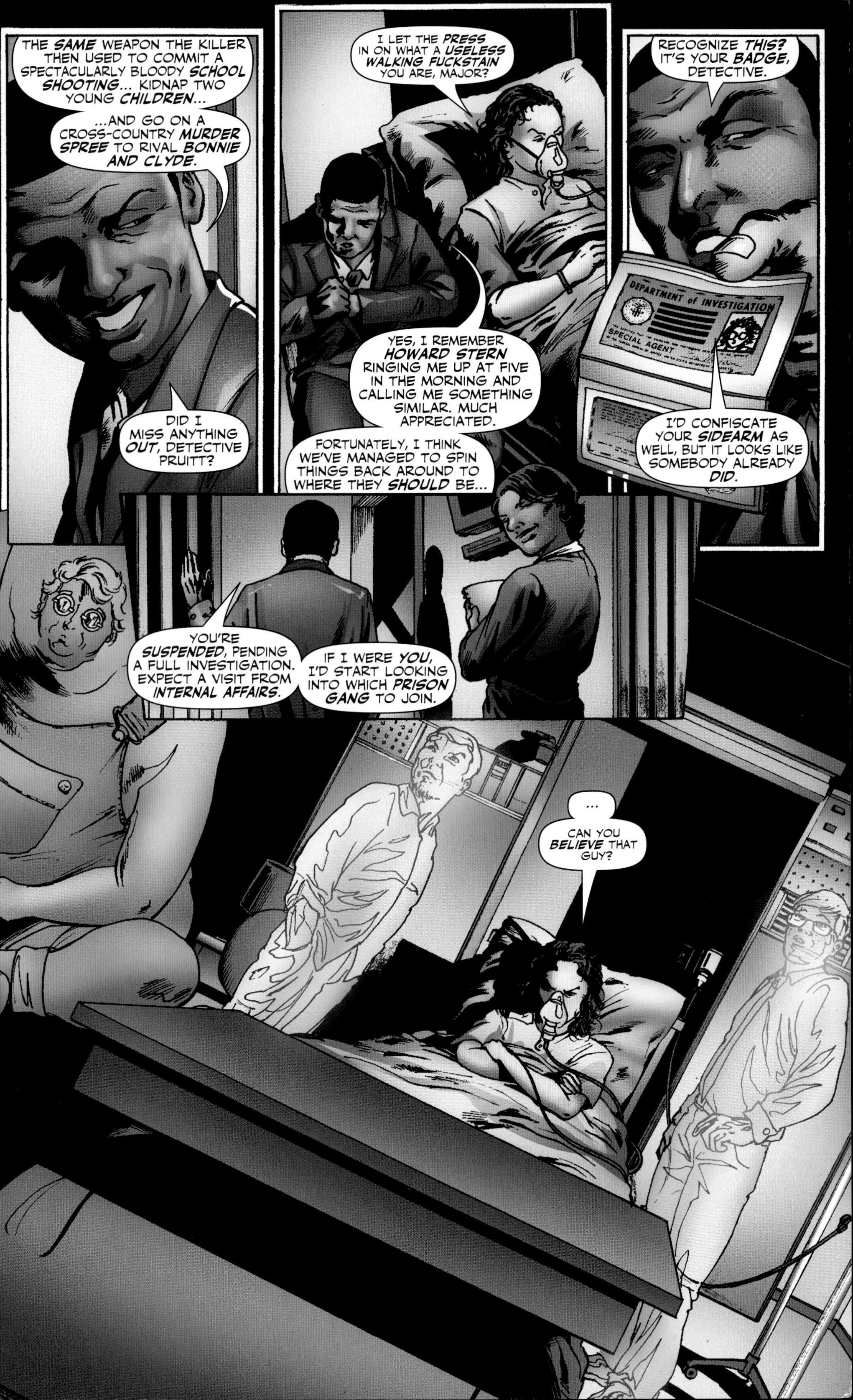
THE SAME WEAPON THE KILLER THEN USED TO COMMIT A SPECTACULARLY BLOODY SCHOOL SHOOTING... KIDNAP TWO YOUNG CHILDREN...
...AND GO ON A CROSS-COUNTRY MURDER SPREE TO RIVAL BONNIE AND CLYDE.
DID I MISS ANYTHING OUT, DETECTIVE PRUITT?
I LET THE PRESS IN ON WHAT A USELESS WALKING FUCKSTAIN YOU ARE, MAJOR?
YES, I REMEMBER HOWARD STERN RINGING ME UP AT FIVE IN THE MORNING AND CALLING ME SOMETHING SIMILAR. MUCH APPRECIATED.
FORTUNATELY, I THINK WE'VE MANAGED TO SPIN THINGS BACK AROUND TO WHERE THEY SHOULD BE...
RECOGNIZE THIS? IT'S YOUR BADGE, DETECTIVE.
DEPARTMENT of INVESTIGATION
SPECIAL AGENT
I'D CONFISCATE YOUR SIDEARM AS WELL, BUT IT LOOKS LIKE SOMEBODY ALREADY DID.
YOU'RE SUSPENDED, PENDING A FULL INVESTIGATION. EXPECT A VISIT FROM INTERNAL AFFAIRS.
IF I WERE YOU, I'D START LOOKING INTO WHICH PRISON GANG TO JOIN.
...
CAN YOU BELIEVE THAT GUY?

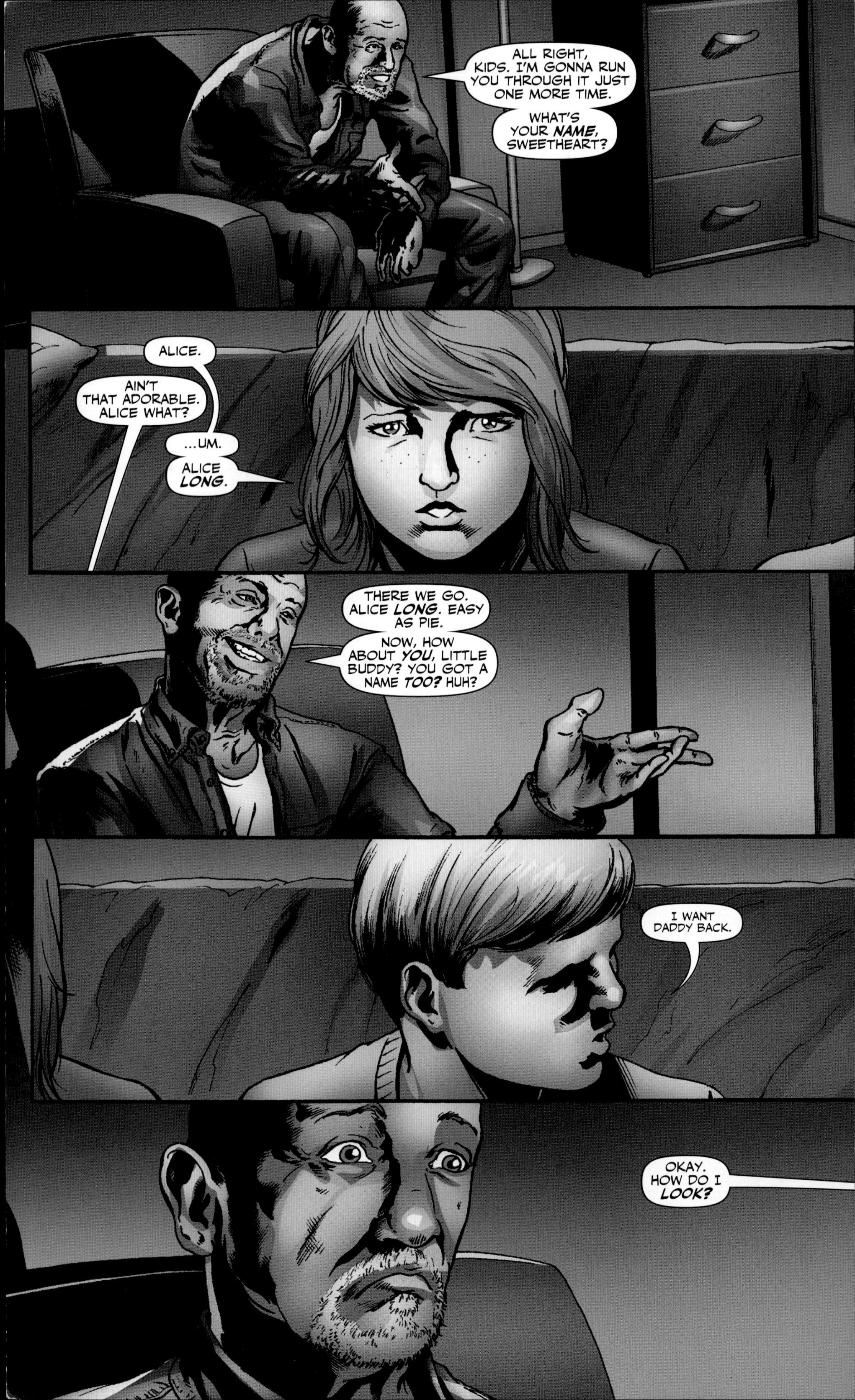
ALL RIGHT, KIDS. I'M GONNA RUN YOU THROUGH IT JUST ONE MORE TIME.
WHAT'S YOUR **NAME,** SWEETHEART?
ALICE.
AIN'T THAT ADORABLE. ALICE WHAT?
...UM.
ALICE **LONG.**
THERE WE GO. ALICE **LONG.** EASY AS PIE.
NOW, HOW ABOUT **YOU,** LITTLE BUDDY? YOU GOT A NAME **TOO?** HUH?
I WANT DADDY BACK.
OKAY. HOW DO I **LOOK?**

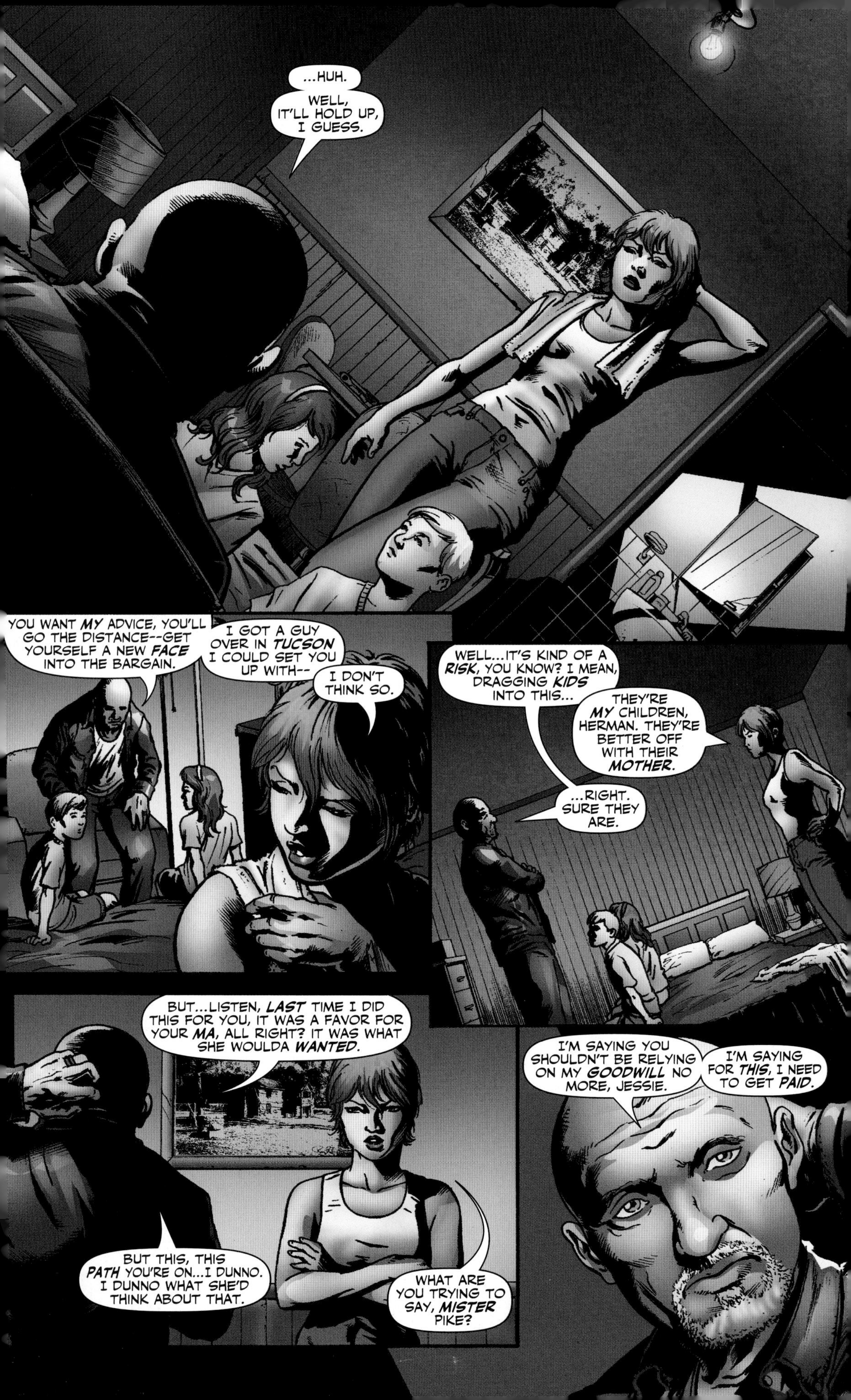
...HUH.
WELL, IT'LL HOLD UP, I GUESS.
YOU WANT MY ADVICE, YOU'LL GO THE DISTANCE--GET YOURSELF A NEW FACE INTO THE BARGAIN.
I GOT A GUY OVER IN TUCSON I COULD SET YOU UP WITH--
I DON'T THINK SO.
WELL...IT'S KIND OF A RISK, YOU KNOW? I MEAN, DRAGGING KIDS INTO THIS...
THEY'RE MY CHILDREN, HERMAN. THEY'RE BETTER OFF WITH THEIR MOTHER.
...RIGHT. SURE THEY ARE.
BUT...LISTEN, LAST TIME I DID THIS FOR YOU, IT WAS A FAVOR FOR YOUR MA, ALL RIGHT? IT WAS WHAT SHE WOULDA WANTED.
BUT THIS, THIS PATH YOU'RE ON...I DUNNO. I DUNNO WHAT SHE'D THINK ABOUT THAT.
WHAT ARE YOU TRYING TO SAY, MISTER PIKE?
I'M SAYING YOU SHOULDN'T BE RELYING ON MY GOODWILL NO MORE, JESSIE.
I'M SAYING FOR THIS, I NEED TO GET PAID.

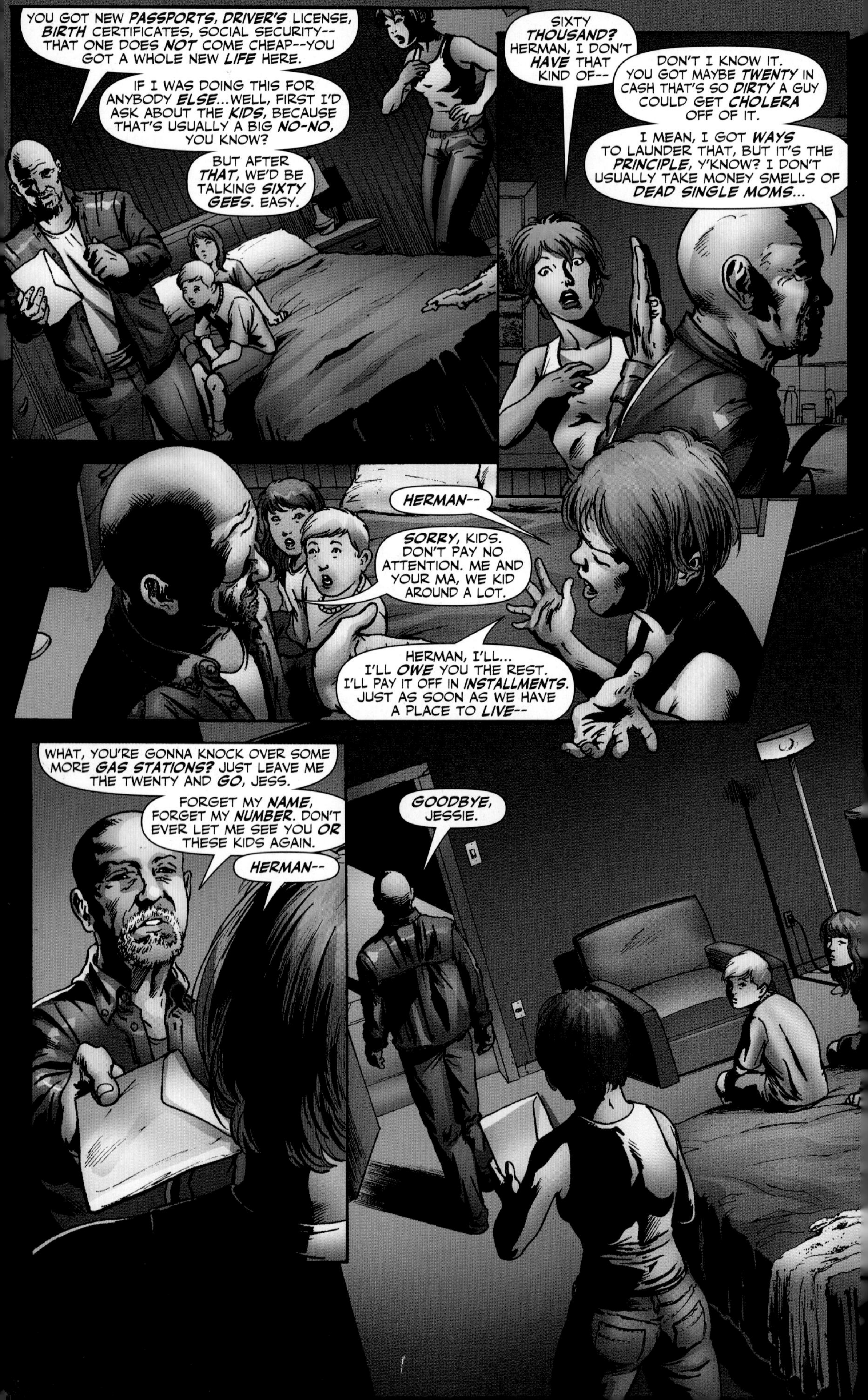
YOU GOT NEW PASSPORTS, DRIVER'S LICENSE, BIRTH CERTIFICATES, SOCIAL SECURITY-- THAT ONE DOES NOT COME CHEAP--YOU GOT A WHOLE NEW LIFE HERE.
IF I WAS DOING THIS FOR ANYBODY ELSE...WELL, FIRST I'D ASK ABOUT THE KIDS, BECAUSE THAT'S USUALLY A BIG NO-NO, YOU KNOW?
BUT AFTER THAT, WE'D BE TALKING SIXTY GEES. EASY.
SIXTY THOUSAND? HERMAN, I DON'T HAVE THAT KIND OF--
DON'T I KNOW IT. YOU GOT MAYBE TWENTY IN CASH THAT'S SO DIRTY A GUY COULD GET CHOLERA OFF OF IT.
I MEAN, I GOT WAYS TO LAUNDER THAT, BUT IT'S THE PRINCIPLE, Y'KNOW? I DON'T USUALLY TAKE MONEY SMELLS OF DEAD SINGLE MOMS...
HERMAN--
SORRY, KIDS. DON'T PAY NO ATTENTION. ME AND YOUR MA, WE KID AROUND A LOT.
HERMAN, I'LL... I'LL OWE YOU THE REST. I'LL PAY IT OFF IN INSTALLMENTS. JUST AS SOON AS WE HAVE A PLACE TO LIVE--
WHAT, YOU'RE GONNA KNOCK OVER SOME MORE GAS STATIONS? JUST LEAVE ME THE TWENTY AND GO, JESS.
FORGET MY NAME, FORGET MY NUMBER. DON'T EVER LET ME SEE YOU OR THESE KIDS AGAIN.
HERMAN--
GOODBYE, JESSIE.

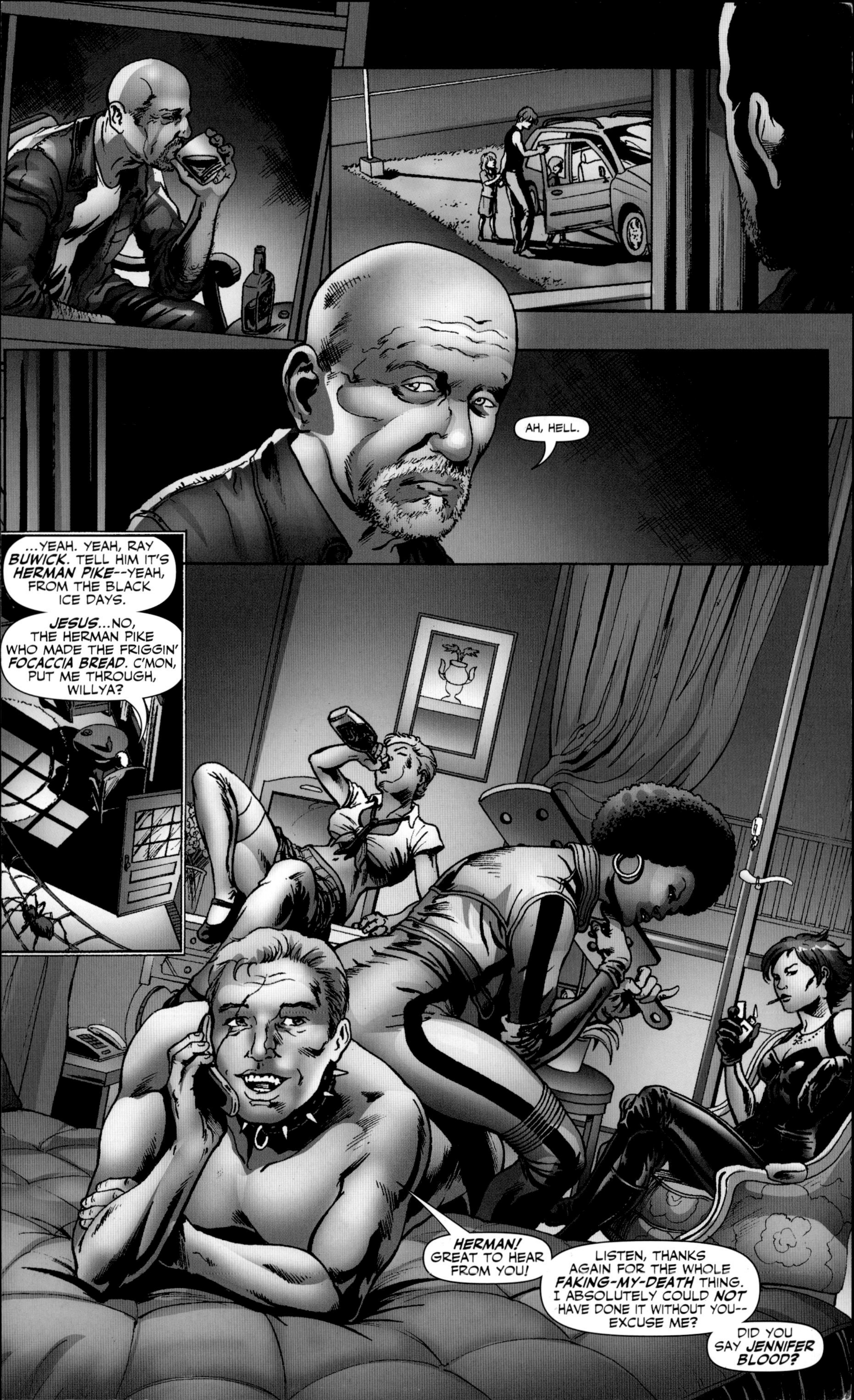
AH, HELL.
...YEAH. YEAH, RAY BUWICK. TELL HIM IT'S HERMAN PIKE--YEAH, FROM THE BLACK ICE DAYS.
JESUS...NO, THE HERMAN PIKE WHO MADE THE FRIGGIN' FOCACCIA BREAD. C'MON, PUT ME THROUGH, WILLYA?
HERMAN! GREAT TO HEAR FROM YOU!
LISTEN, THANKS AGAIN FOR THE WHOLE FAKING-MY-DEATH THING. I ABSOLUTELY COULD NOT HAVE DONE IT WITHOUT YOU-- EXCUSE ME?
DID YOU SAY JENNIFER BLOOD?

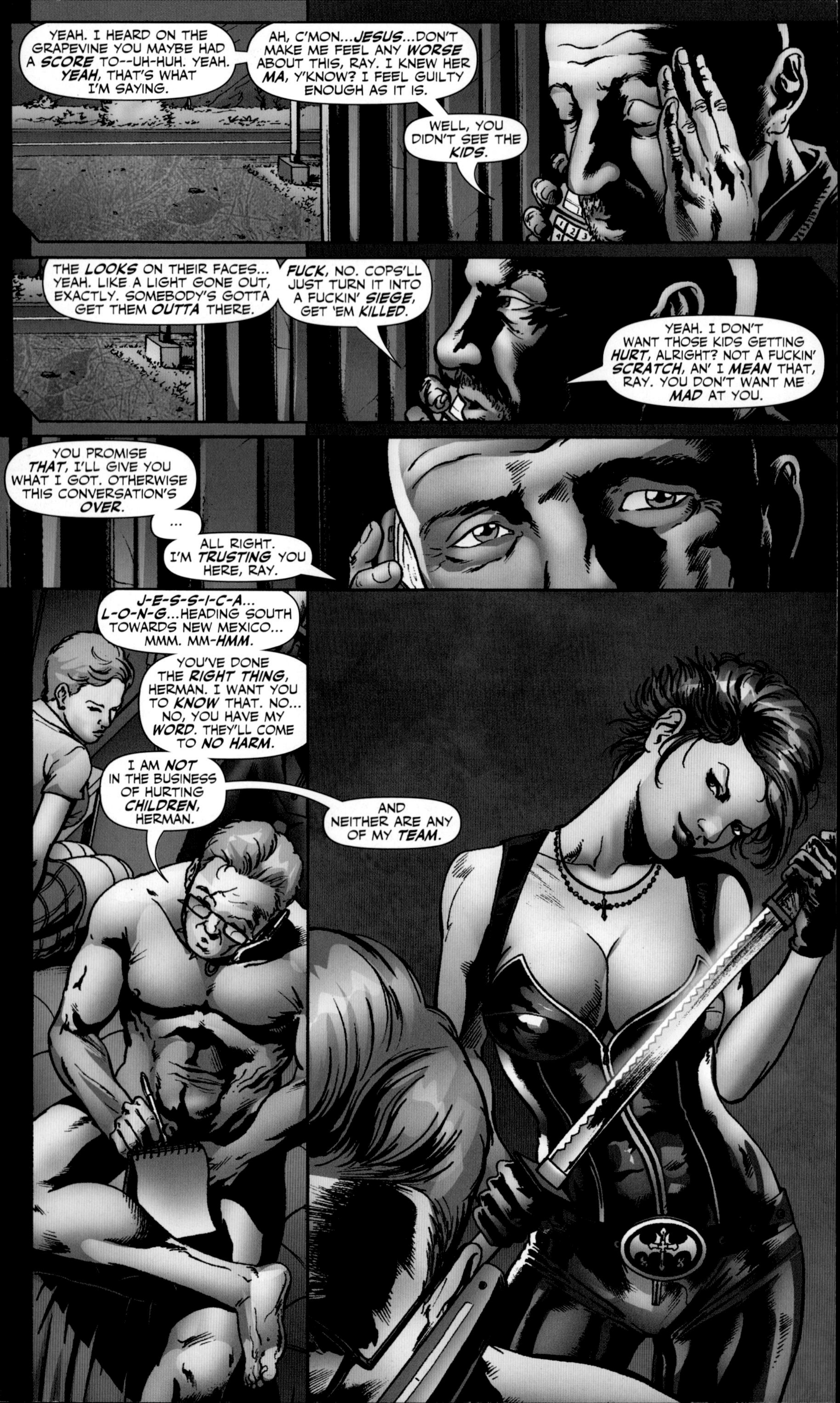
YEAH. I HEARD ON THE GRAPEVINE YOU MAYBE HAD A SCORE TO--UH-HUH. YEAH. YEAH, THAT'S WHAT I'M SAYING.
AH, C'MON...JESUS...DON'T MAKE ME FEEL ANY WORSE ABOUT THIS, RAY. I KNEW HER MA, Y'KNOW? I FEEL GUILTY ENOUGH AS IT IS.
WELL, YOU DIDN'T SEE THE KIDS.
THE LOOKS ON THEIR FACES... YEAH. LIKE A LIGHT GONE OUT, EXACTLY. SOMEBODY'S GOTTA GET THEM OUTTA THERE.
FUCK, NO. COPS'LL JUST TURN IT INTO A FUCKIN' SIEGE, GET 'EM KILLED.
YEAH. I DON'T WANT THOSE KIDS GETTING HURT, ALRIGHT? NOT A FUCKIN' SCRATCH, AN' I MEAN THAT, RAY. YOU DON'T WANT ME MAD AT YOU.
YOU PROMISE THAT, I'LL GIVE YOU WHAT I GOT. OTHERWISE THIS CONVERSATION'S OVER.
...
ALL RIGHT. I'M TRUSTING YOU HERE, RAY.
J-E-S-S-I-C-A... L-O-N-G...HEADING SOUTH TOWARDS NEW MEXICO... MMM. MM-HMM.
YOU'VE DONE THE RIGHT THING, HERMAN. I WANT YOU TO KNOW THAT. NO... NO, YOU HAVE MY WORD. THEY'LL COME TO NO HARM.
I AM NOT IN THE BUSINESS OF HURTING CHILDREN, HERMAN.
AND NEITHER ARE ANY OF MY TEAM.

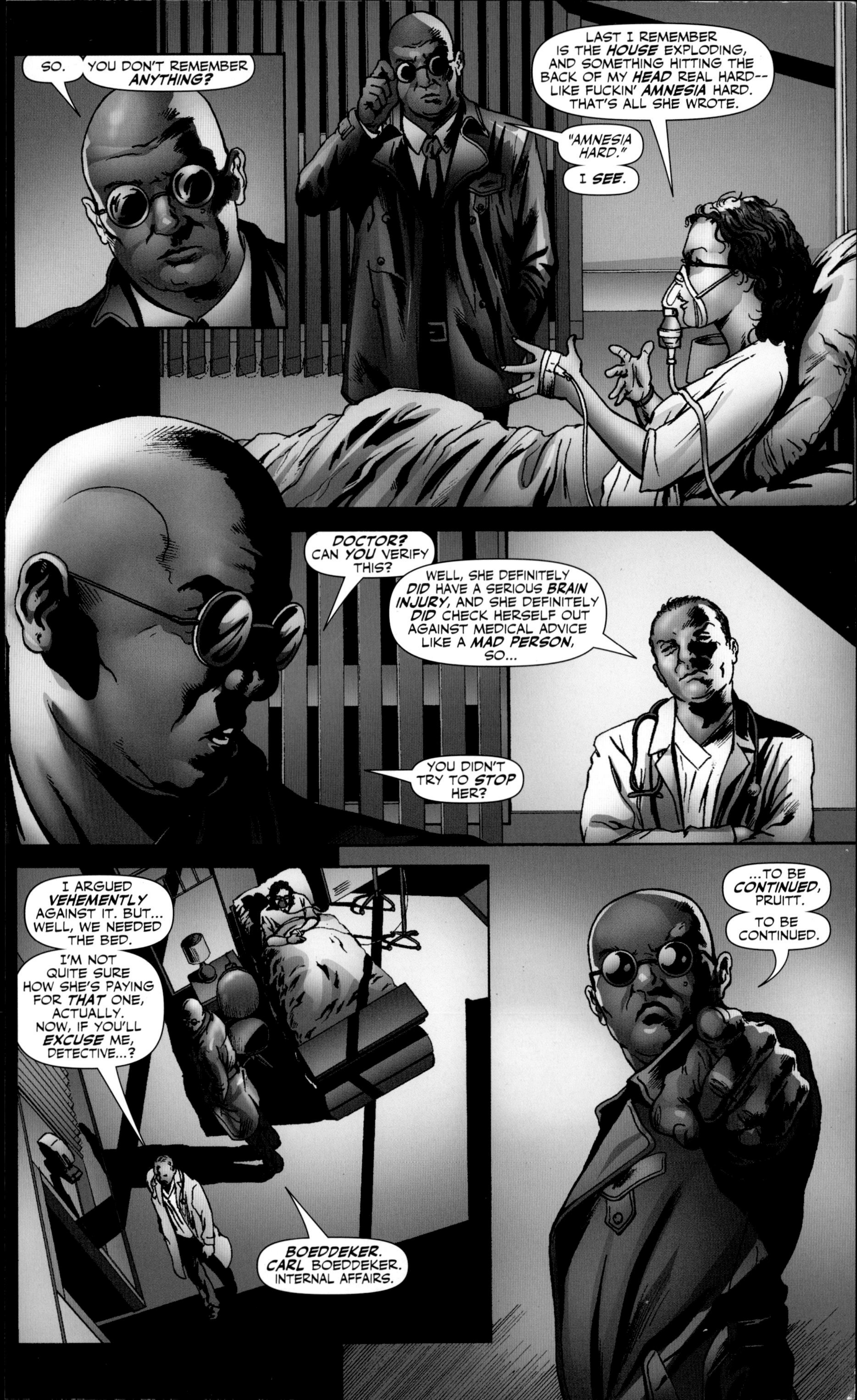
SO.
YOU DON'T REMEMBER ANYTHING?
LAST I REMEMBER IS THE HOUSE EXPLODING, AND SOMETHING HITTING THE BACK OF MY HEAD REAL HARD-- LIKE FUCKIN' AMNESIA HARD. THAT'S ALL SHE WROTE.
"AMNESIA HARD."
I SEE.
DOCTOR? CAN YOU VERIFY THIS?
WELL, SHE DEFINITELY DID HAVE A SERIOUS BRAIN INJURY, AND SHE DEFINITELY DID CHECK HERSELF OUT AGAINST MEDICAL ADVICE LIKE A MAD PERSON, SO...
YOU DIDN'T TRY TO STOP HER?
I ARGUED VEHEMENTLY AGAINST IT. BUT... WELL, WE NEEDED THE BED.
I'M NOT QUITE SURE HOW SHE'S PAYING FOR THAT ONE, ACTUALLY. NOW, IF YOU'LL EXCUSE ME, DETECTIVE...?
BOEDDEKER. CARL BOEDDEKER. INTERNAL AFFAIRS.
...TO BE CONTINUED, PRUITT.
TO BE CONTINUED.

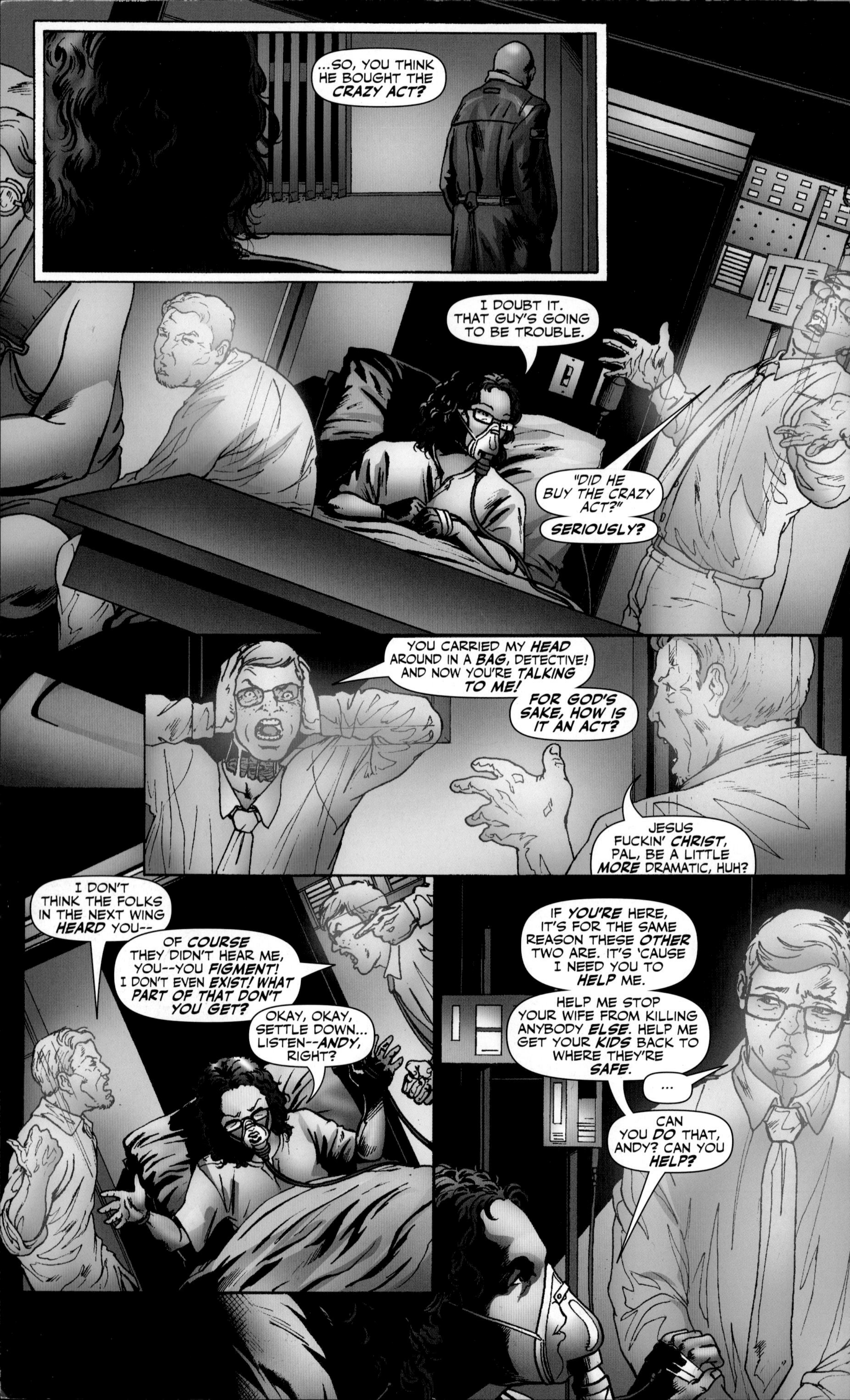
...SO, YOU THINK HE BOUGHT THE CRAZY ACT?
I DOUBT IT. THAT GUY'S GOING TO BE TROUBLE.
"DID HE BUY THE CRAZY ACT?" SERIOUSLY?
YOU CARRIED MY HEAD AROUND IN A BAG, DETECTIVE! AND NOW YOU'RE TALKING TO ME!
FOR GOD'S SAKE, HOW IS IT AN ACT?
JESUS FUCKIN' CHRIST, PAL, BE A LITTLE MORE DRAMATIC, HUH?
I DON'T THINK THE FOLKS IN THE NEXT WING HEARD YOU--
OF COURSE THEY DIDN'T HEAR ME, YOU--YOU FIGMENT! I DON'T EVEN EXIST! WHAT PART OF THAT DON'T YOU GET?
OKAY, OKAY, SETTLE DOWN... LISTEN--ANDY, RIGHT?
IF YOU'RE HERE, IT'S FOR THE SAME REASON THESE OTHER TWO ARE. IT'S 'CAUSE I NEED YOU TO HELP ME.
HELP ME STOP YOUR WIFE FROM KILLING ANYBODY ELSE. HELP ME GET YOUR KIDS BACK TO WHERE THEY'RE SAFE.
...
CAN YOU DO THAT, ANDY? CAN YOU HELP?

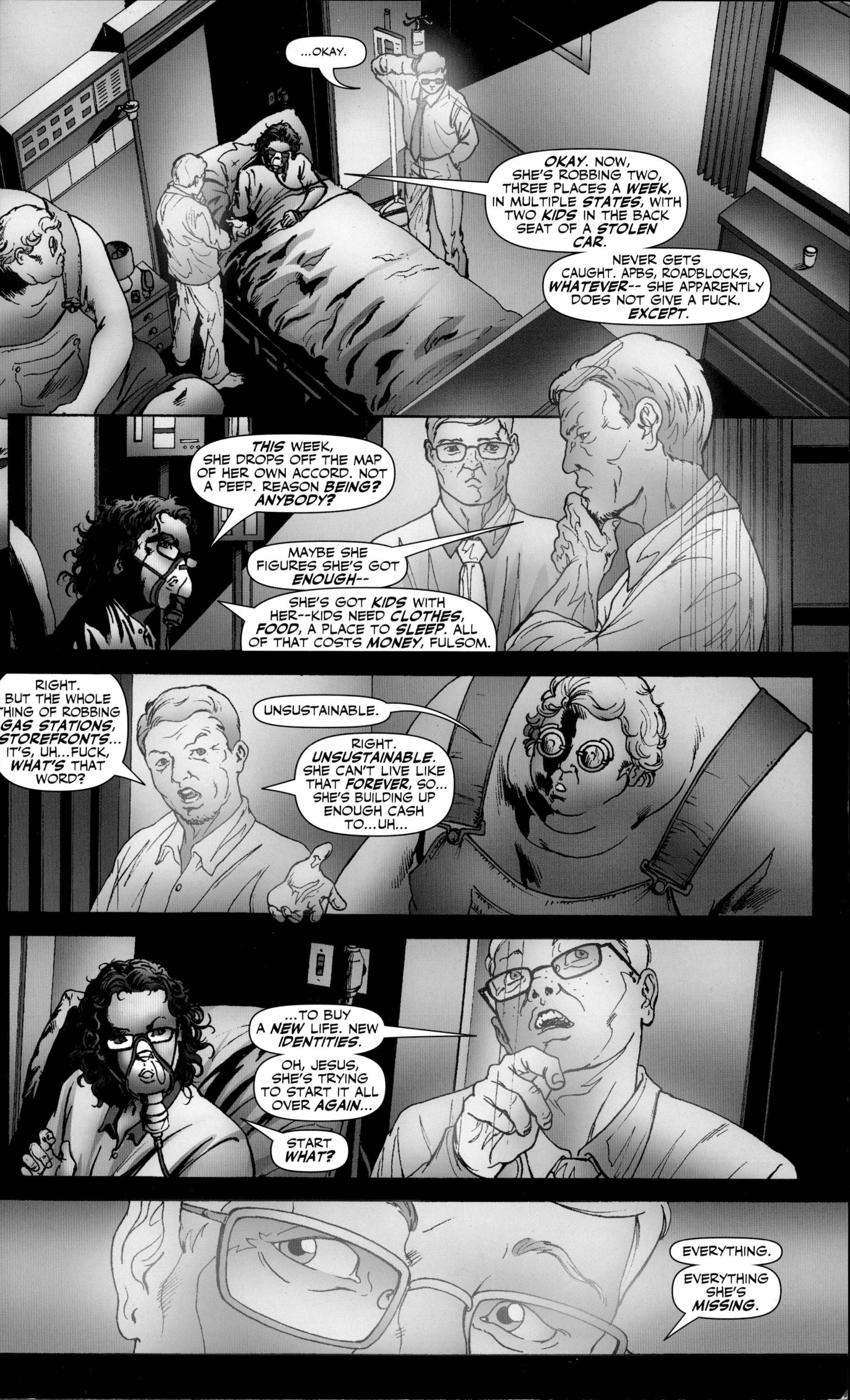
...OKAY.
OKAY. NOW, SHE'S ROBBING TWO, THREE PLACES A WEEK, IN MULTIPLE STATES, WITH TWO KIDS IN THE BACK SEAT OF A STOLEN CAR.
NEVER GETS CAUGHT. APBS, ROADBLOCKS, WHATEVER-- SHE APPARENTLY DOES NOT GIVE A FUCK. EXCEPT.
THIS WEEK, SHE DROPS OFF THE MAP OF HER OWN ACCORD. NOT A PEEP. REASON BEING? ANYBODY?
MAYBE SHE FIGURES SHE'S GOT ENOUGH--
SHE'S GOT KIDS WITH HER--KIDS NEED CLOTHES, FOOD, A PLACE TO SLEEP. ALL OF THAT COSTS MONEY, FULSOM.
RIGHT. BUT THE WHOLE THING OF ROBBING GAS STATIONS, STOREFRONTS... IT'S, UH...FUCK, WHAT'S THAT WORD?
UNSUSTAINABLE.
RIGHT. UNSUSTAINABLE. SHE CAN'T LIVE LIKE THAT FOREVER, SO... SHE'S BUILDING UP ENOUGH CASH TO...UH...
...TO BUY A NEW LIFE. NEW IDENTITIES.
OH, JESUS, SHE'S TRYING TO START IT ALL OVER AGAIN...
START WHAT?
EVERYTHING.
EVERYTHING SHE'S MISSING.

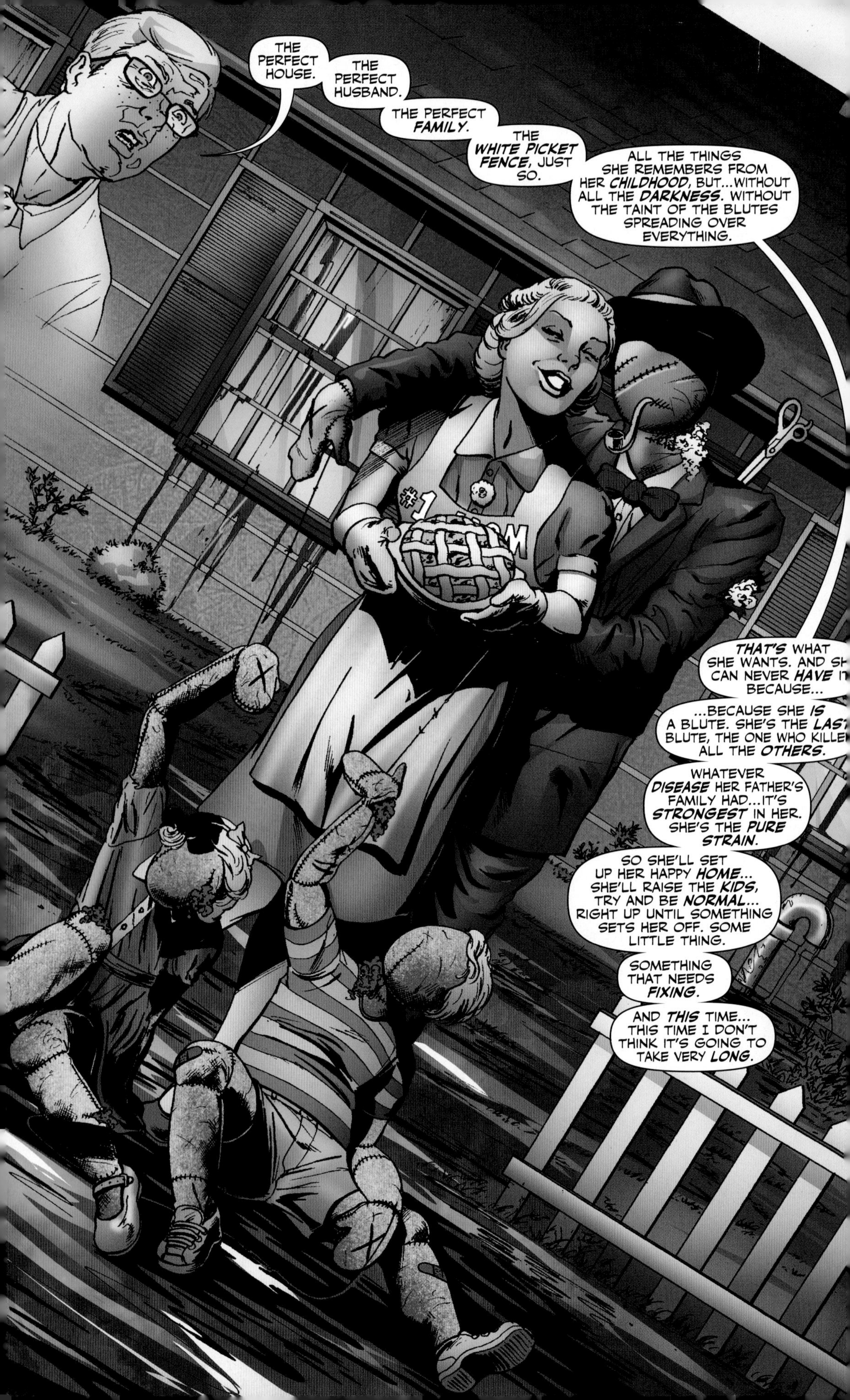
THE PERFECT HOUSE.
THE PERFECT HUSBAND.
THE PERFECT *FAMILY*.
THE *WHITE PICKET FENCE*, JUST SO.
ALL THE THINGS SHE REMEMBERS FROM HER *CHILDHOOD*, BUT...WITHOUT ALL THE *DARKNESS*. WITHOUT THE TAINT OF THE BLUTES SPREADING OVER EVERYTHING.
THAT'S WHAT SHE WANTS. AND SH CAN NEVER *HAVE* IT BECAUSE...
...BECAUSE SHE *IS* A BLUTE. SHE'S THE *LAST* BLUTE, THE ONE WHO KILLE ALL THE *OTHERS*.
WHATEVER *DISEASE* HER FATHER'S FAMILY HAD...IT'S *STRONGEST* IN HER. SHE'S THE *PURE STRAIN*.
SO SHE'LL SET UP HER HAPPY *HOME*... SHE'LL RAISE THE *KIDS*, TRY AND BE *NORMAL*... RIGHT UP UNTIL SOMETHING SETS HER OFF. SOME LITTLE THING.
SOMETHING THAT NEEDS *FIXING*.
AND *THIS* TIME... THIS TIME I DON'T THINK IT'S GOING TO TAKE VERY *LONG*.

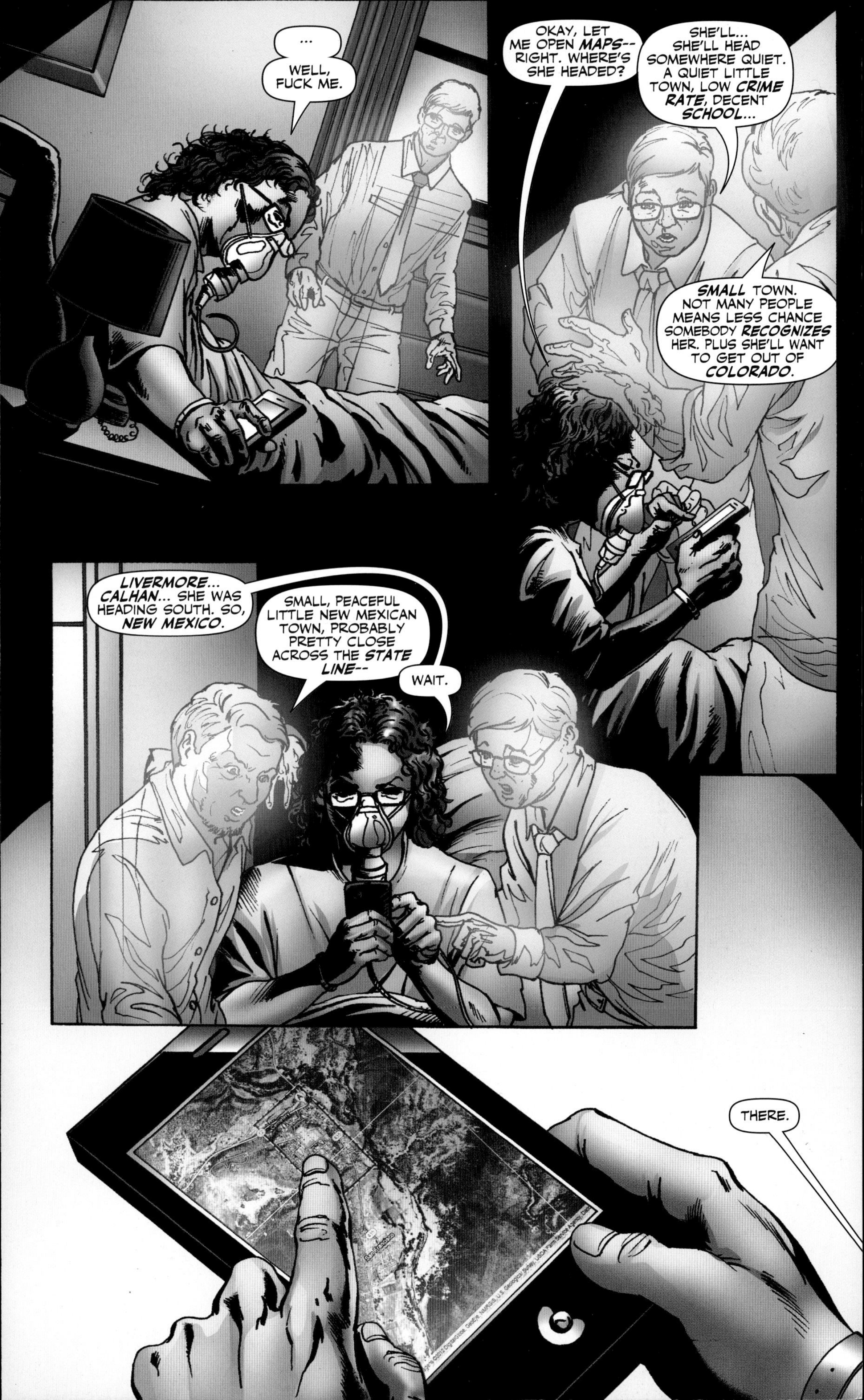
...
WELL, FUCK ME.
OKAY, LET ME OPEN MAPS-- RIGHT. WHERE'S SHE HEADED?
SHE'LL... SHE'LL HEAD SOMEWHERE QUIET. A QUIET LITTLE TOWN, LOW CRIME RATE, DECENT SCHOOL...
SMALL TOWN. NOT MANY PEOPLE MEANS LESS CHANCE SOMEBODY RECOGNIZES HER. PLUS SHE'LL WANT TO GET OUT OF COLORADO.
LIVERMORE... CALHAN... SHE WAS HEADING SOUTH. SO, NEW MEXICO.
SMALL, PEACEFUL LITTLE NEW MEXICAN TOWN, PROBABLY PRETTY CLOSE ACROSS THE STATE LINE--
WAIT.
THERE.

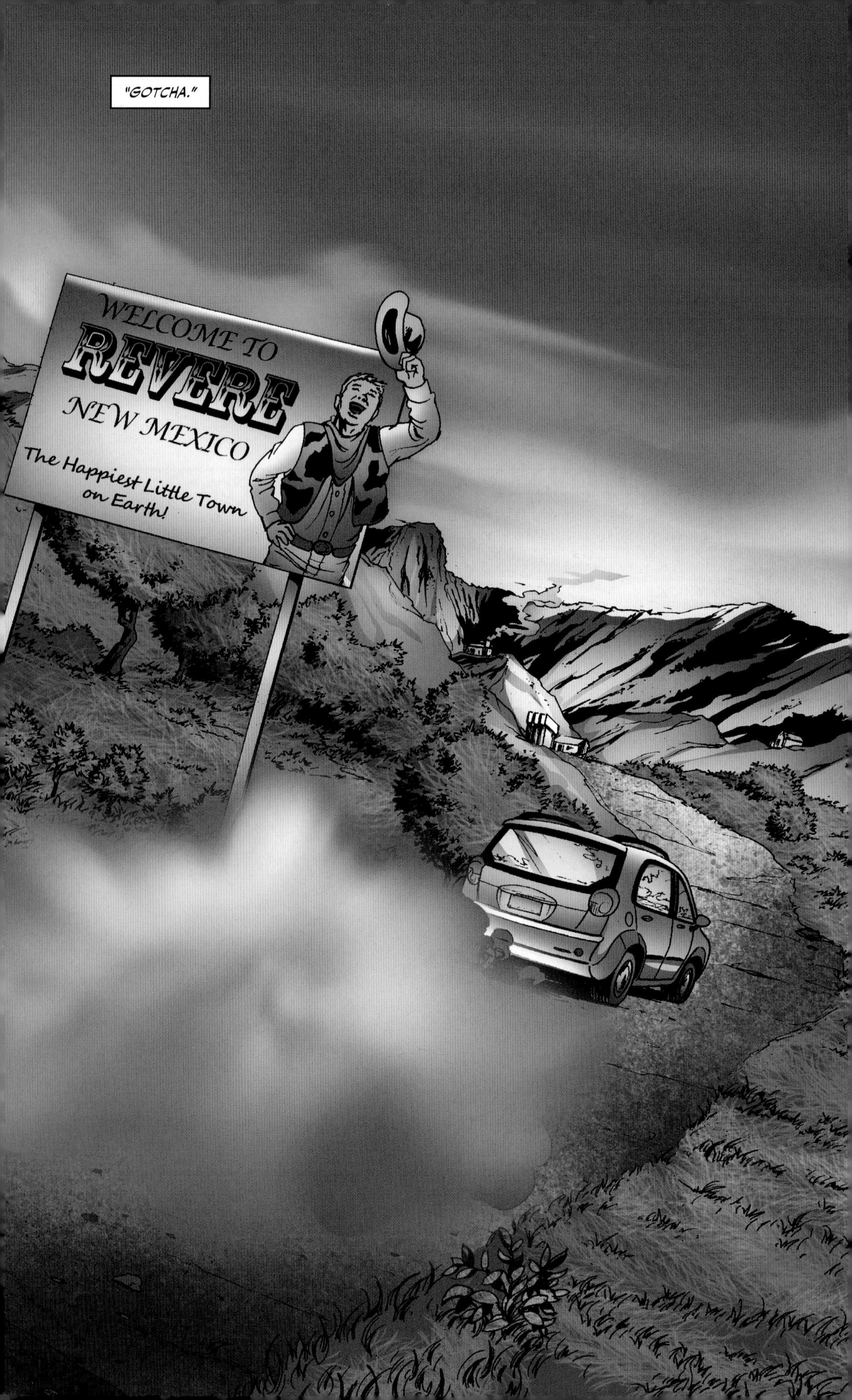
"GOTCHA."
WELCOME TO
REVERE
NEW MEXICO
The Happiest Little Town on Earth!

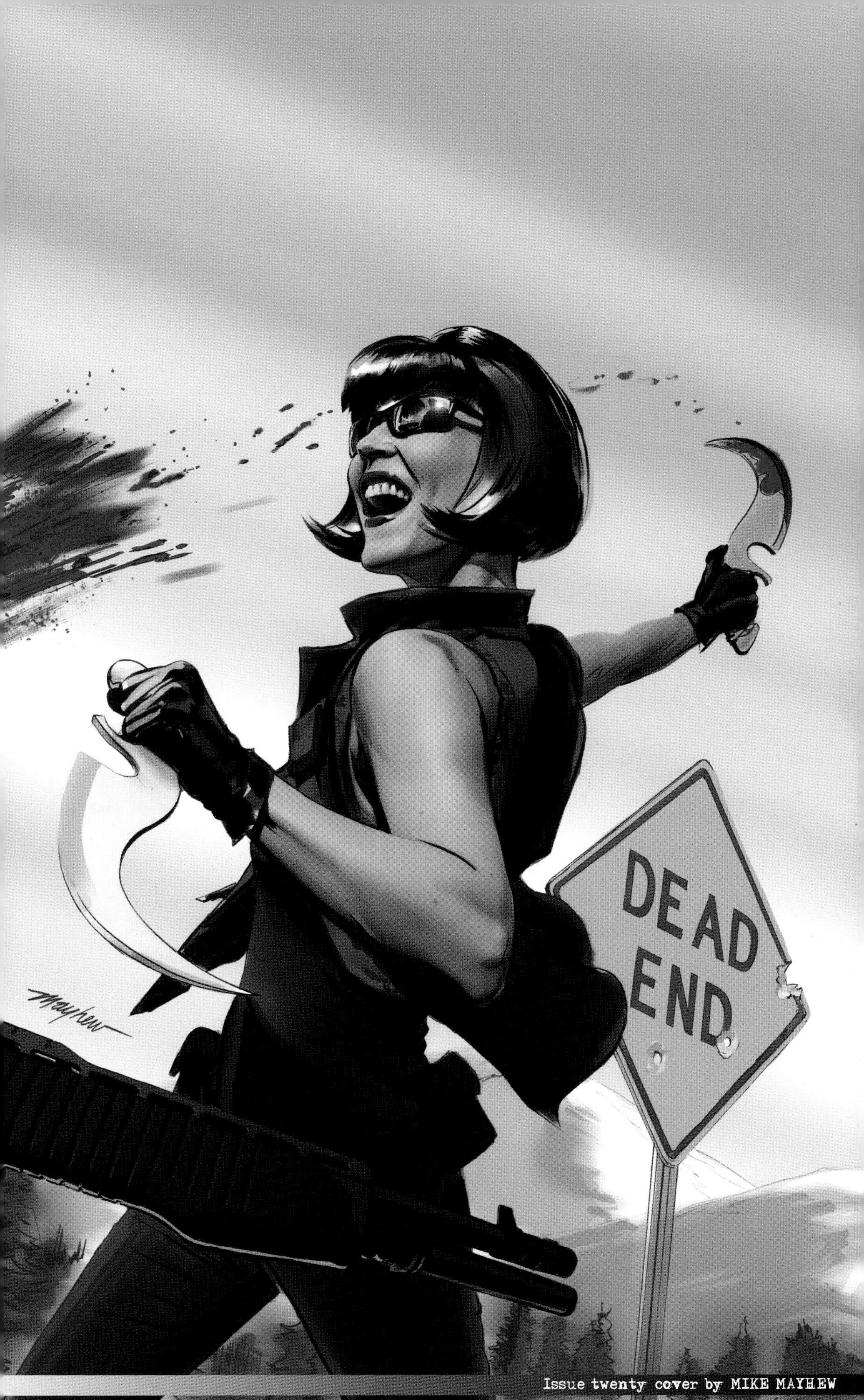
mayhew
DEAD END

Issue twenty cover by MIKE MAYHEW

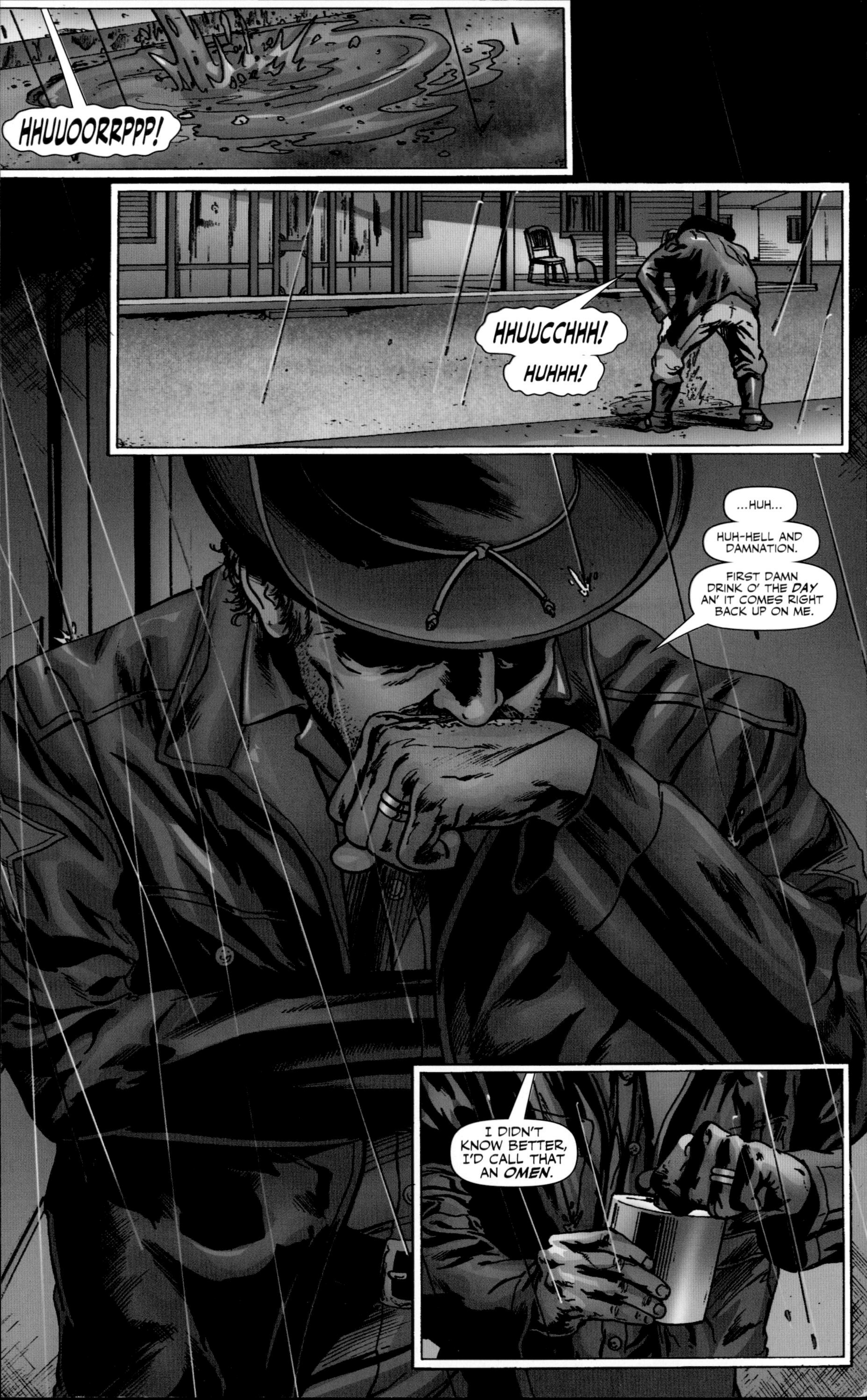

HHUUOORRPPP!
HHUUCCHHH!
HUHHH!
...HUH...
HUH-HELL AND DAMNATION.
FIRST DAMN DRINK O' THE *DAY* AN' IT COMES RIGHT BACK UP ON ME.
I DIDN'T KNOW BETTER, I'D CALL THAT AN *OMEN*.

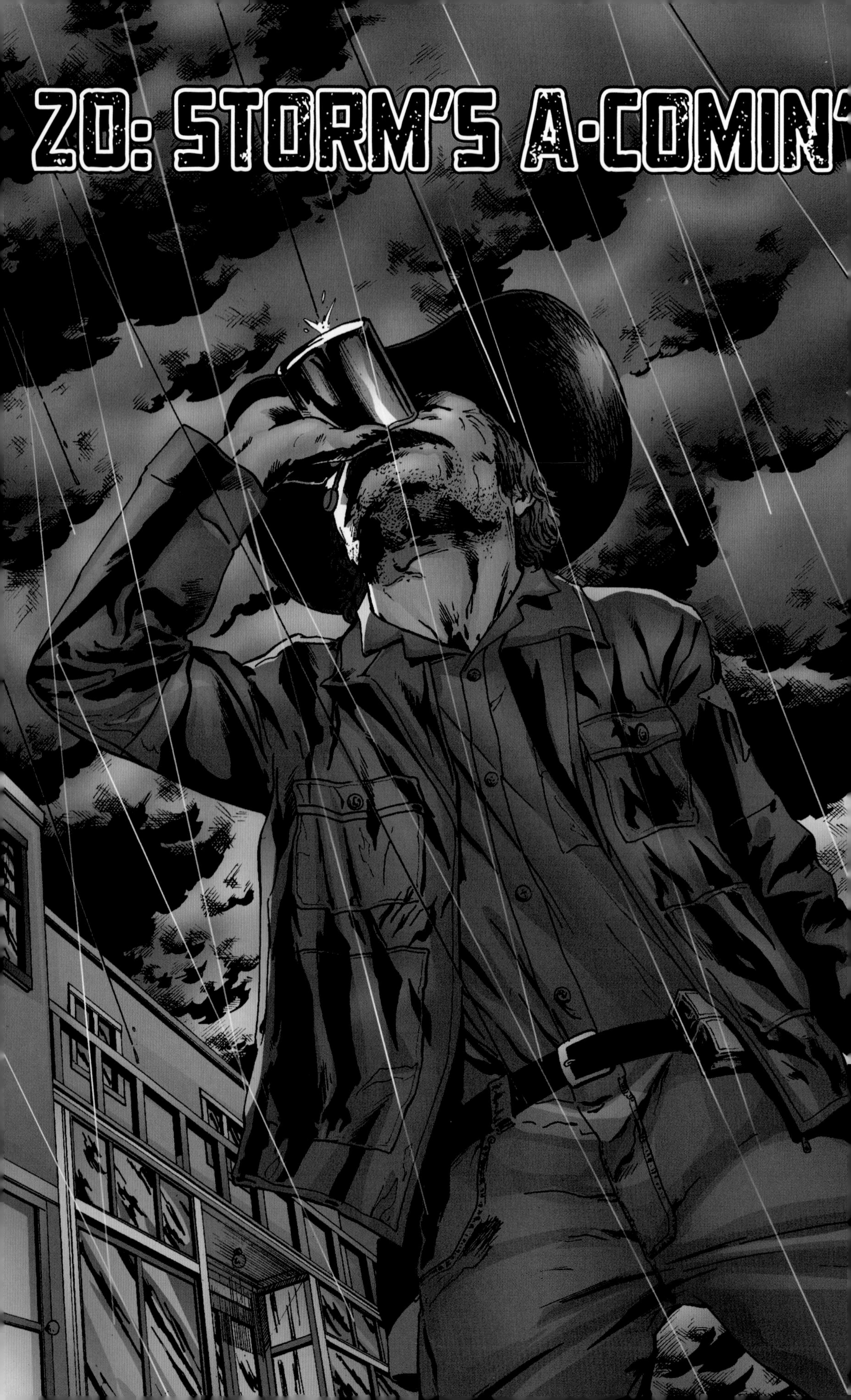
20: STORM'S A-COMIN'

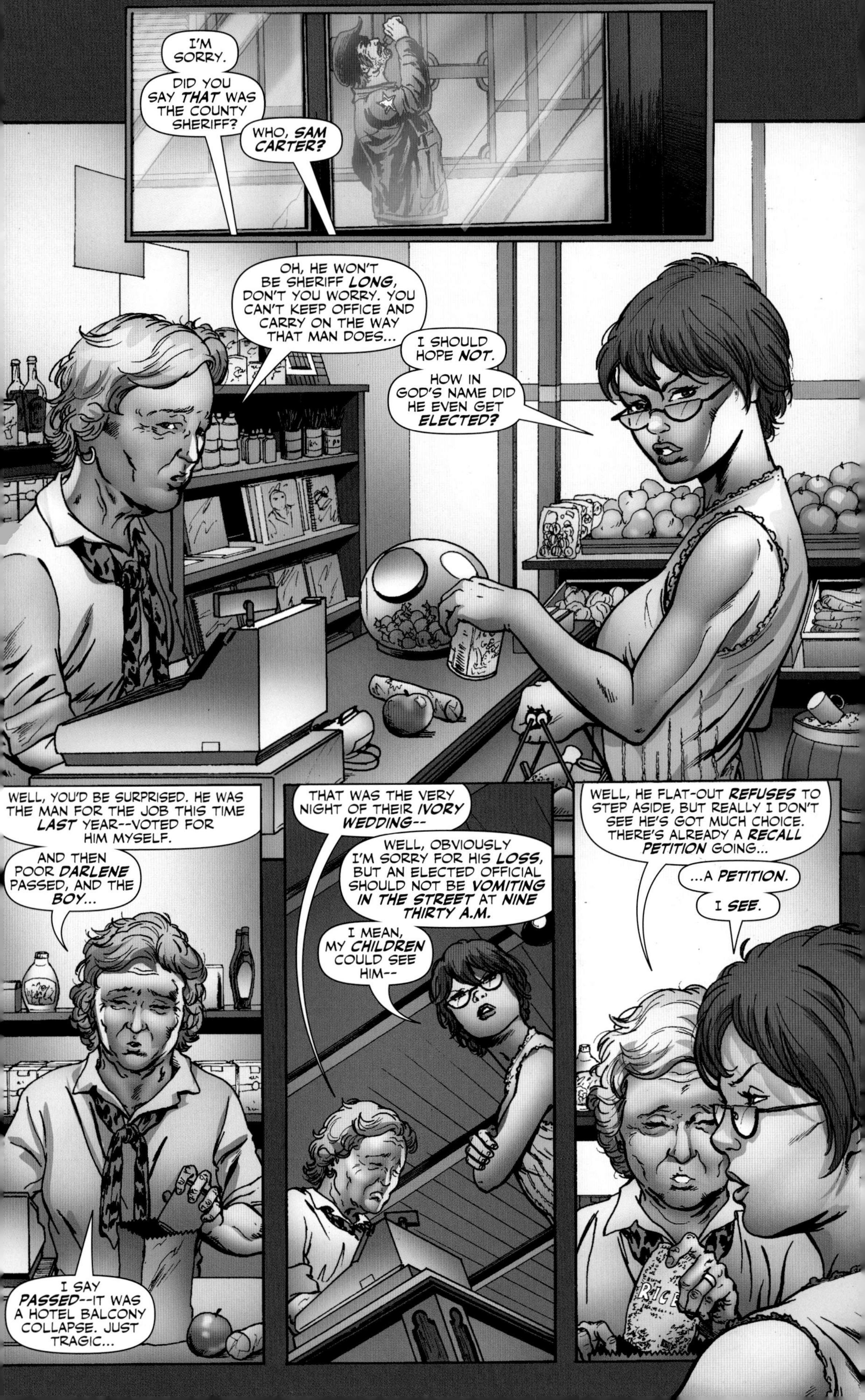
I'M SORRY.
DID YOU SAY THAT WAS THE COUNTY SHERIFF?
WHO, SAM CARTER?
OH, HE WON'T BE SHERIFF LONG, DON'T YOU WORRY. YOU CAN'T KEEP OFFICE AND CARRY ON THE WAY THAT MAN DOES...
I SHOULD HOPE NOT.
HOW IN GOD'S NAME DID HE EVEN GET ELECTED?
WELL, YOU'D BE SURPRISED. HE WAS THE MAN FOR THE JOB THIS TIME LAST YEAR--VOTED FOR HIM MYSELF.
AND THEN POOR DARLENE PASSED, AND THE BOY...
I SAY PASSED--IT WAS A HOTEL BALCONY COLLAPSE. JUST TRAGIC...
THAT WAS THE VERY NIGHT OF THEIR IVORY WEDDING--
WELL, OBVIOUSLY I'M SORRY FOR HIS LOSS, BUT AN ELECTED OFFICIAL SHOULD NOT BE VOMITING IN THE STREET AT NINE THIRTY A.M.
I MEAN, MY CHILDREN COULD SEE HIM--
WELL, HE FLAT-OUT REFUSES TO STEP ASIDE, BUT REALLY I DON'T SEE HE'S GOT MUCH CHOICE. THERE'S ALREADY A RECALL PETITION GOING...
...A PETITION.
I SEE.
RICE

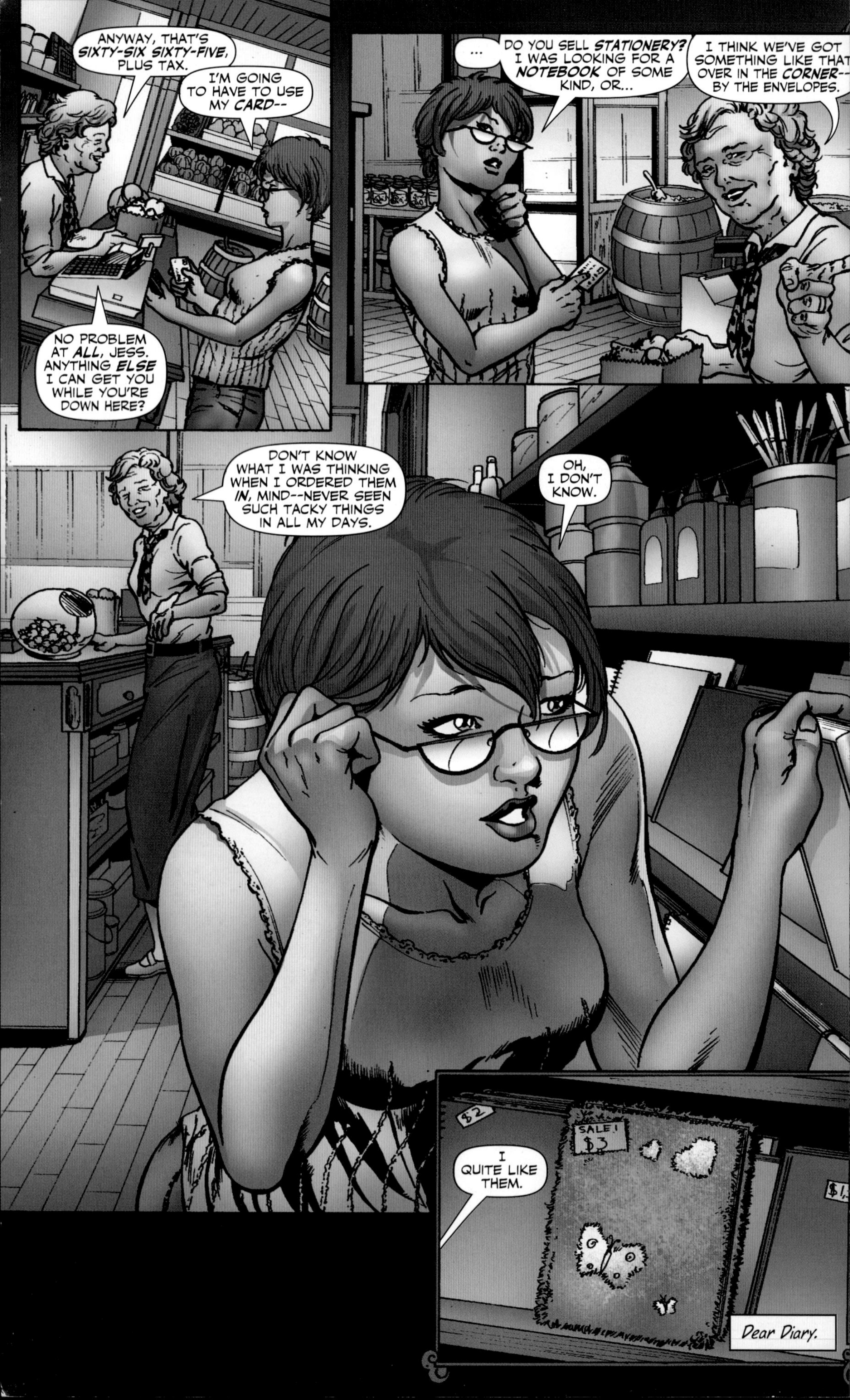

ANYWAY, THAT'S *SIXTY-SIX SIXTY-FIVE,* PLUS TAX.
I'M GOING TO HAVE TO USE MY *CARD*--
NO PROBLEM AT *ALL,* JESS. ANYTHING *ELSE* I CAN GET YOU WHILE YOU'RE DOWN HERE?
...
DO YOU SELL *STATIONERY?* I WAS LOOKING FOR A *NOTEBOOK* OF SOME KIND, OR...
I THINK WE'VE GOT SOMETHING LIKE THAT OVER IN THE *CORNER*-- BY THE ENVELOPES.
DON'T KNOW WHAT I WAS THINKING WHEN I ORDERED THEM *IN,* MIND--NEVER SEEN SUCH TACKY THINGS IN ALL MY DAYS.
OH, I DON'T KNOW.
$2
SALE! $3
I QUITE LIKE THEM.
Dear Diary.

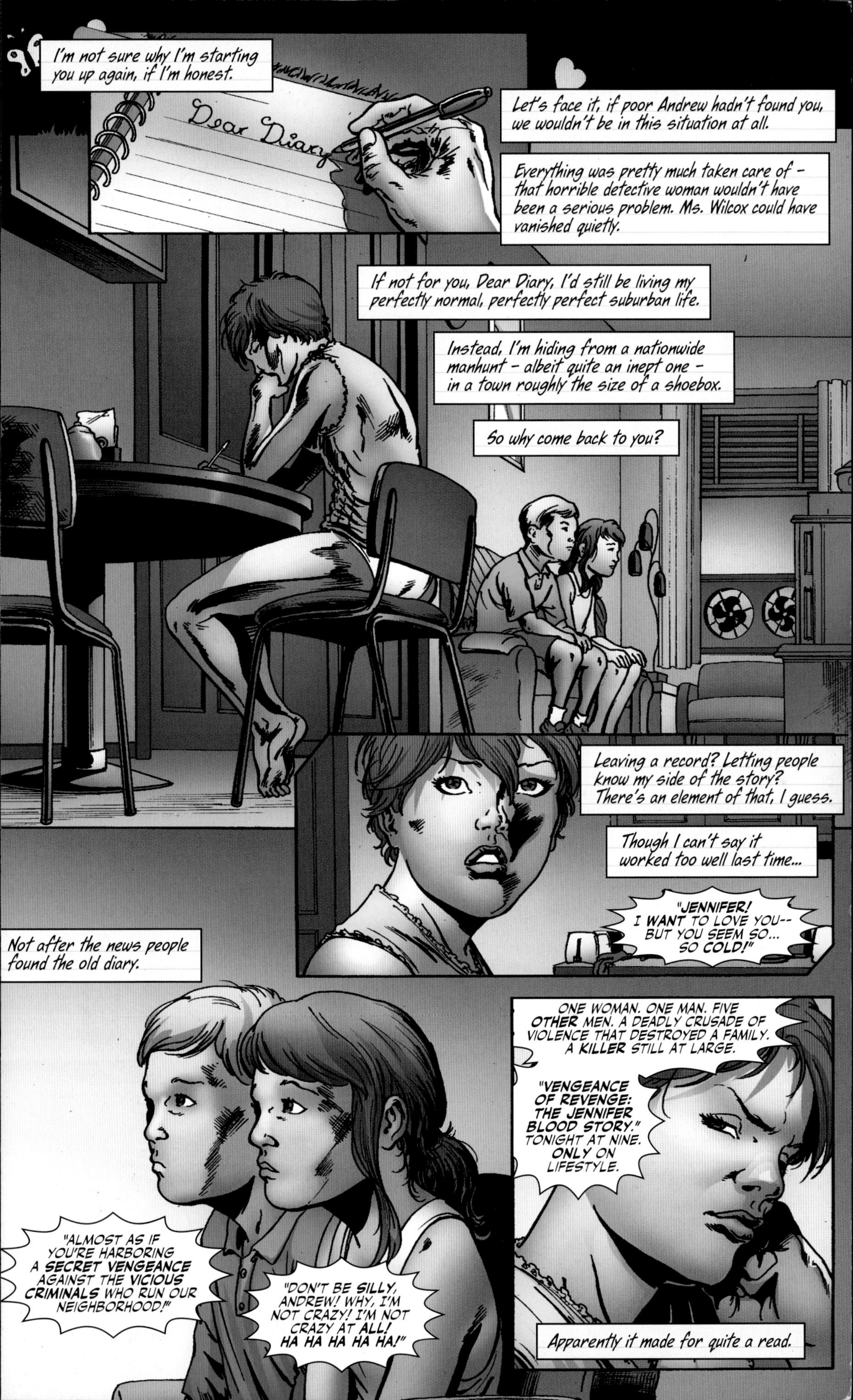
I'm not sure why I'm starting you up again, if I'm honest.
Dear Diary
Let's face it, if poor Andrew hadn't found you, we wouldn't be in this situation at all.
Everything was pretty much taken care of - that horrible detective woman wouldn't have been a serious problem. Ms. Wilcox could have vanished quietly.
If not for you, Dear Diary, I'd still be living my perfectly normal, perfectly perfect suburban life.
Instead, I'm hiding from a nationwide manhunt - albeit quite an inept one - in a town roughly the size of a shoebox.
So why come back to you?
Leaving a record? Letting people know my side of the story? There's an element of that, I guess.
Though I can't say it worked too well last time...
"JENNIFER! I WANT TO LOVE YOU-- BUT YOU SEEM SO... SO COLD!"
Not after the news people found the old diary.
ONE WOMAN. ONE MAN. FIVE OTHER MEN. A DEADLY CRUSADE OF VIOLENCE THAT DESTROYED A FAMILY. A KILLER STILL AT LARGE.
"VENGEANCE OF REVENGE: THE JENNIFER BLOOD STORY." TONIGHT AT NINE. ONLY ON LIFESTYLE.
"ALMOST AS IF YOU'RE HARBORING A SECRET VENGEANCE AGAINST THE VICIOUS CRIMINALS WHO RUN OUR NEIGHBORHOOD!"
"DON'T BE SILLY, ANDREW! WHY, I'M NOT CRAZY! I'M NOT CRAZY AT ALL! HA HA HA HA HA!"
Apparently it made for quite a read.

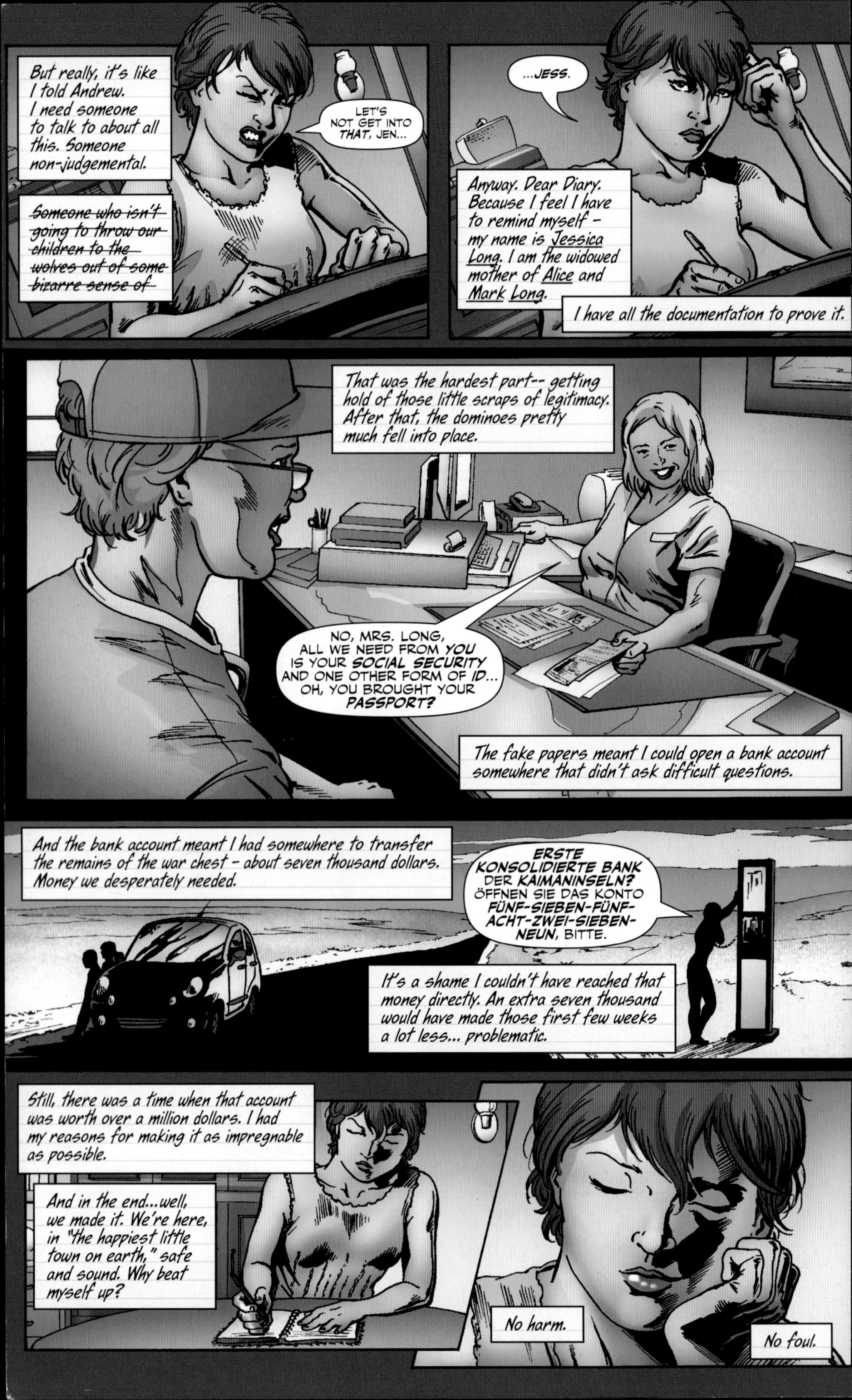
But really, it's like I told Andrew. I need someone to talk to about all this. Someone non-judgemental.
~~Someone who isn't going to throw our children to the wolves out of some bizarre sense of~~
LET'S NOT GET INTO THAT, JEN...
...JESS.
Anyway. Dear Diary. Because I feel I have to remind myself – my name is Jessica Long. I am the widowed mother of Alice and Mark Long.
I have all the documentation to prove it.
That was the hardest part-- getting hold of those little scraps of legitimacy. After that, the dominoes pretty much fell into place.
NO, MRS. LONG, ALL WE NEED FROM YOU IS YOUR SOCIAL SECURITY AND ONE OTHER FORM OF ID... OH, YOU BROUGHT YOUR PASSPORT?
The fake papers meant I could open a bank account somewhere that didn't ask difficult questions.
And the bank account meant I had somewhere to transfer the remains of the war chest – about seven thousand dollars. Money we desperately needed.
ERSTE KONSOLIDIERTE BANK DER KAIMANINSELN? ÖFFNEN SIE DAS KONTO FÜNF-SIEBEN-FÜNF-ACHT-ZWEI-SIEBEN-NEUN, BITTE.
It's a shame I couldn't have reached that money directly. An extra seven thousand would have made those first few weeks a lot less... problematic.
Still, there was a time when that account was worth over a million dollars. I had my reasons for making it as impregnable as possible.
And in the end...well, we made it. We're here, in "the happiest little town on earth," safe and sound. Why beat myself up?
No harm.
No foul.

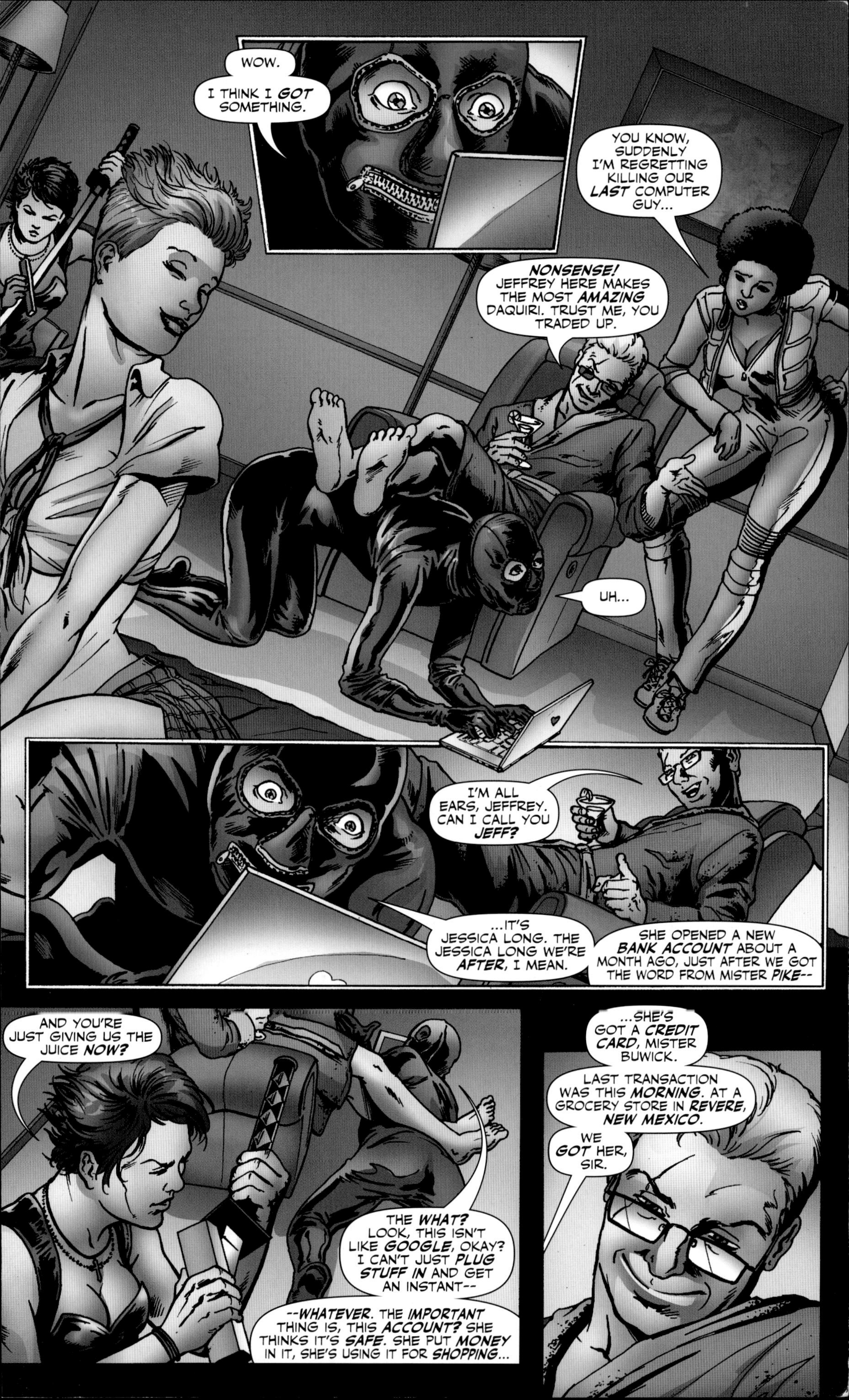
WOW.
I THINK I GOT SOMETHING.
YOU KNOW, SUDDENLY I'M REGRETTING KILLING OUR LAST COMPUTER GUY...
NONSENSE! JEFFREY HERE MAKES THE MOST AMAZING DAQUIRI. TRUST ME, YOU TRADED UP.
UH...
I'M ALL EARS, JEFFREY. CAN I CALL YOU JEFF?
...IT'S JESSICA LONG. THE JESSICA LONG WE'RE AFTER, I MEAN.
SHE OPENED A NEW BANK ACCOUNT ABOUT A MONTH AGO, JUST AFTER WE GOT THE WORD FROM MISTER PIKE--
AND YOU'RE JUST GIVING US THE JUICE NOW?
THE WHAT? LOOK, THIS ISN'T LIKE GOOGLE, OKAY? I CAN'T JUST PLUG STUFF IN AND GET AN INSTANT--
--WHATEVER. THE IMPORTANT THING IS, THIS ACCOUNT? SHE THINKS IT'S SAFE. SHE PUT MONEY IN IT, SHE'S USING IT FOR SHOPPING...
...SHE'S GOT A CREDIT CARD, MISTER BUWICK.
LAST TRANSACTION WAS THIS MORNING. AT A GROCERY STORE IN REVERE, NEW MEXICO.
WE GOT HER, SIR.

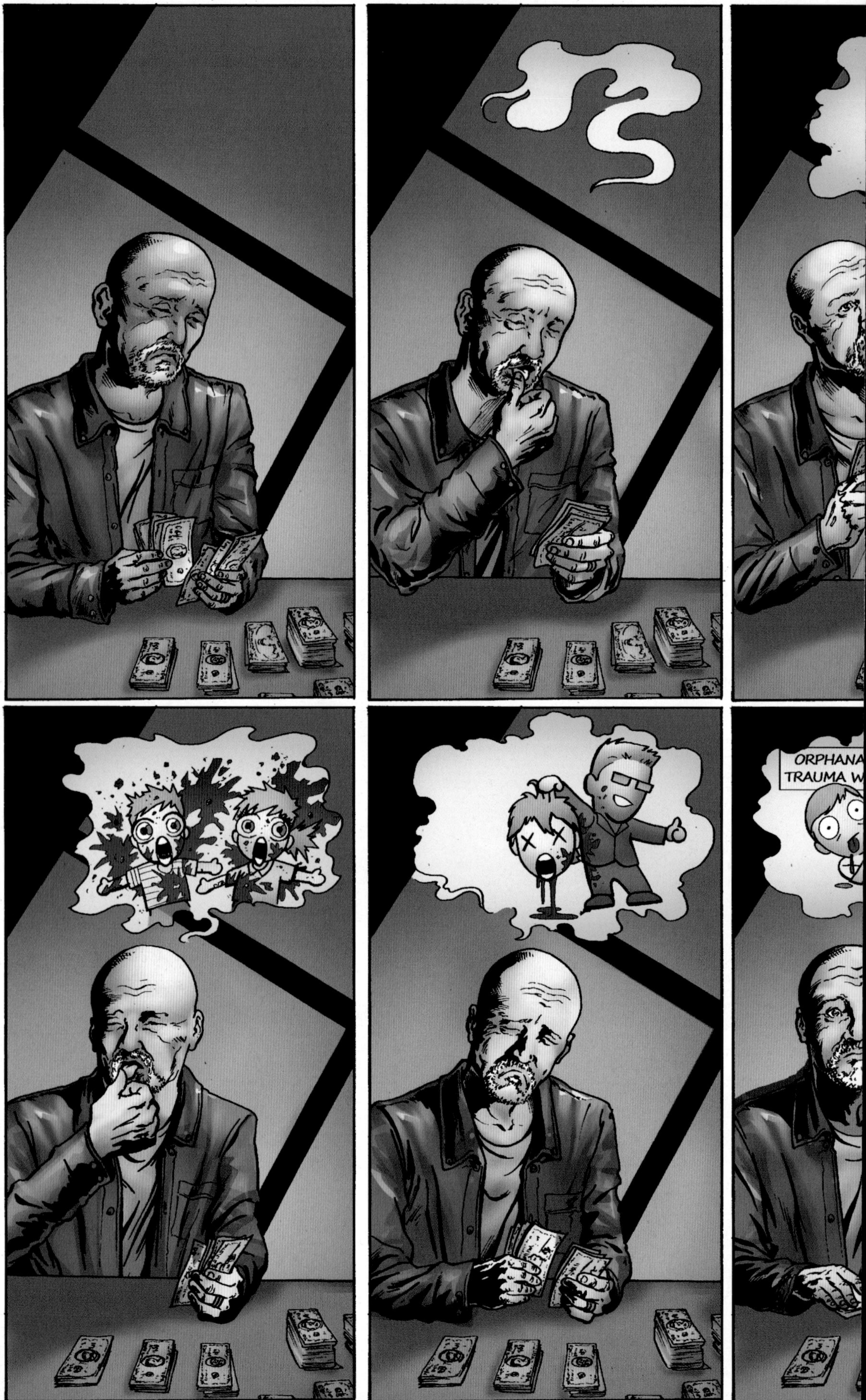
ORPHANA
TRAUMA W

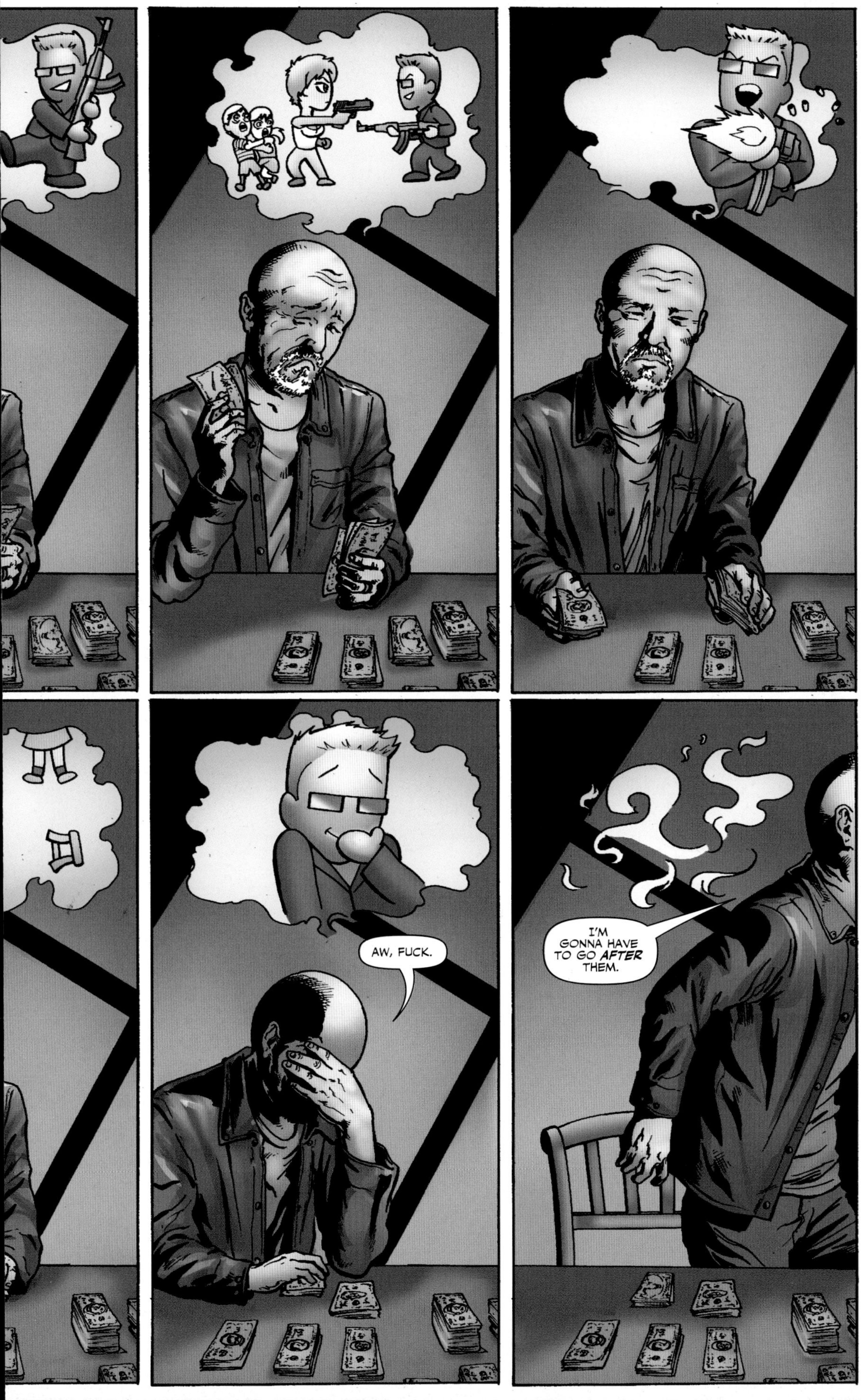
AW, FUCK.
I'M GONNA HAVE TO GO AFTER THEM.

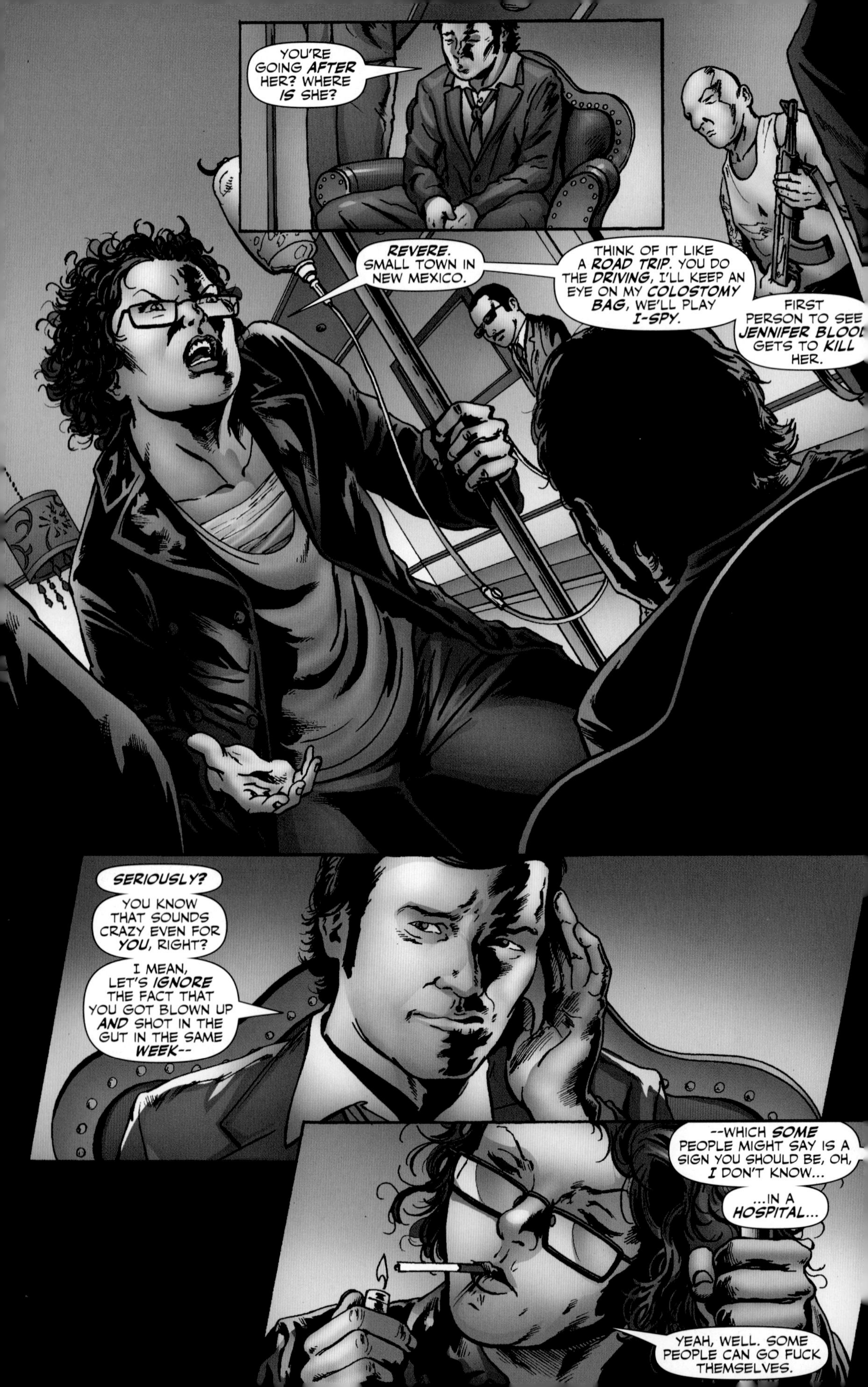
YOU'RE GOING AFTER HER? WHERE IS SHE?
REVERE. SMALL TOWN IN NEW MEXICO.
THINK OF IT LIKE A ROAD TRIP. YOU DO THE DRIVING, I'LL KEEP AN EYE ON MY COLOSTOMY BAG, WE'LL PLAY I-SPY.
FIRST PERSON TO SEE JENNIFER BLOOD GETS TO KILL HER.
SERIOUSLY?
YOU KNOW THAT SOUNDS CRAZY EVEN FOR YOU, RIGHT?
I MEAN, LET'S IGNORE THE FACT THAT YOU GOT BLOWN UP AND SHOT IN THE GUT IN THE SAME WEEK--
--WHICH SOME PEOPLE MIGHT SAY IS A SIGN YOU SHOULD BE, OH, I DON'T KNOW...
...IN A HOSPITAL...
YEAH, WELL. SOME PEOPLE CAN GO FUCK THEMSELVES.

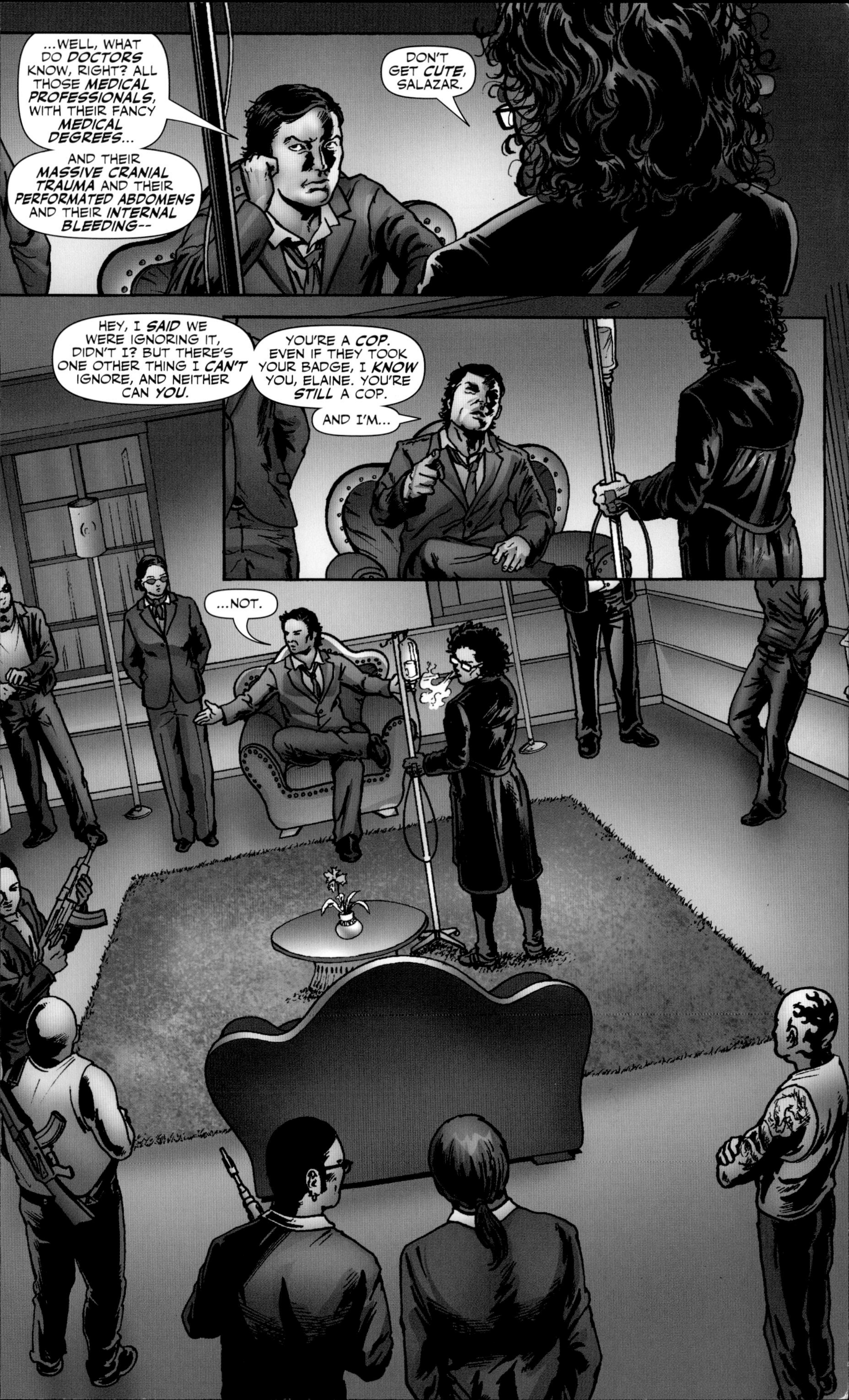

...WELL, WHAT DO DOCTORS KNOW, RIGHT? ALL THOSE MEDICAL PROFESSIONALS, WITH THEIR FANCY MEDICAL DEGREES...
AND THEIR MASSIVE CRANIAL TRAUMA AND THEIR PERFORMATED ABDOMENS AND THEIR INTERNAL BLEEDING--
DON'T GET CUTE, SALAZAR.
HEY, I SAID WE WERE IGNORING IT, DIDN'T I? BUT THERE'S ONE OTHER THING I CAN'T IGNORE, AND NEITHER CAN YOU.
YOU'RE A COP. EVEN IF THEY TOOK YOUR BADGE, I KNOW YOU, ELAINE. YOU'RE STILL A COP.
AND I'M...
...NOT.

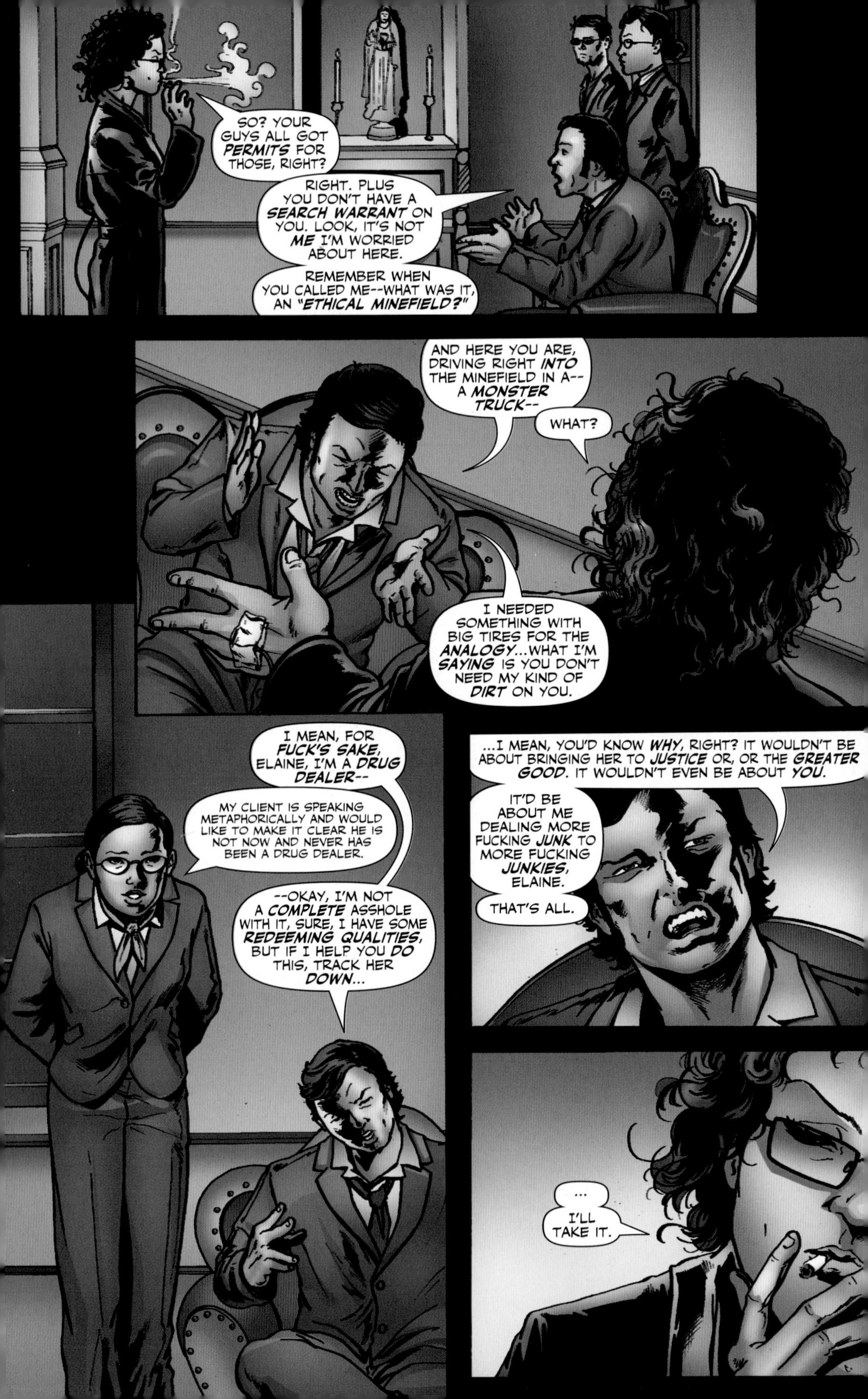
SO? YOUR GUYS ALL GOT PERMITS FOR THOSE, RIGHT?
RIGHT. PLUS YOU DON'T HAVE A SEARCH WARRANT ON YOU. LOOK, IT'S NOT ME I'M WORRIED ABOUT HERE.
REMEMBER WHEN YOU CALLED ME--WHAT WAS IT, AN "ETHICAL MINEFIELD?"
AND HERE YOU ARE, DRIVING RIGHT INTO THE MINEFIELD IN A-- A MONSTER TRUCK--
WHAT?
I NEEDED SOMETHING WITH BIG TIRES FOR THE ANALOGY...WHAT I'M SAYING IS YOU DON'T NEED MY KIND OF DIRT ON YOU.
I MEAN, FOR FUCK'S SAKE, ELAINE, I'M A DRUG DEALER--
MY CLIENT IS SPEAKING METAPHORICALLY AND WOULD LIKE TO MAKE IT CLEAR HE IS NOT NOW AND NEVER HAS BEEN A DRUG DEALER.
--OKAY, I'M NOT A COMPLETE ASSHOLE WITH IT, SURE, I HAVE SOME REDEEMING QUALITIES, BUT IF I HELP YOU DO THIS, TRACK HER DOWN...
...I MEAN, YOU'D KNOW WHY, RIGHT? IT WOULDN'T BE ABOUT BRINGING HER TO JUSTICE OR, OR THE GREATER GOOD. IT WOULDN'T EVEN BE ABOUT YOU.
IT'D BE ABOUT ME DEALING MORE FUCKING JUNK TO MORE FUCKING JUNKIES, ELAINE.
THAT'S ALL.
...
I'LL TAKE IT.

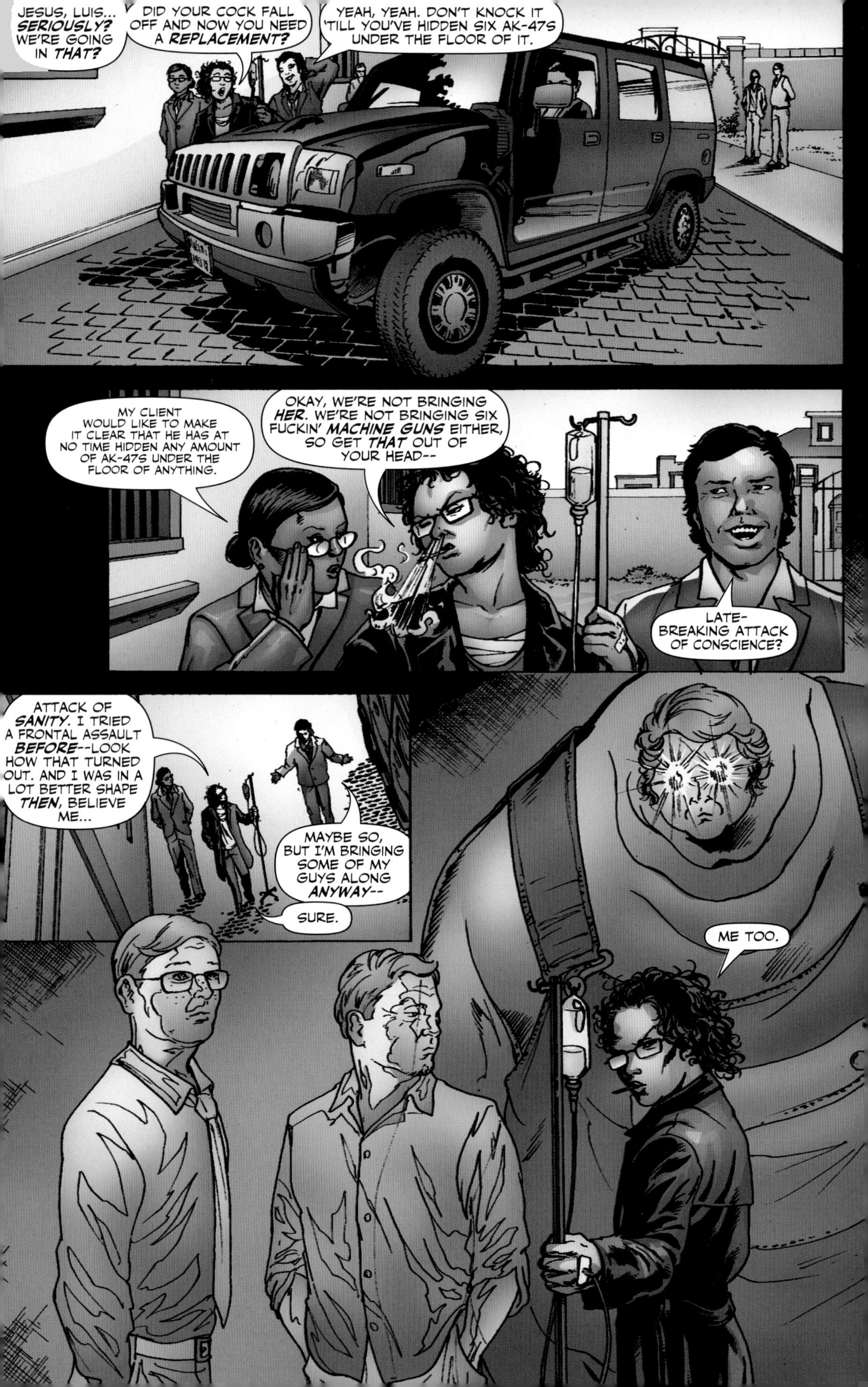
JESUS, LUIS... SERIOUSLY? WE'RE GOING IN THAT?
DID YOUR COCK FALL OFF AND NOW YOU NEED A REPLACEMENT?
YEAH, YEAH. DON'T KNOCK IT 'TILL YOU'VE HIDDEN SIX AK-47S UNDER THE FLOOR OF IT.
MY CLIENT WOULD LIKE TO MAKE IT CLEAR THAT HE HAS AT NO TIME HIDDEN ANY AMOUNT OF AK-47S UNDER THE FLOOR OF ANYTHING.
OKAY, WE'RE NOT BRINGING HER. WE'RE NOT BRINGING SIX FUCKIN' MACHINE GUNS EITHER, SO GET THAT OUT OF YOUR HEAD--
LATE-BREAKING ATTACK OF CONSCIENCE?
ATTACK OF SANITY. I TRIED A FRONTAL ASSAULT BEFORE--LOOK HOW THAT TURNED OUT. AND I WAS IN A LOT BETTER SHAPE THEN, BELIEVE ME...
MAYBE SO, BUT I'M BRINGING SOME OF MY GUYS ALONG ANYWAY--
SURE.
ME TOO.

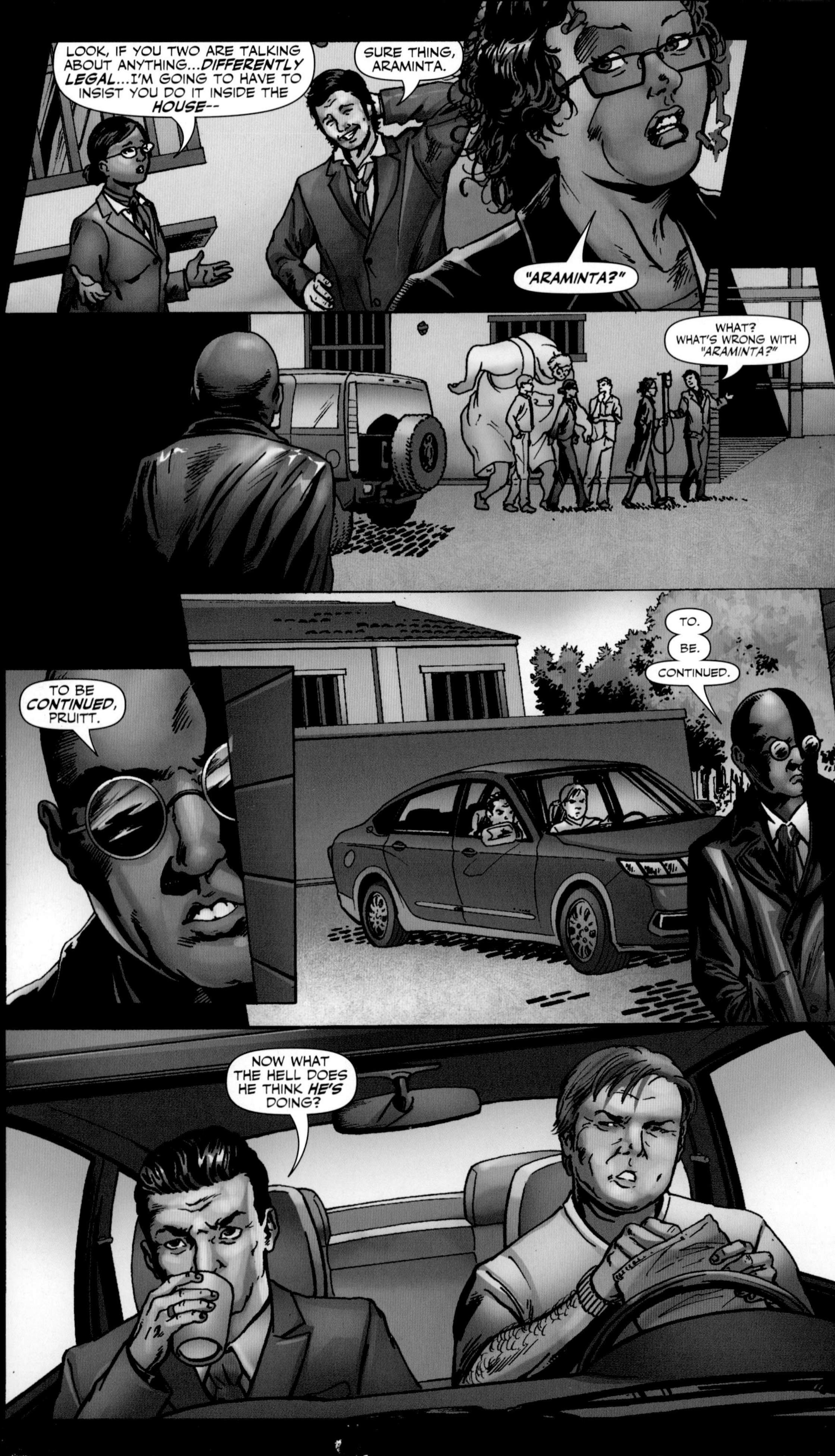
LOOK, IF YOU TWO ARE TALKING ABOUT ANYTHING...DIFFERENTLY LEGAL...I'M GOING TO HAVE TO INSIST YOU DO IT INSIDE THE HOUSE--
SURE THING, ARAMINTA.
"ARAMINTA?"
WHAT? WHAT'S WRONG WITH "ARAMINTA?"
TO.
BE.
CONTINUED.
TO BE CONTINUED, PRUITT.
NOW WHAT THE HELL DOES HE THINK HE'S DOING?

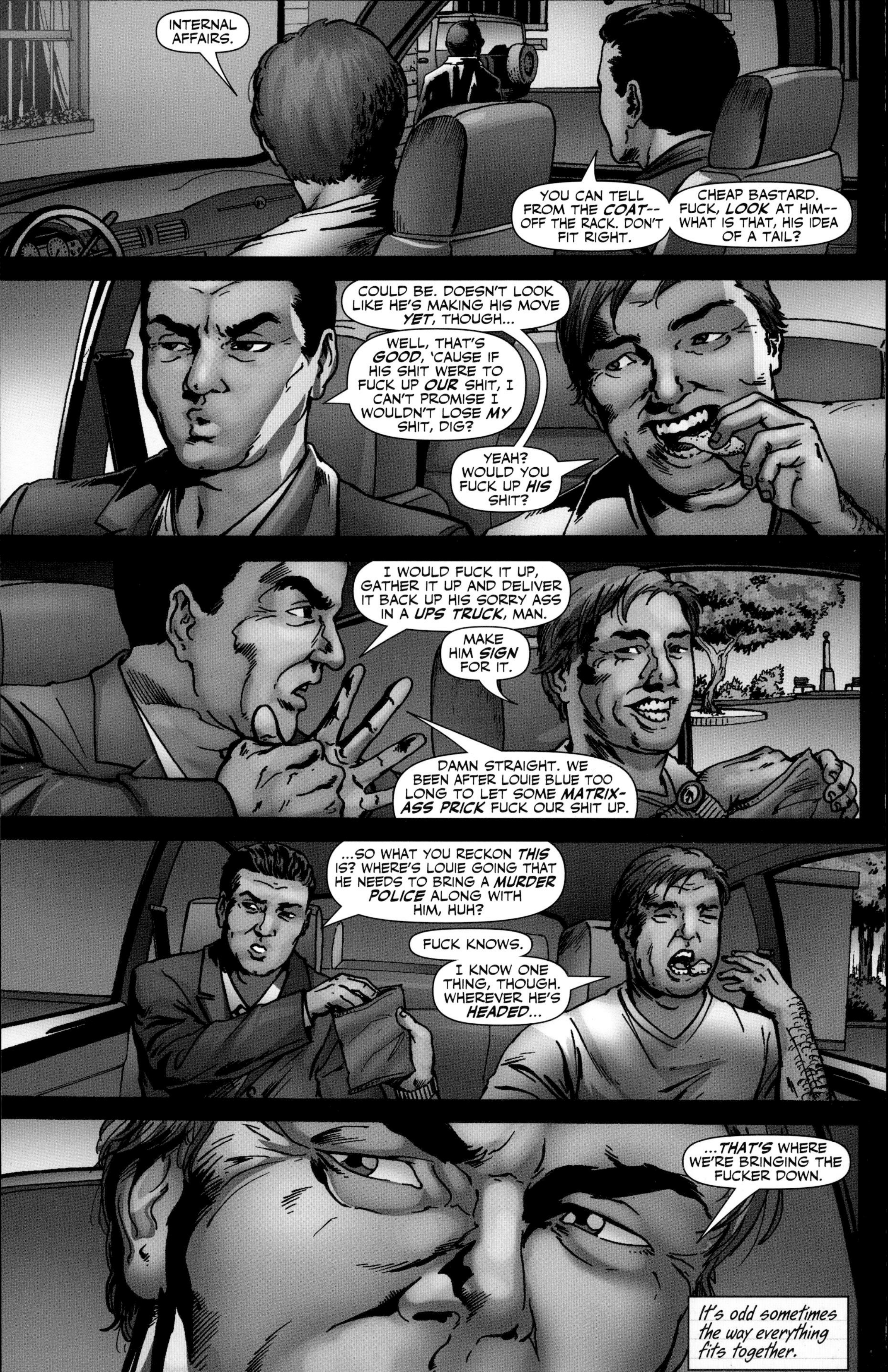
INTERNAL AFFAIRS.
YOU CAN TELL FROM THE COAT-- OFF THE RACK. DON'T FIT RIGHT.
CHEAP BASTARD. FUCK, LOOK AT HIM-- WHAT IS THAT, HIS IDEA OF A TAIL?
COULD BE. DOESN'T LOOK LIKE HE'S MAKING HIS MOVE YET, THOUGH...
WELL, THAT'S GOOD, 'CAUSE IF HIS SHIT WERE TO FUCK UP OUR SHIT, I CAN'T PROMISE I WOULDN'T LOSE MY SHIT, DIG?
YEAH? WOULD YOU FUCK UP HIS SHIT?
I WOULD FUCK IT UP, GATHER IT UP AND DELIVER IT BACK UP HIS SORRY ASS IN A UPS TRUCK, MAN.
MAKE HIM SIGN FOR IT.
DAMN STRAIGHT. WE BEEN AFTER LOUIE BLUE TOO LONG TO LET SOME MATRIX-ASS PRICK FUCK OUR SHIT UP.
...SO WHAT YOU RECKON THIS IS? WHERE'S LOUIE GOING THAT HE NEEDS TO BRING A MURDER POLICE ALONG WITH HIM, HUH?
FUCK KNOWS.
I KNOW ONE THING, THOUGH. WHEREVER HE'S HEADED...
...THAT'S WHERE WE'RE BRINGING THE FUCKER DOWN.
It's odd sometimes the way everything fits together.

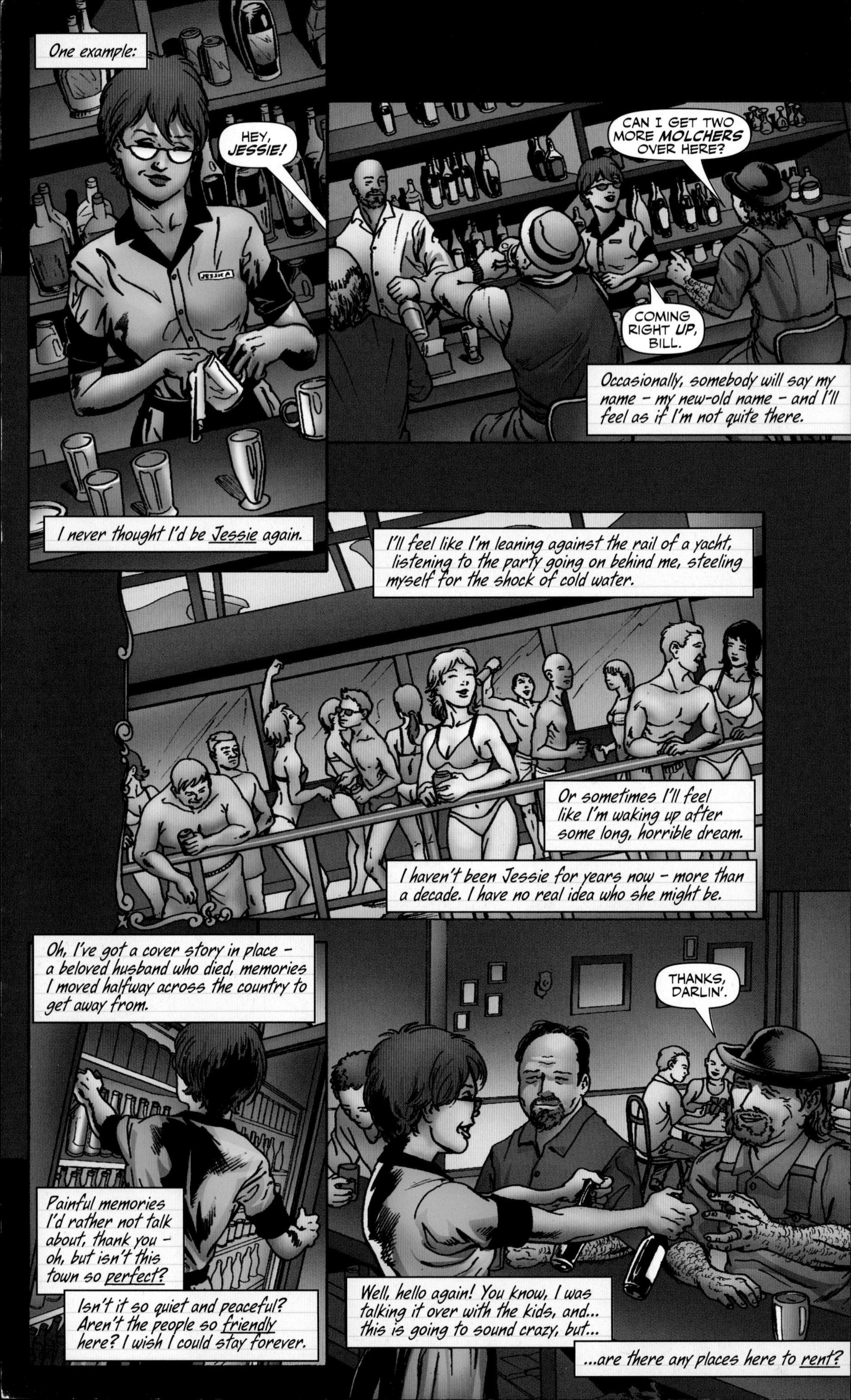
One example:
HEY, JESSIE!
I never thought I'd be Jessie again.
CAN I GET TWO MORE MOLCHERS OVER HERE?
COMING RIGHT UP, BILL.
Occasionally, somebody will say my name – my new-old name – and I'll feel as if I'm not quite there.
I'll feel like I'm leaning against the rail of a yacht, listening to the party going on behind me, steeling myself for the shock of cold water.
Or sometimes I'll feel like I'm waking up after some long, horrible dream.
I haven't been Jessie for years now – more than a decade. I have no real idea who she might be.
Oh, I've got a cover story in place – a beloved husband who died, memories I moved halfway across the country to get away from.
Painful memories I'd rather not talk about, thank you – oh, but isn't this town so perfect?
Isn't it so quiet and peaceful? Aren't the people so friendly here? I wish I could stay forever.
THANKS, DARLIN'.
Well, hello again! You know, I was talking it over with the kids, and... this is going to sound crazy, but...
...are there any places here to rent?

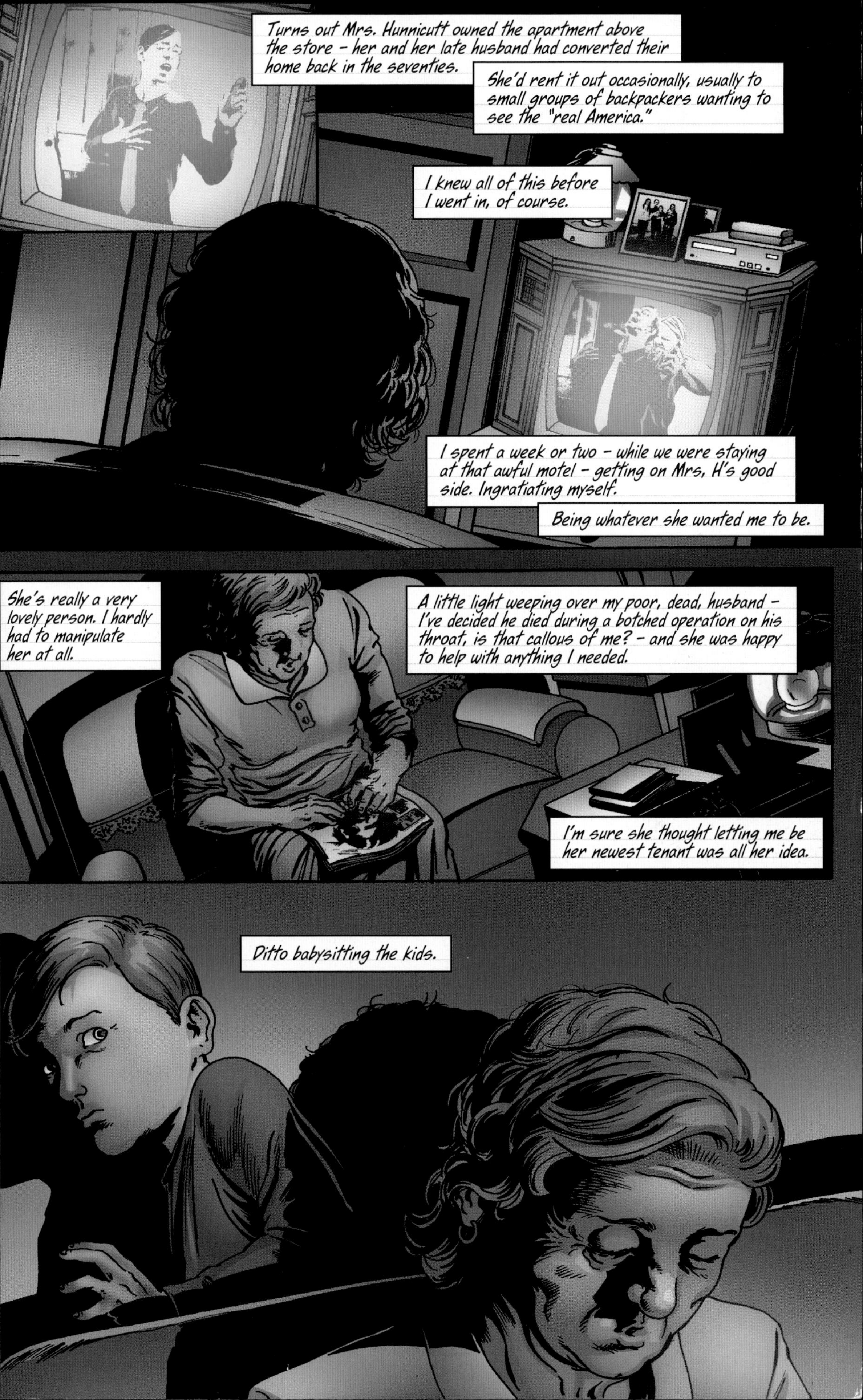

Turns out Mrs. Hunnicutt owned the apartment above the store - her and her late husband had converted their home back in the seventies.
She'd rent it out occasionally, usually to small groups of backpackers wanting to see the "real America."
I knew all of this before I went in, of course.
I spent a week or two - while we were staying at that awful motel - getting on Mrs, H's good side. Ingratiating myself.
Being whatever she wanted me to be.
She's really a very lovely person. I hardly had to manipulate her at all.
A little light weeping over my poor, dead, husband - I've decided he died during a botched operation on his throat, is that callous of me? - and she was happy to help with anything I needed.
I'm sure she thought letting me be her newest tenant was all her idea.
Ditto babysitting the kids.

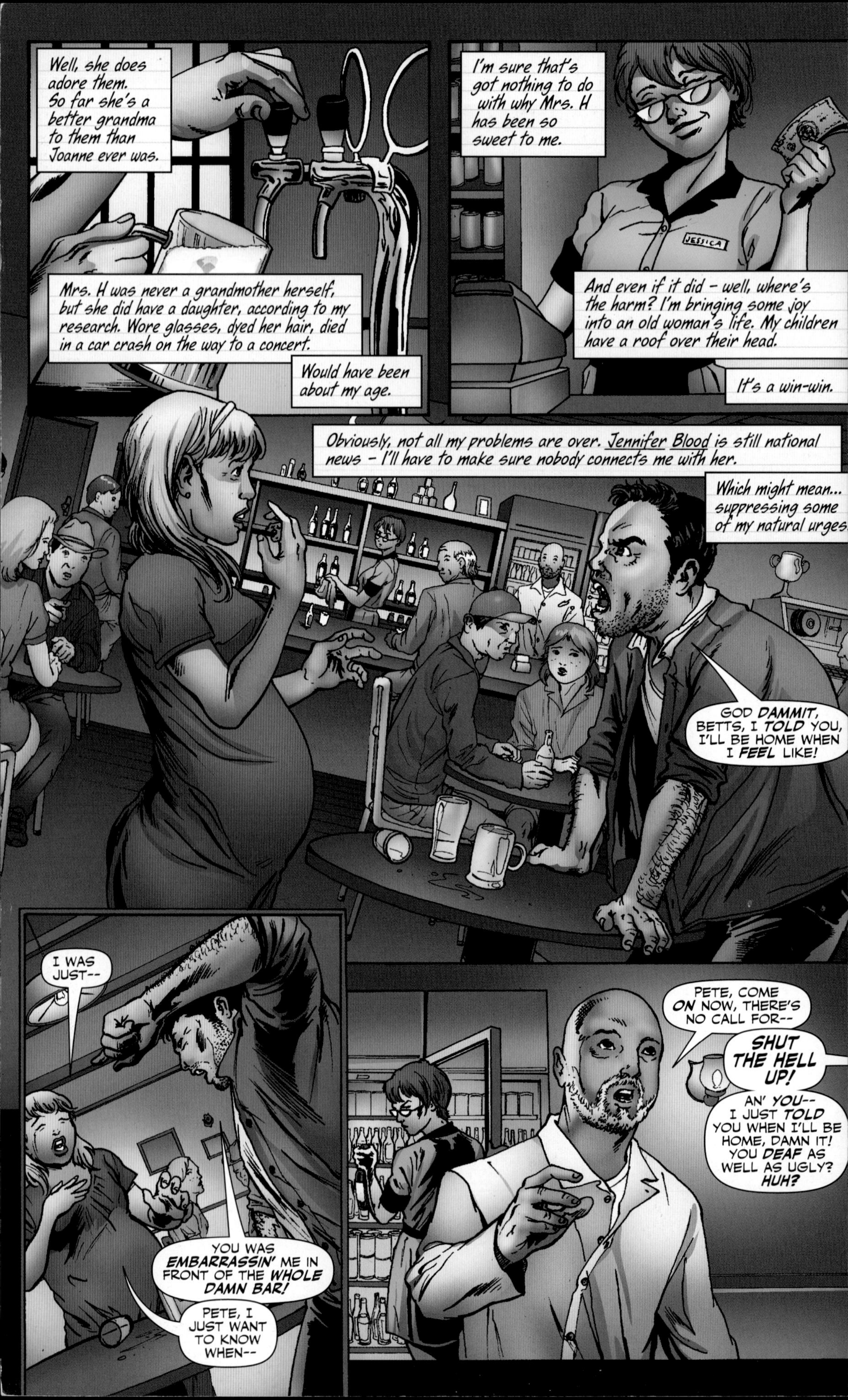

Well, she does adore them. So far she's a better grandma to them than Joanne ever was.
Mrs. H was never a grandmother herself, but she did have a daughter, according to my research. Wore glasses, dyed her hair, died in a car crash on the way to a concert.
Would have been about my age.
I'm sure that's got nothing to do with why Mrs. H has been so sweet to me.
JESSICA
And even if it did - well, where's the harm? I'm bringing some joy into an old woman's life. My children have a roof over their head.
It's a win-win.
Obviously, not all my problems are over. Jennifer Blood is still national news - I'll have to make sure nobody connects me with her.
Which might mean... suppressing some of my natural urges.
GOD DAMMIT, BETTS, I TOLD YOU, I'LL BE HOME WHEN I FEEL LIKE!
I WAS JUST--
YOU WAS EMBARRASSIN' ME IN FRONT OF THE WHOLE DAMN BAR!
PETE, I JUST WANT TO KNOW WHEN--
PETE, COME ON NOW, THERE'S NO CALL FOR--
SHUT THE HELL UP!
AN' YOU-- I JUST TOLD YOU WHEN I'LL BE HOME, DAMN IT! YOU DEAF AS WELL AS UGLY? HUH?

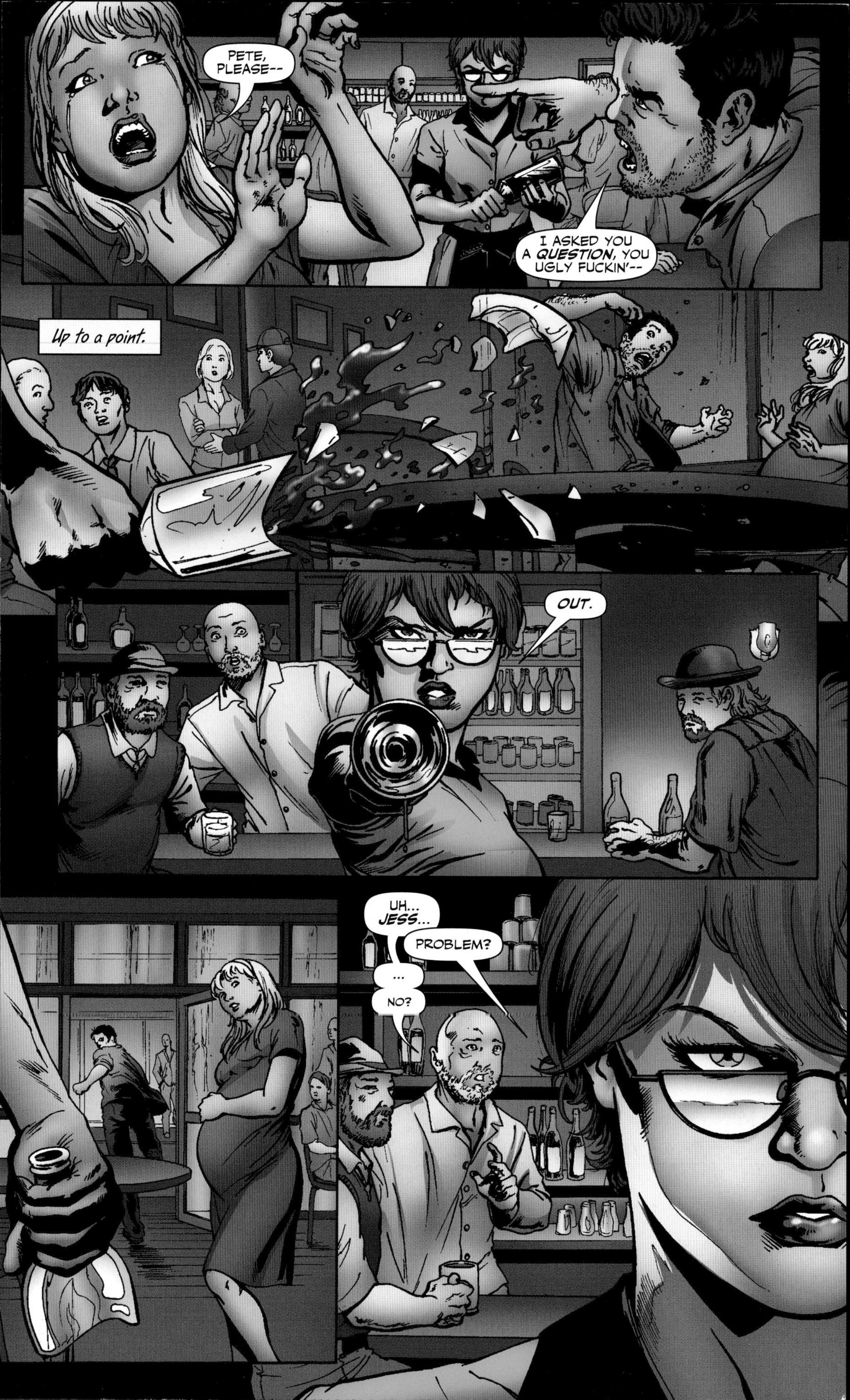
PETE, PLEASE--
I ASKED YOU A QUESTION, YOU UGLY FUCKIN'--
Up to a point.
OUT.
UH... JESS...
PROBLEM?
...
NO?

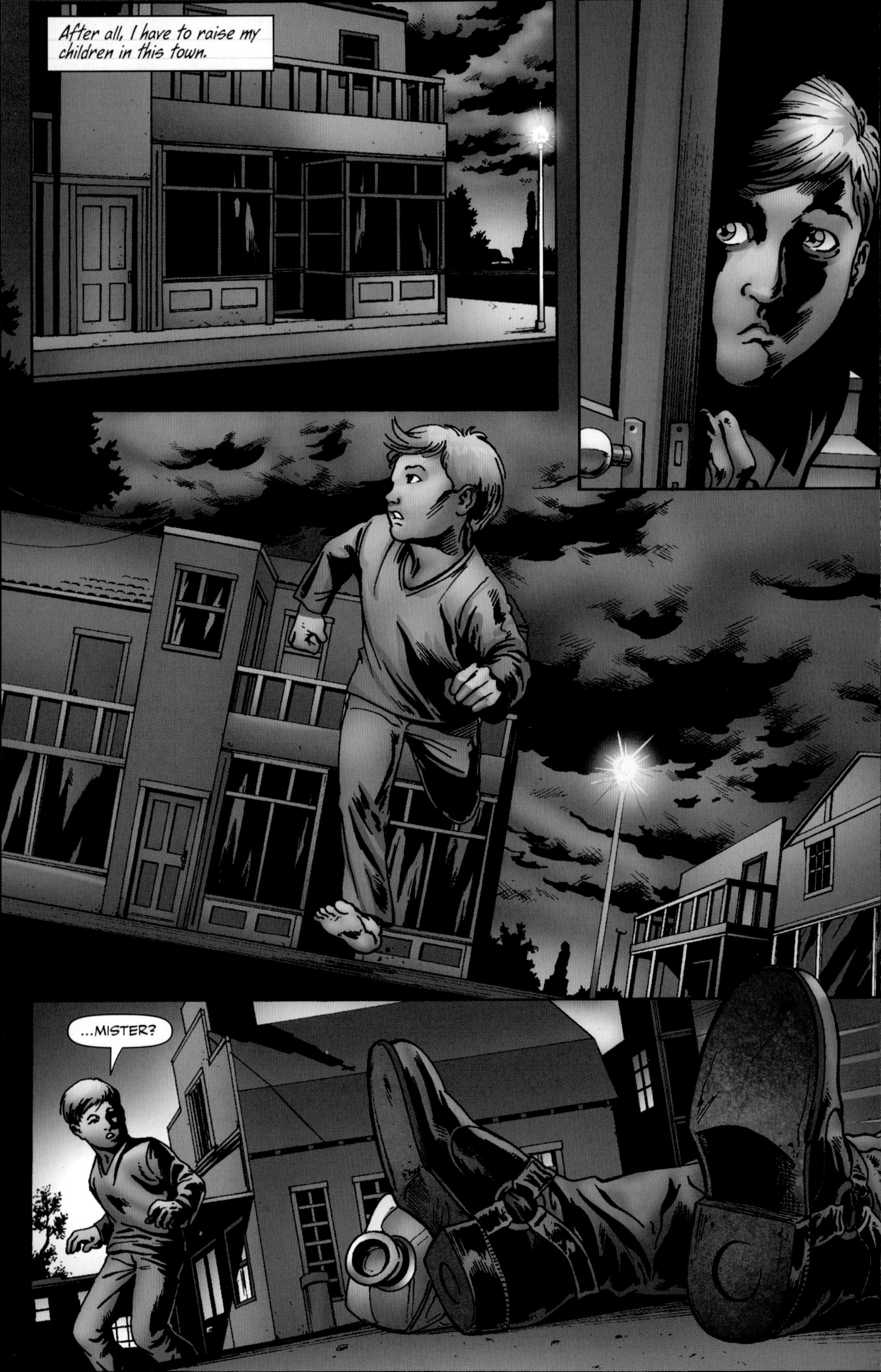
After all, I have to raise my children in this town.
...MISTER?

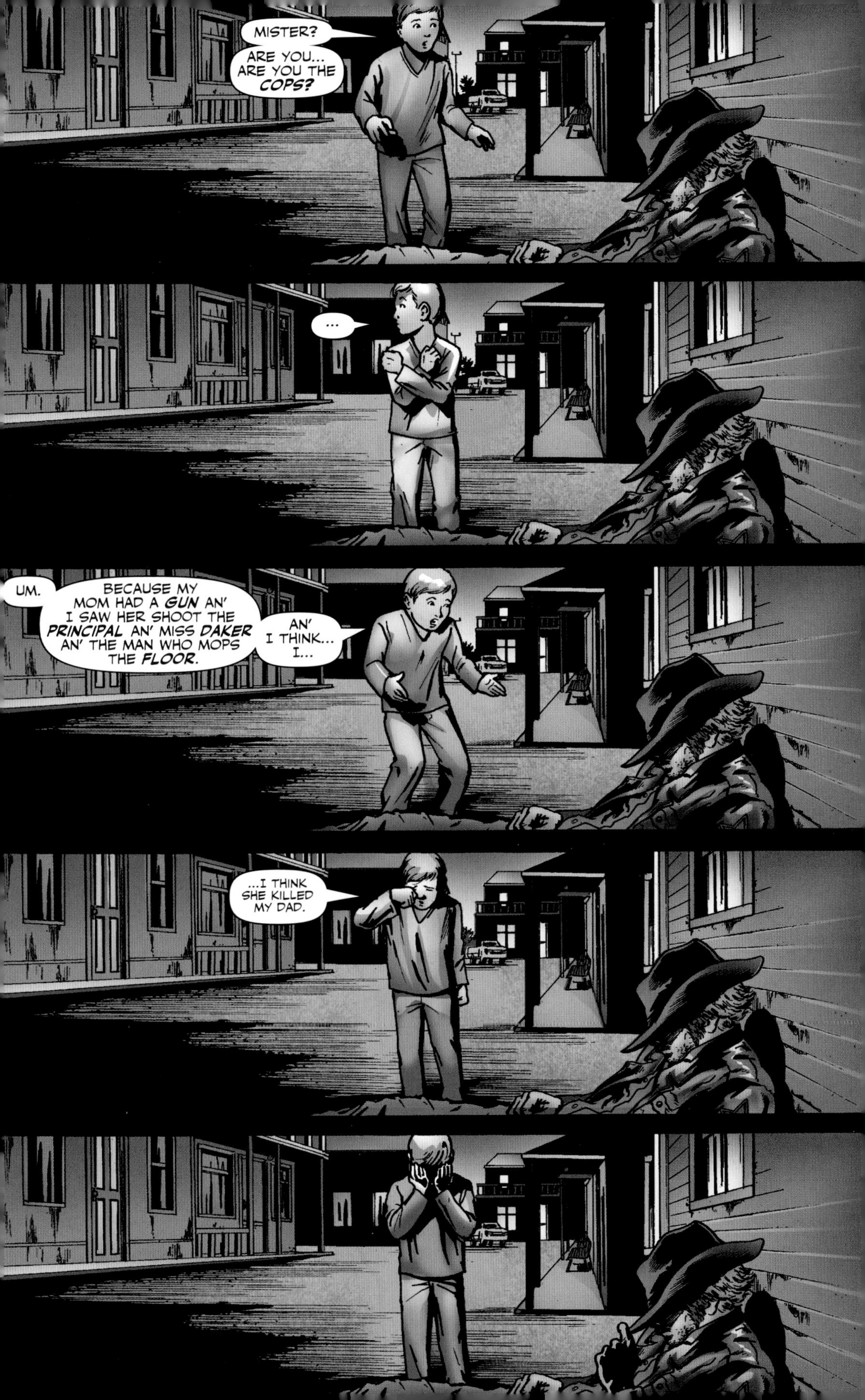
MISTER?
ARE YOU... ARE YOU THE COPS?
...
UM.
BECAUSE MY MOM HAD A GUN AN' I SAW HER SHOOT THE PRINCIPAL AN' MISS DAKER AN' THE MAN WHO MOPS THE FLOOR.
AN' I THINK... I...
...I THINK SHE KILLED MY DAD.

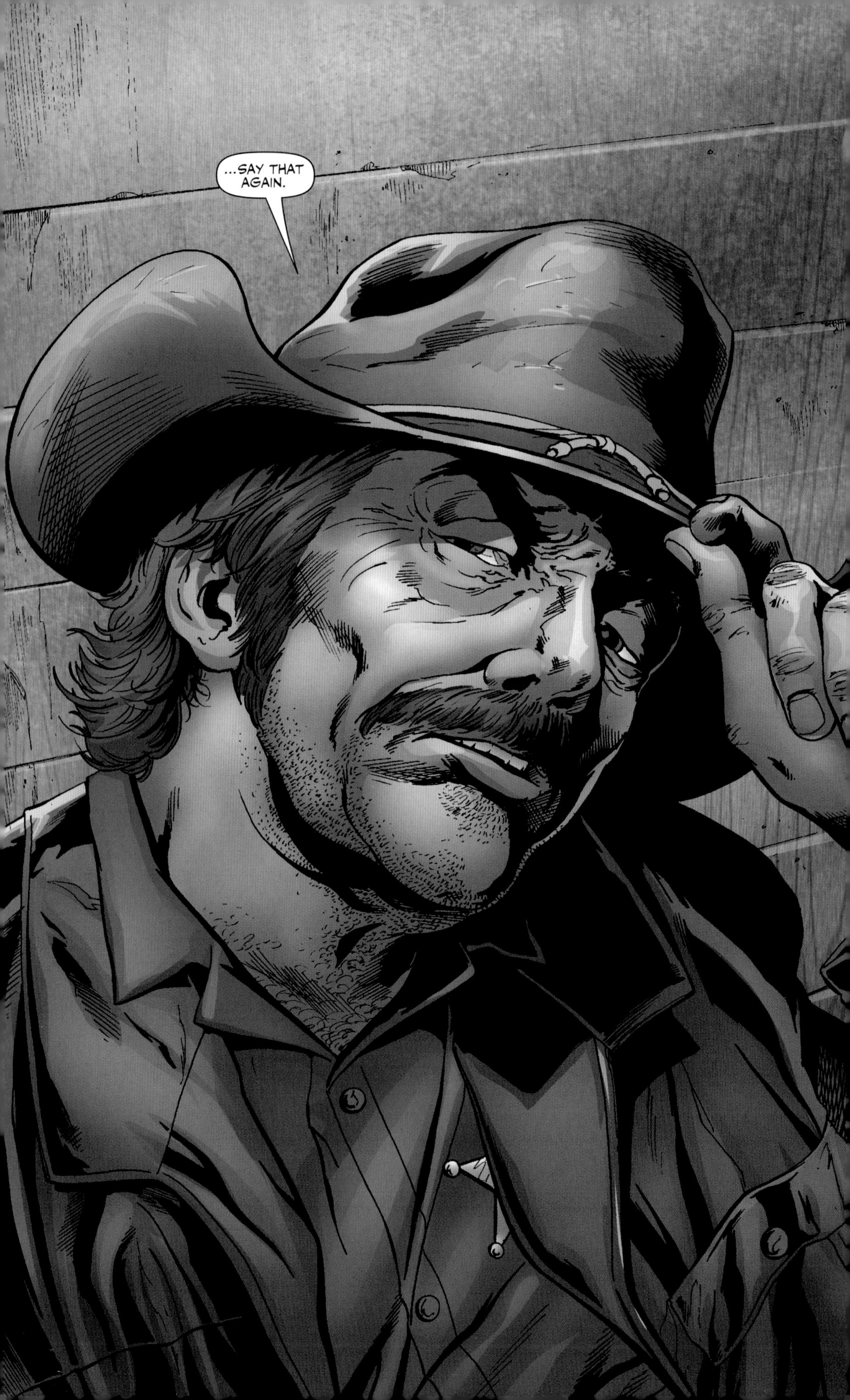
...SAY THAT AGAIN.

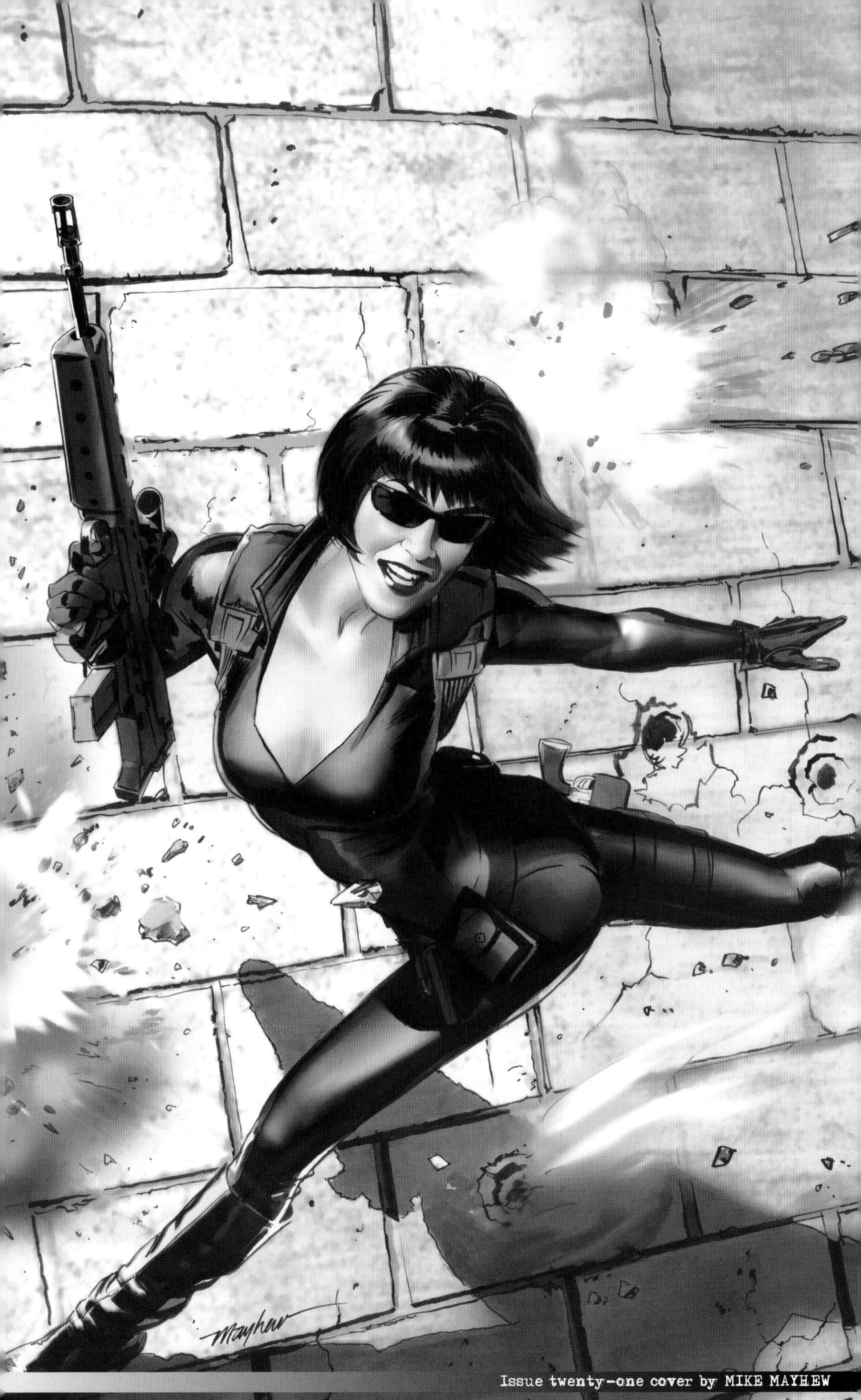
Mayhew

Issue twenty-one cover by MIKE MAYHEW

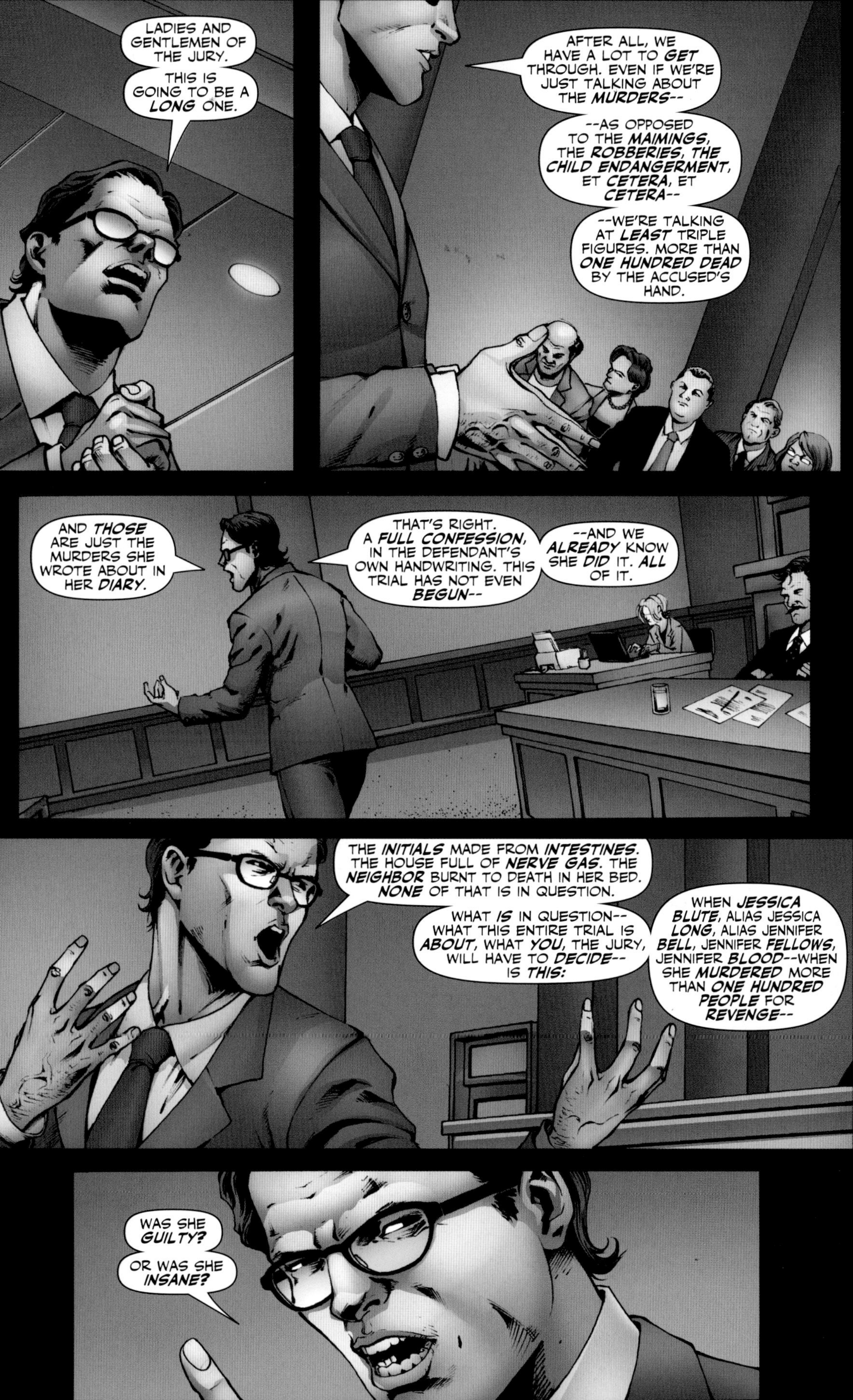
LADIES AND GENTLEMEN OF THE JURY.
THIS IS GOING TO BE A LONG ONE.
AFTER ALL, WE HAVE A LOT TO GET THROUGH. EVEN IF WE'RE JUST TALKING ABOUT THE MURDERS--
--AS OPPOSED TO THE MAIMINGS, THE ROBBERIES, THE CHILD ENDANGERMENT, ET CETERA, ET CETERA--
--WE'RE TALKING AT LEAST TRIPLE FIGURES. MORE THAN ONE HUNDRED DEAD BY THE ACCUSED'S HAND.
AND THOSE ARE JUST THE MURDERS SHE WROTE ABOUT IN HER DIARY.
THAT'S RIGHT. A FULL CONFESSION, IN THE DEFENDANT'S OWN HANDWRITING. THIS TRIAL HAS NOT EVEN BEGUN--
--AND WE ALREADY KNOW SHE DID IT. ALL OF IT.
THE INITIALS MADE FROM INTESTINES. THE HOUSE FULL OF NERVE GAS. THE NEIGHBOR BURNT TO DEATH IN HER BED. NONE OF THAT IS IN QUESTION.
WHAT IS IN QUESTION-- WHAT THIS ENTIRE TRIAL IS ABOUT, WHAT YOU, THE JURY, WILL HAVE TO DECIDE-- IS THIS:
WHEN JESSICA BLUTE, ALIAS JESSICA LONG, ALIAS JENNIFER BELL, JENNIFER FELLOWS, JENNIFER BLOOD--WHEN SHE MURDERED MORE THAN ONE HUNDRED PEOPLE FOR REVENGE--
WAS SHE GUILTY?
OR WAS SHE INSANE?

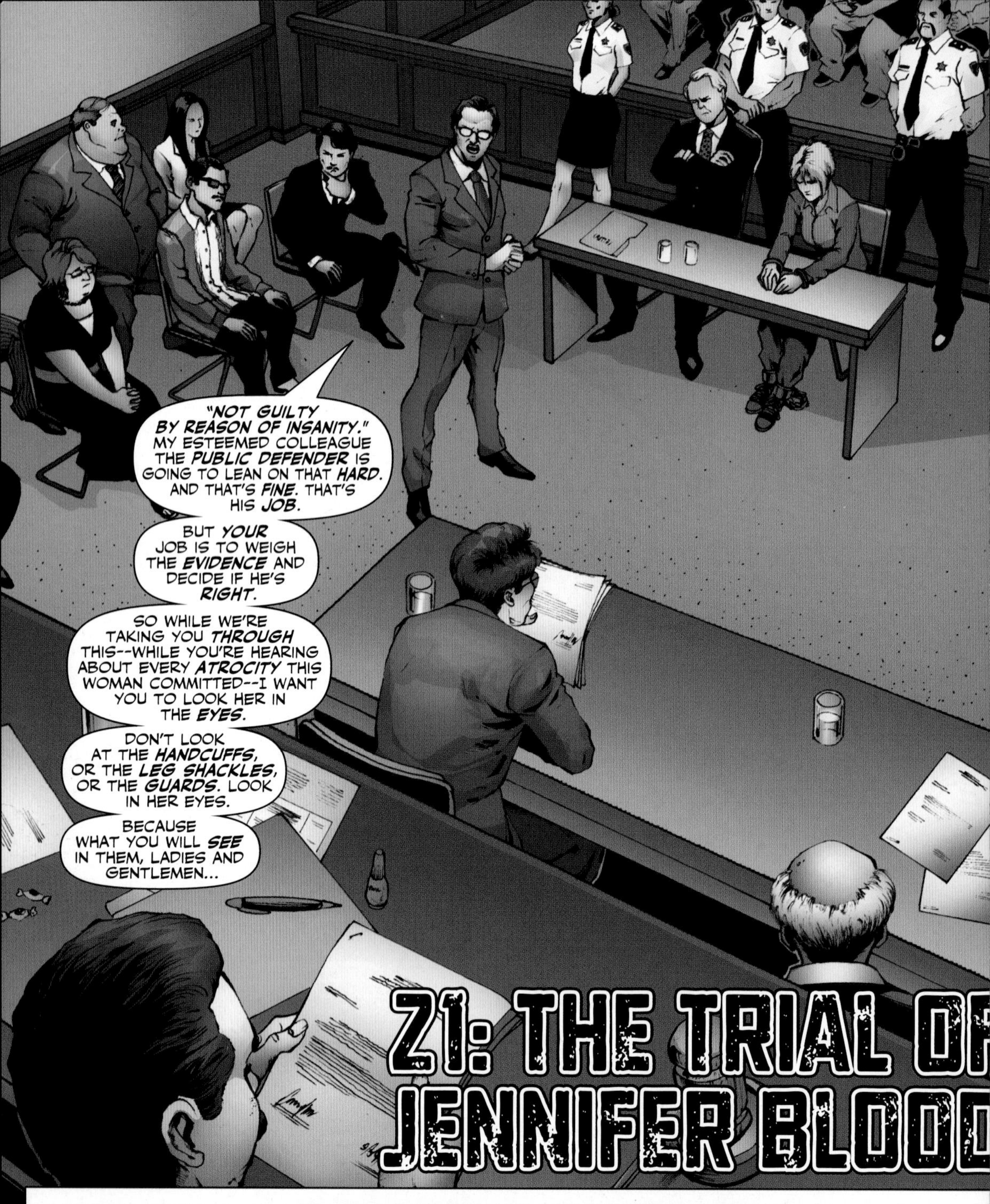
"NOT GUILTY BY REASON OF INSANITY." MY ESTEEMED COLLEAGUE THE PUBLIC DEFENDER IS GOING TO LEAN ON THAT HARD. AND THAT'S FINE. THAT'S HIS JOB.
BUT YOUR JOB IS TO WEIGH THE EVIDENCE AND DECIDE IF HE'S RIGHT.
SO WHILE WE'RE TAKING YOU THROUGH THIS--WHILE YOU'RE HEARING ABOUT EVERY ATROCITY THIS WOMAN COMMITTED--I WANT YOU TO LOOK HER IN THE EYES.
DON'T LOOK AT THE HANDCUFFS, OR THE LEG SHACKLES, OR THE GUARDS. LOOK IN HER EYES.
BECAUSE WHAT YOU WILL SEE IN THEM, LADIES AND GENTLEMEN...
21: THE TRIAL OF
JENNIFER BLOOD

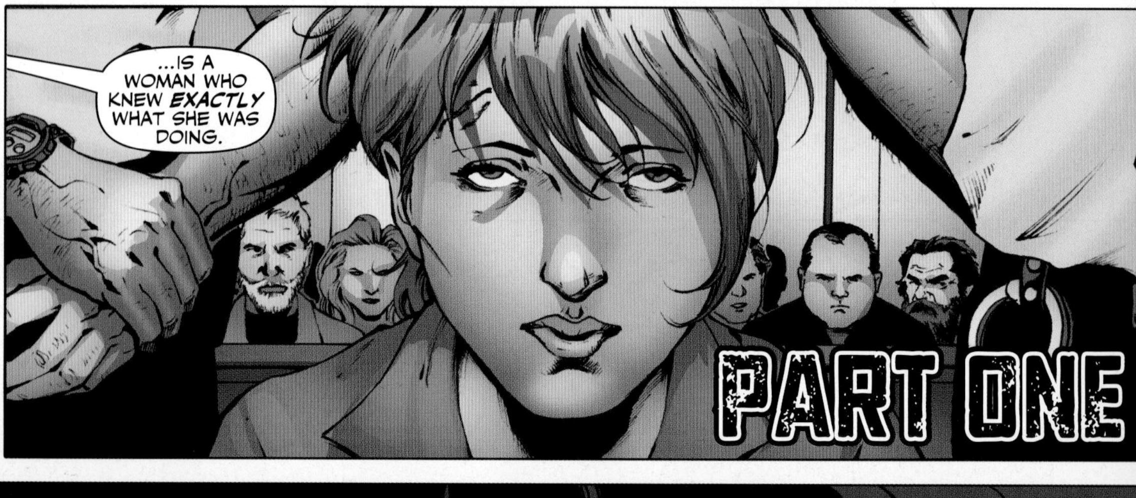
...IS A WOMAN WHO KNEW EXACTLY WHAT SHE WAS DOING.
PART ONE

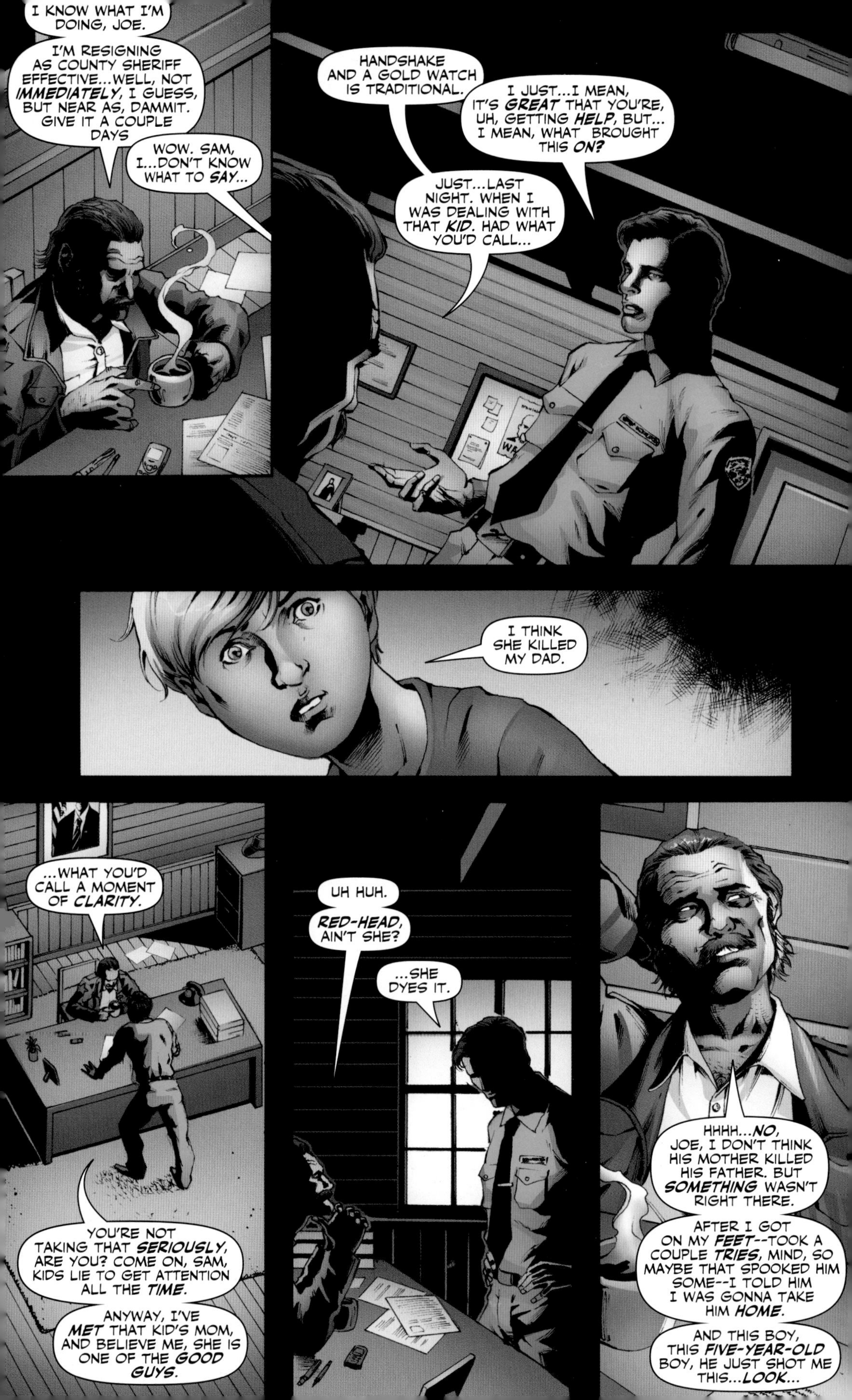
I KNOW WHAT I'M DOING, JOE.
I'M RESIGNING AS COUNTY SHERIFF EFFECTIVE...WELL, NOT IMMEDIATELY, I GUESS, BUT NEAR AS, DAMMIT. GIVE IT A COUPLE DAYS
WOW. SAM, I...DON'T KNOW WHAT TO SAY...
HANDSHAKE AND A GOLD WATCH IS TRADITIONAL.
I JUST...I MEAN, IT'S GREAT THAT YOU'RE, UH, GETTING HELP, BUT... I MEAN, WHAT BROUGHT THIS ON?
JUST...LAST NIGHT. WHEN I WAS DEALING WITH THAT KID. HAD WHAT YOU'D CALL...
I THINK SHE KILLED MY DAD.
...WHAT YOU'D CALL A MOMENT OF CLARITY.
YOU'RE NOT TAKING THAT SERIOUSLY, ARE YOU? COME ON, SAM, KIDS LIE TO GET ATTENTION ALL THE TIME.
ANYWAY, I'VE MET THAT KID'S MOM, AND BELIEVE ME, SHE IS ONE OF THE GOOD GUYS.
UH HUH.
RED-HEAD, AIN'T SHE?
...SHE DYES IT.
HHHH...NO, JOE, I DON'T THINK HIS MOTHER KILLED HIS FATHER. BUT SOMETHING WASN'T RIGHT THERE.
AFTER I GOT ON MY FEET--TOOK A COUPLE TRIES, MIND, SO MAYBE THAT SPOOKED HIM SOME--I TOLD HIM I WAS GONNA TAKE HIM HOME.
AND THIS BOY, THIS FIVE-YEAR-OLD BOY, HE JUST SHOT ME THIS...LOOK...

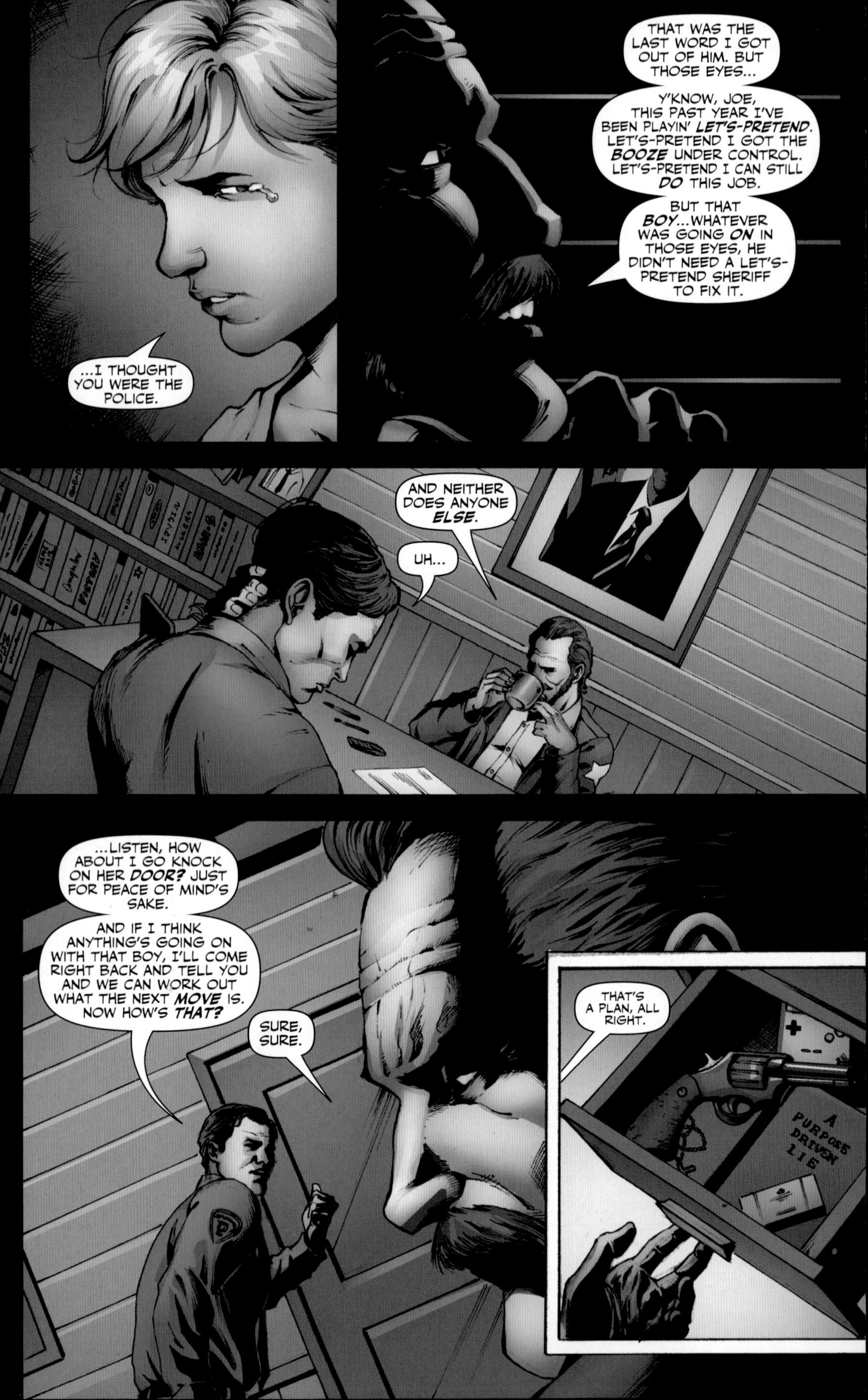
...I THOUGHT YOU WERE THE POLICE.
THAT WAS THE LAST WORD I GOT OUT OF HIM. BUT THOSE EYES...
Y'KNOW, JOE, THIS PAST YEAR I'VE BEEN PLAYIN' *LET'S-PRETEND*. LET'S-PRETEND I GOT THE *BOOZE* UNDER CONTROL. LET'S-PRETEND I CAN STILL *DO* THIS JOB.
BUT THAT *BOY*...WHATEVER WAS GOING *ON* IN THOSE EYES, HE DIDN'T NEED A LET'S-PRETEND SHERIFF TO FIX IT.
AND NEITHER DOES ANYONE *ELSE*.
UH...
...LISTEN, HOW ABOUT I GO KNOCK ON HER *DOOR?* JUST FOR PEACE OF MIND'S SAKE.
AND IF I THINK ANYTHING'S GOING ON WITH THAT BOY, I'LL COME RIGHT BACK AND TELL YOU AND WE CAN WORK OUT WHAT THE NEXT *MOVE* IS. NOW HOW'S *THAT?*
SURE, SURE.
THAT'S A PLAN, ALL RIGHT.
VICTORY
A PURPOSE DRIVEN LIE

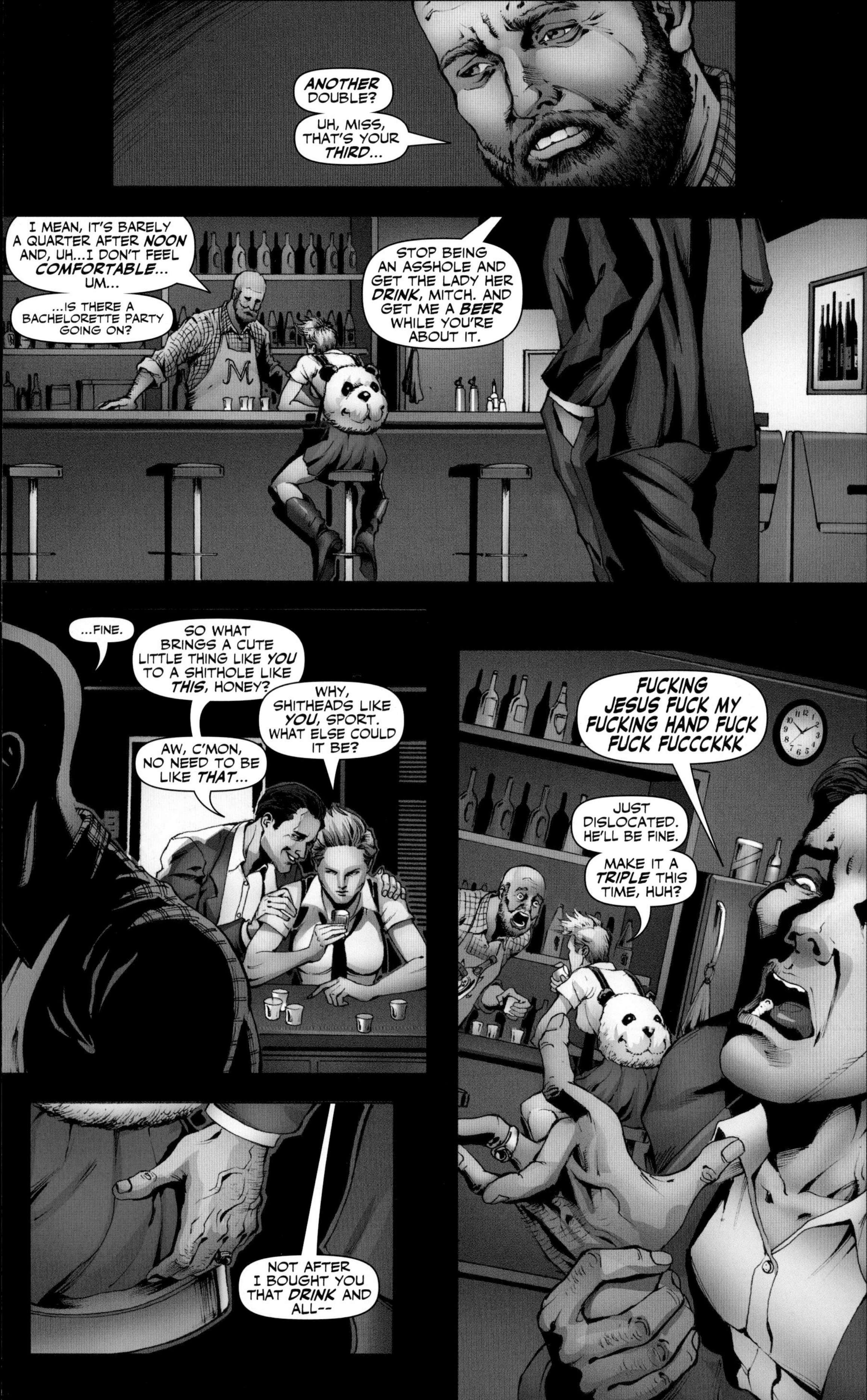
ANOTHER DOUBLE?
UH, MISS, THAT'S YOUR THIRD...
I MEAN, IT'S BARELY A QUARTER AFTER NOON AND, UH...I DON'T FEEL COMFORTABLE... UM...
...IS THERE A BACHELORETTE PARTY GOING ON?
STOP BEING AN ASSHOLE AND GET THE LADY HER DRINK, MITCH. AND GET ME A BEER WHILE YOU'RE ABOUT IT.
...FINE.
SO WHAT BRINGS A CUTE LITTLE THING LIKE YOU TO A SHITHOLE LIKE THIS, HONEY?
WHY, SHITHEADS LIKE YOU, SPORT. WHAT ELSE COULD IT BE?
AW, C'MON, NO NEED TO BE LIKE THAT...
NOT AFTER I BOUGHT YOU THAT DRINK AND ALL--
FUCKING JESUS FUCK MY FUCKING HAND FUCK FUCK FUCCCKKK
JUST DISLOCATED. HE'LL BE FINE.
MAKE IT A TRIPLE THIS TIME, HUH?

THERE YOU ARE, OFFICER DOLLAND...

LISTEN, "OFFICER DOLLAND" WAS MY FATHER. HOW ABOUT YOU CALL ME *JOE?*

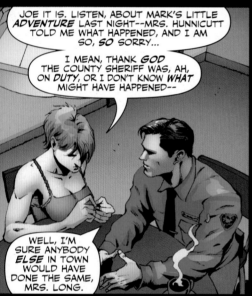

JOE IT IS. LISTEN, ABOUT MARK'S LITTLE *ADVENTURE* LAST NIGHT--MRS. HUNNICUTT TOLD ME WHAT HAPPENED, AND I AM SO, *SO* SORRY...

I MEAN, THANK *GOD* THE COUNTY SHERIFF WAS, AH, ON *DUTY,* OR I DON'T KNOW *WHAT* MIGHT HAVE HAPPENED--

WELL, I'M SURE ANYBODY *ELSE* IN TOWN WOULD HAVE DONE THE SAME, MRS. LONG.

PLEASE, IT'S--IT'S *JESSICA.* JESSIE. IF I'M CALLING YOU *JOE,* I MEAN.

LISTEN, JESSIE, I KNOW YOU CAME HERE FROM THE *CITY,* BUT *REVERE* AIN'T SUCH A DANGEROUS PLACE FOR A BOY TO GROW UP IN.

I MEAN, *SURE,* HE SHOULDN'T BE RUNNING AROUND THE STREETS SO LATE AT *NIGHT,* NOT WITHOUT *SUPERVISION...*

...BUT, YOU KNOW, NOTHING BAD CAME OF IT *THIS* TIME, SO LET'S CHALK IT UP AS A *LESSON LEARNED* AND, UH... MRS. *LONG?*

...JESSIE? YOU *OKAY?*

NO. NO, I'M NOT.

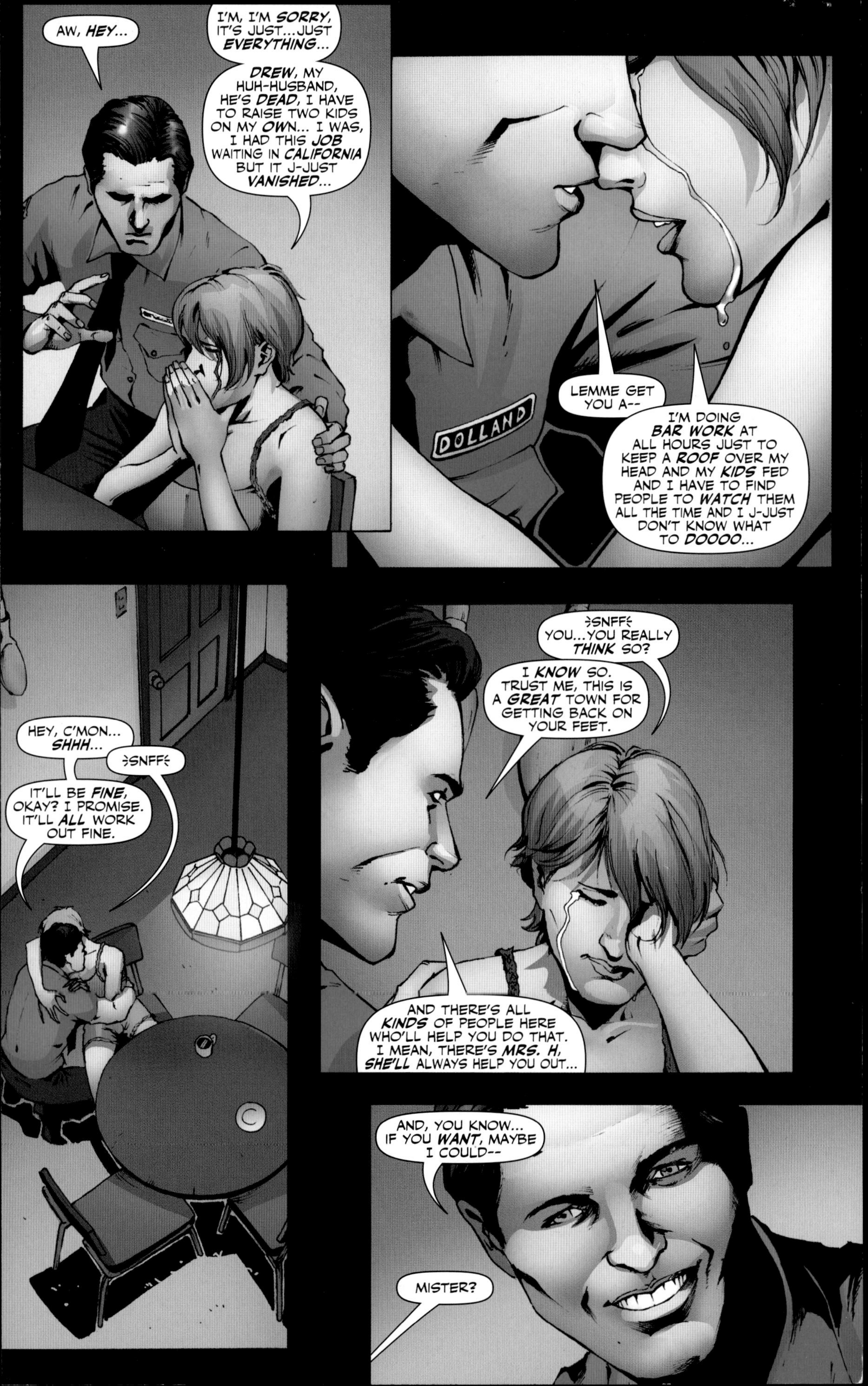
AW, HEY...
I'M, I'M SORRY, IT'S JUST...JUST EVERYTHING...
DREW, MY HUH-HUSBAND, HE'S DEAD, I HAVE TO RAISE TWO KIDS ON MY OWN... I WAS, I HAD THIS JOB WAITING IN CALIFORNIA BUT IT J-JUST VANISHED...
LEMME GET YOU A--
DOLLAND
I'M DOING BAR WORK AT ALL HOURS JUST TO KEEP A ROOF OVER MY HEAD AND MY KIDS FED AND I HAVE TO FIND PEOPLE TO WATCH THEM ALL THE TIME AND I J-JUST DON'T KNOW WHAT TO DOOOO...
HEY, C'MON... SHHH...
SNFF
IT'LL BE FINE, OKAY? I PROMISE. IT'LL ALL WORK OUT FINE.
SNFF
YOU...YOU REALLY THINK SO?
I KNOW SO. TRUST ME, THIS IS A GREAT TOWN FOR GETTING BACK ON YOUR FEET.
AND THERE'S ALL KINDS OF PEOPLE HERE WHO'LL HELP YOU DO THAT. I MEAN, THERE'S MRS. H, SHE'LL ALWAYS HELP YOU OUT...
AND, YOU KNOW... IF YOU WANT, MAYBE I COULD--
MISTER?

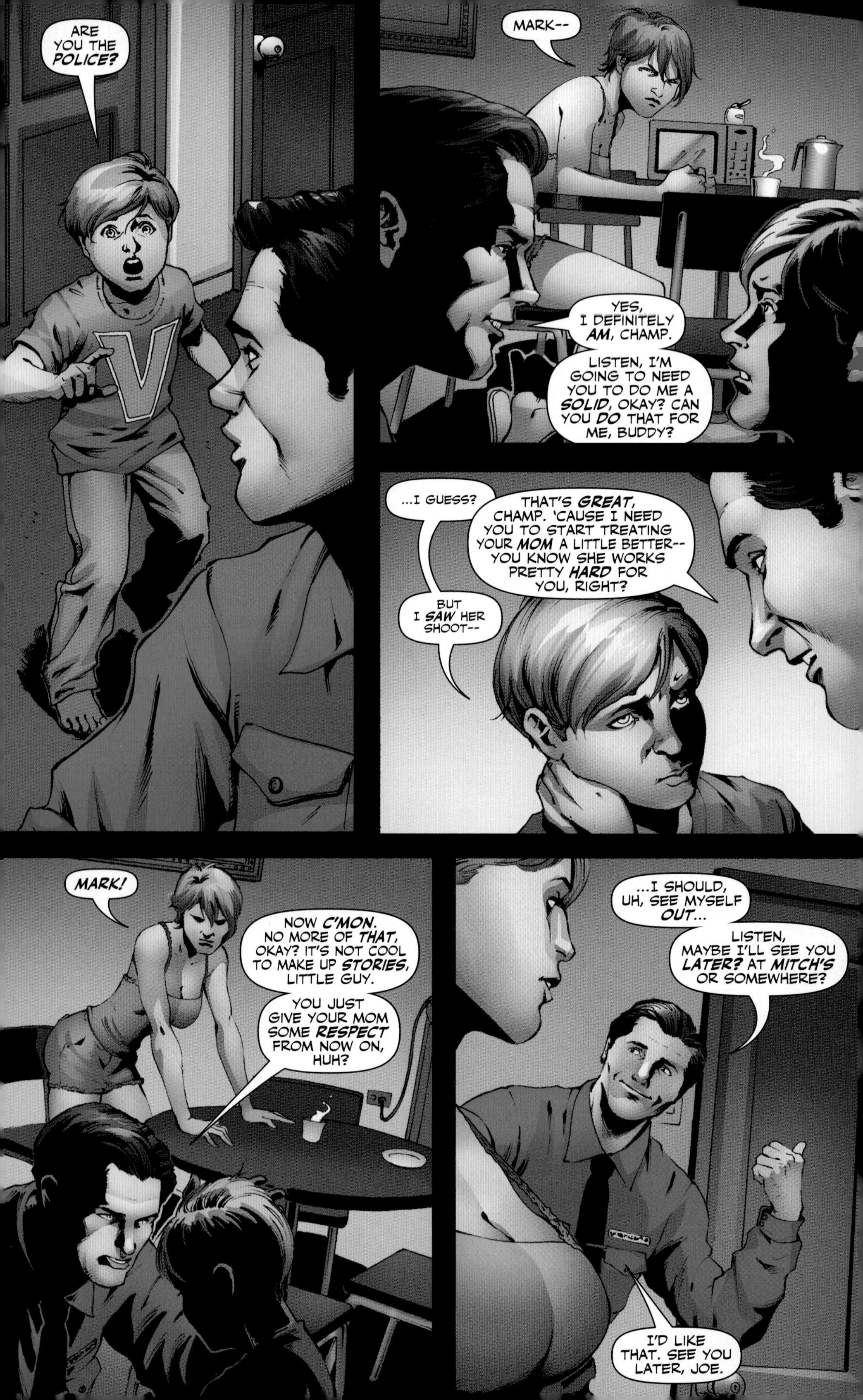

ARE YOU THE *POLICE?*
MARK--
YES, I DEFINITELY *AM*, CHAMP.
LISTEN, I'M GOING TO NEED YOU TO DO ME A *SOLID*, OKAY? CAN YOU *DO* THAT FOR ME, BUDDY?
...I GUESS?
THAT'S *GREAT*, CHAMP. 'CAUSE I NEED YOU TO START TREATING YOUR *MOM* A LITTLE BETTER-- YOU KNOW SHE WORKS PRETTY *HARD* FOR YOU, RIGHT?
BUT I *SAW* HER SHOOT--
MARK!
NOW *C'MON*. NO MORE OF *THAT*, OKAY? IT'S NOT COOL TO MAKE UP *STORIES*, LITTLE GUY.
YOU JUST GIVE YOUR MOM SOME *RESPECT* FROM NOW ON, HUH?
...I SHOULD, UH, SEE MYSELF *OUT*...
LISTEN, MAYBE I'LL SEE YOU *LATER?* AT *MITCH'S* OR SOMEWHERE?
I'D LIKE THAT. SEE YOU LATER, JOE.

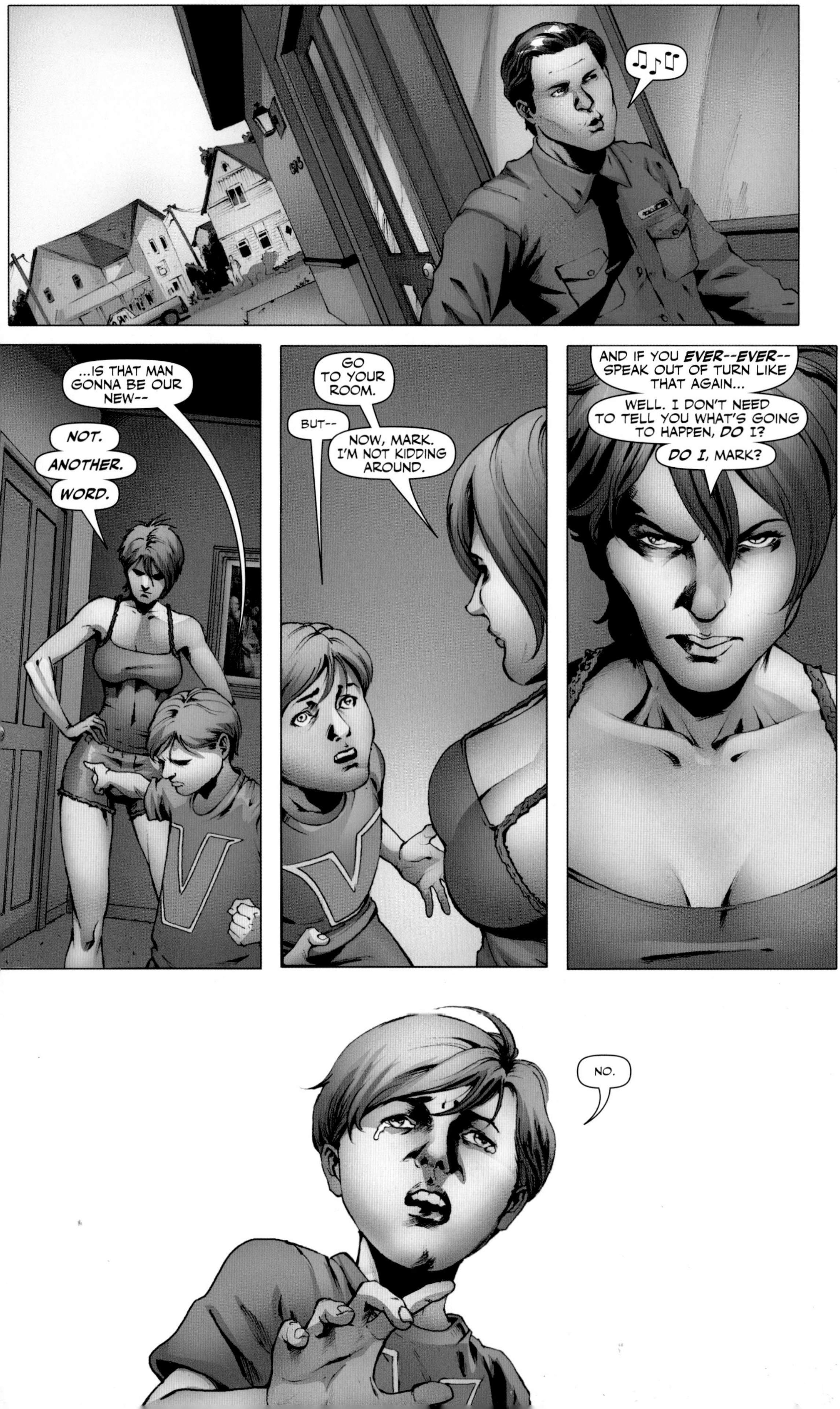
...IS THAT MAN GONNA BE OUR NEW--
NOT.
ANOTHER.
WORD.
GO TO YOUR ROOM.
BUT--
NOW, MARK. I'M NOT KIDDING AROUND.
AND IF YOU EVER--EVER-- SPEAK OUT OF TURN LIKE THAT AGAIN...
WELL. I DON'T NEED TO TELL YOU WHAT'S GOING TO HAPPEN, DO I?
DO I, MARK?
NO.

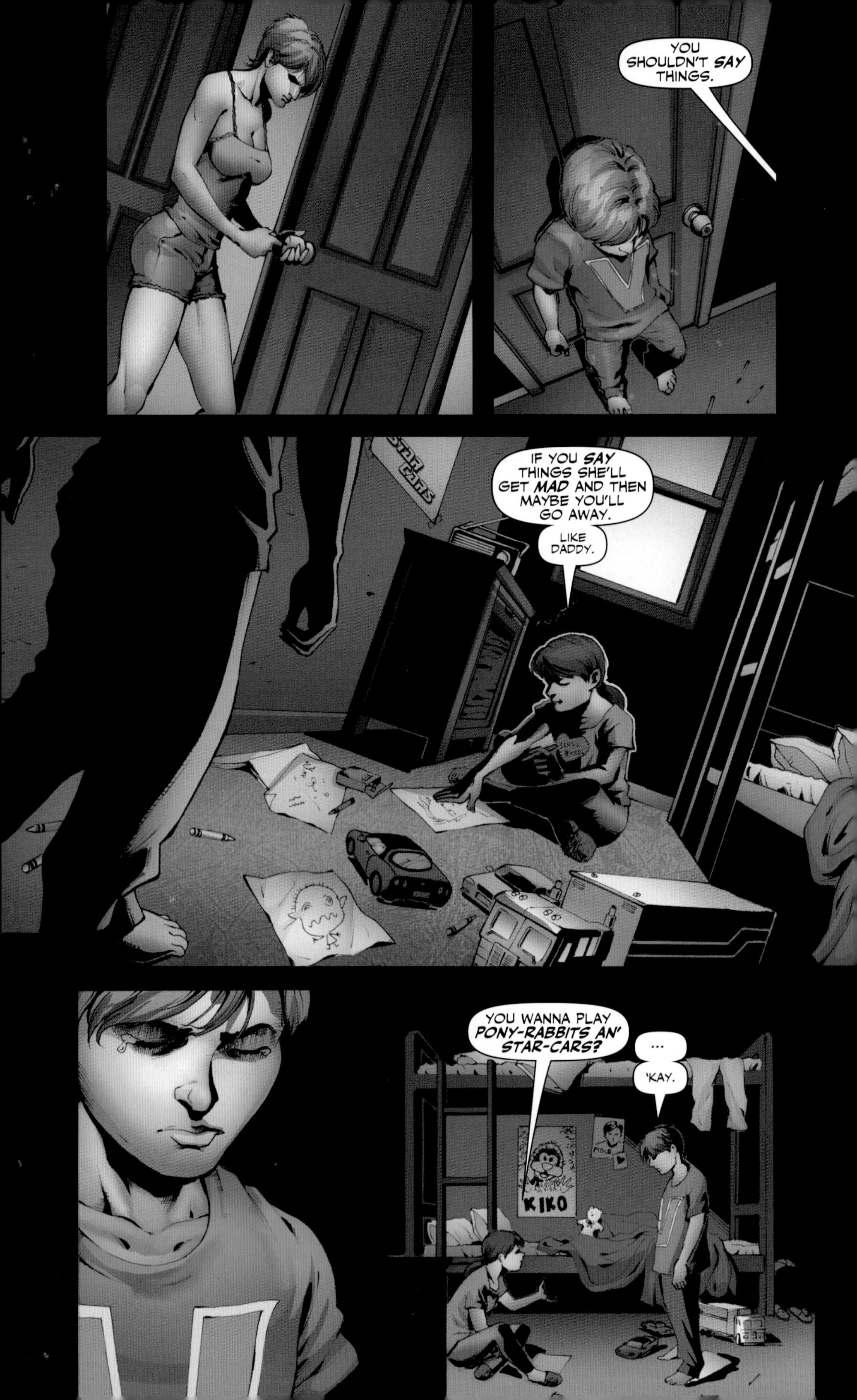

YOU SHOULDN'T SAY THINGS.
IF YOU SAY THINGS SHE'LL GET MAD AND THEN MAYBE YOU'LL GO AWAY.
LIKE DADDY.
YOU WANNA PLAY PONY-RABBITS AN' STAR-CARS?
...
'KAY.

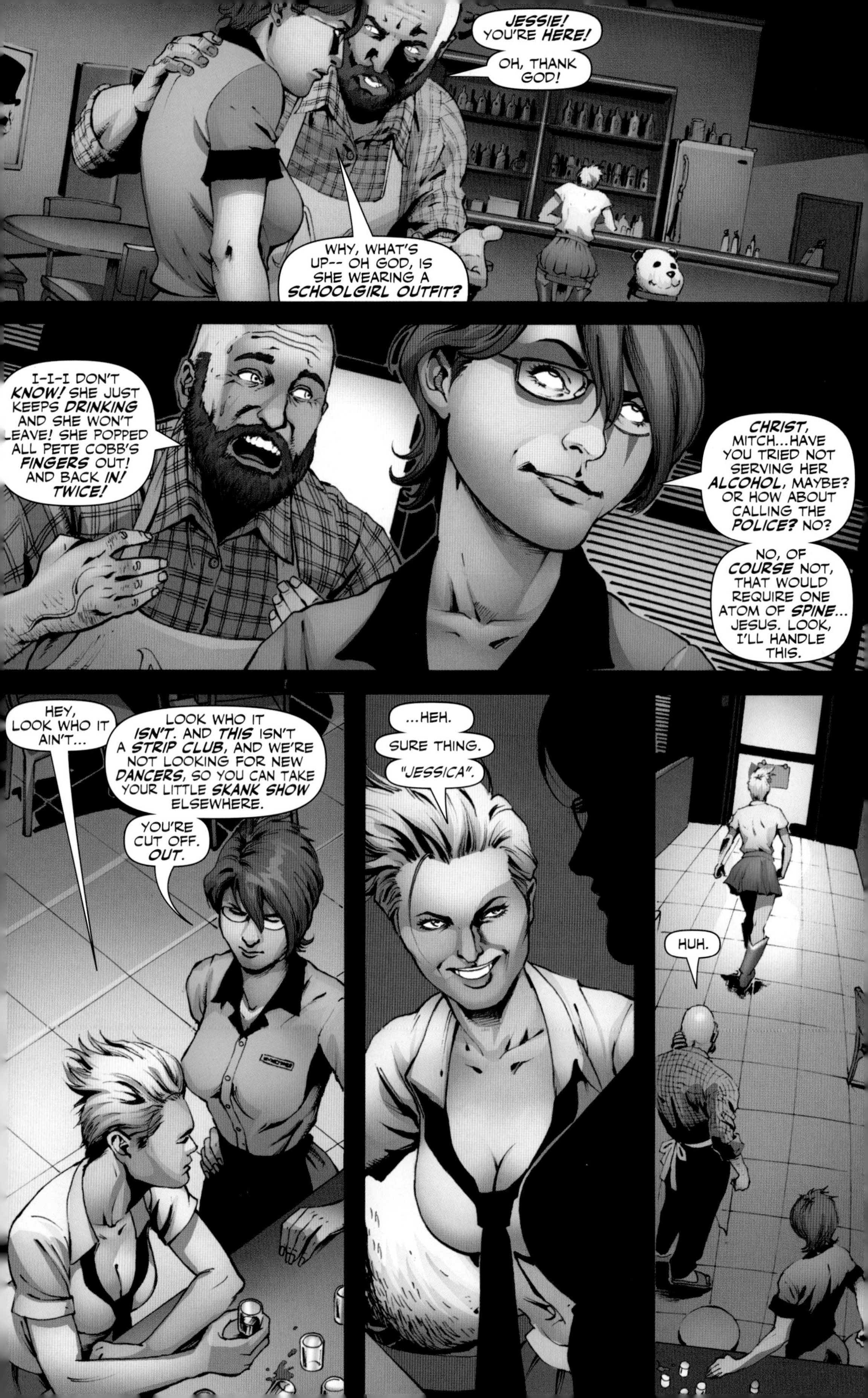
JESSIE! YOU'RE HERE!
OH, THANK GOD!
WHY, WHAT'S UP-- OH GOD, IS SHE WEARING A SCHOOLGIRL OUTFIT?
I-I-I DON'T KNOW! SHE JUST KEEPS DRINKING AND SHE WON'T LEAVE! SHE POPPED ALL PETE COBB'S FINGERS OUT! AND BACK IN! TWICE!
CHRIST, MITCH...HAVE YOU TRIED NOT SERVING HER ALCOHOL, MAYBE? OR HOW ABOUT CALLING THE POLICE? NO?
NO, OF COURSE NOT, THAT WOULD REQUIRE ONE ATOM OF SPINE... JESUS. LOOK, I'LL HANDLE THIS.
HEY, LOOK WHO IT AIN'T...
LOOK WHO IT ISN'T. AND THIS ISN'T A STRIP CLUB, AND WE'RE NOT LOOKING FOR NEW DANCERS, SO YOU CAN TAKE YOUR LITTLE SKANK SHOW ELSEWHERE.
YOU'RE CUT OFF. OUT.
...HEH.
SURE THING.
"JESSICA".
HUH.

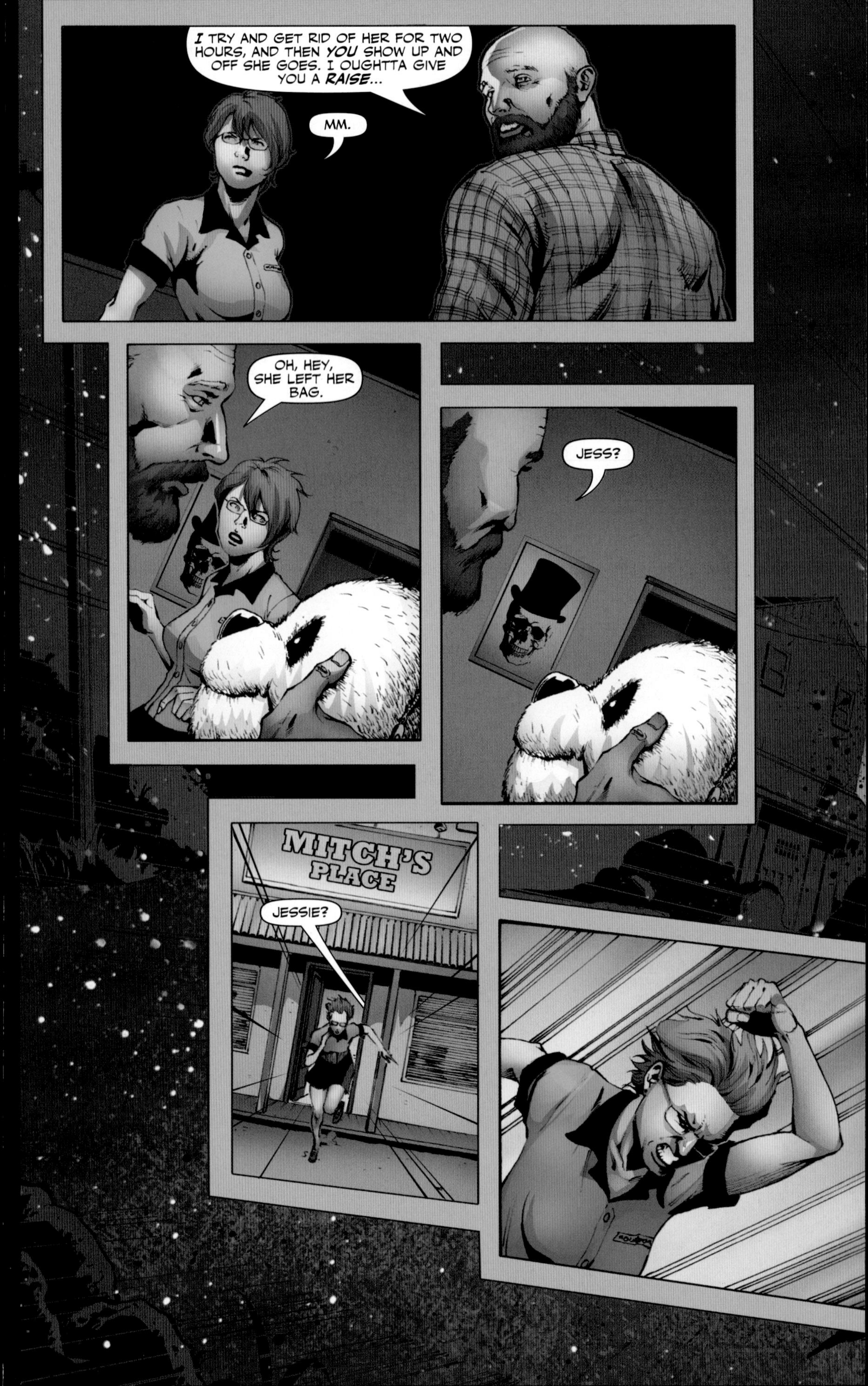
I TRY AND GET RID OF HER FOR TWO HOURS, AND THEN YOU SHOW UP AND OFF SHE GOES. I OUGHTTA GIVE YOU A RAISE...
MM.
OH, HEY, SHE LEFT HER BAG.
JESS?
MITCH'S PLACE
JESSIE?

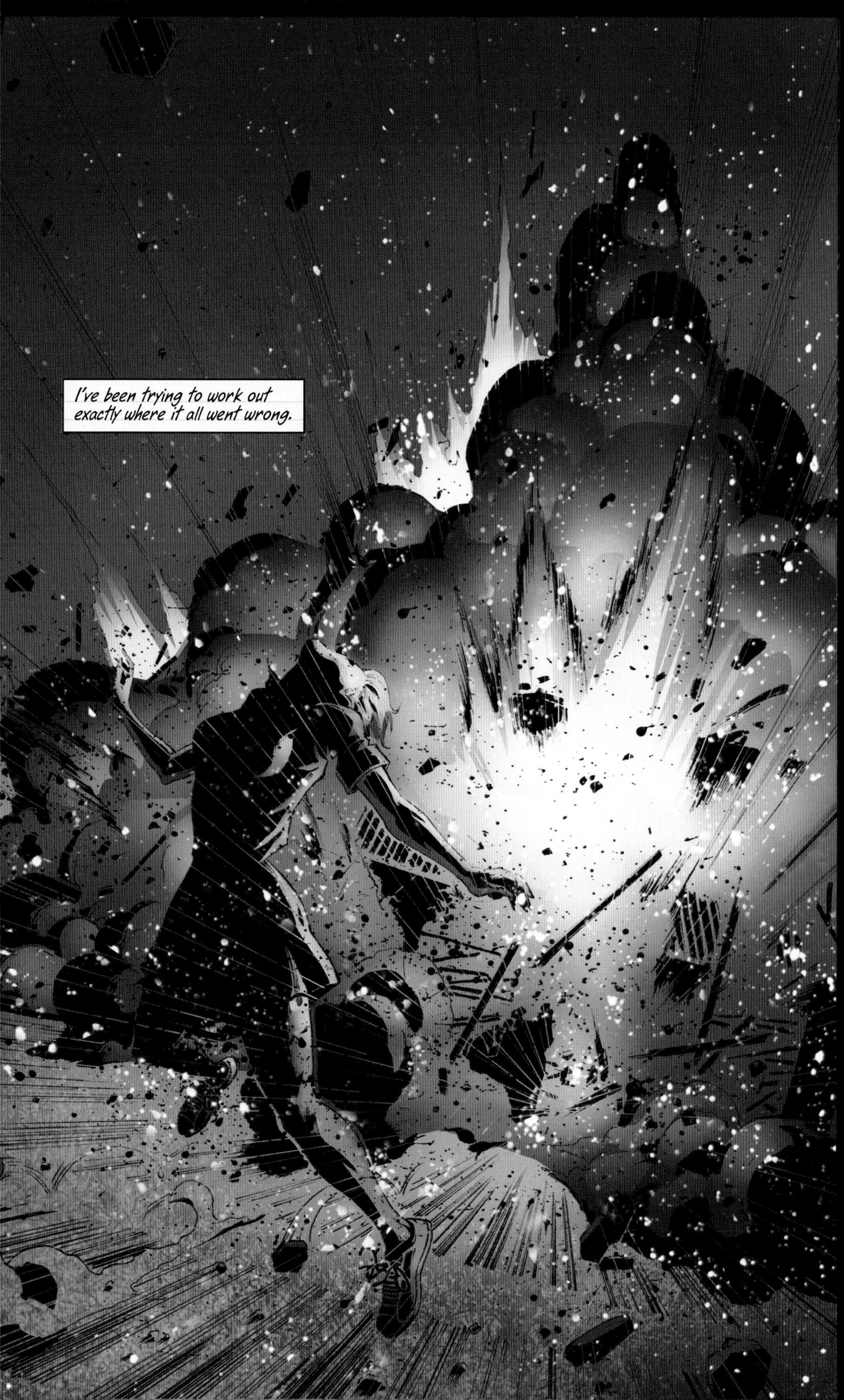
I've been trying to work out exactly where it all went wrong.

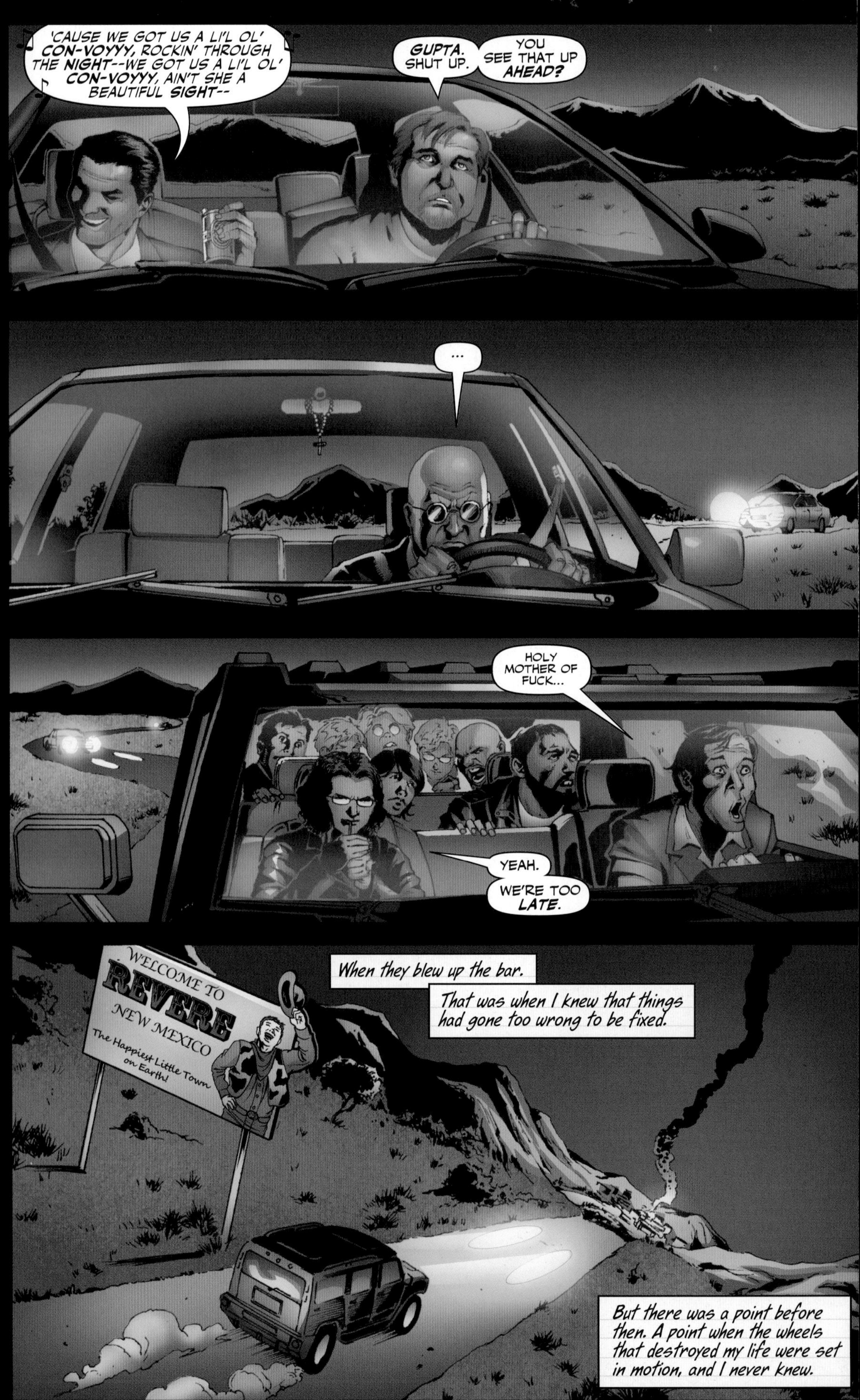
'CAUSE WE GOT US A LI'L OL' CON-VOYYY, ROCKIN' THROUGH THE NIGHT--WE GOT US A LI'L OL' CON-VOYYY, AIN'T SHE A BEAUTIFUL SIGHT--
GUPTA. SHUT UP.
YOU SEE THAT UP AHEAD?
...
HOLY MOTHER OF FUCK...
YEAH.
WE'RE TOO LATE.
WELCOME TO REVERE NEW MEXICO
The Happiest Little Town on Earth!
When they blew up the bar.
That was when I knew that things had gone too wrong to be fixed.
But there was a point before then. A point when the wheels that destroyed my life were set in motion, and I never knew.

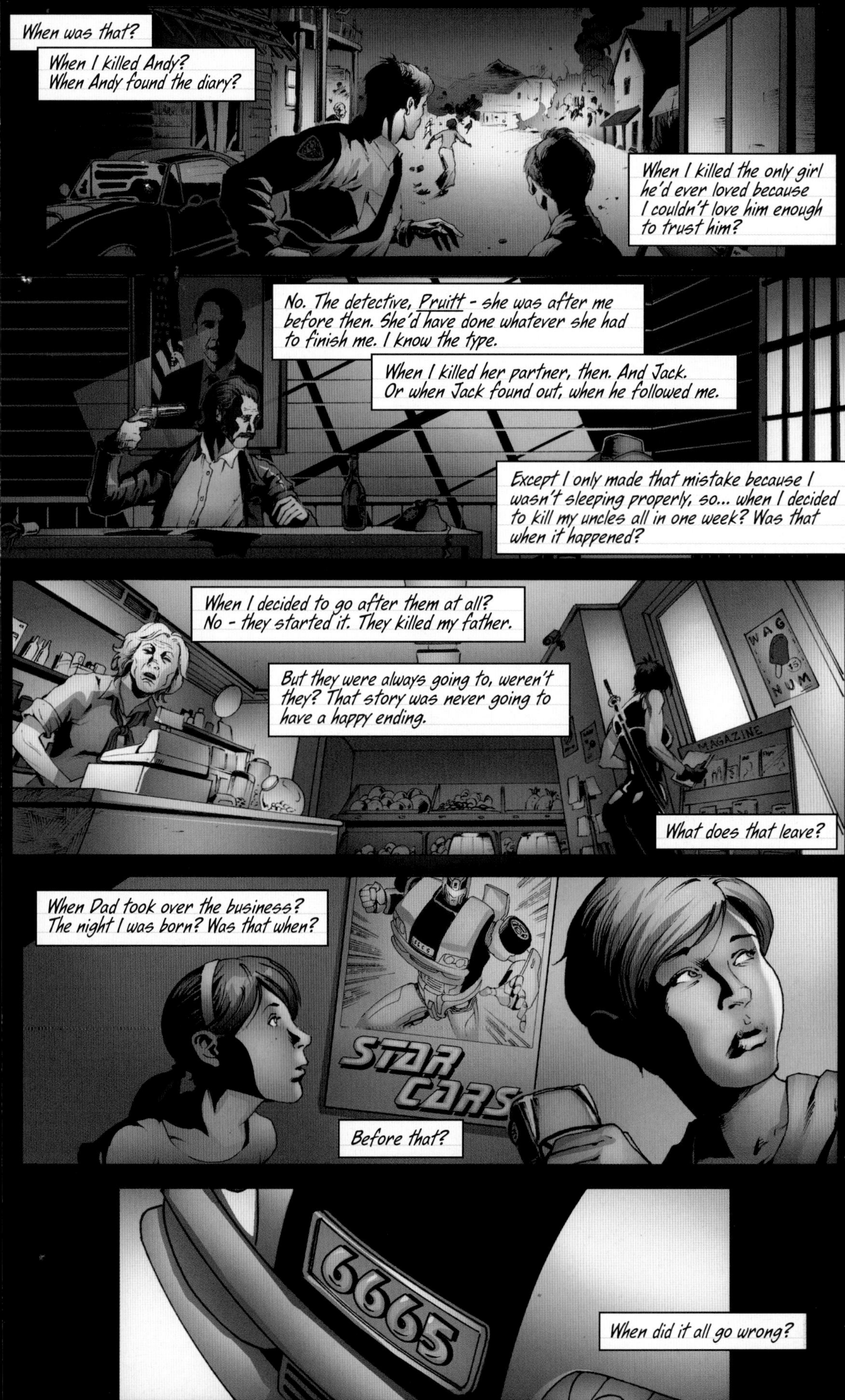

When was that?
When I killed Andy? When Andy found the diary?
When I killed the only girl he'd ever loved because I couldn't love him enough to trust him?
No. The detective, Pruitt - she was after me before then. She'd have done whatever she had to finish me. I know the type.
When I killed her partner, then. And Jack. Or when Jack found out, when he followed me.
Except I only made that mistake because I wasn't sleeping properly, so... when I decided to kill my uncles all in one week? Was that when it happened?
When I decided to go after them at all? No - they started it. They killed my father.
But they were always going to, weren't they? That story was never going to have a happy ending.
WAG
NUM
MAGAZINE
What does that leave?
When Dad took over the business? The night I was born? Was that when?
STAR CARS
Before that?
6665
When did it all go wrong?

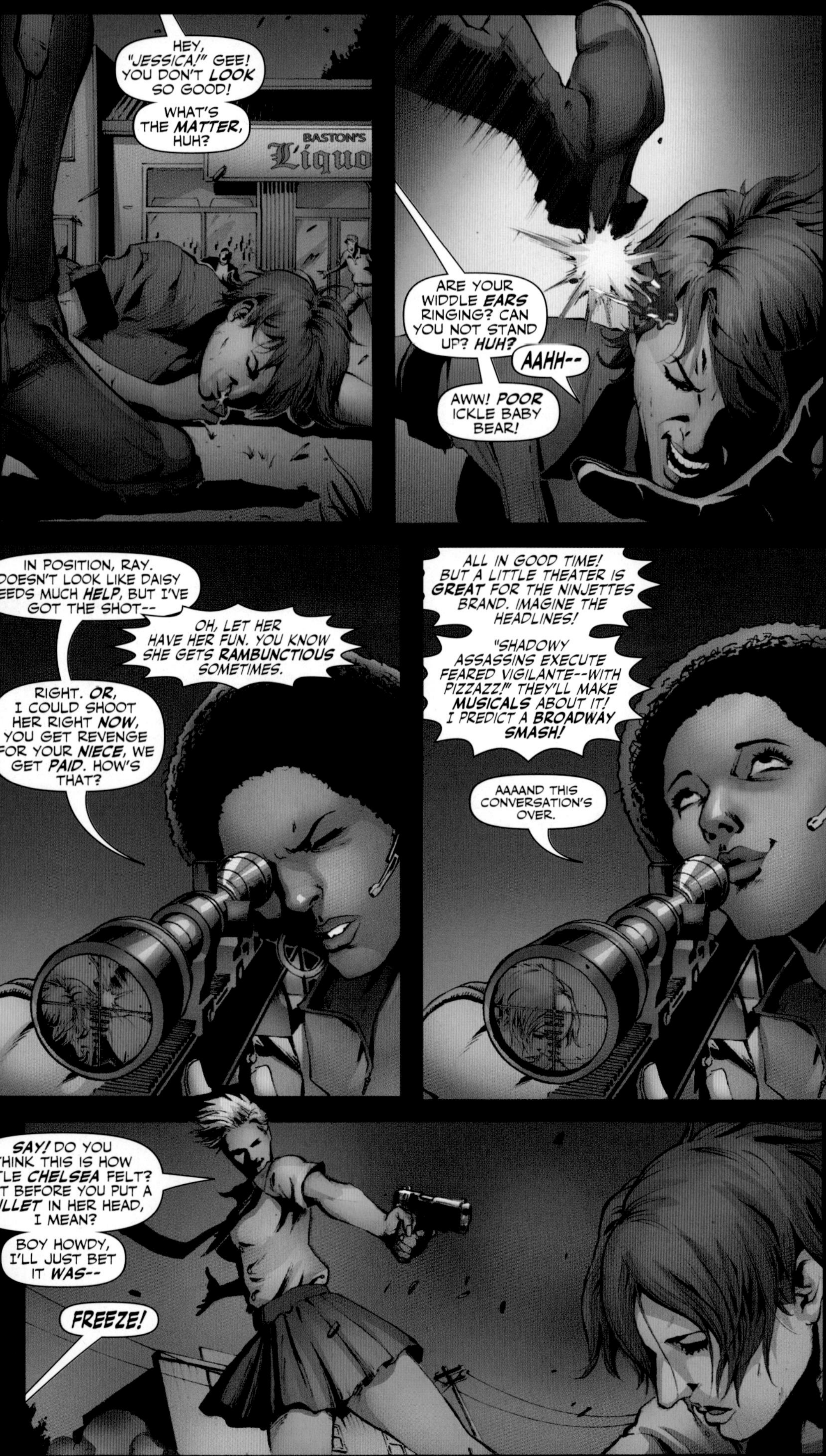
HEY, "JESSICA!" GEE! YOU DON'T LOOK SO GOOD!
WHAT'S THE MATTER, HUH?
BASTON'S Liquo
ARE YOUR WIDDLE EARS RINGING? CAN YOU NOT STAND UP? HUH?
AAHH--
AWW! POOR ICKLE BABY BEAR!
IN POSITION, RAY. DOESN'T LOOK LIKE DAISY NEEDS MUCH HELP, BUT I'VE GOT THE SHOT--
OH, LET HER HAVE HER FUN. YOU KNOW SHE GETS RAMBUNCTIOUS SOMETIMES.
RIGHT. OR, I COULD SHOOT HER RIGHT NOW, YOU GET REVENGE FOR YOUR NIECE, WE GET PAID. HOW'S THAT?
ALL IN GOOD TIME! BUT A LITTLE THEATER IS GREAT FOR THE NINJETTES BRAND. IMAGINE THE HEADLINES!
"SHADOWY ASSASSINS EXECUTE FEARED VIGILANTE--WITH PIZZAZZ!" THEY'LL MAKE MUSICALS ABOUT IT! I PREDICT A BROADWAY SMASH!
AAAAND THIS CONVERSATION'S OVER.
SAY! DO YOU THINK THIS IS HOW LITTLE CHELSEA FELT? JUST BEFORE YOU PUT A BULLET IN HER HEAD, I MEAN?
BOY HOWDY, I'LL JUST BET IT WAS--
FREEZE!

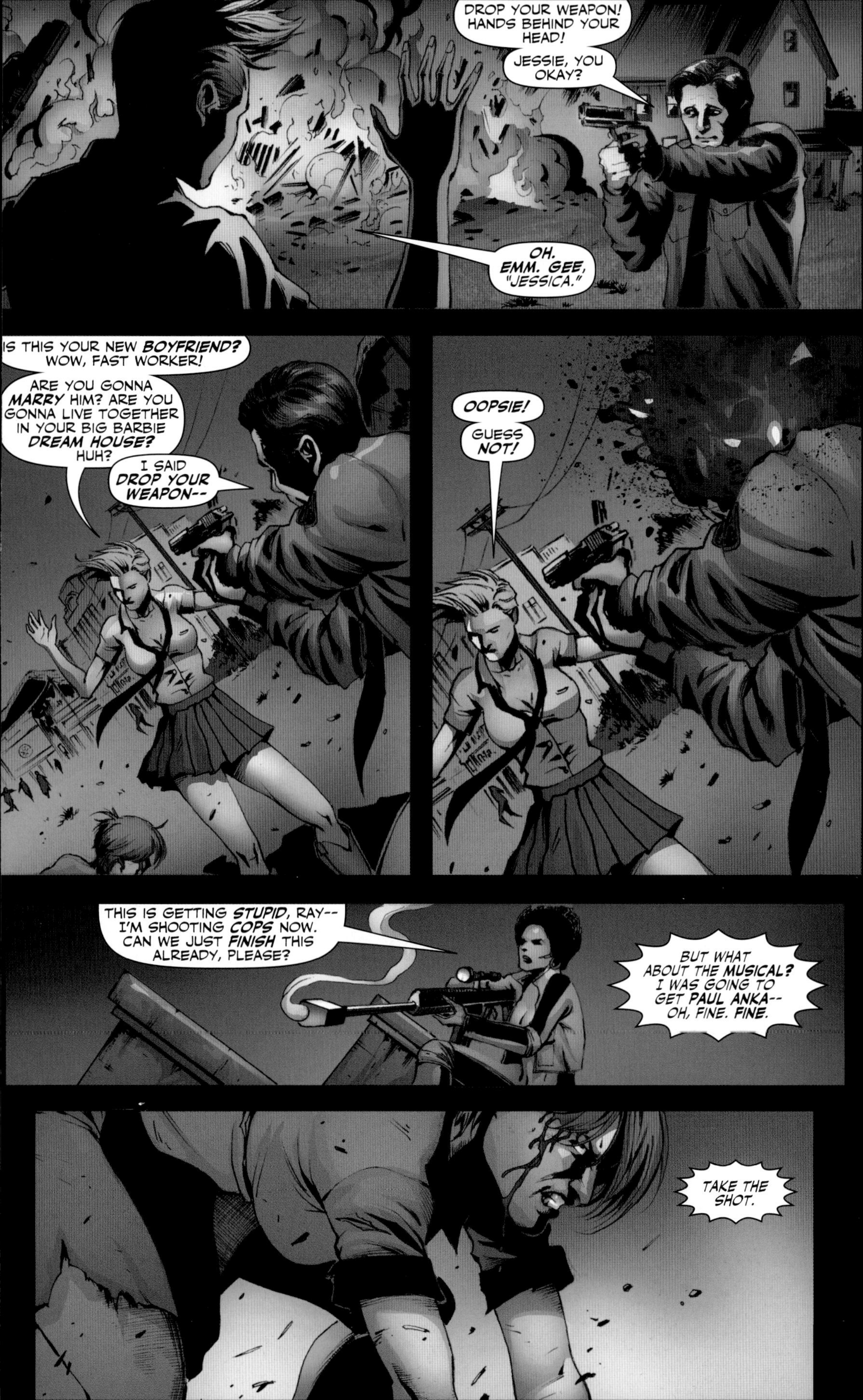
DROP YOUR WEAPON! HANDS BEHIND YOUR HEAD!
JESSIE, YOU OKAY?
OH. EMM. GEE, "JESSICA."
IS THIS YOUR NEW BOYFRIEND? WOW, FAST WORKER!
ARE YOU GONNA MARRY HIM? ARE YOU GONNA LIVE TOGETHER IN YOUR BIG BARBIE DREAM HOUSE? HUH?
I SAID DROP YOUR WEAPON--
OOPSIE!
GUESS NOT!
THIS IS GETTING STUPID, RAY-- I'M SHOOTING COPS NOW. CAN WE JUST FINISH THIS ALREADY, PLEASE?
BUT WHAT ABOUT THE MUSICAL? I WAS GOING TO GET PAUL ANKA-- OH, FINE. FINE.
TAKE THE SHOT.

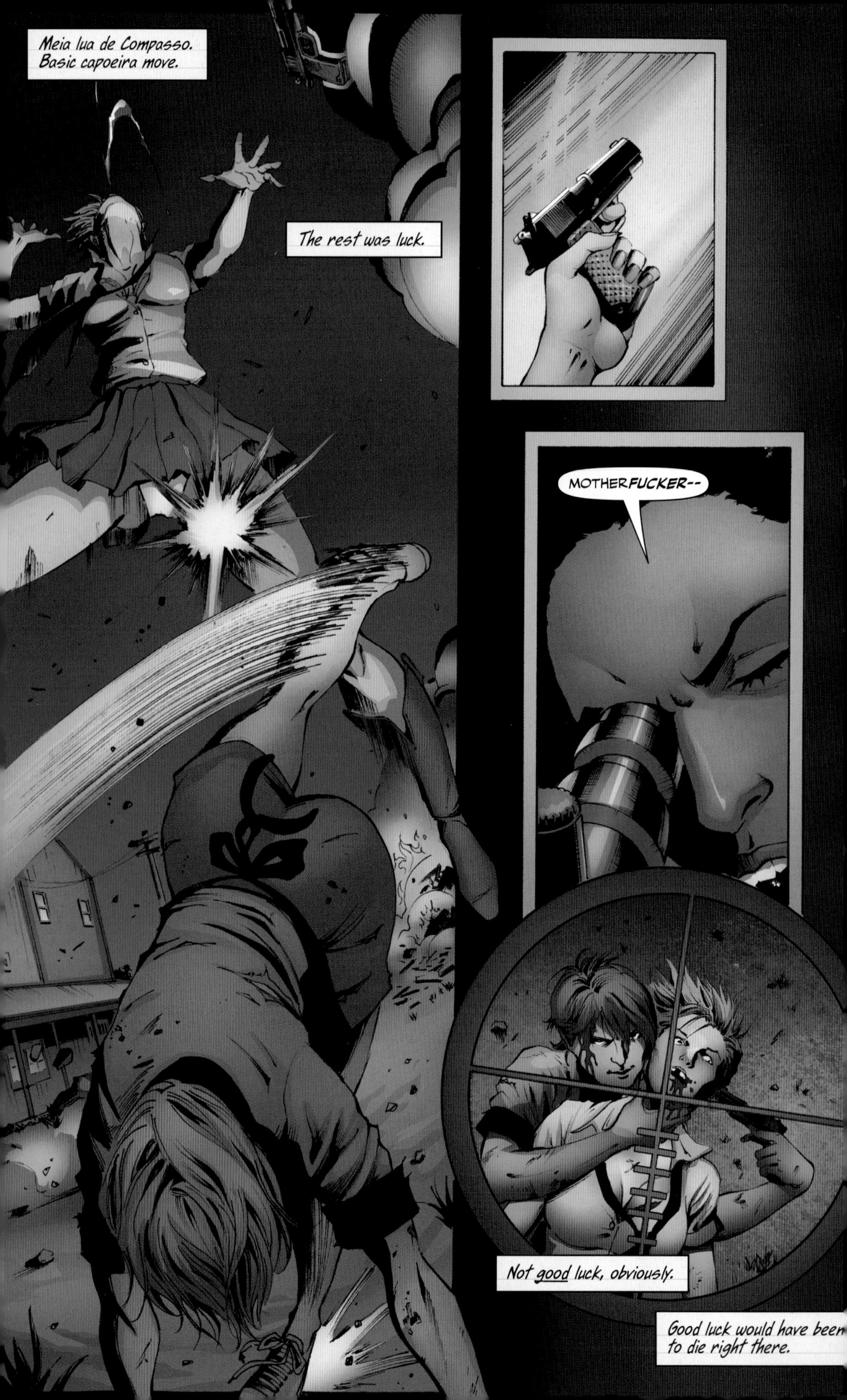
Meia lua de Compasso. Basic capoeira move.
The rest was luck.
MOTHERFUCKER--
Not good luck, obviously.
Good luck would have been to die right there.

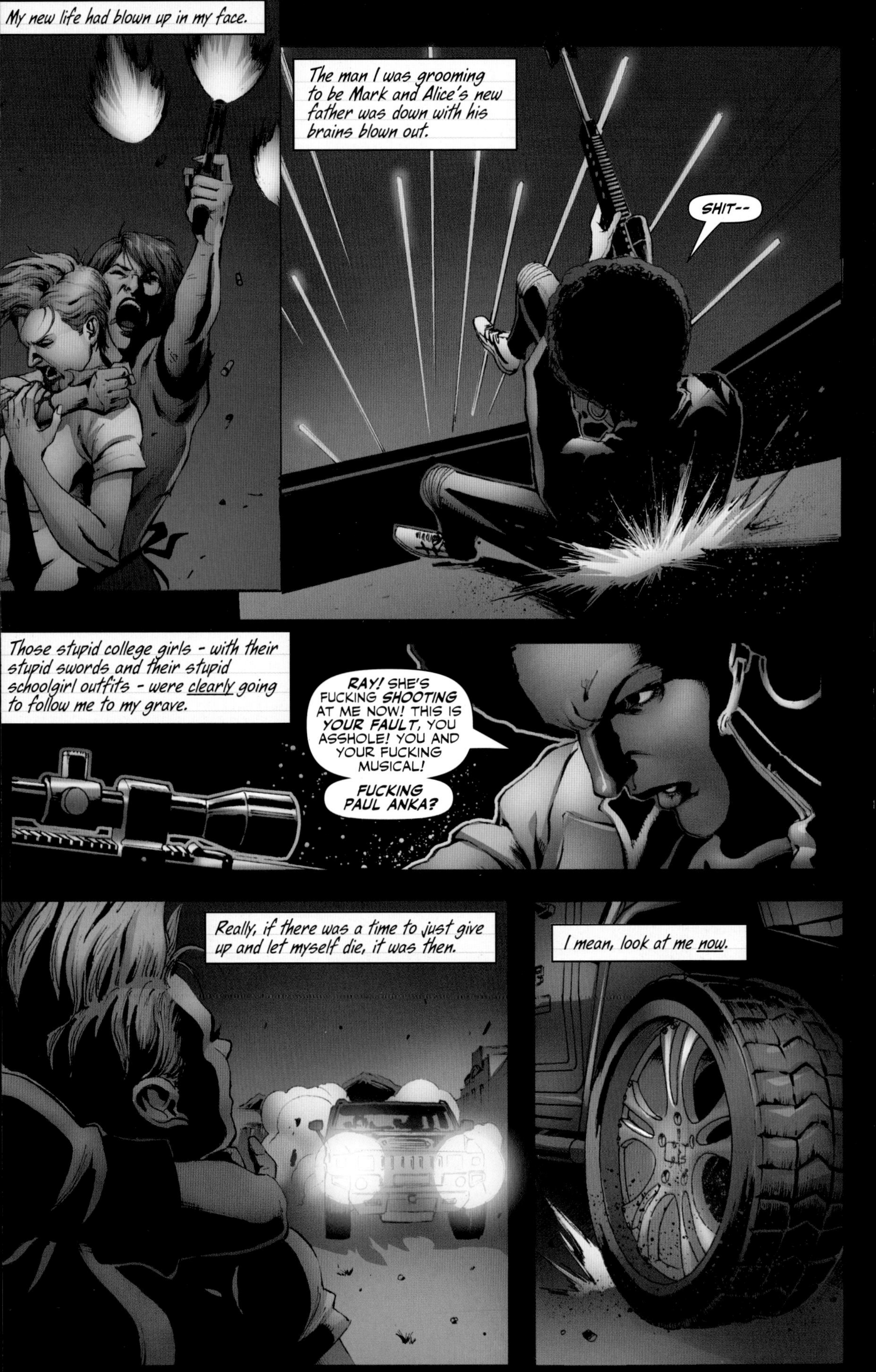
My new life had blown up in my face.
The man I was grooming to be Mark and Alice's new father was down with his brains blown out.
SHIT--
Those stupid college girls - with their stupid swords and their stupid schoolgirl outfits - were clearly going to follow me to my grave.
RAY! SHE'S FUCKING SHOOTING AT ME NOW! THIS IS YOUR FAULT, YOU ASSHOLE! YOU AND YOUR FUCKING MUSICAL!
FUCKING PAUL ANKA?
Really, if there was a time to just give up and let myself die, it was then.
I mean, look at me now.

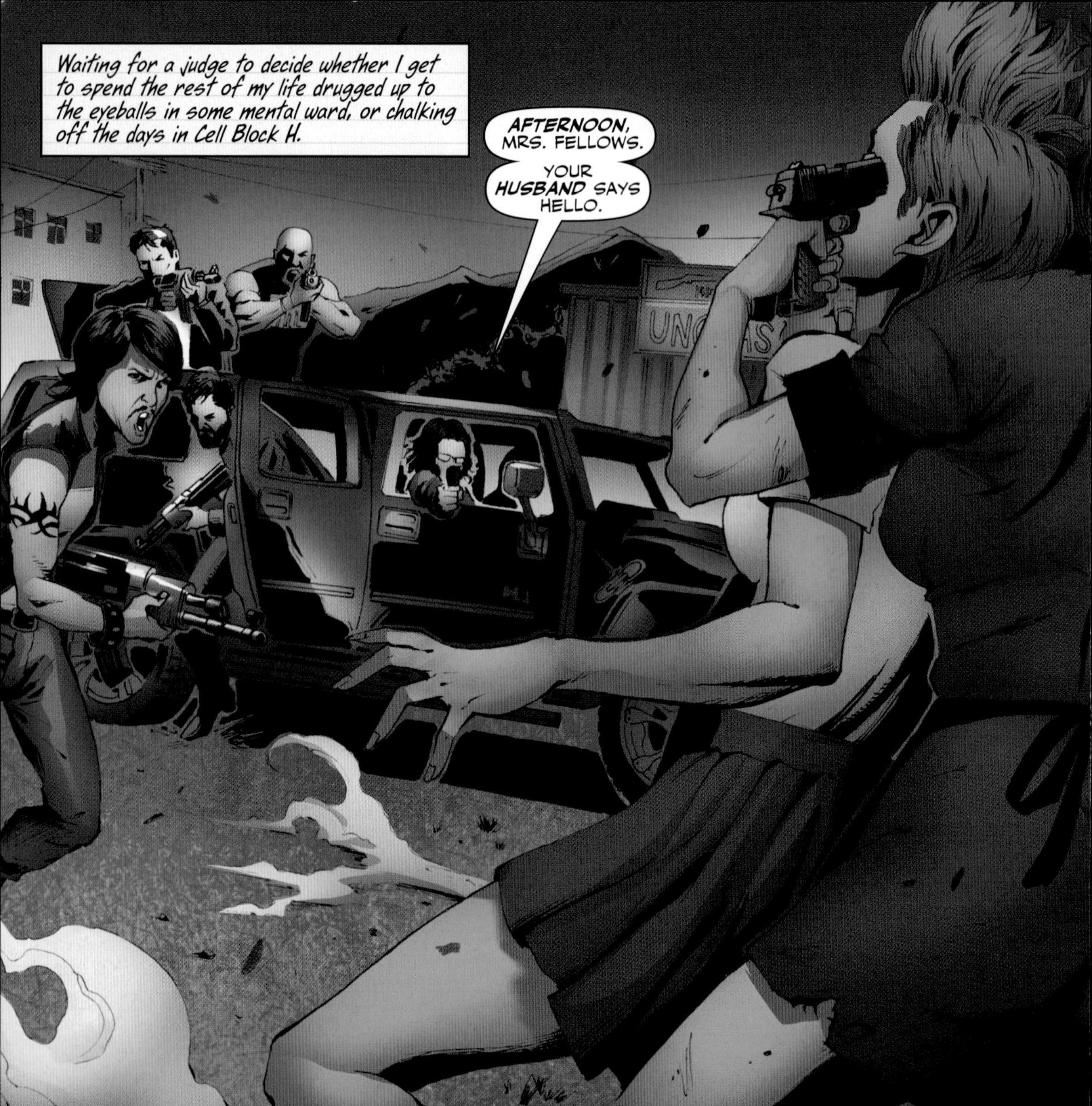

Waiting for a judge to decide whether I get to spend the rest of my life drugged up to the eyeballs in some mental ward, or chalking off the days in Cell Block H.
AFTERNOON, MRS. FELLOWS.
YOUR HUSBAND SAYS HELLO.

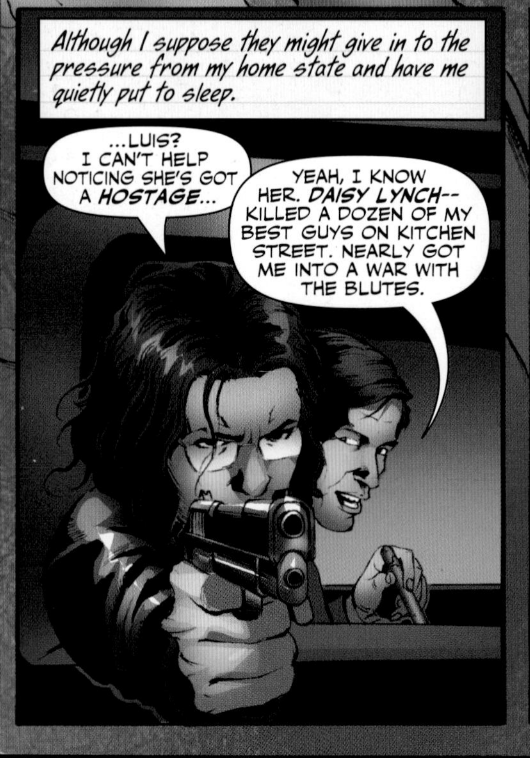

Although I suppose they might give in to the pressure from my home state and have me quietly put to sleep.
...LUIS? I CAN'T HELP NOTICING SHE'S GOT A HOSTAGE...
YEAH, I KNOW HER. DAISY LYNCH-- KILLED A DOZEN OF MY BEST GUYS ON KITCHEN STREET. NEARLY GOT ME INTO A WAR WITH THE BLUTES.

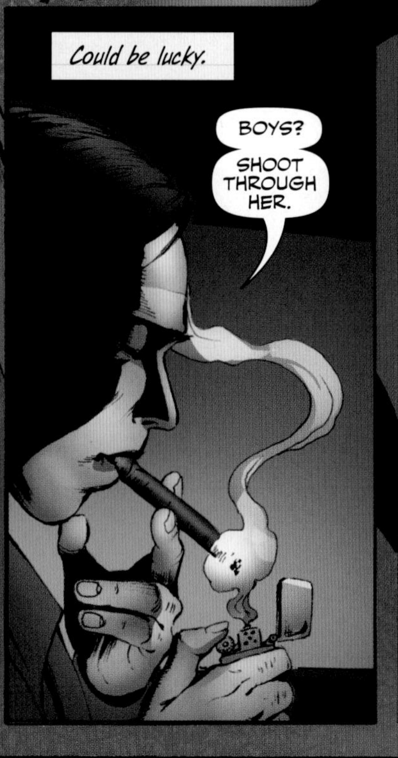

Could be lucky.
BOYS?
SHOOT THROUGH HER.

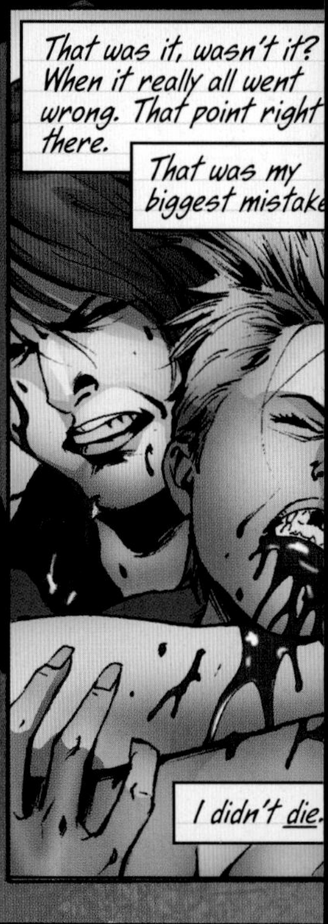

That was it, wasn't it? When it really all went wrong. That point right there.
That was my biggest mistake
I didn't die.

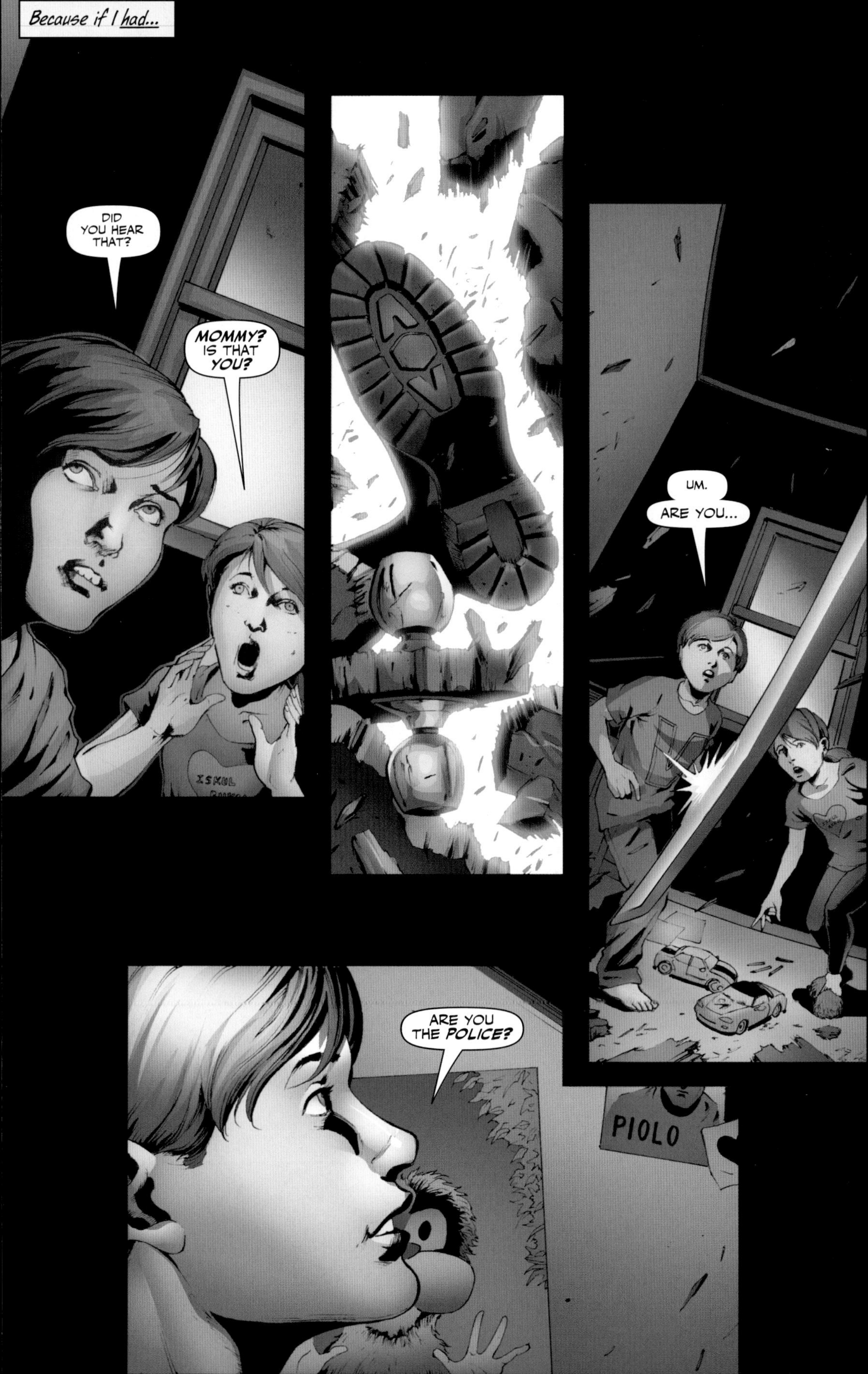
Because if I had...
DID YOU HEAR THAT?
MOMMY? IS THAT YOU?
UM.
ARE YOU...
ARE YOU THE POLICE?
PIOLO

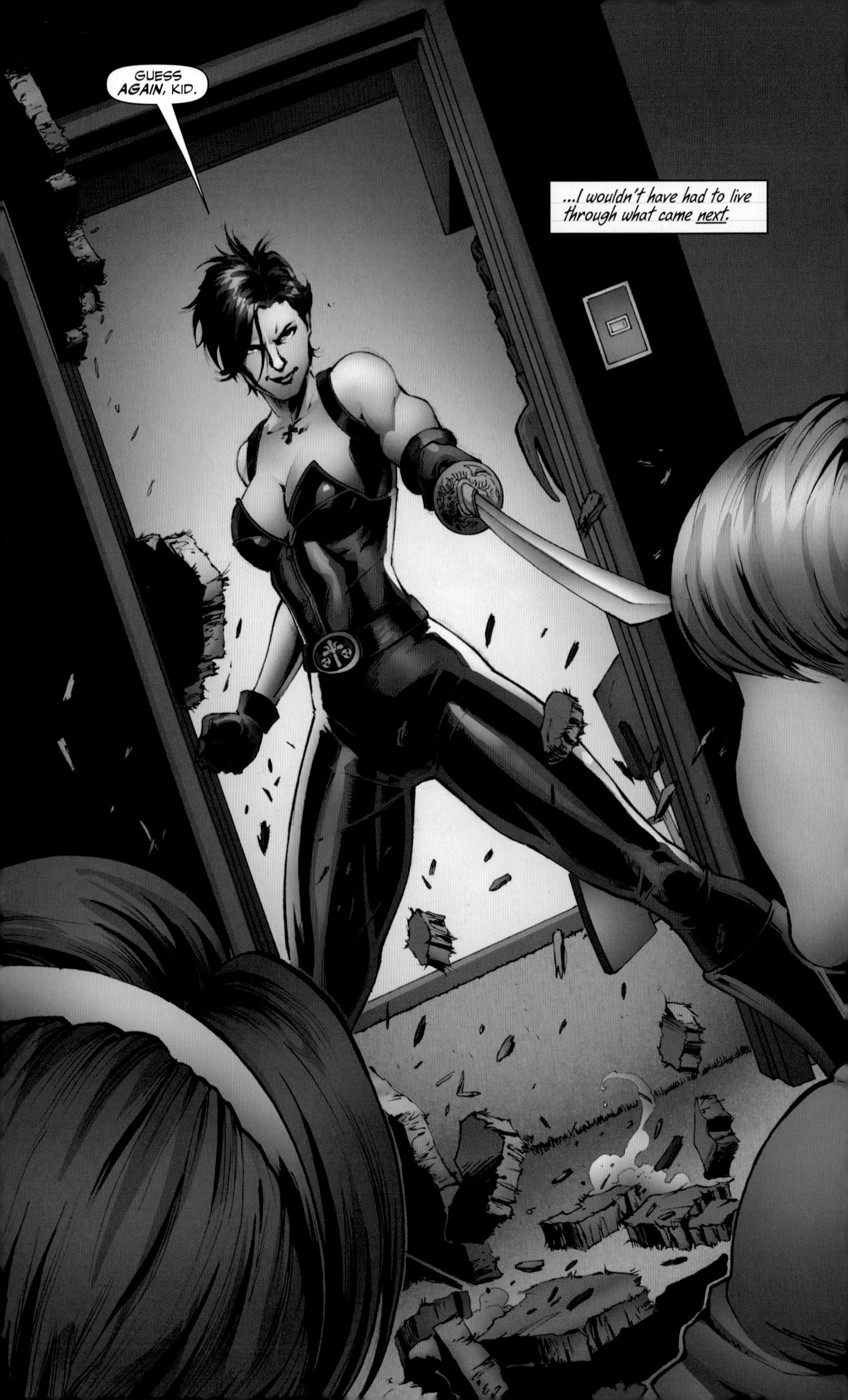
GUESS AGAIN, KID.
...I wouldn't have had to live through what came next.

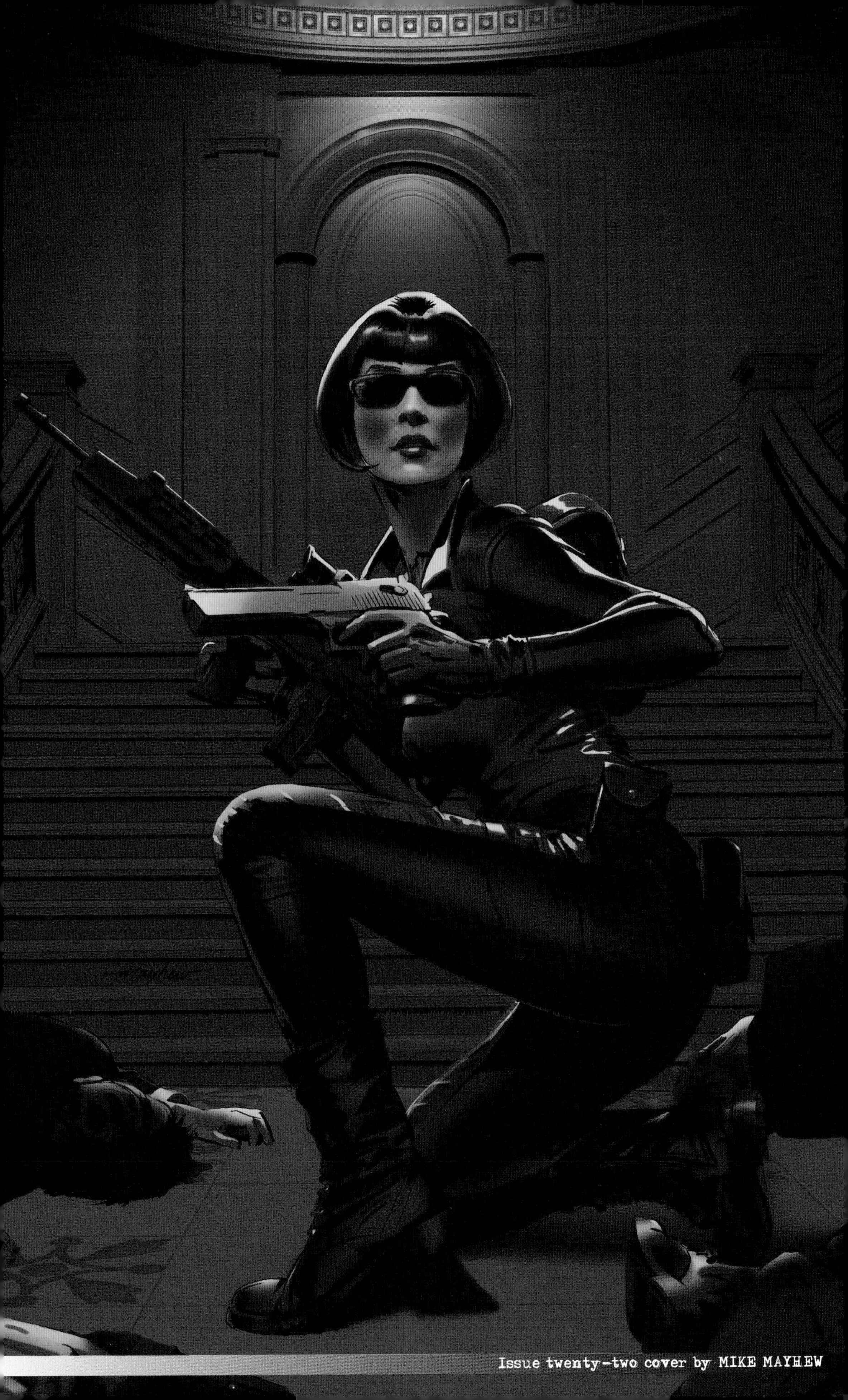

Issue twenty-two cover by MIKE MAYHEW

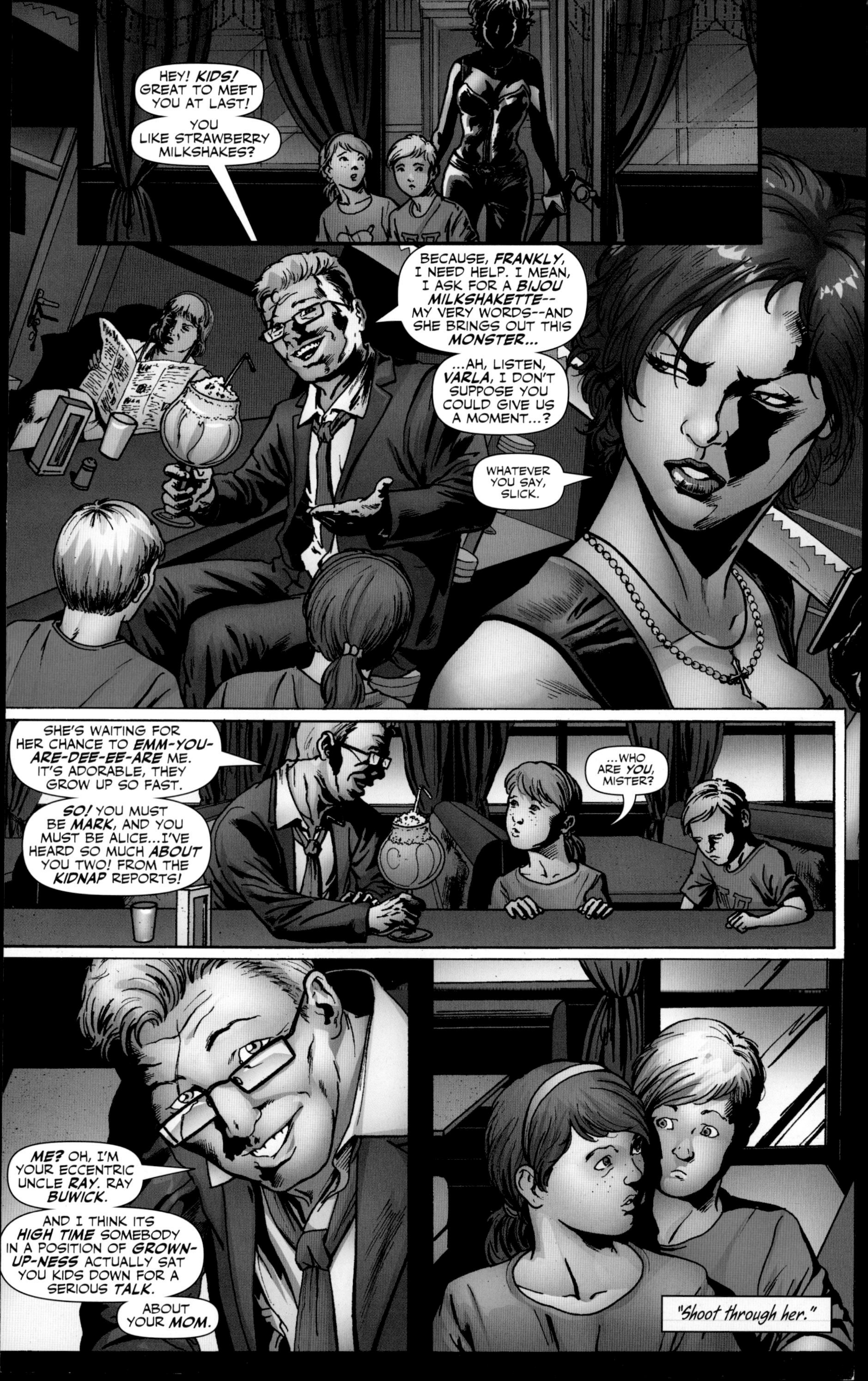
HEY! KIDS! GREAT TO MEET YOU AT LAST!
YOU LIKE STRAWBERRY MILKSHAKES?
BECAUSE, FRANKLY, I NEED HELP. I MEAN, I ASK FOR A BIJOU MILKSHAKETTE-- MY VERY WORDS--AND SHE BRINGS OUT THIS MONSTER...
...AH, LISTEN, VARLA, I DON'T SUPPOSE YOU COULD GIVE US A MOMENT...?
WHATEVER YOU SAY, SLICK.
SHE'S WAITING FOR HER CHANCE TO EMM-YOU-ARE-DEE-EE-ARE ME. IT'S ADORABLE, THEY GROW UP SO FAST.
SO! YOU MUST BE MARK, AND YOU MUST BE ALICE...I'VE HEARD SO MUCH ABOUT YOU TWO! FROM THE KIDNAP REPORTS!
...WHO ARE YOU, MISTER?
ME? OH, I'M YOUR ECCENTRIC UNCLE RAY. RAY BUWICK.
AND I THINK ITS HIGH TIME SOMEBODY IN A POSITION OF GROWN-UP-NESS ACTUALLY SAT YOU KIDS DOWN FOR A SERIOUS TALK.
ABOUT YOUR MOM.
"Shoot through her."

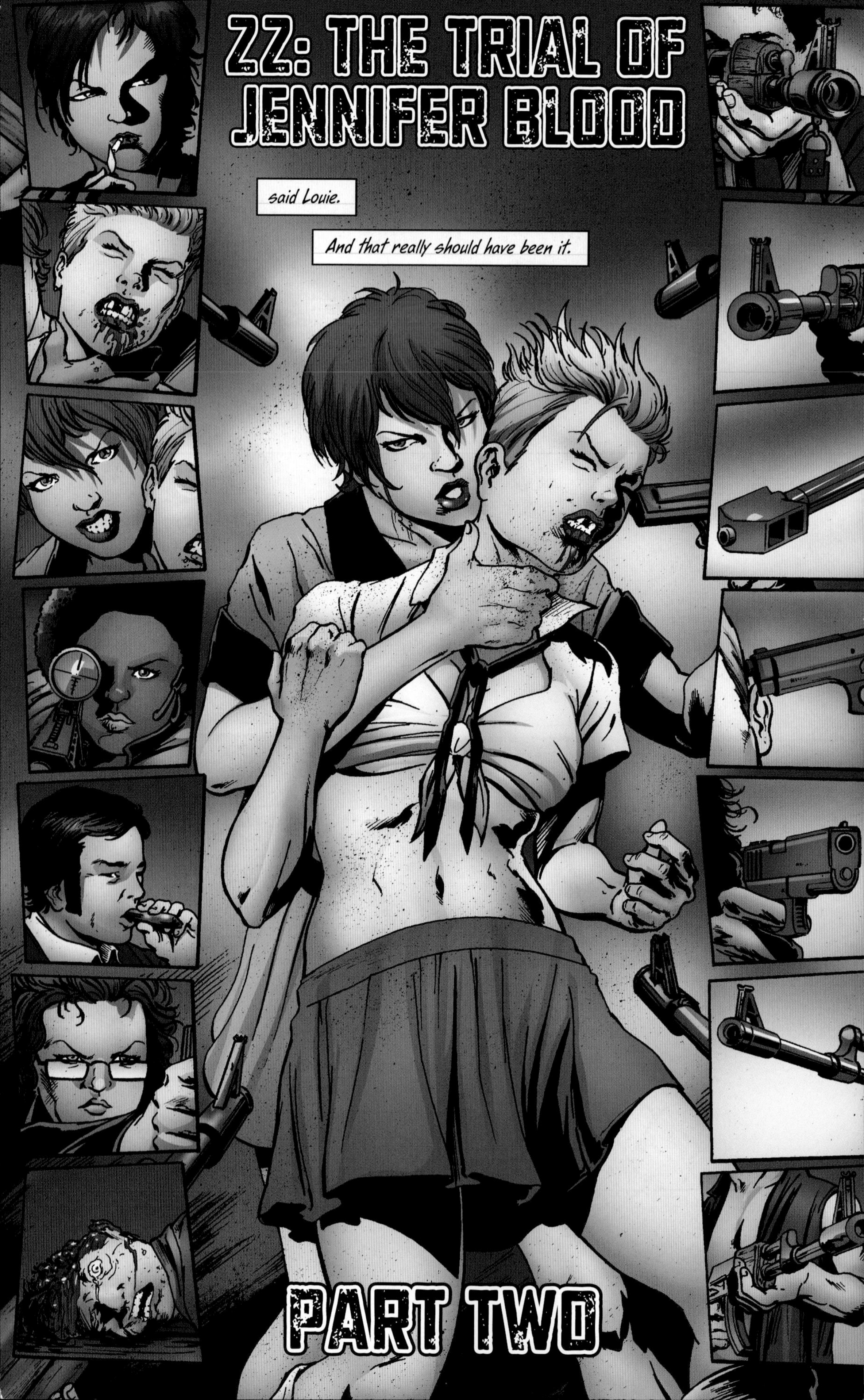
ZZ: THE TRIAL OF JENNIFER BLOOD
said Louie.
And that really should have been it.
PART TWO

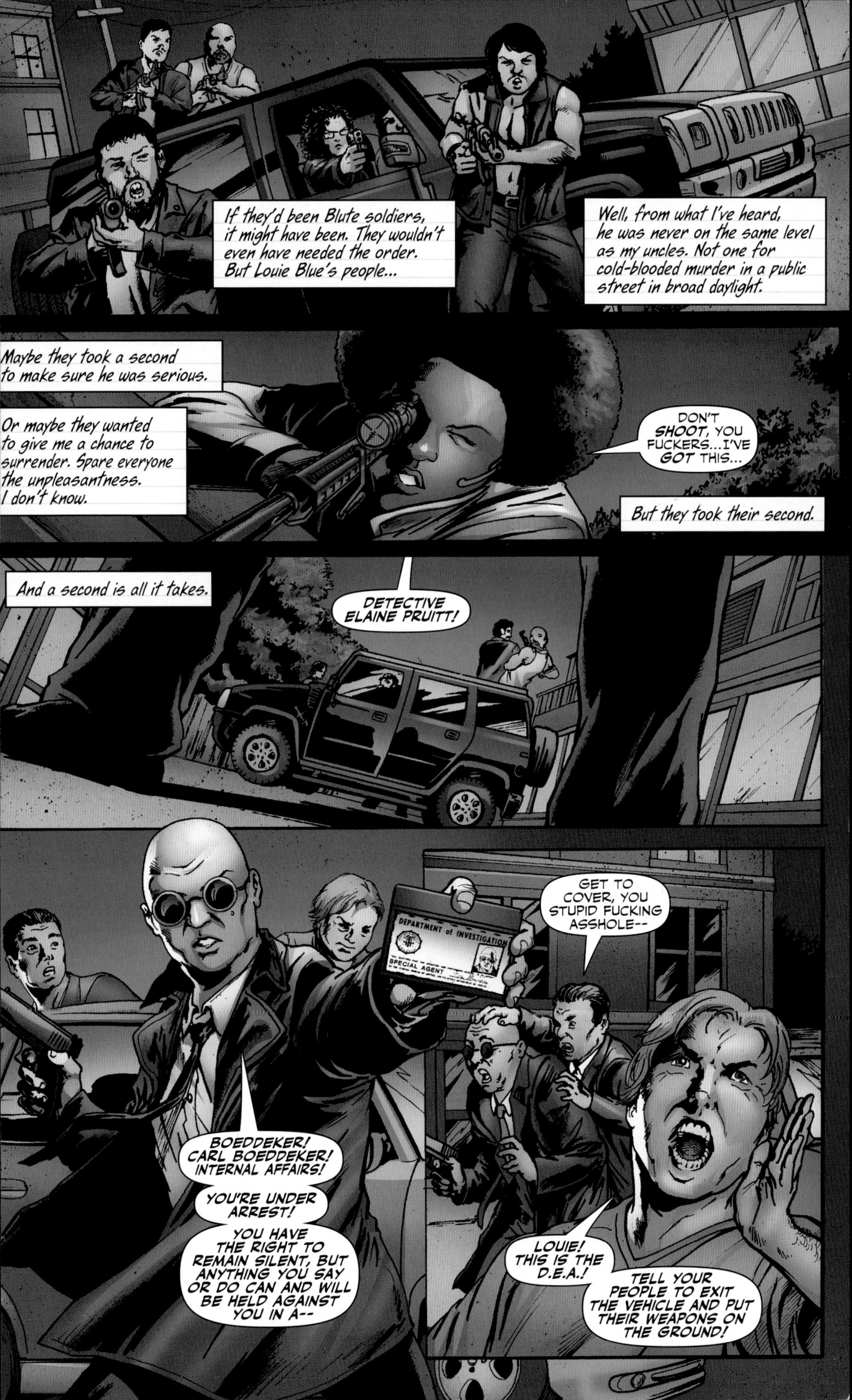
If they'd been Blute soldiers, it might have been. They wouldn't even have needed the order. But Louie Blue's people...
Well, from what I've heard, he was never on the same level as my uncles. Not one for cold-blooded murder in a public street in broad daylight.
Maybe they took a second to make sure he was serious.
Or maybe they wanted to give me a chance to surrender. Spare everyone the unpleasantness. I don't know.
DON'T SHOOT, YOU FUCKERS...I'VE GOT THIS...
But they took their second.
And a second is all it takes.
DETECTIVE ELAINE PRUITT!
DEPARTMENT of INVESTIGATION
SPECIAL AGENT
GET TO COVER, YOU STUPID FUCKING ASSHOLE--
BOEDDEKER! CARL BOEDDEKER! INTERNAL AFFAIRS!
YOU'RE UNDER ARREST!
YOU HAVE THE RIGHT TO REMAIN SILENT, BUT ANYTHING YOU SAY OR DO CAN AND WILL BE HELD AGAINST YOU IN A--
LOUIE! THIS IS THE D.E.A.!
TELL YOUR PEOPLE TO EXIT THE VEHICLE AND PUT THEIR WEAPONS ON THE GROUND!

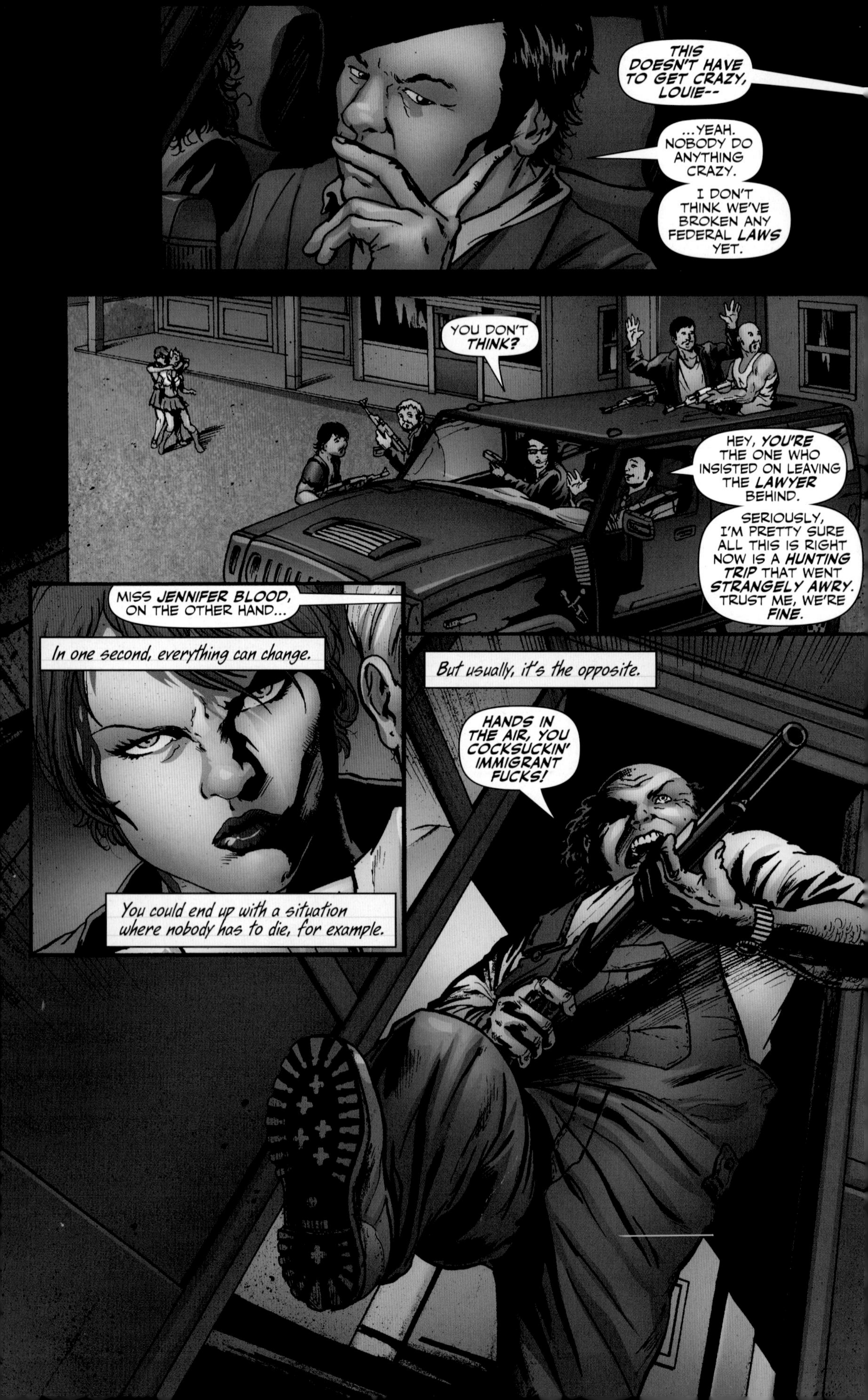
THIS DOESN'T HAVE TO GET CRAZY, LOUIE--
...YEAH. NOBODY DO ANYTHING CRAZY.
I DON'T THINK WE'VE BROKEN ANY FEDERAL LAWS YET.
YOU DON'T THINK?
HEY, YOU'RE THE ONE WHO INSISTED ON LEAVING THE LAWYER BEHIND.
SERIOUSLY, I'M PRETTY SURE ALL THIS IS RIGHT NOW IS A HUNTING TRIP THAT WENT STRANGELY AWRY. TRUST ME, WE'RE FINE.
MISS JENNIFER BLOOD, ON THE OTHER HAND...
In one second, everything can change.
You could end up with a situation where nobody has to die, for example.
But usually, it's the opposite.
HANDS IN THE AIR, YOU COCKSUCKIN' IMMIGRANT FUCKS!

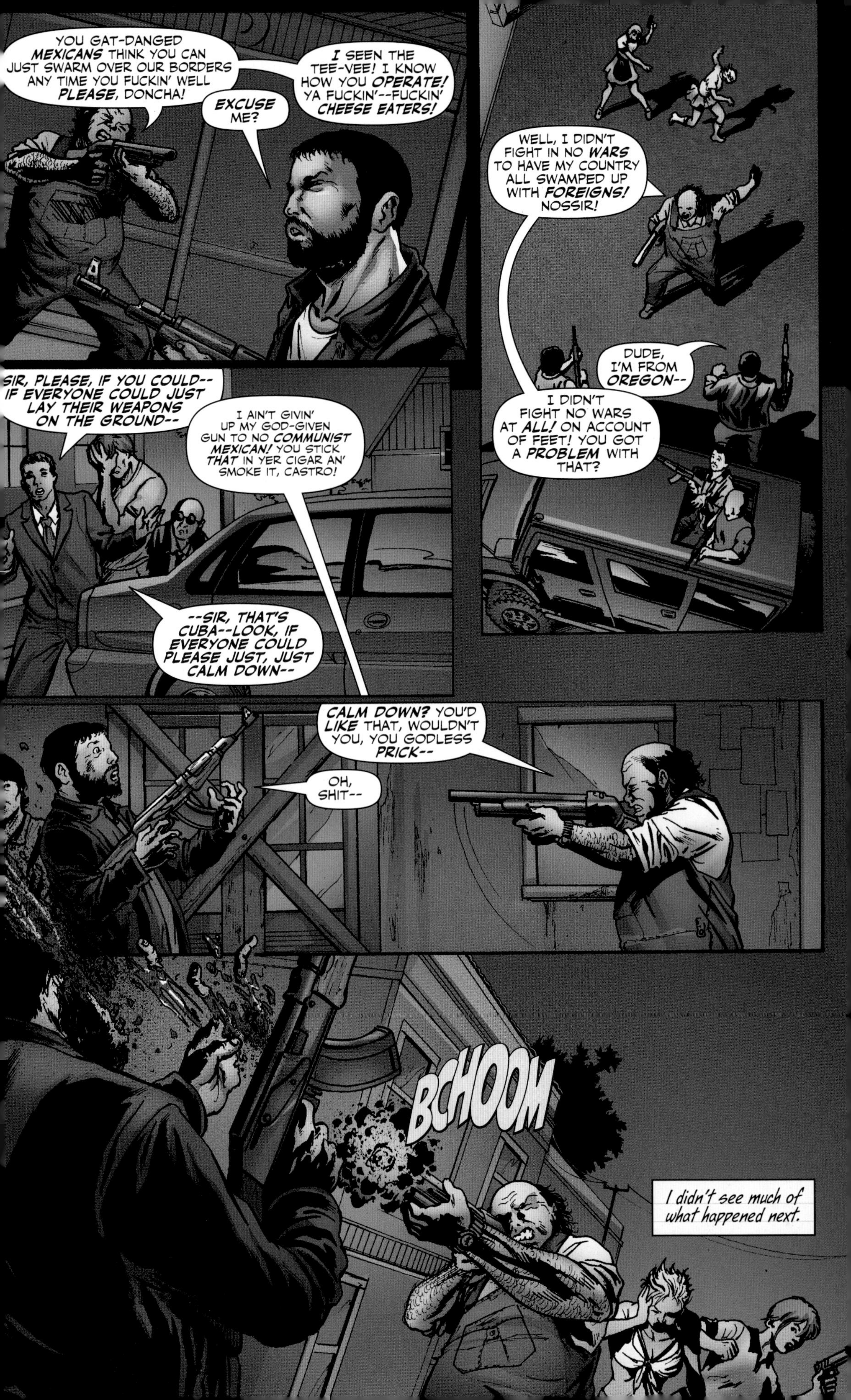
YOU GAT-DANGED MEXICANS THINK YOU CAN JUST SWARM OVER OUR BORDERS ANY TIME YOU FUCKIN' WELL PLEASE, DONCHA!
EXCUSE ME?
I SEEN THE TEE-VEE! I KNOW HOW YOU OPERATE! YA FUCKIN'--FUCKIN' CHEESE EATERS!
WELL, I DIDN'T FIGHT IN NO WARS TO HAVE MY COUNTRY ALL SWAMPED UP WITH FOREIGNS! NOSSIR!
DUDE, I'M FROM OREGON--
I DIDN'T FIGHT NO WARS AT ALL! ON ACCOUNT OF FEET! YOU GOT A PROBLEM WITH THAT?
SIR, PLEASE, IF YOU COULD-- IF EVERYONE COULD JUST LAY THEIR WEAPONS ON THE GROUND--
I AIN'T GIVIN' UP MY GOD-GIVEN GUN TO NO COMMUNIST MEXICAN! YOU STICK THAT IN YER CIGAR AN' SMOKE IT, CASTRO!
--SIR, THAT'S CUBA--LOOK, IF EVERYONE COULD PLEASE JUST, JUST CALM DOWN--
CALM DOWN? YOU'D LIKE THAT, WOULDN'T YOU, YOU GODLESS PRICK--
OH, SHIT--
BCHOOM
I didn't see much of what happened next.

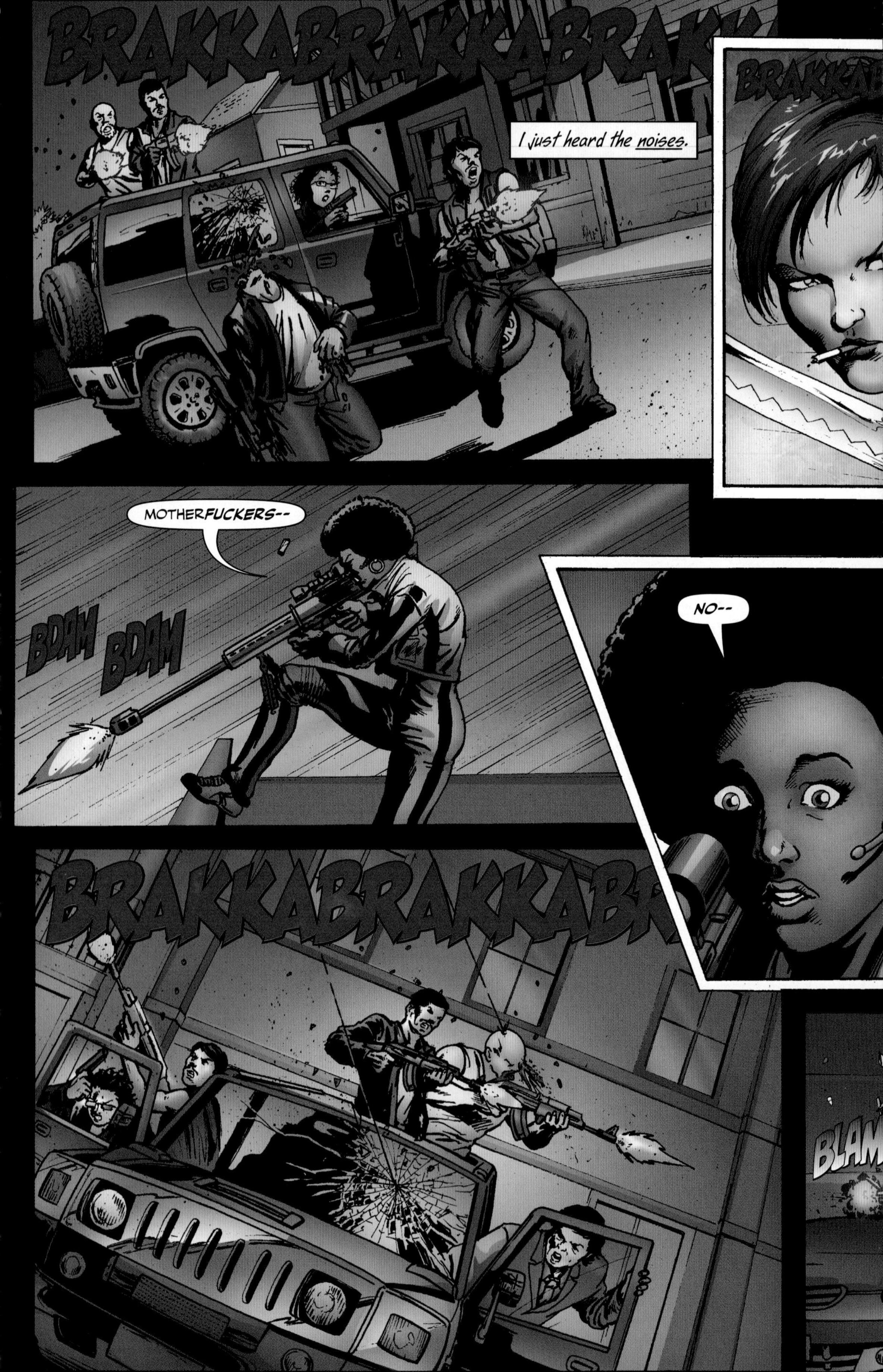

BRAKKABRAKKABRAKKABRAK
I just heard the noises.
MOTHERFUCKERS--
BDAM
BDAM
NO--
BRAKKABRAKKABR
BLAM

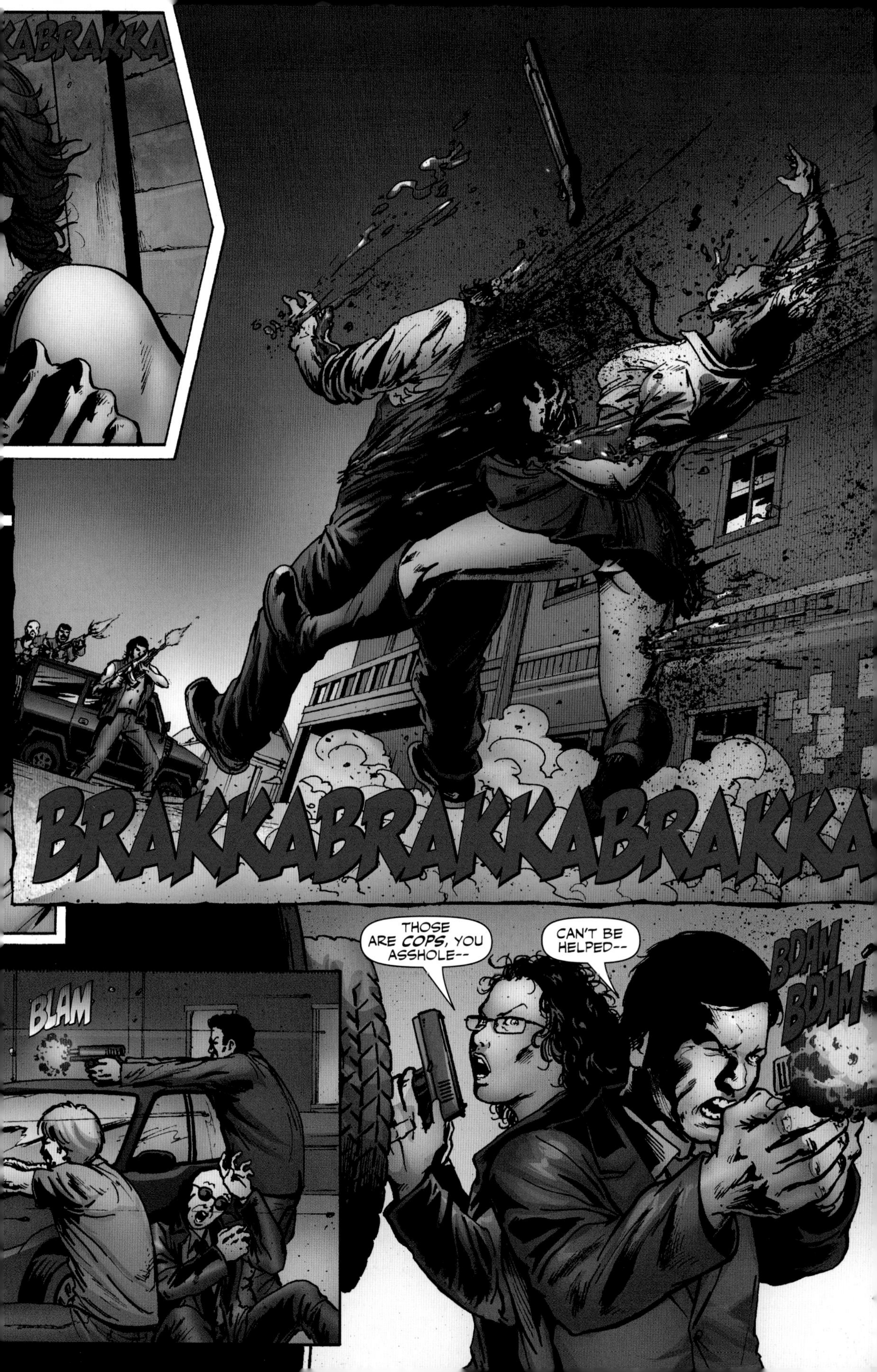

KABRAKKA
BRAKKABRAKKABRAKKA
BLAM
THOSE ARE COPS, YOU ASSHOLE--
CAN'T BE HELPED--
BDAM BDAM

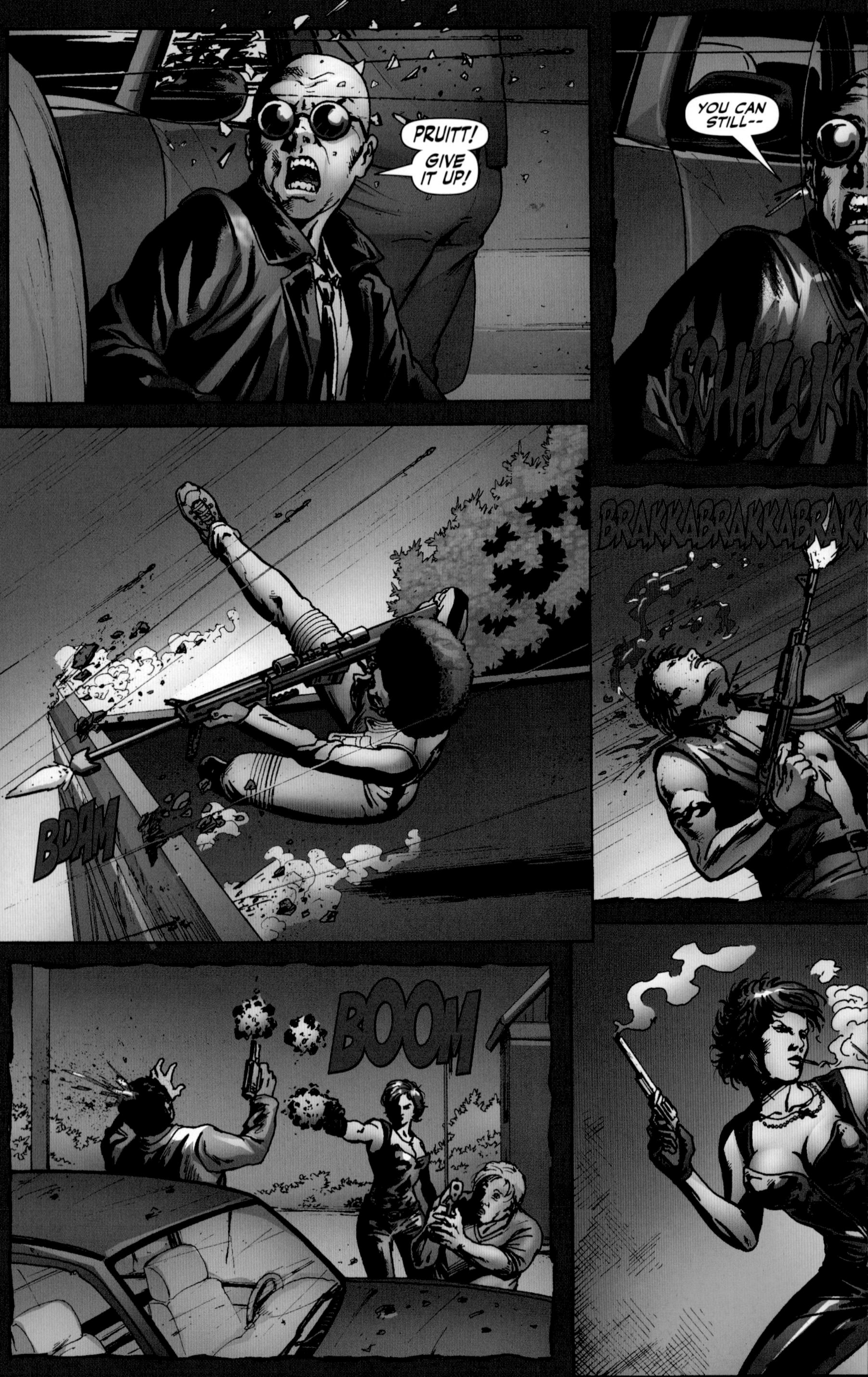
PRUITT!
GIVE IT UP!
YOU CAN STILL--
SCHLUKK
BDAM
BRAKKABRAKKABRAKK
BOOM

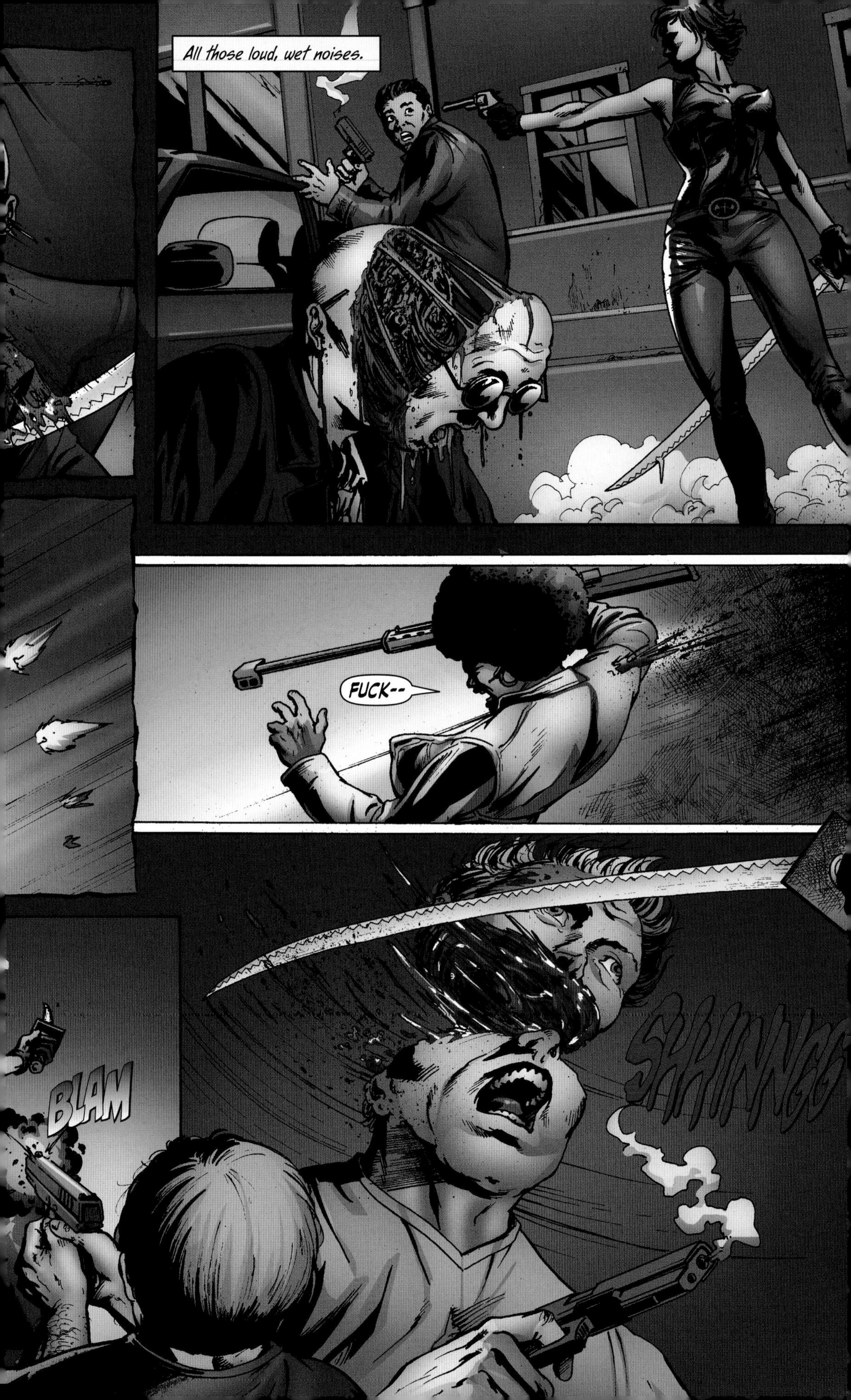

All those loud, wet noises.
FUCK--
BLAM

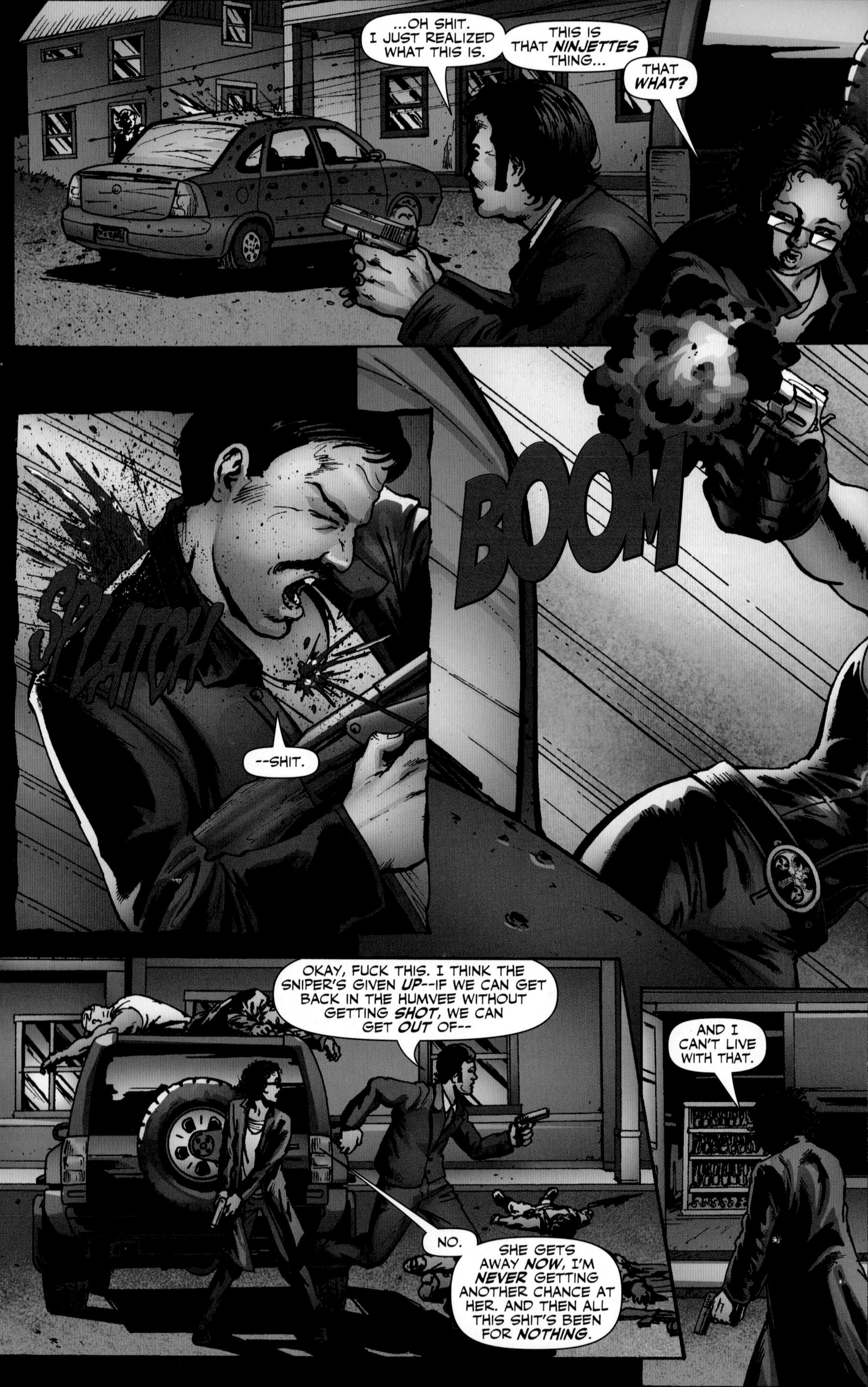
...OH SHIT. I JUST REALIZED WHAT THIS IS.
THIS IS THAT NINJETTES THING...
THAT WHAT?
SPLATCH
--SHIT.
BOOM
OKAY, FUCK THIS. I THINK THE SNIPER'S GIVEN UP--IF WE CAN GET BACK IN THE HUMVEE WITHOUT GETTING SHOT, WE CAN GET OUT OF--
NO.
SHE GETS AWAY NOW, I'M NEVER GETTING ANOTHER CHANCE AT HER. AND THEN ALL THIS SHIT'S BEEN FOR NOTHING.
AND I CAN'T LIVE WITH THAT.

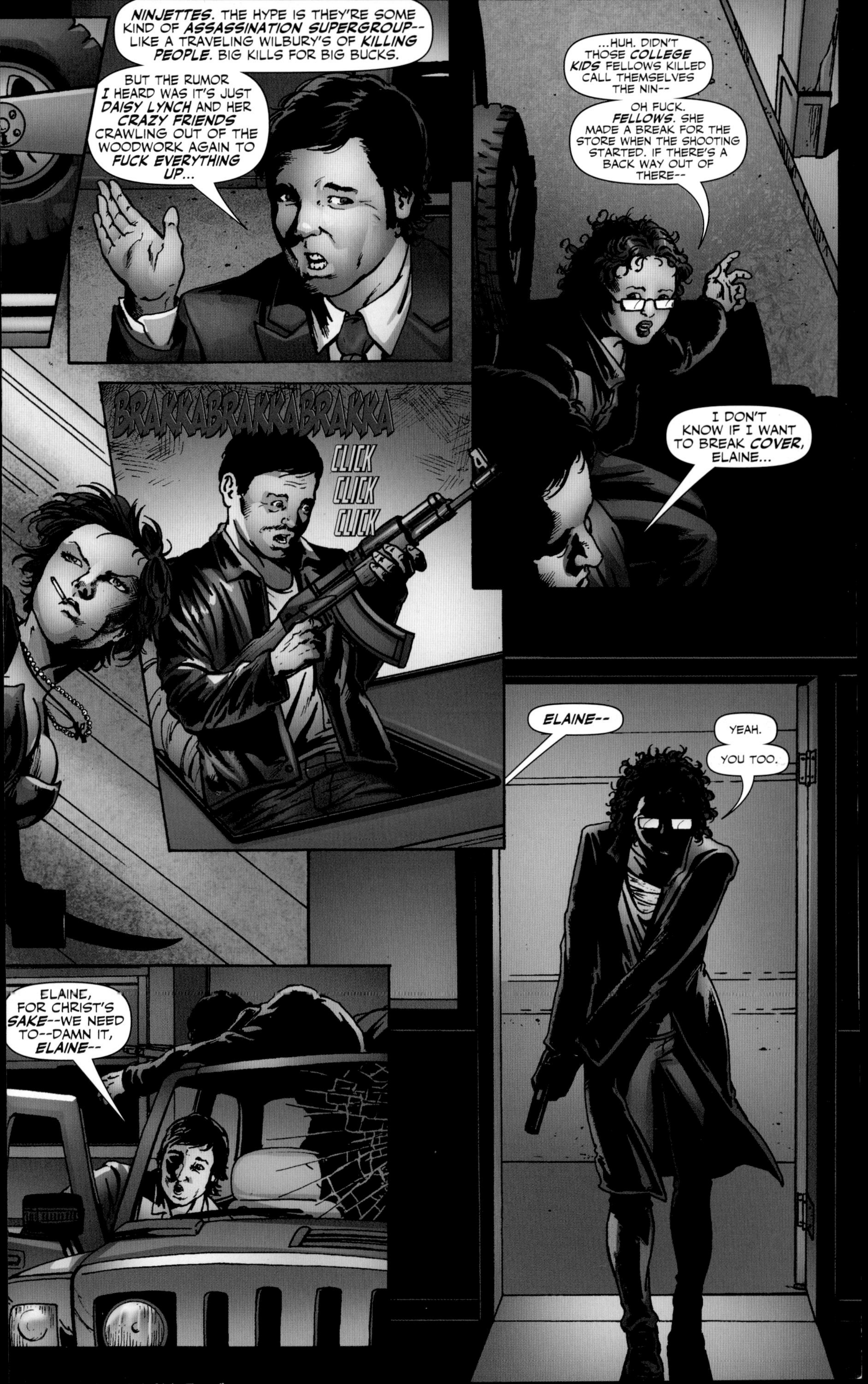
NINJETTES. THE HYPE IS THEY'RE SOME KIND OF ASSASSINATION SUPERGROUP-- LIKE A TRAVELING WILBURY'S OF KILLING PEOPLE. BIG KILLS FOR BIG BUCKS.
BUT THE RUMOR I HEARD WAS IT'S JUST DAISY LYNCH AND HER CRAZY FRIENDS CRAWLING OUT OF THE WOODWORK AGAIN TO FUCK EVERYTHING UP...
...HUH. DIDN'T THOSE COLLEGE KIDS FELLOWS KILLED CALL THEMSELVES THE NIN--
OH FUCK. FELLOWS. SHE MADE A BREAK FOR THE STORE WHEN THE SHOOTING STARTED. IF THERE'S A BACK WAY OUT OF THERE--
BRAKKABRAKKABRAKKA
CLICK CLICK CLICK
I DON'T KNOW IF I WANT TO BREAK COVER, ELAINE...
ELAINE--
YEAH.
YOU TOO.
ELAINE, FOR CHRIST'S SAKE--WE NEED TO--DAMN IT, ELAINE--

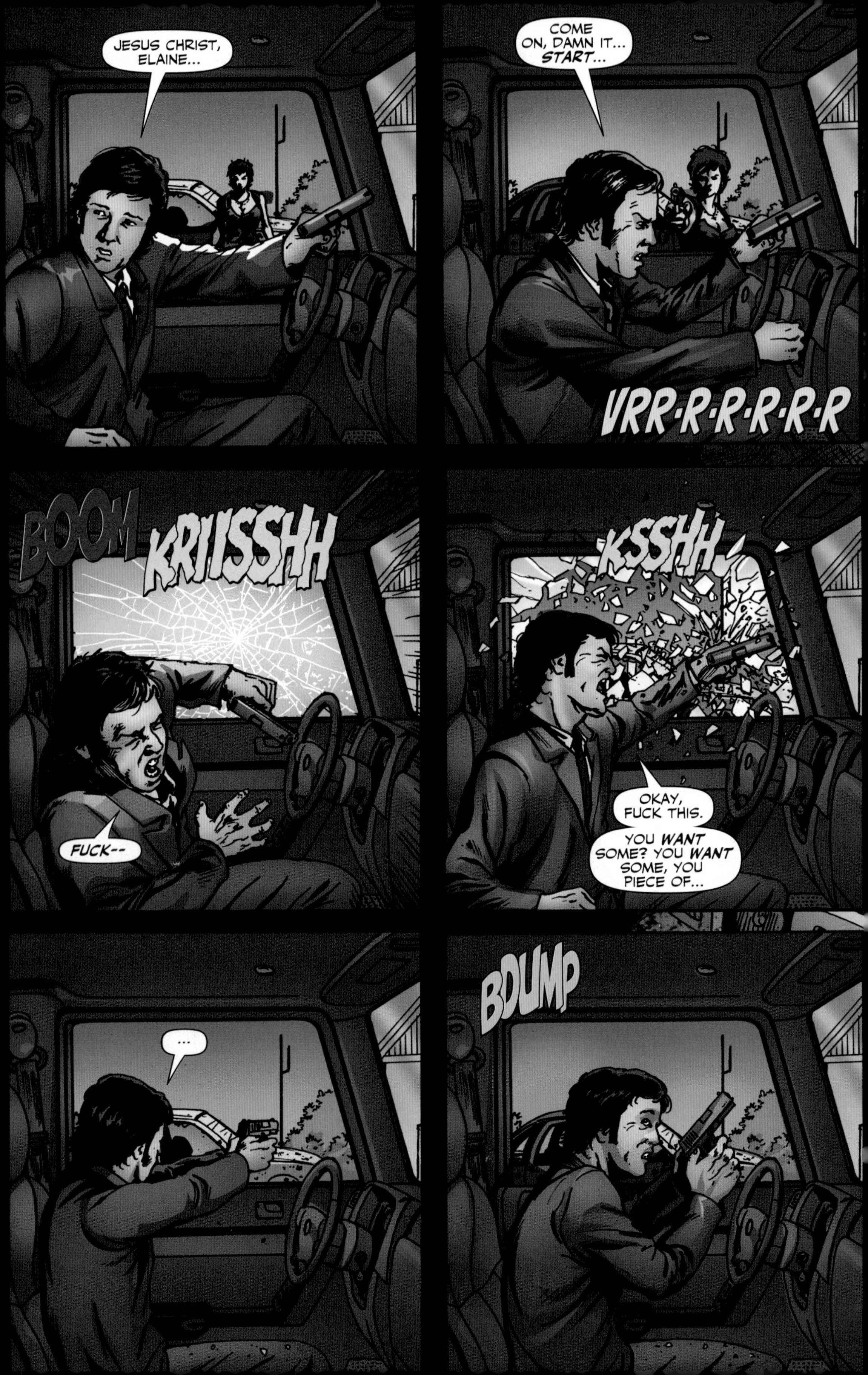
JESUS CHRIST, ELAINE...
COME ON, DAMN IT... *START*...
VRR·R·R·R·R·R
BOOM
KRIISSHH
FUCK--
KSSHH
OKAY, FUCK THIS.
YOU *WANT* SOME? YOU *WANT* SOME, YOU PIECE OF...
...
BDUMP

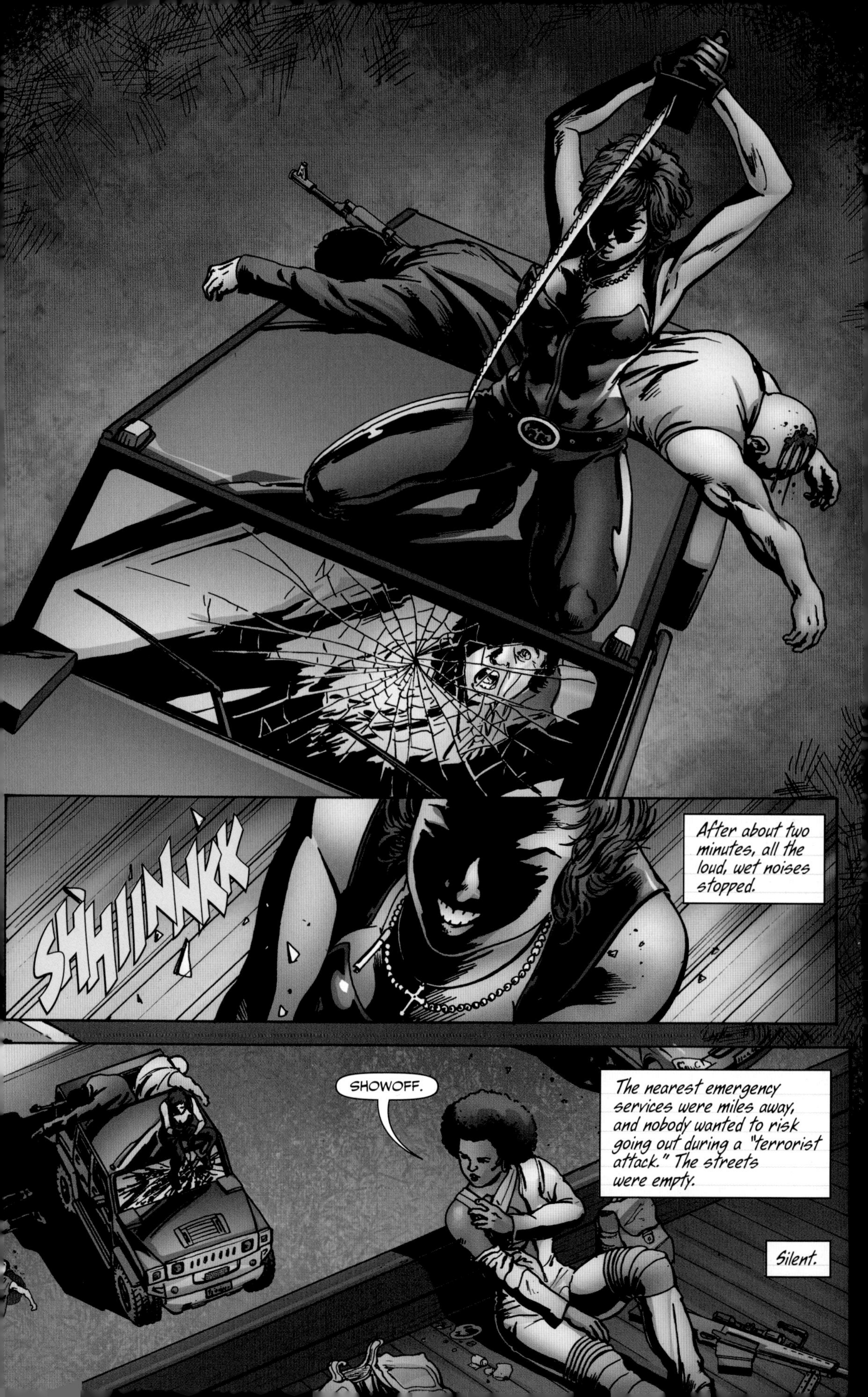
SHHINNKK
After about two minutes, all the loud, wet noises stopped.
SHOWOFF.
The nearest emergency services were miles away, and nobody wanted to risk going out during a "terrorist attack." The streets were empty.
Silent.

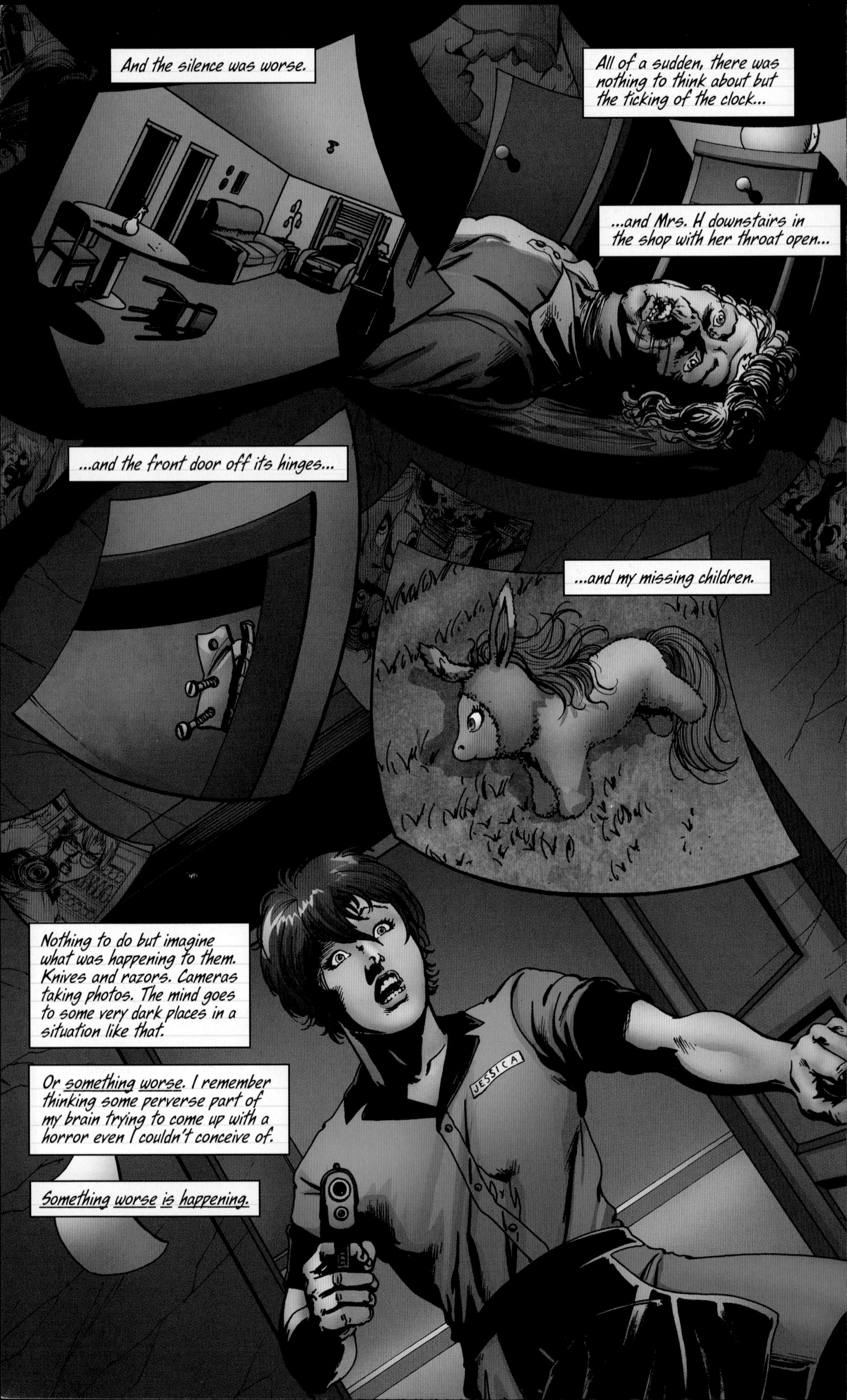
And the silence was worse.
All of a sudden, there was nothing to think about but the ticking of the clock...
...and Mrs. H downstairs in the shop with her throat open...
...and the front door off its hinges...
...and my missing children.
Nothing to do but imagine what was happening to them. Knives and razors. Cameras taking photos. The mind goes to some very dark places in a situation like that.
Or something worse. I remember thinking some perverse part of my brain trying to come up with a horror even I couldn't conceive of.
Something worse is happening.
JESSICA

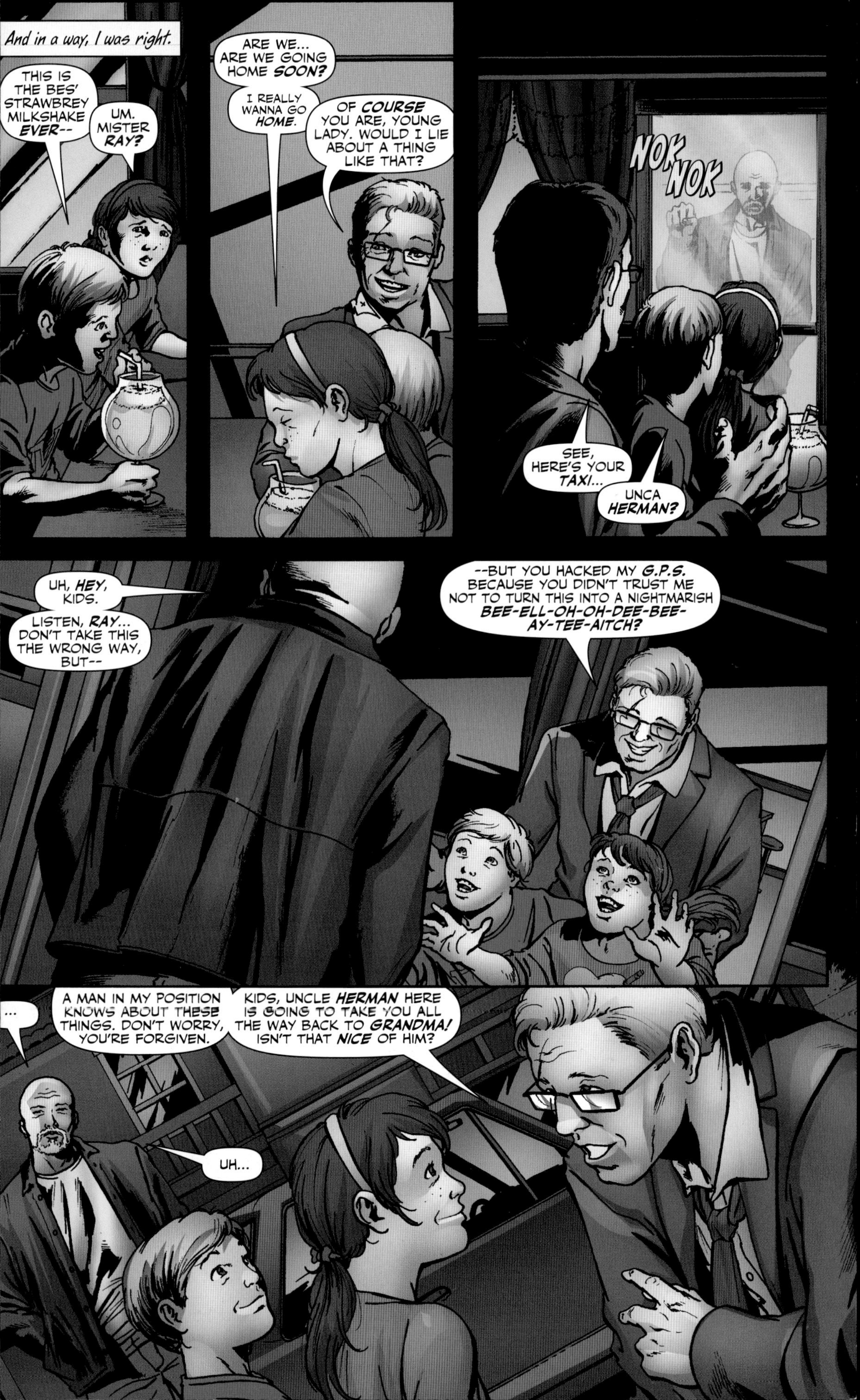
And in a way, I was right.
THIS IS THE BES' STRAWBREY MILKSHAKE EVER--
UM. MISTER RAY?
ARE WE... ARE WE GOING HOME SOON?
I REALLY WANNA GO HOME.
OF COURSE YOU ARE, YOUNG LADY. WOULD I LIE ABOUT A THING LIKE THAT?
NOK NOK
SEE, HERE'S YOUR TAXI...
UNCA HERMAN?
UH, HEY, KIDS.
LISTEN, RAY... DON'T TAKE THIS THE WRONG WAY, BUT--
--BUT YOU HACKED MY G.P.S. BECAUSE YOU DIDN'T TRUST ME NOT TO TURN THIS INTO A NIGHTMARISH BEE-ELL-OH-OH-DEE-BEE-AY-TEE-AITCH?
...
A MAN IN MY POSITION KNOWS ABOUT THESE THINGS. DON'T WORRY, YOU'RE FORGIVEN.
KIDS, UNCLE HERMAN HERE IS GOING TO TAKE YOU ALL THE WAY BACK TO GRANDMA! ISN'T THAT NICE OF HIM?
UH...

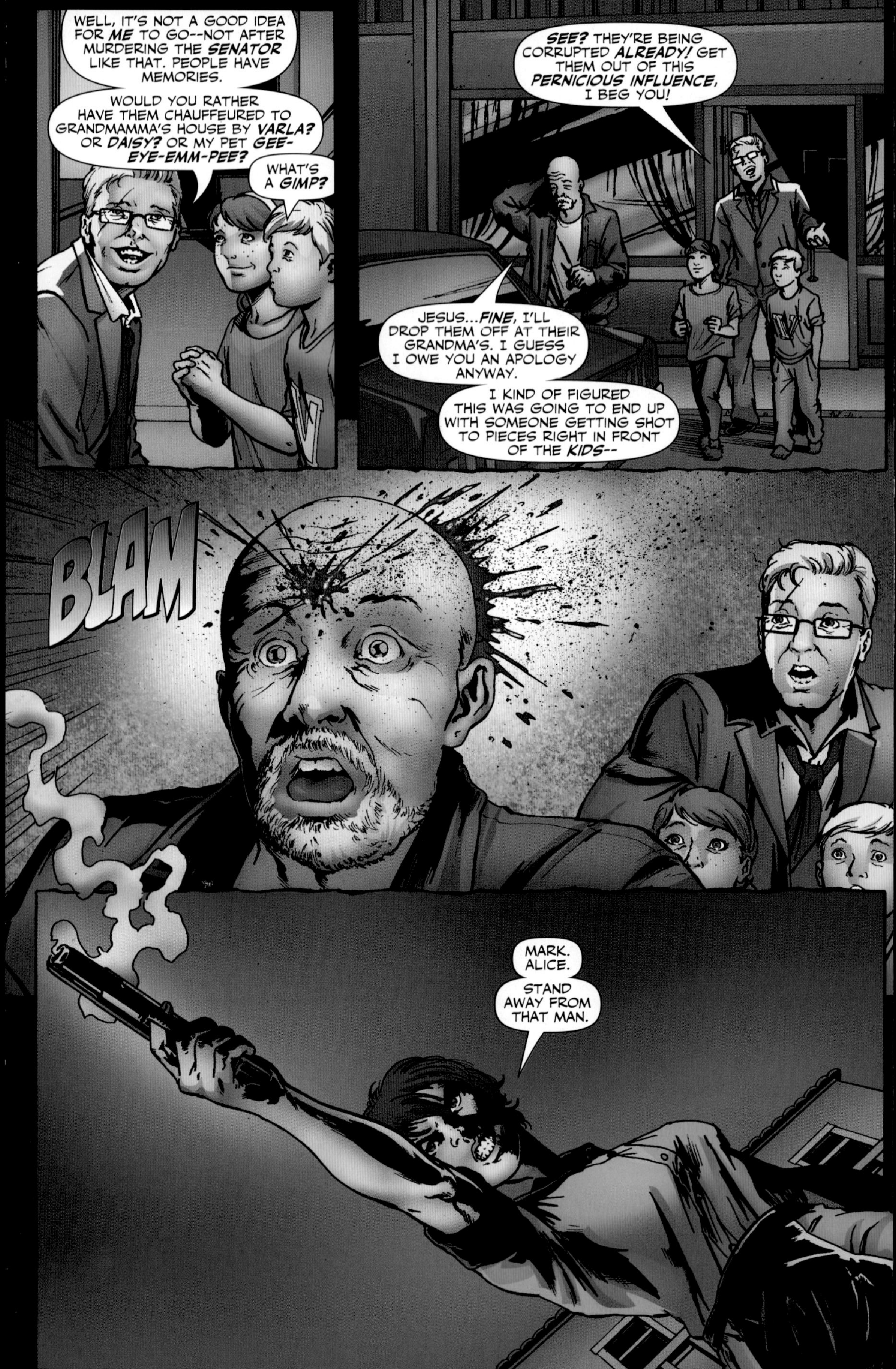
WELL, IT'S NOT A GOOD IDEA FOR ME TO GO--NOT AFTER MURDERING THE SENATOR LIKE THAT. PEOPLE HAVE MEMORIES.
WOULD YOU RATHER HAVE THEM CHAUFFEURED TO GRANDMAMMA'S HOUSE BY VARLA? OR DAISY? OR MY PET GEE-EYE-EMM-PEE?
WHAT'S A GIMP?
SEE? THEY'RE BEING CORRUPTED ALREADY! GET THEM OUT OF THIS PERNICIOUS INFLUENCE, I BEG YOU!
JESUS...FINE, I'LL DROP THEM OFF AT THEIR GRANDMA'S. I GUESS I OWE YOU AN APOLOGY ANYWAY.
I KIND OF FIGURED THIS WAS GOING TO END UP WITH SOMEONE GETTING SHOT TO PIECES RIGHT IN FRONT OF THE KIDS--
BLAM
MARK. ALICE.
STAND AWAY FROM THAT MAN.

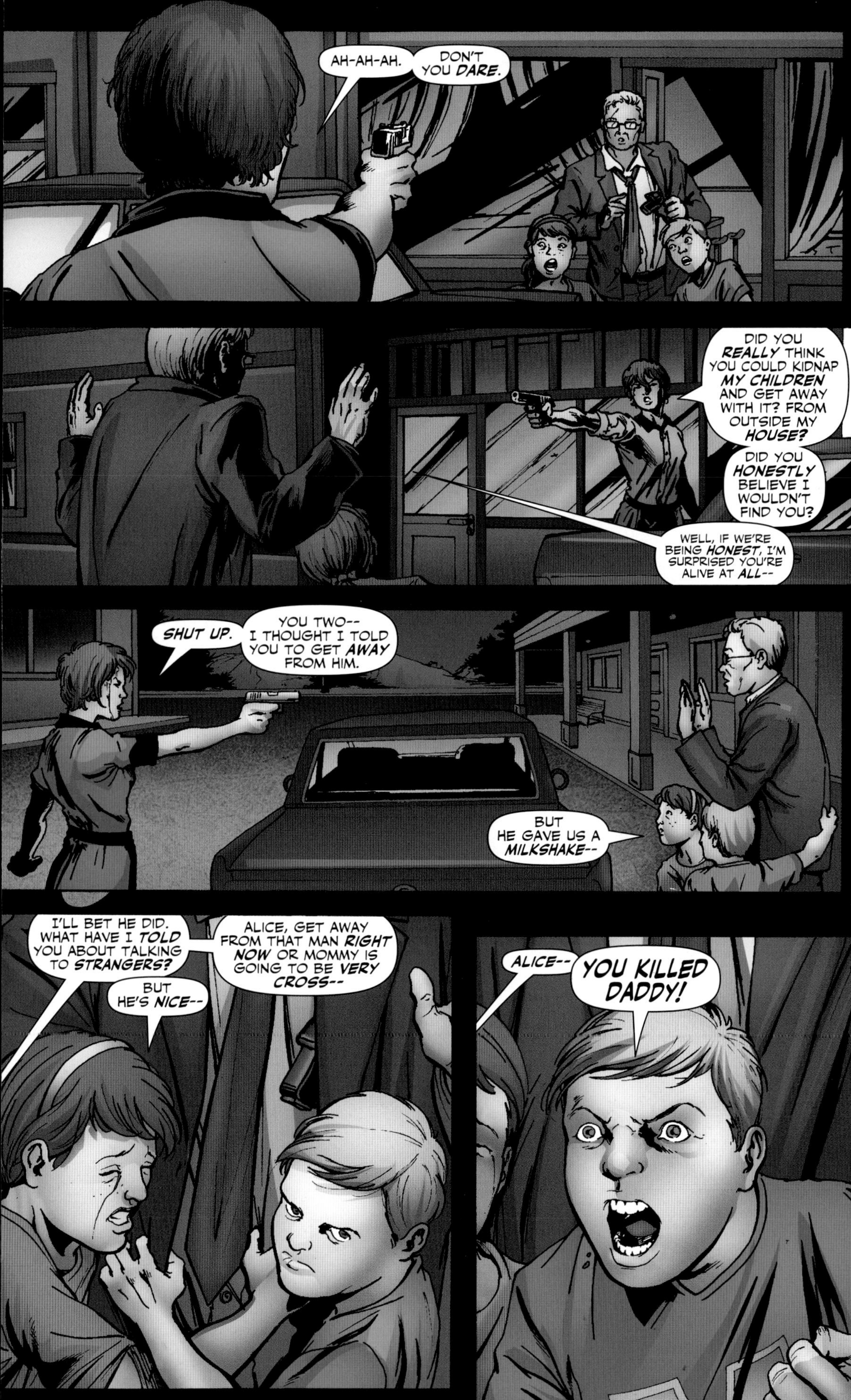
AH-AH-AH.
DON'T YOU DARE.
DID YOU REALLY THINK YOU COULD KIDNAP MY CHILDREN AND GET AWAY WITH IT? FROM OUTSIDE MY HOUSE?
DID YOU HONESTLY BELIEVE I WOULDN'T FIND YOU?
WELL, IF WE'RE BEING HONEST, I'M SURPRISED YOU'RE ALIVE AT ALL--
SHUT UP.
YOU TWO-- I THOUGHT I TOLD YOU TO GET AWAY FROM HIM.
BUT HE GAVE US A MILKSHAKE--
I'LL BET HE DID. WHAT HAVE I TOLD YOU ABOUT TALKING TO STRANGERS?
BUT HE'S NICE--
ALICE, GET AWAY FROM THAT MAN RIGHT NOW OR MOMMY IS GOING TO BE VERY CROSS--
ALICE--
YOU KILLED DADDY!

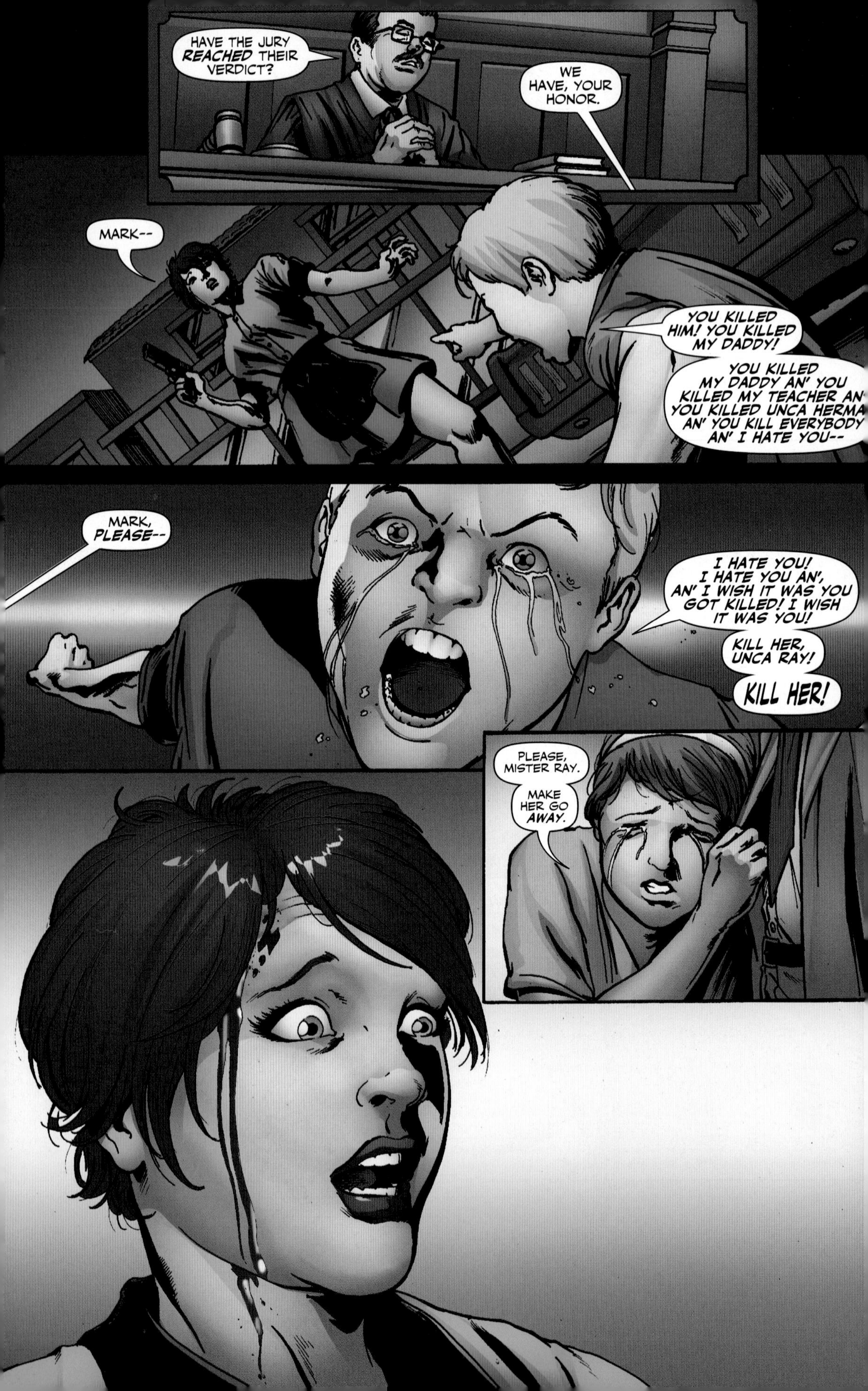
HAVE THE JURY REACHED THEIR VERDICT?
WE HAVE, YOUR HONOR.
MARK--
YOU KILLED HIM! YOU KILLED MY DADDY!
YOU KILLED MY DADDY AN' YOU KILLED MY TEACHER AN' YOU KILLED UNCA HERMA AN' YOU KILL EVERYBODY AN' I HATE YOU--
MARK, PLEASE--
I HATE YOU! I HATE YOU AN', AN' I WISH IT WAS YOU GOT KILLED! I WISH IT WAS YOU!
KILL HER, UNCA RAY!
KILL HER!
PLEASE, MISTER RAY.
MAKE HER GO AWAY.

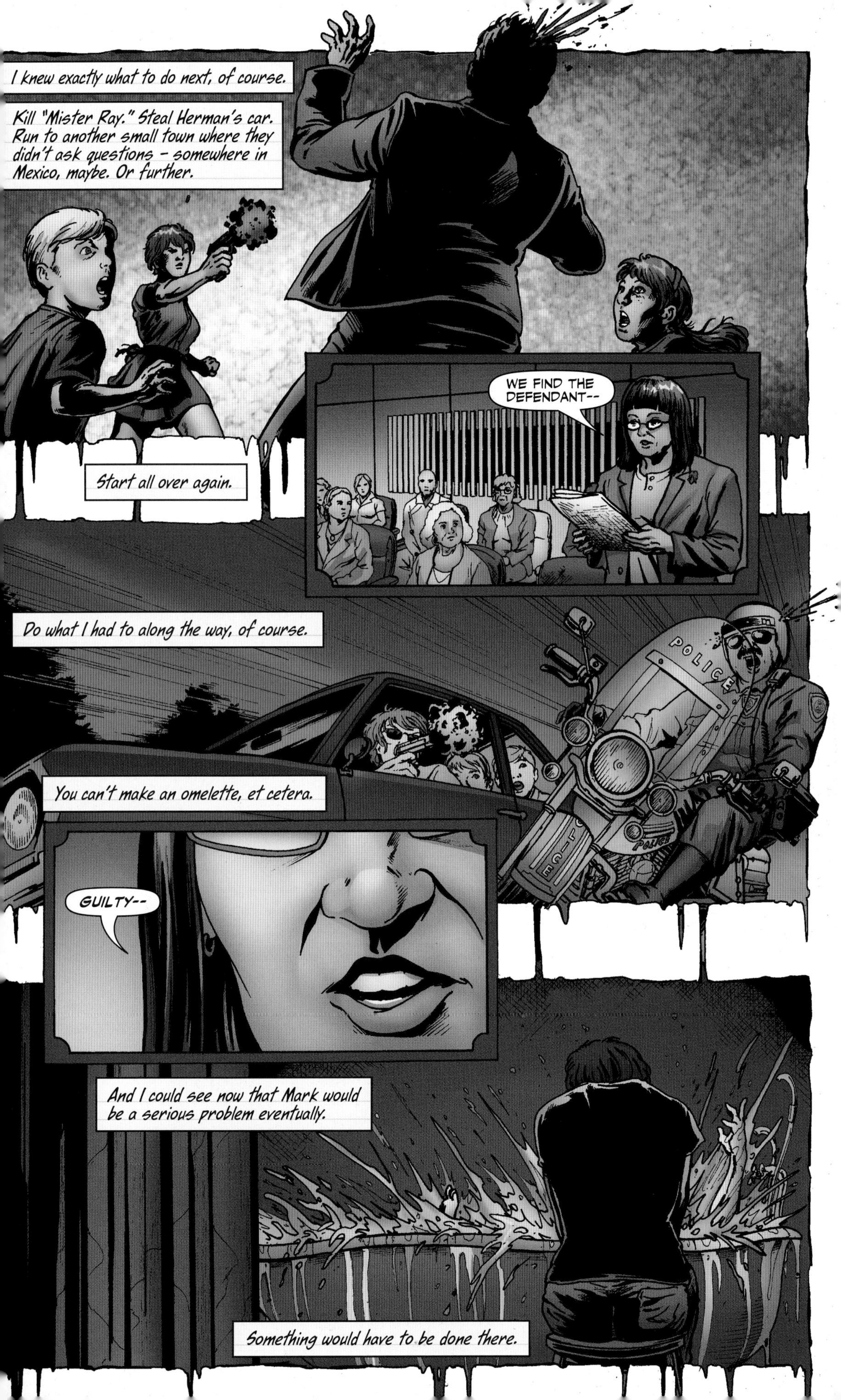
I knew exactly what to do next, of course.
Kill "Mister Ray." Steal Herman's car. Run to another small town where they didn't ask questions - somewhere in Mexico, maybe. Or further.
Start all over again.
WE FIND THE DEFENDANT--
Do what I had to along the way, of course.
POLICE
You can't make an omelette, et cetera.
GUILTY--
And I could see now that Mark would be a serious problem eventually.
Something would have to be done there.

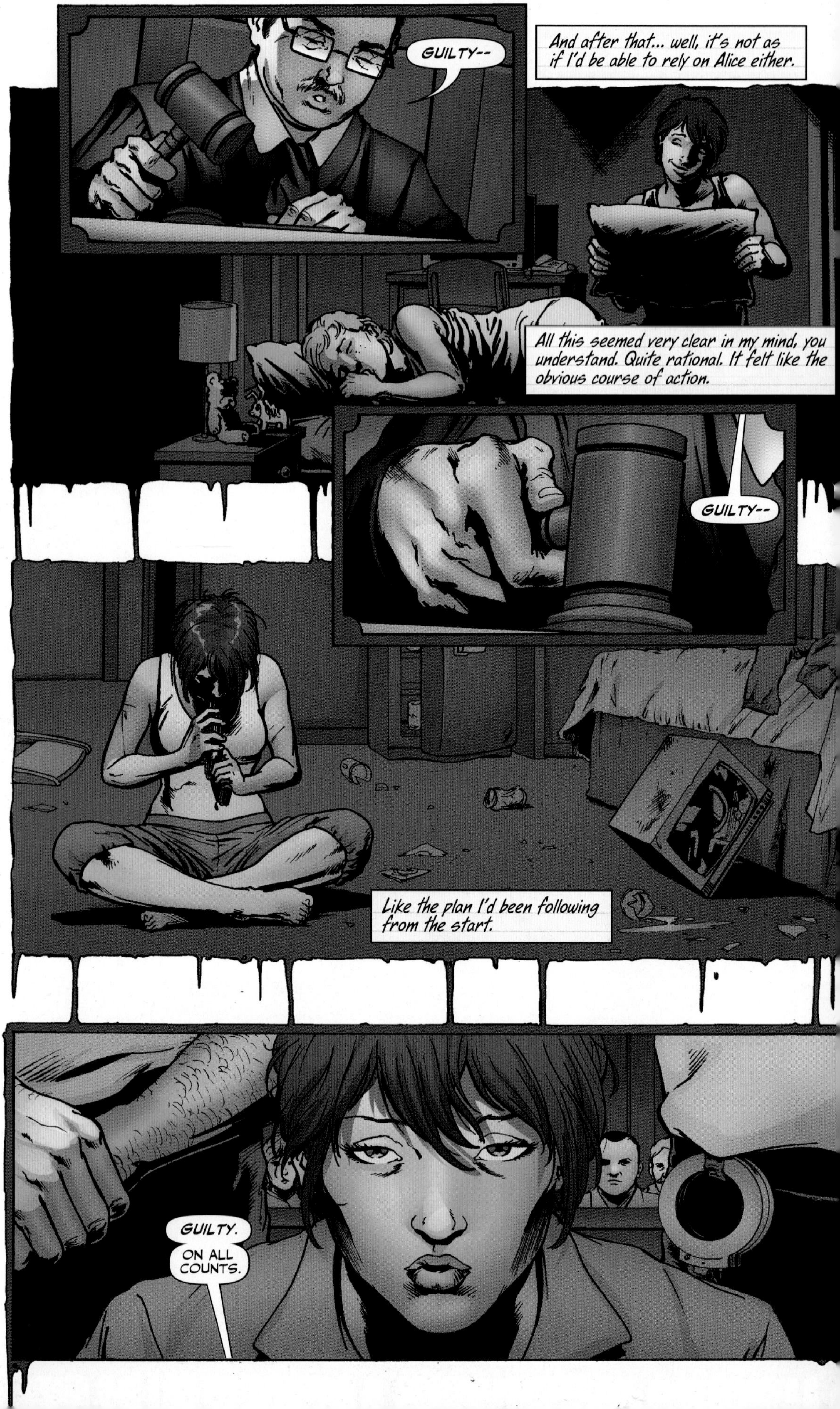
GUILTY--
And after that... well, it's not as if I'd be able to rely on Alice either.
All this seemed very clear in my mind, you understand. Quite rational. It felt like the obvious course of action.
GUILTY--
Like the plan I'd been following from the start.
GUILTY.
ON ALL COUNTS.

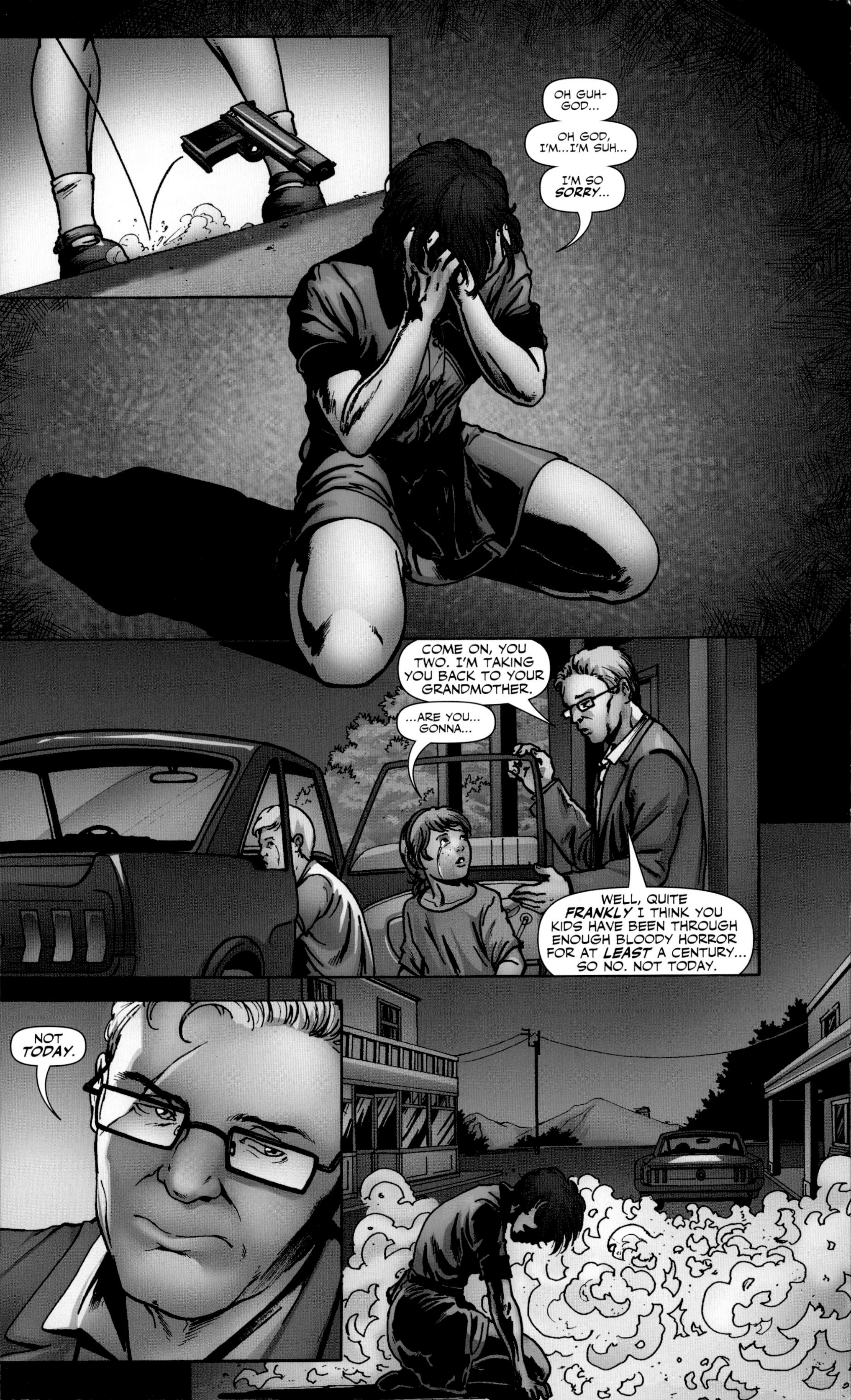
OH GUH-GOD...
OH GOD, I'M...I'M SUH...
I'M SO SORRY...
COME ON, YOU TWO. I'M TAKING YOU BACK TO YOUR GRANDMOTHER.
...ARE YOU... GONNA...
WELL, QUITE FRANKLY I THINK YOU KIDS HAVE BEEN THROUGH ENOUGH BLOODY HORROR FOR AT LEAST A CENTURY... SO NO. NOT TODAY.
NOT TODAY.

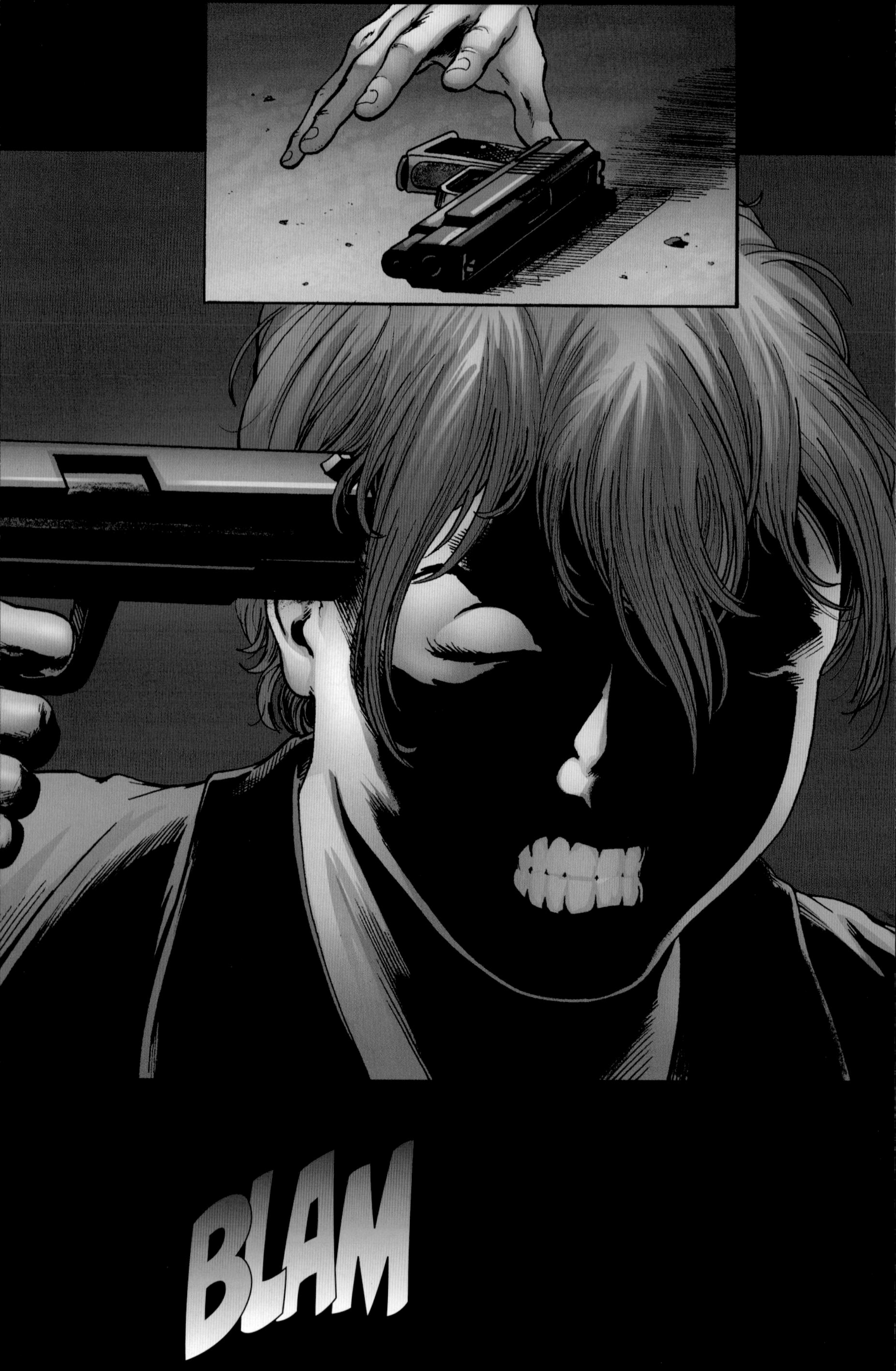
BLAM

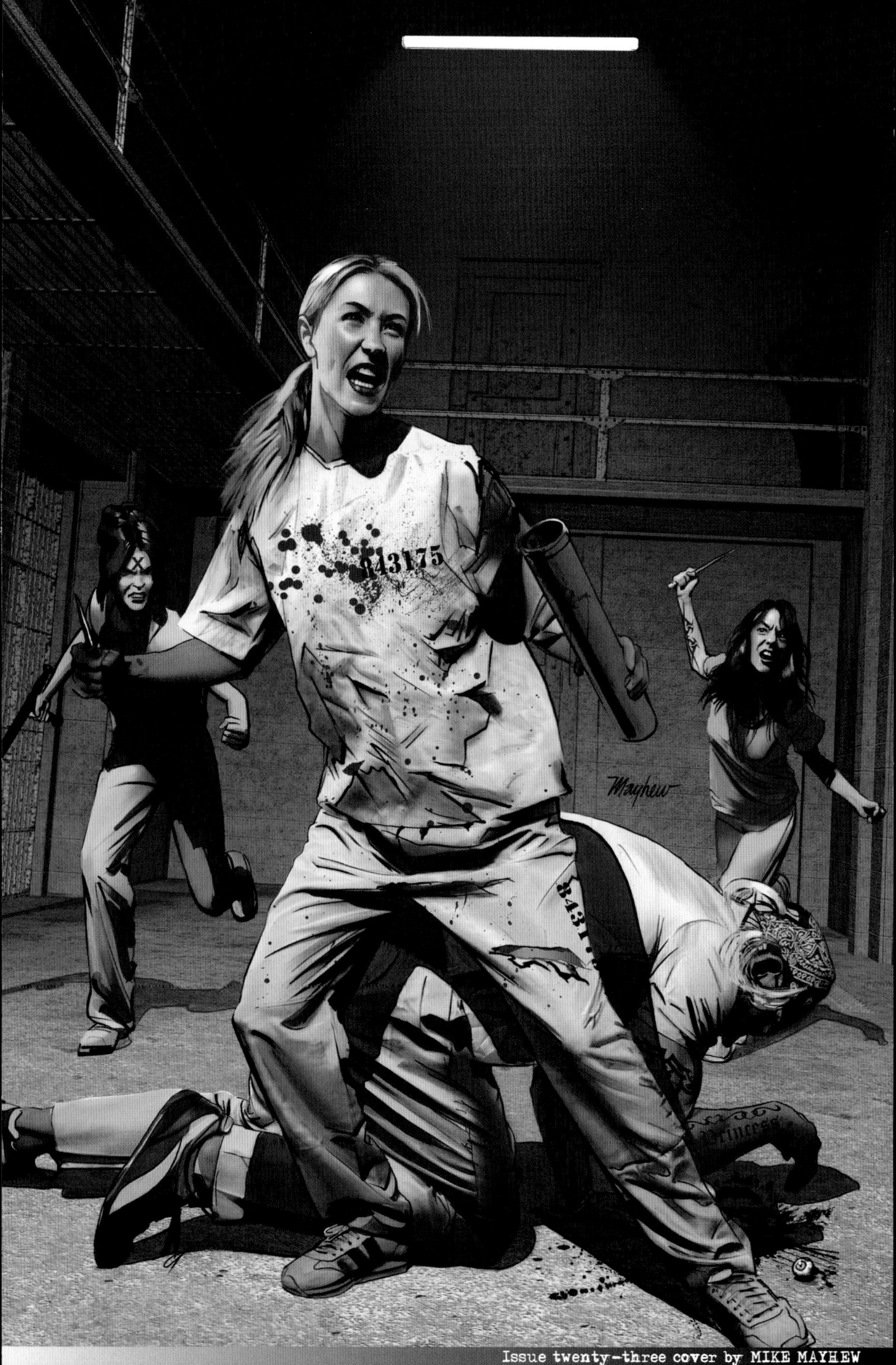
843175
Mayhew

Issue twenty-three cover by MIKE MAYHEW

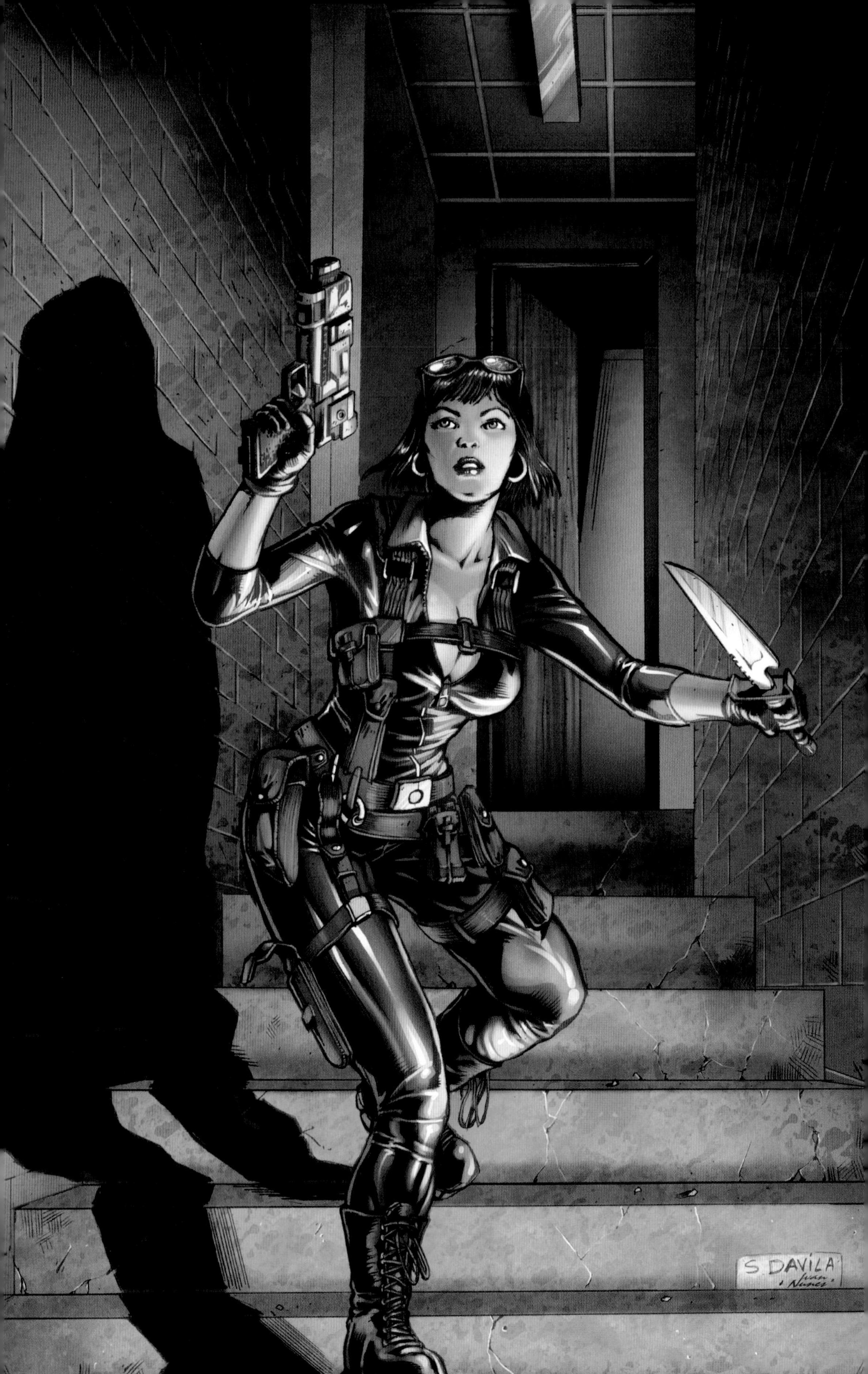
S. DAVILA

Issue twenty-three cover by SERGIO FERNANDEZ DAVILLA

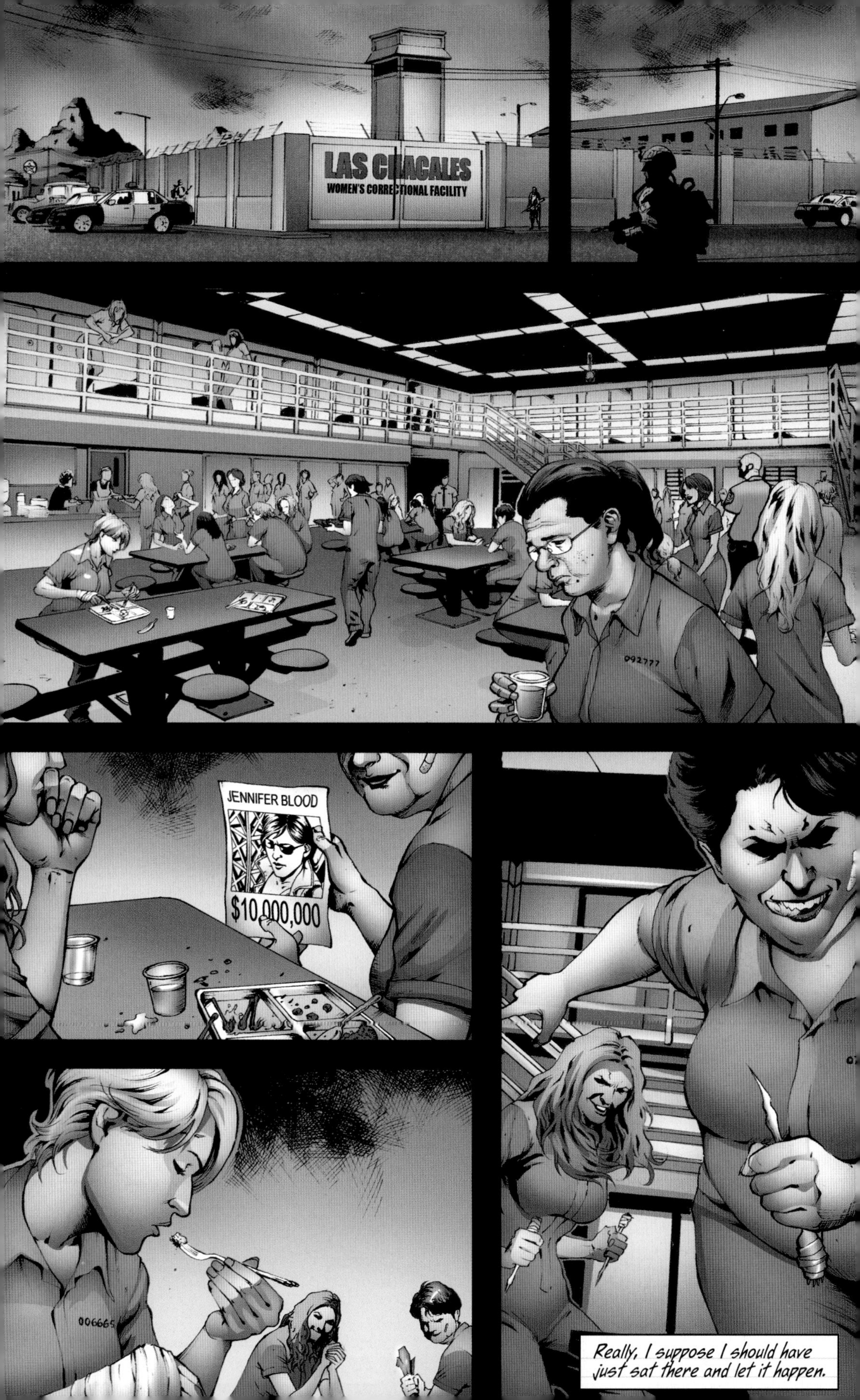
LAS CHACALES
WOMEN'S CORRECTIONAL FACILITY
092777
JENNIFER BLOOD
$10,000,000
006665
Really, I suppose I should have just sat there and let it happen.

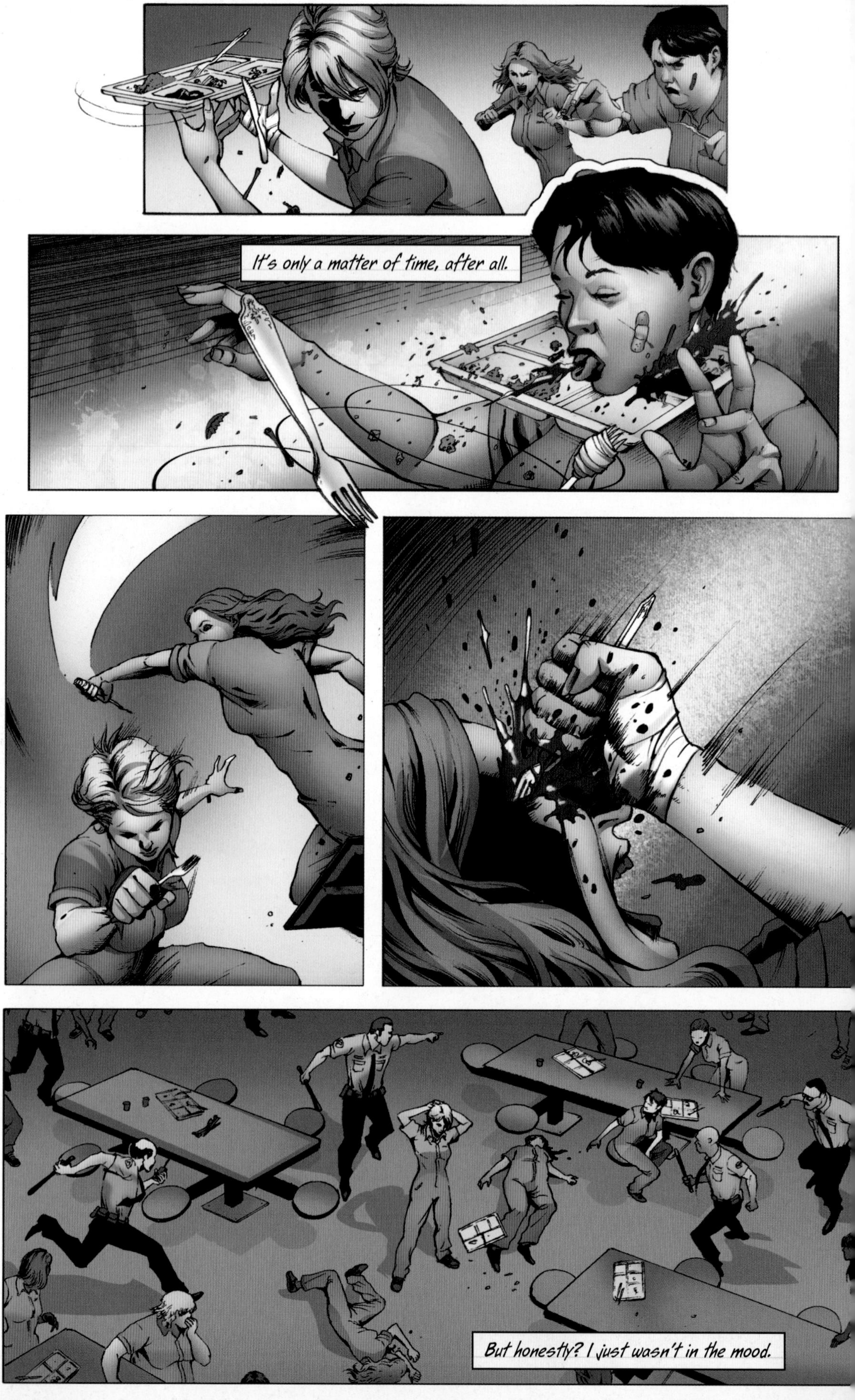
It's only a matter of time, after all.
But honestly? I just wasn't in the mood.

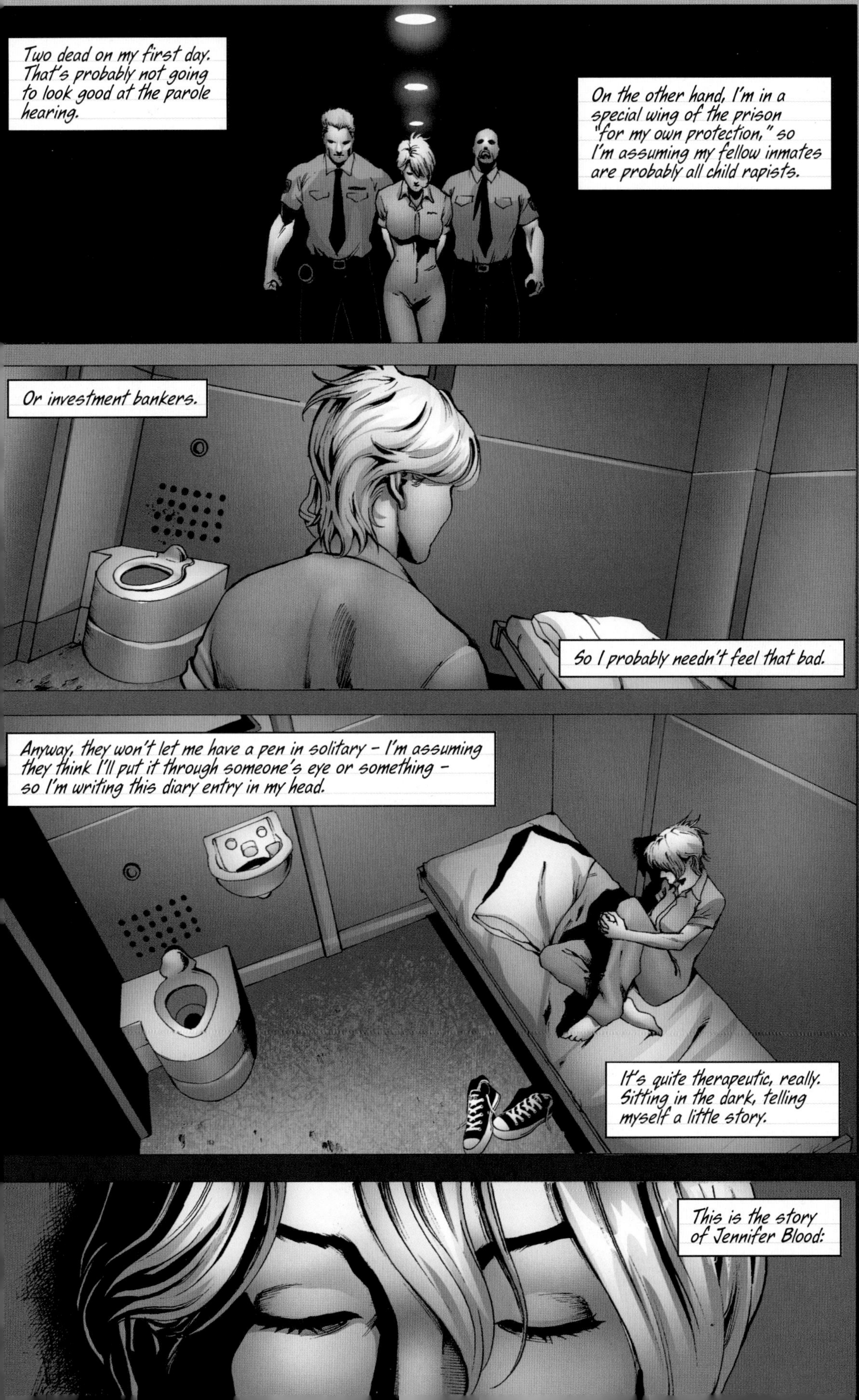

Two dead on my first day. That's probably not going to look good at the parole hearing.
On the other hand, I'm in a special wing of the prison "for my own protection," so I'm assuming my fellow inmates are probably all child rapists.
Or investment bankers.
So I probably needn't feel that bad.
Anyway, they won't let me have a pen in solitary - I'm assuming they think I'll put it through someone's eye or something - so I'm writing this diary entry in my head.
It's quite therapeutic, really. Sitting in the dark, telling myself a little story.
This is the story of Jennifer Blood:

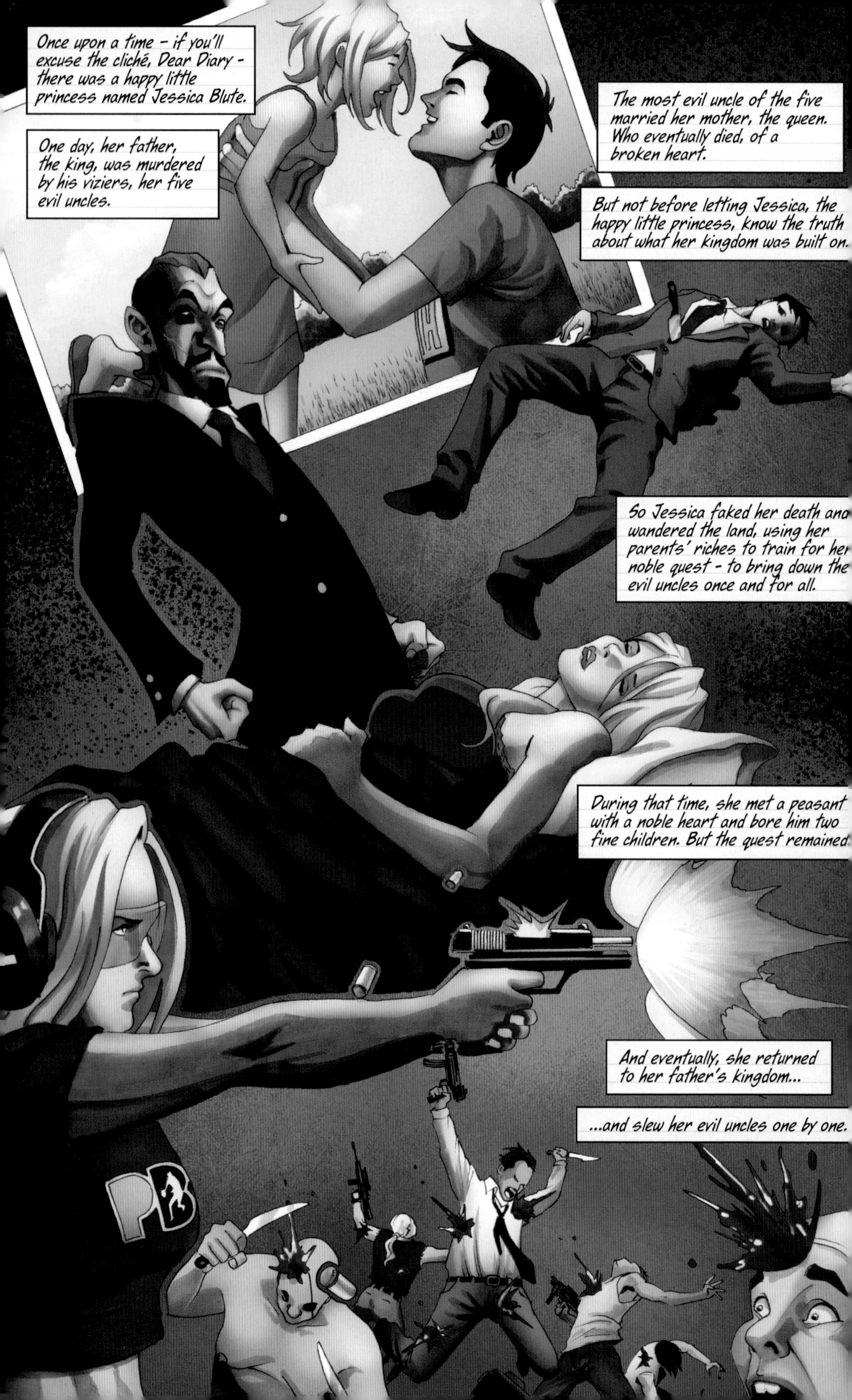
Once upon a time - if you'll excuse the cliché, Dear Diary - there was a happy little princess named Jessica Blute.
One day, her father, the king, was murdered by his viziers, her five evil uncles.
The most evil uncle of the five married her mother, the queen. Who eventually died, of a broken heart.
But not before letting Jessica, the happy little princess, know the truth about what her kingdom was built on.
So Jessica faked her death and wandered the land, using her parents' riches to train for her noble quest - to bring down the evil uncles once and for all.
During that time, she met a peasant with a noble heart and bore him two fine children. But the quest remained.
And eventually, she returned to her father's kingdom...
...and slew her evil uncles one by one.

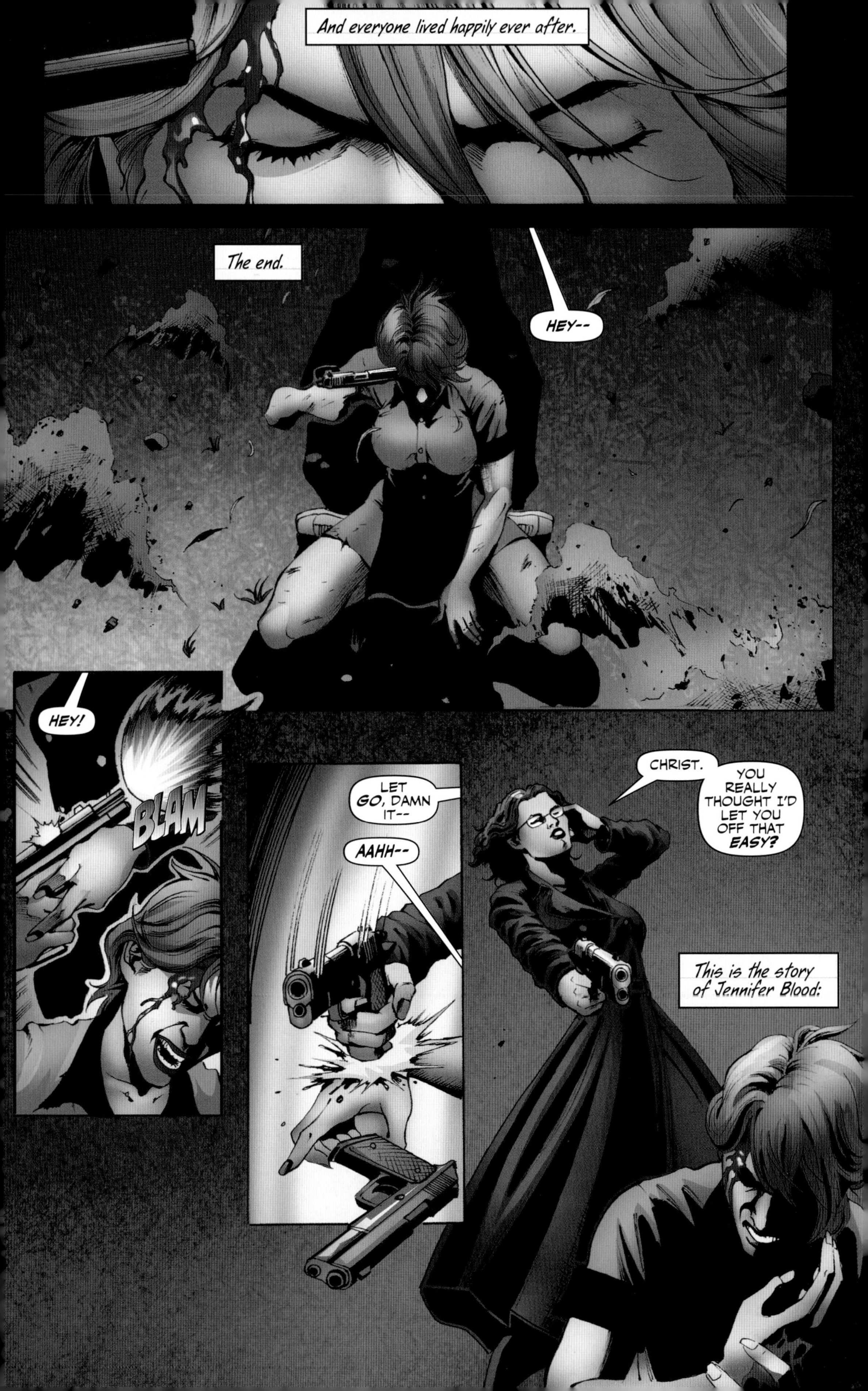
And everyone lived happily ever after.
The end.
HEY--
HEY!
BLAM
LET GO, DAMN IT--
AAHH--
CHRIST.
YOU REALLY THOUGHT I'D LET YOU OFF THAT EASY?
This is the story of Jennifer Blood:

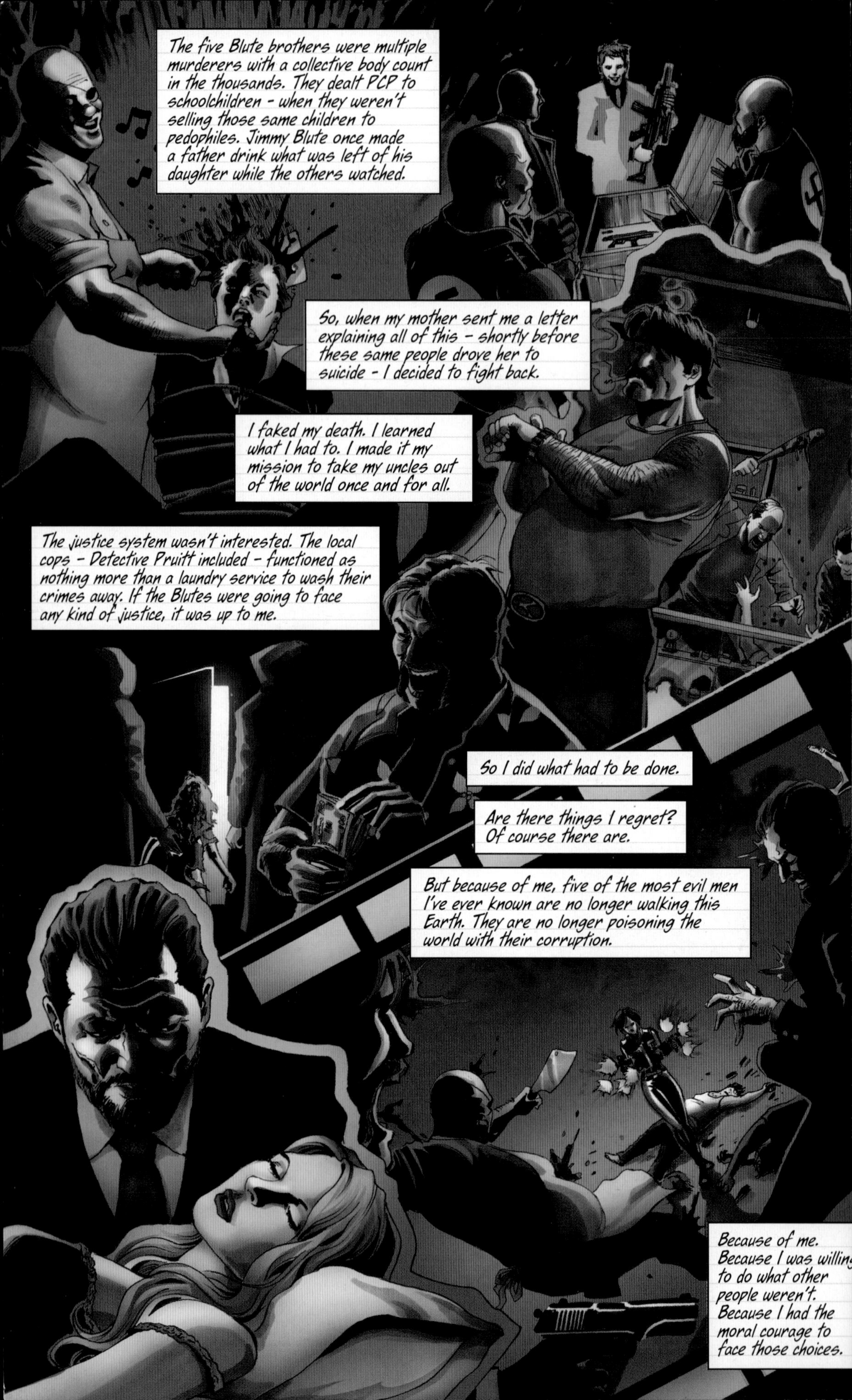
The five Blute brothers were multiple murderers with a collective body count in the thousands. They dealt PCP to schoolchildren - when they weren't selling those same children to pedophiles. Jimmy Blute once made a father drink what was left of his daughter while the others watched.
So, when my mother sent me a letter explaining all of this - shortly before these same people drove her to suicide - I decided to fight back.
I faked my death. I learned what I had to. I made it my mission to take my uncles out of the world once and for all.
The justice system wasn't interested. The local cops - Detective Pruitt included - functioned as nothing more than a laundry service to wash their crimes away. If the Blutes were going to face any kind of justice, it was up to me.
So I did what had to be done.
Are there things I regret? Of course there are.
But because of me, five of the most evil men I've ever known are no longer walking this Earth. They are no longer poisoning the world with their corruption.
Because of me. Because I was willing to do what other people weren't. Because I had the moral courage to face those choices.

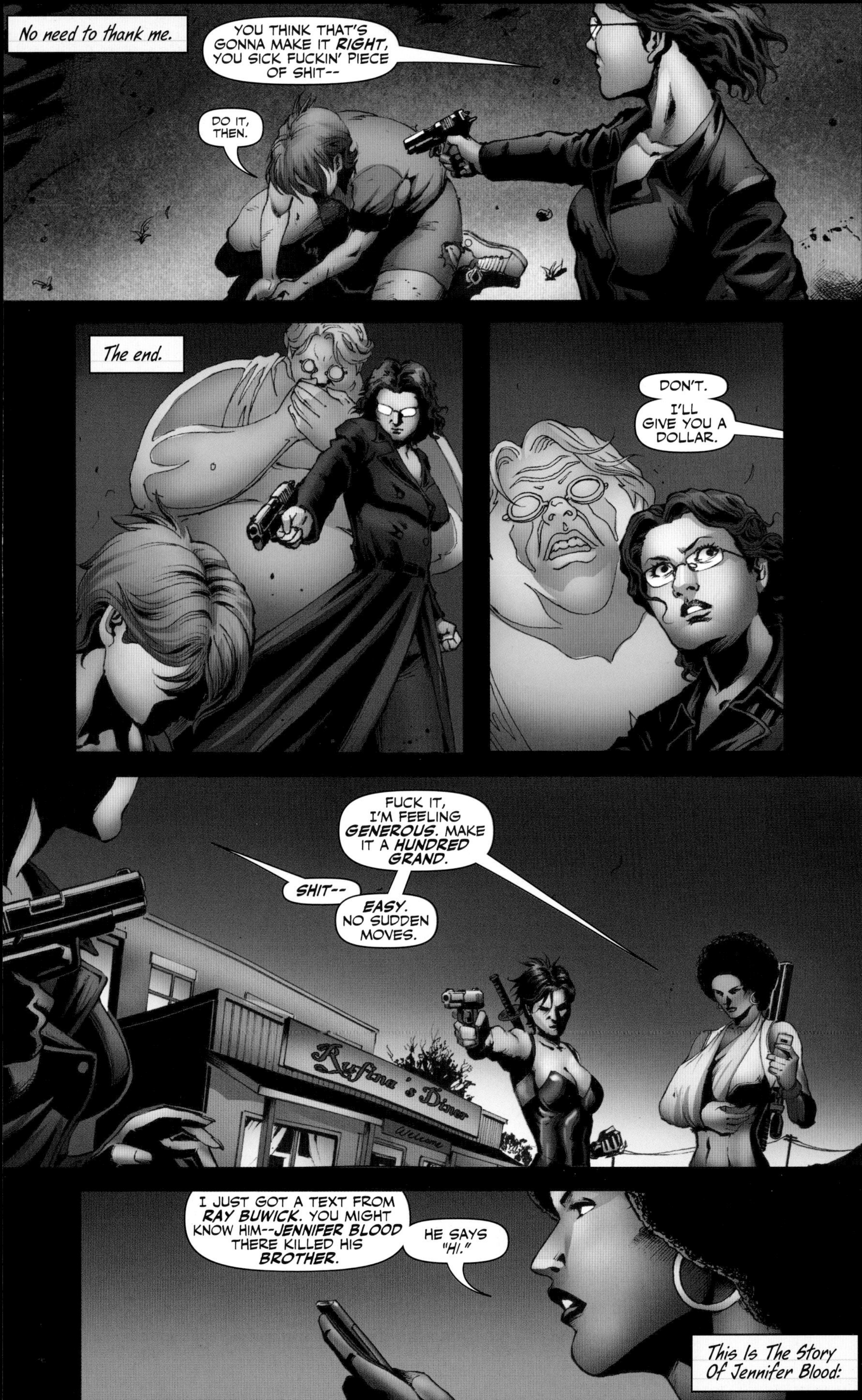
No need to thank me.
YOU THINK THAT'S GONNA MAKE IT RIGHT, YOU SICK FUCKIN' PIECE OF SHIT--
DO IT, THEN.
The end.
DON'T.
I'LL GIVE YOU A DOLLAR.
FUCK IT, I'M FEELING GENEROUS. MAKE IT A HUNDRED GRAND.
SHIT--
EASY. NO SUDDEN MOVES.
Rufina's Diner
I JUST GOT A TEXT FROM RAY BUWICK. YOU MIGHT KNOW HIM--JENNIFER BLOOD THERE KILLED HIS BROTHER.
HE SAYS "HI."
This Is The Story Of Jennifer Blood:

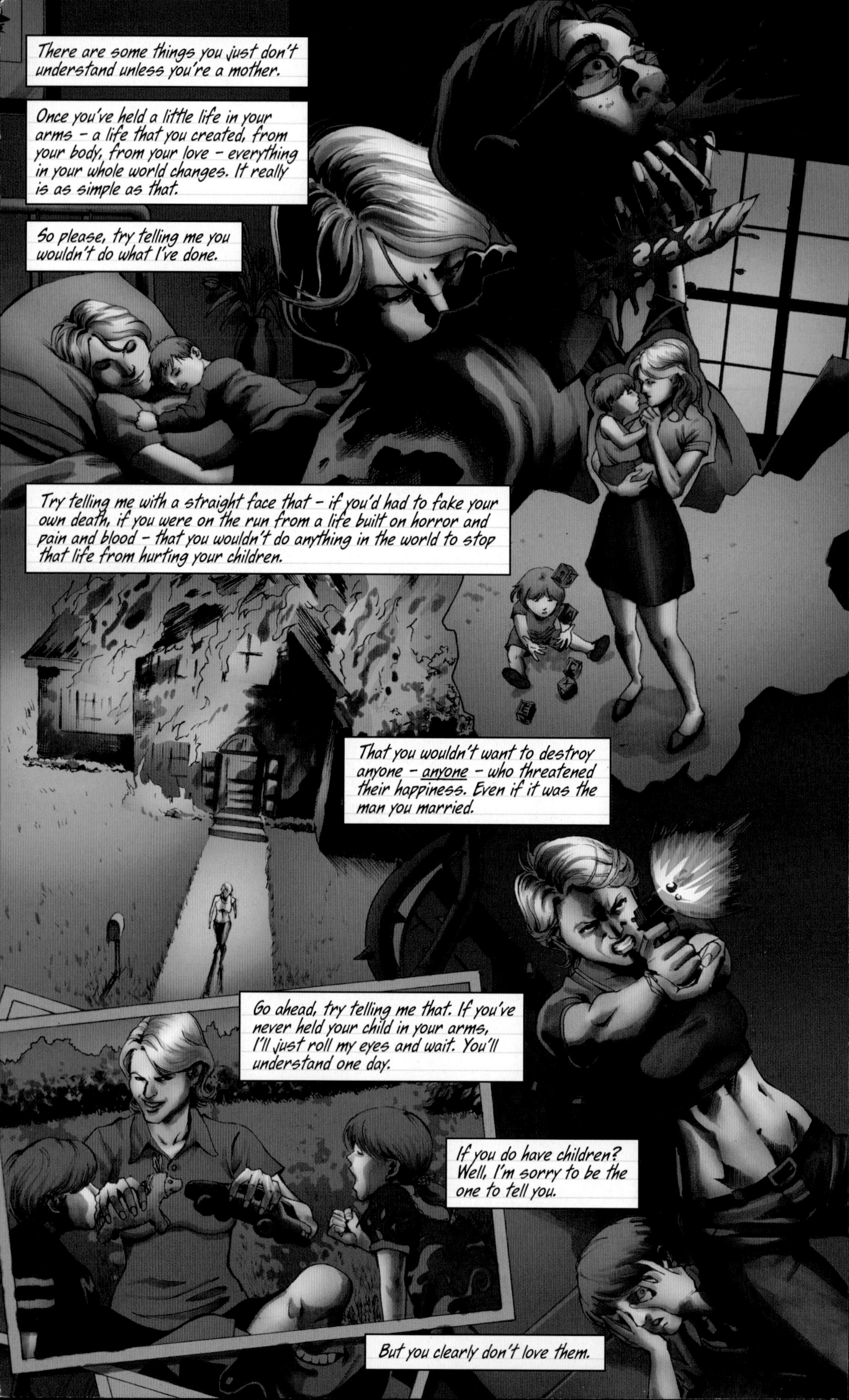
There are some things you just don't understand unless you're a mother.
Once you've held a little life in your arms – a life that you created, from your body, from your love – everything in your whole world changes. It really is as simple as that.
So please, try telling me you wouldn't do what I've done.
Try telling me with a straight face that – if you'd had to fake your own death, if you were on the run from a life built on horror and pain and blood – that you wouldn't do anything in the world to stop that life from hurting your children.
That you wouldn't want to destroy anyone – anyone – who threatened their happiness. Even if it was the man you married.
Go ahead, try telling me that. If you've never held your child in your arms, I'll just roll my eyes and wait. You'll understand one day.
If you do have children? Well, I'm sorry to be the one to tell you.
But you clearly don't love them.

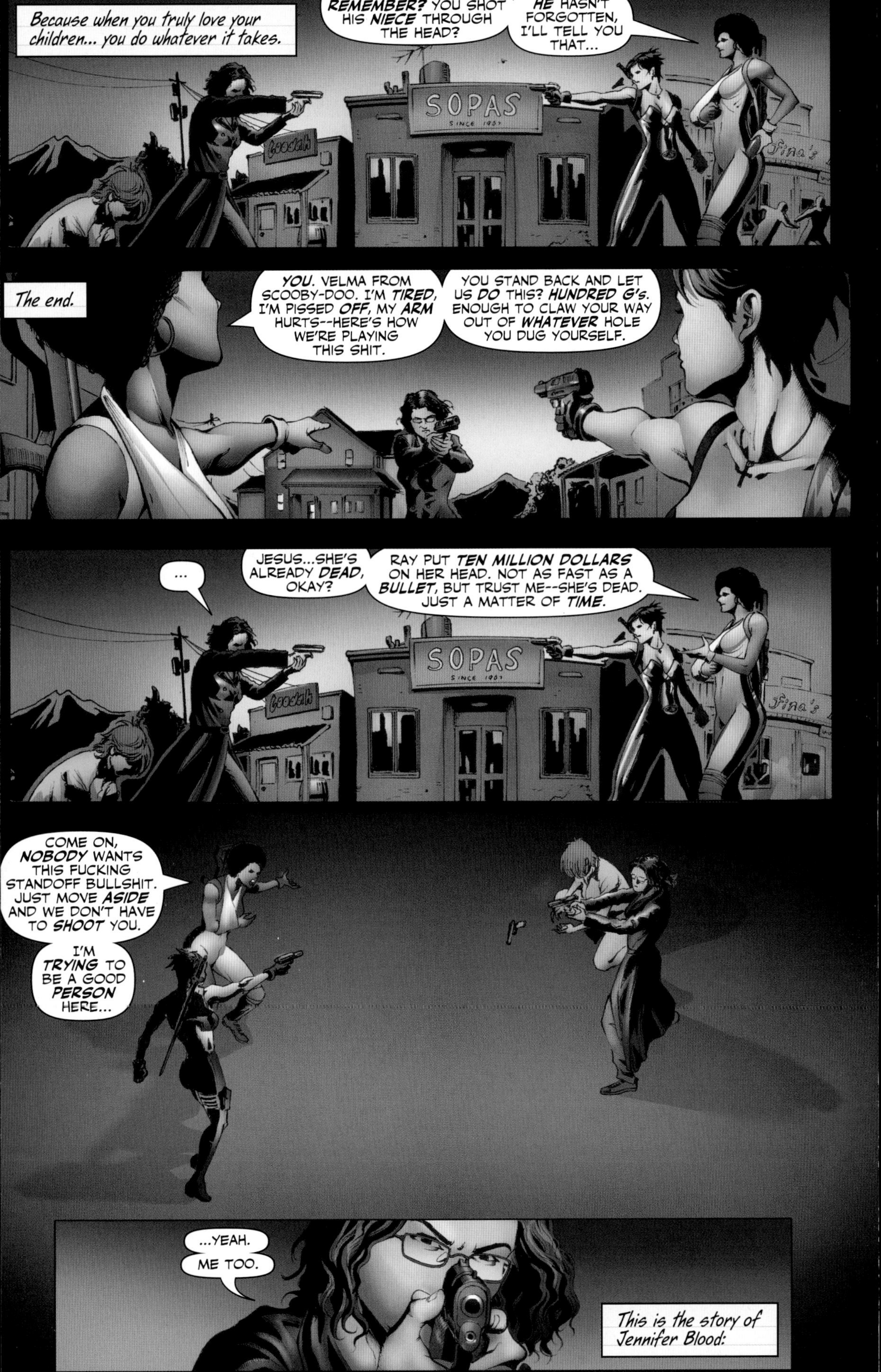

Because when you truly love your children... you do whatever it takes.
REMEMBER? YOU SHOT HIS NIECE THROUGH THE HEAD?
HE HASN'T FORGOTTEN, I'LL TELL YOU THAT...
SOPAS
SINCE 1907
Goodah
Fina's
The end.
YOU. VELMA FROM SCOOBY-DOO. I'M TIRED, I'M PISSED OFF, MY ARM HURTS--HERE'S HOW WE'RE PLAYING THIS SHIT.
YOU STAND BACK AND LET US DO THIS? HUNDRED G's. ENOUGH TO CLAW YOUR WAY OUT OF WHATEVER HOLE YOU DUG YOURSELF.
...
JESUS...SHE'S ALREADY DEAD, OKAY?
RAY PUT TEN MILLION DOLLARS ON HER HEAD. NOT AS FAST AS A BULLET, BUT TRUST ME--SHE'S DEAD. JUST A MATTER OF TIME.
SOPAS
SINCE 1907
Goodah
Fina's
COME ON, NOBODY WANTS THIS FUCKING STANDOFF BULLSHIT. JUST MOVE ASIDE AND WE DON'T HAVE TO SHOOT YOU.
I'M TRYING TO BE A GOOD PERSON HERE...
...YEAH.
ME TOO.
This is the story of Jennifer Blood:

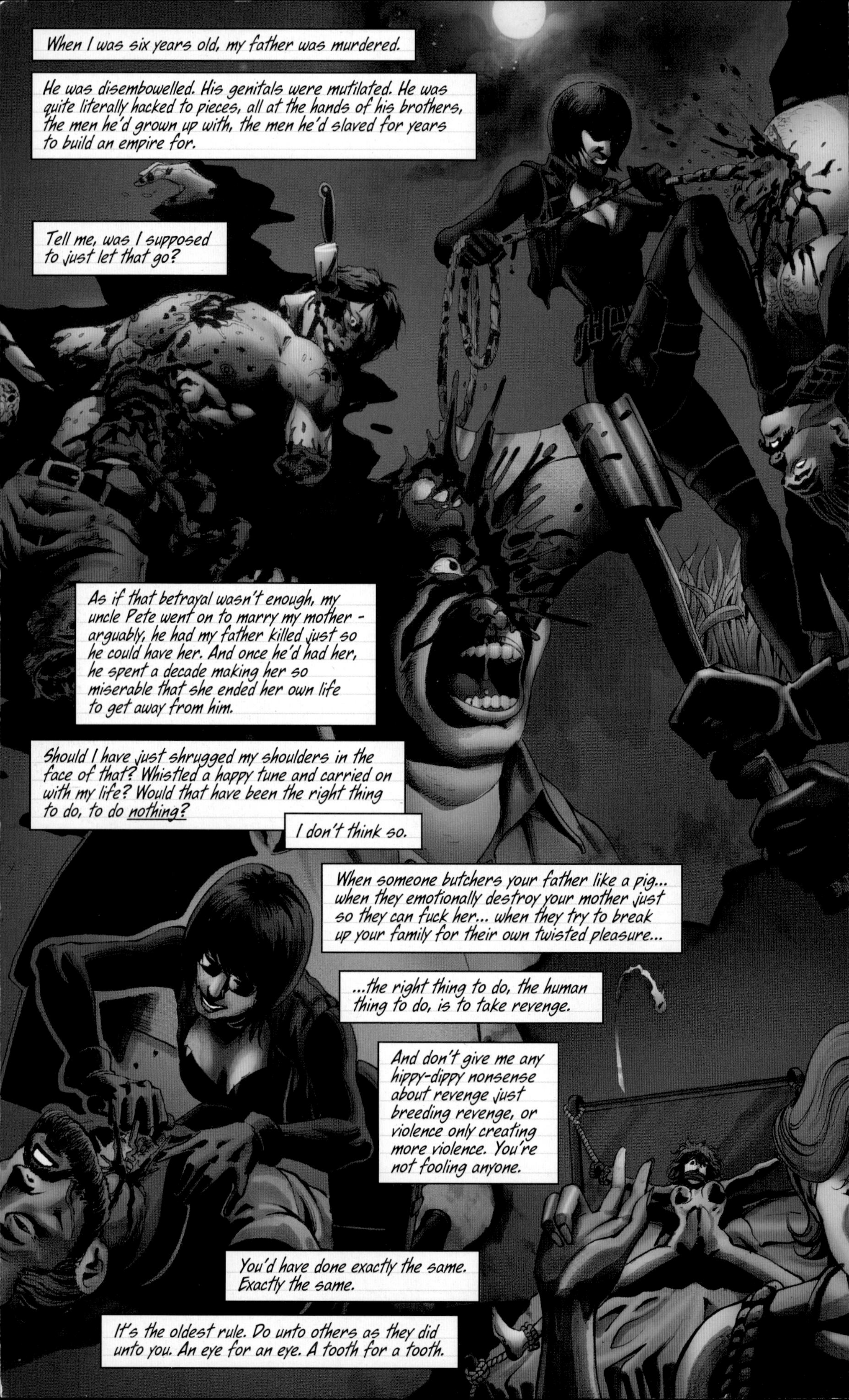
When I was six years old, my father was murdered.
He was disembowelled. His genitals were mutilated. He was quite literally hacked to pieces, all at the hands of his brothers, the men he'd grown up with, the men he'd slaved for years to build an empire for.
Tell me, was I supposed to just let that go?
As if that betrayal wasn't enough, my uncle Pete went on to marry my mother - arguably, he had my father killed just so he could have her. And once he'd had her, he spent a decade making her so miserable that she ended her own life to get away from him.
Should I have just shrugged my shoulders in the face of that? Whistled a happy tune and carried on with my life? Would that have been the right thing to do, to do nothing?
I don't think so.
When someone butchers your father like a pig... when they emotionally destroy your mother just so they can fuck her... when they try to break up your family for their own twisted pleasure...
...the right thing to do, the human thing to do, is to take revenge.
And don't give me any hippy-dippy nonsense about revenge just breeding revenge, or violence only creating more violence. You're not fooling anyone.
You'd have done exactly the same. Exactly the same.
It's the oldest rule. Do unto others as they did unto you. An eye for an eye. A tooth for a tooth.

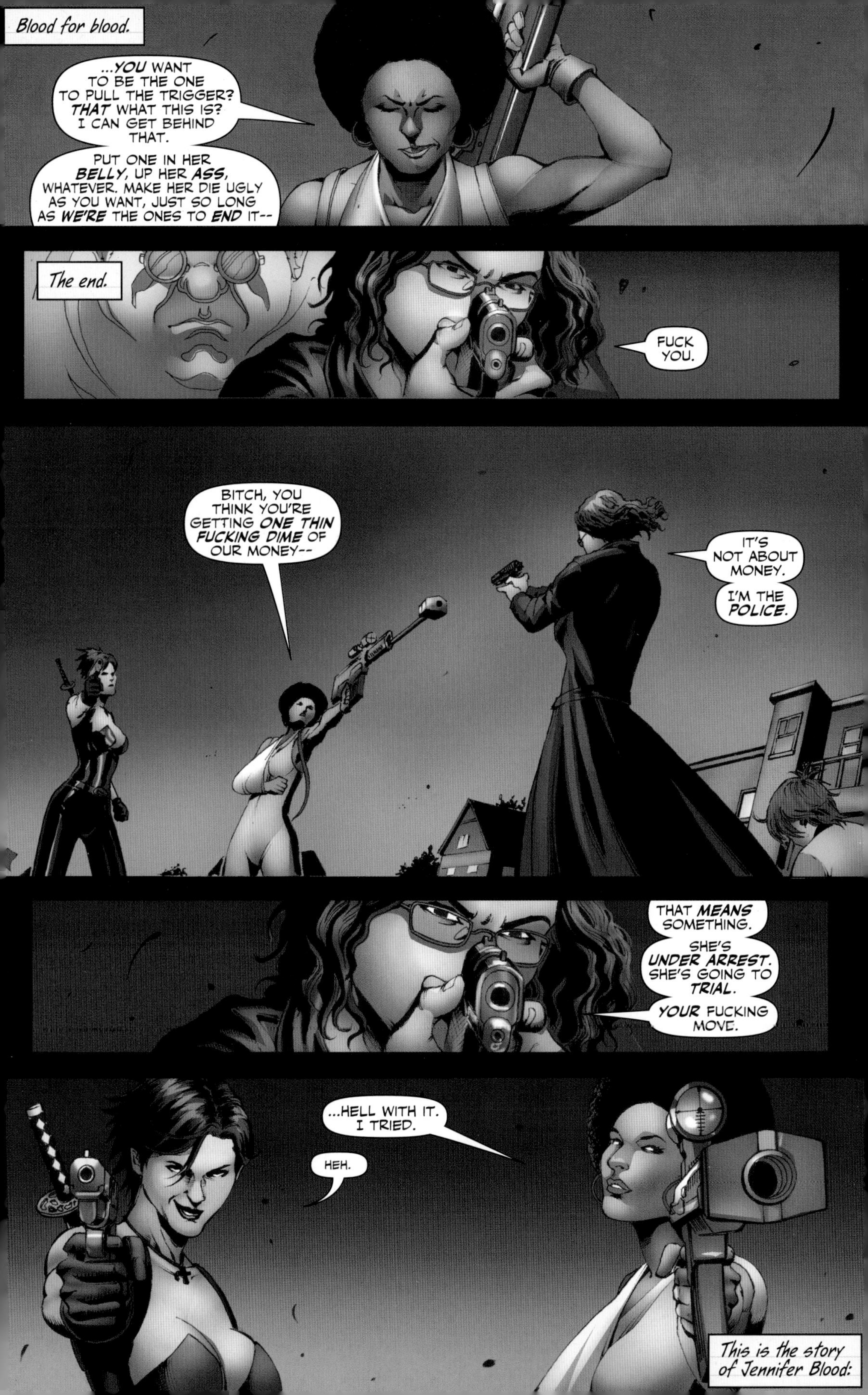
Blood for blood.
...YOU WANT TO BE THE ONE TO PULL THE TRIGGER? THAT WHAT THIS IS? I CAN GET BEHIND THAT.
PUT ONE IN HER BELLY, UP HER ASS, WHATEVER. MAKE HER DIE UGLY AS YOU WANT, JUST SO LONG AS WE'RE THE ONES TO END IT--
The end.
FUCK YOU.
BITCH, YOU THINK YOU'RE GETTING ONE THIN FUCKING DIME OF OUR MONEY--
IT'S NOT ABOUT MONEY.
I'M THE POLICE.
THAT MEANS SOMETHING.
SHE'S UNDER ARREST. SHE'S GOING TO TRIAL.
YOUR FUCKING MOVE.
...HELL WITH IT. I TRIED.
HEH.
This is the story of Jennifer Blood:

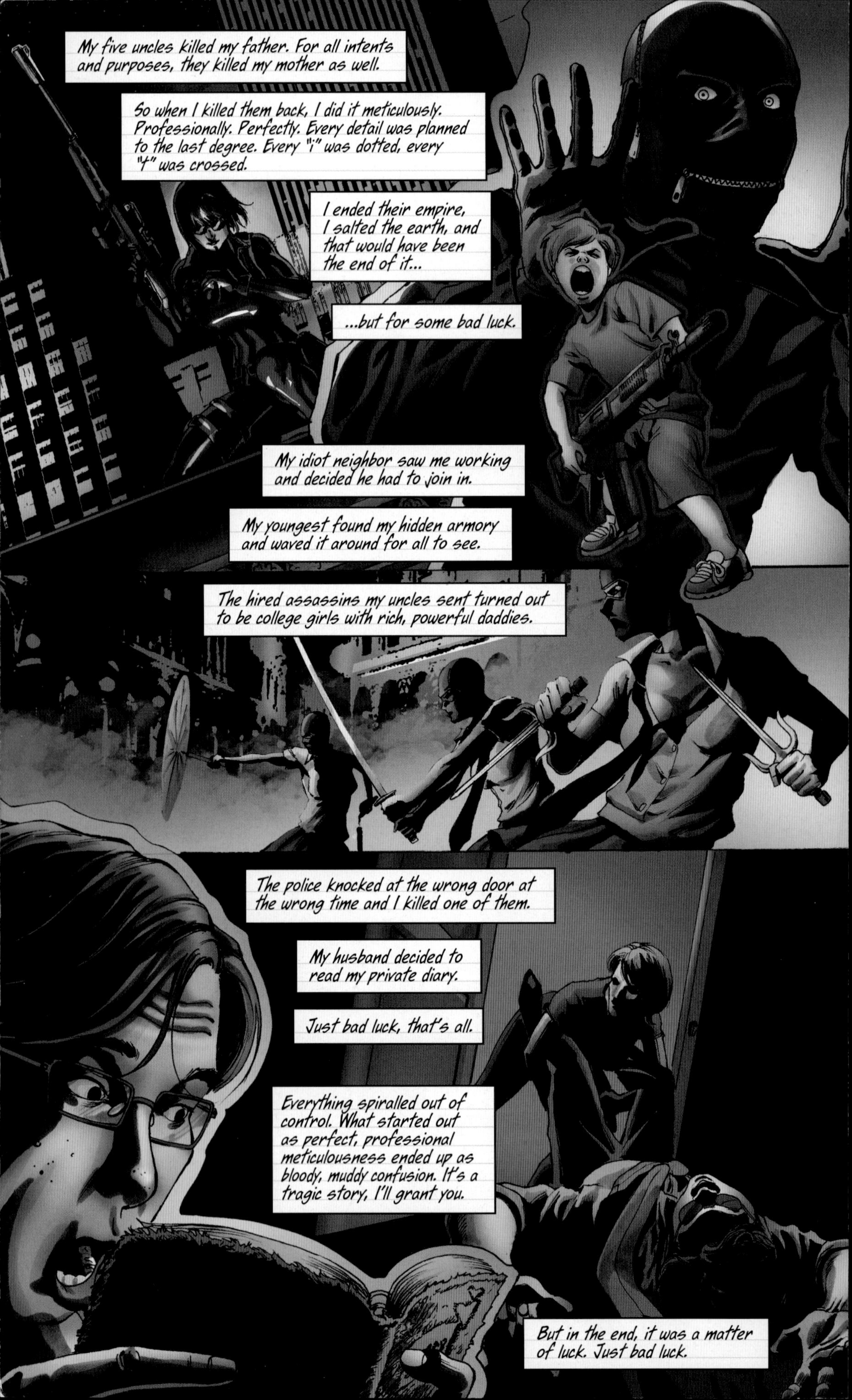

My five uncles killed my father. For all intents and purposes, they killed my mother as well.
So when I killed them back, I did it meticulously. Professionally. Perfectly. Every detail was planned to the last degree. Every "i" was dotted, every "t" was crossed.
I ended their empire, I salted the earth, and that would have been the end of it...
...but for some bad luck.
My idiot neighbor saw me working and decided he had to join in.
My youngest found my hidden armory and waved it around for all to see.
The hired assassins my uncles sent turned out to be college girls with rich, powerful daddies.
The police knocked at the wrong door at the wrong time and I killed one of them.
My husband decided to read my private diary.
Just bad luck, that's all.
Everything spiralled out of control. What started out as perfect, professional meticulousness ended up as bloody, muddy confusion. It's a tragic story, I'll grant you.
But in the end, it was a matter of luck. Just bad luck.

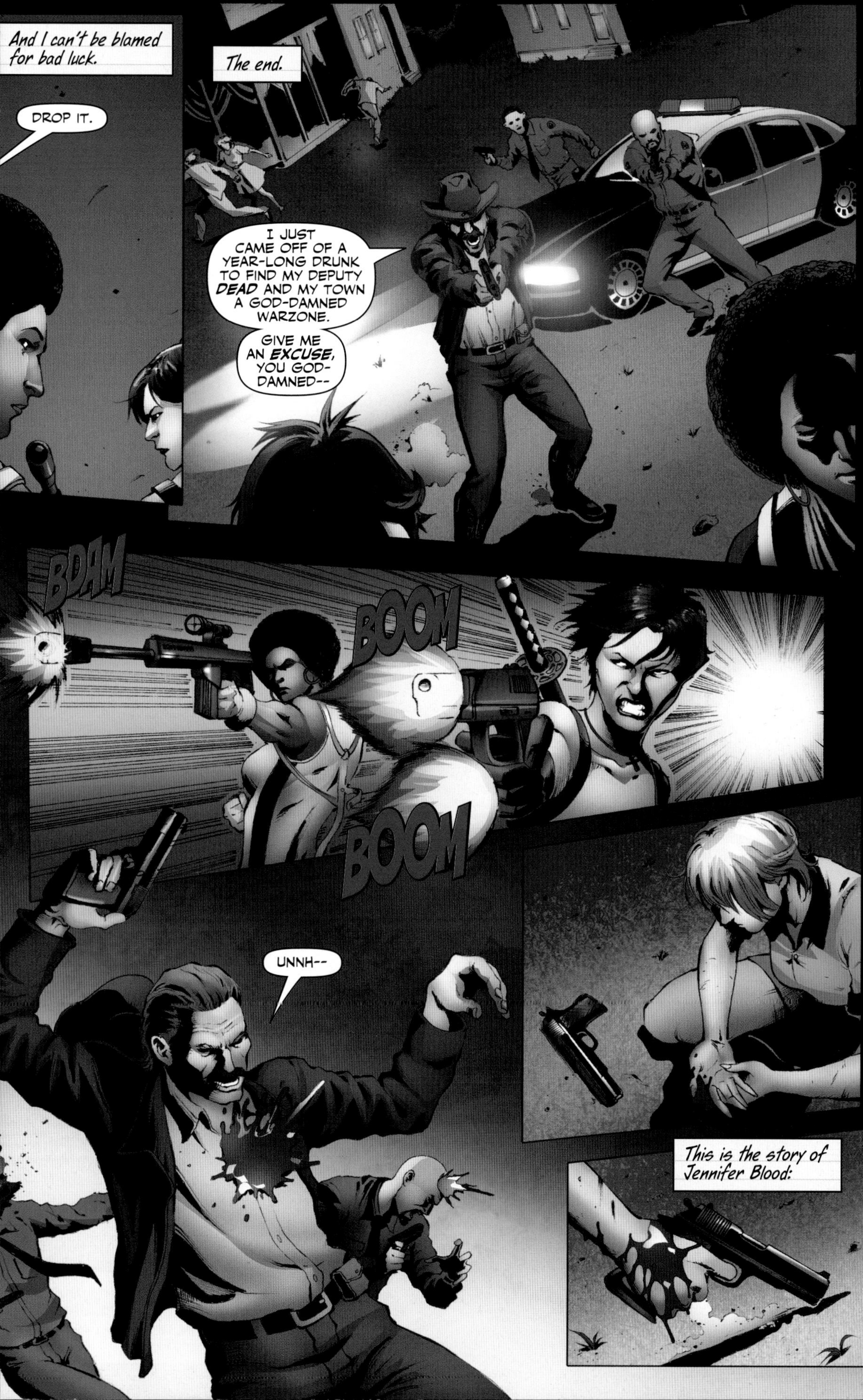
And I can't be blamed for bad luck.
DROP IT.
The end.
I JUST CAME OFF OF A YEAR-LONG DRUNK TO FIND MY DEPUTY DEAD AND MY TOWN A GOD-DAMNED WARZONE.
GIVE ME AN EXCUSE, YOU GOD-DAMNED--
BDAM
BOOM
BOOM
UNNH--
This is the story of Jennifer Blood:

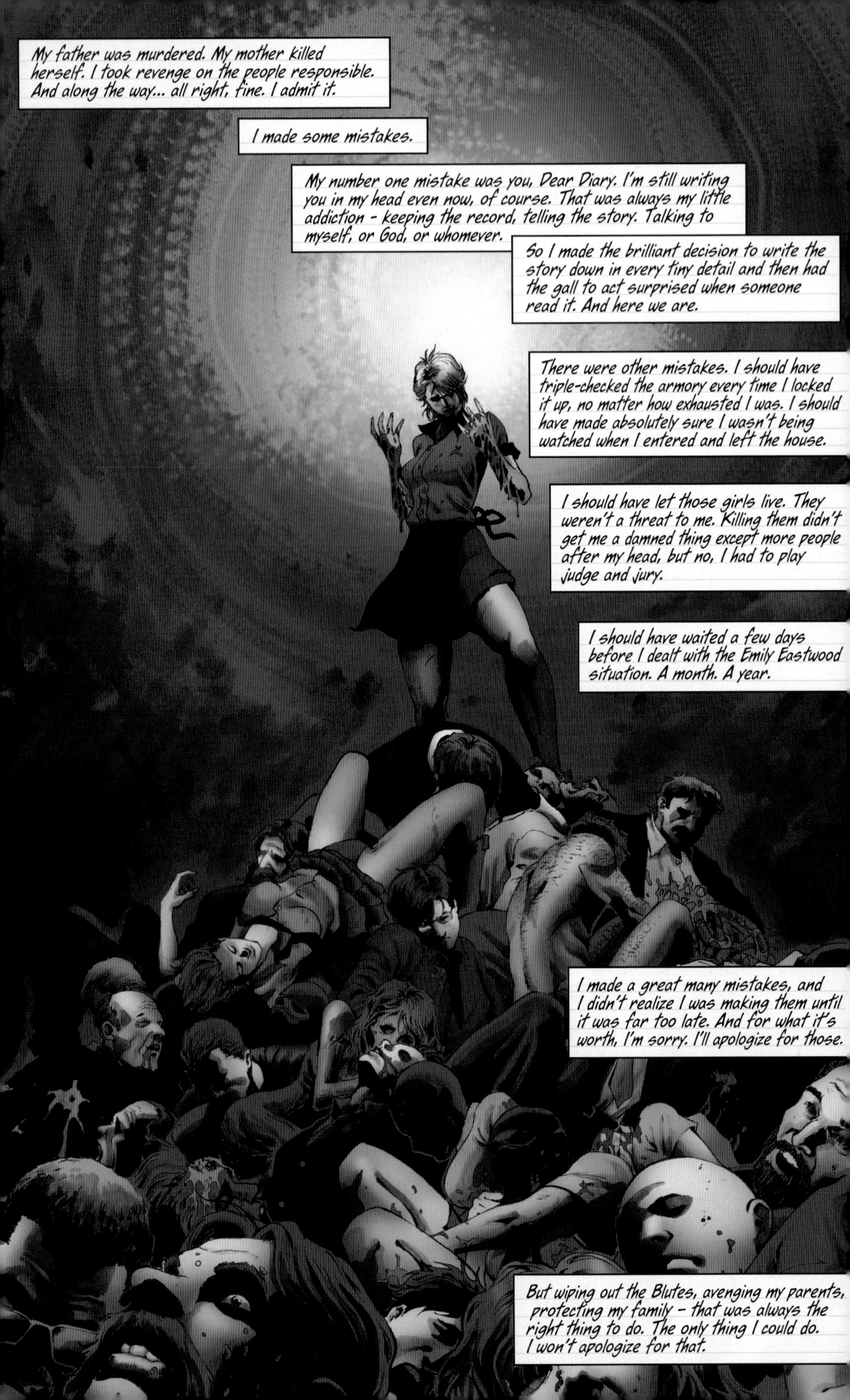
My father was murdered. My mother killed herself. I took revenge on the people responsible. And along the way... all right, fine. I admit it.
I made some mistakes.
My number one mistake was you, Dear Diary. I'm still writing you in my head even now, of course. That was always my little addiction - keeping the record, telling the story. Talking to myself, or God, or whomever.
So I made the brilliant decision to write the story down in every tiny detail and then had the gall to act surprised when someone read it. And here we are.
There were other mistakes. I should have triple-checked the armory every time I locked it up, no matter how exhausted I was. I should have made absolutely sure I wasn't being watched when I entered and left the house.
I should have let those girls live. They weren't a threat to me. Killing them didn't get me a damned thing except more people after my head, but no, I had to play judge and jury.
I should have waited a few days before I dealt with the Emily Eastwood situation. A month. A year.
I made a great many mistakes, and I didn't realize I was making them until it was far too late. And for what it's worth, I'm sorry. I'll apologize for those.
But wiping out the Blutes, avenging my parents, protecting my family – that was always the right thing to do. The only thing I could do. I won't apologize for that.

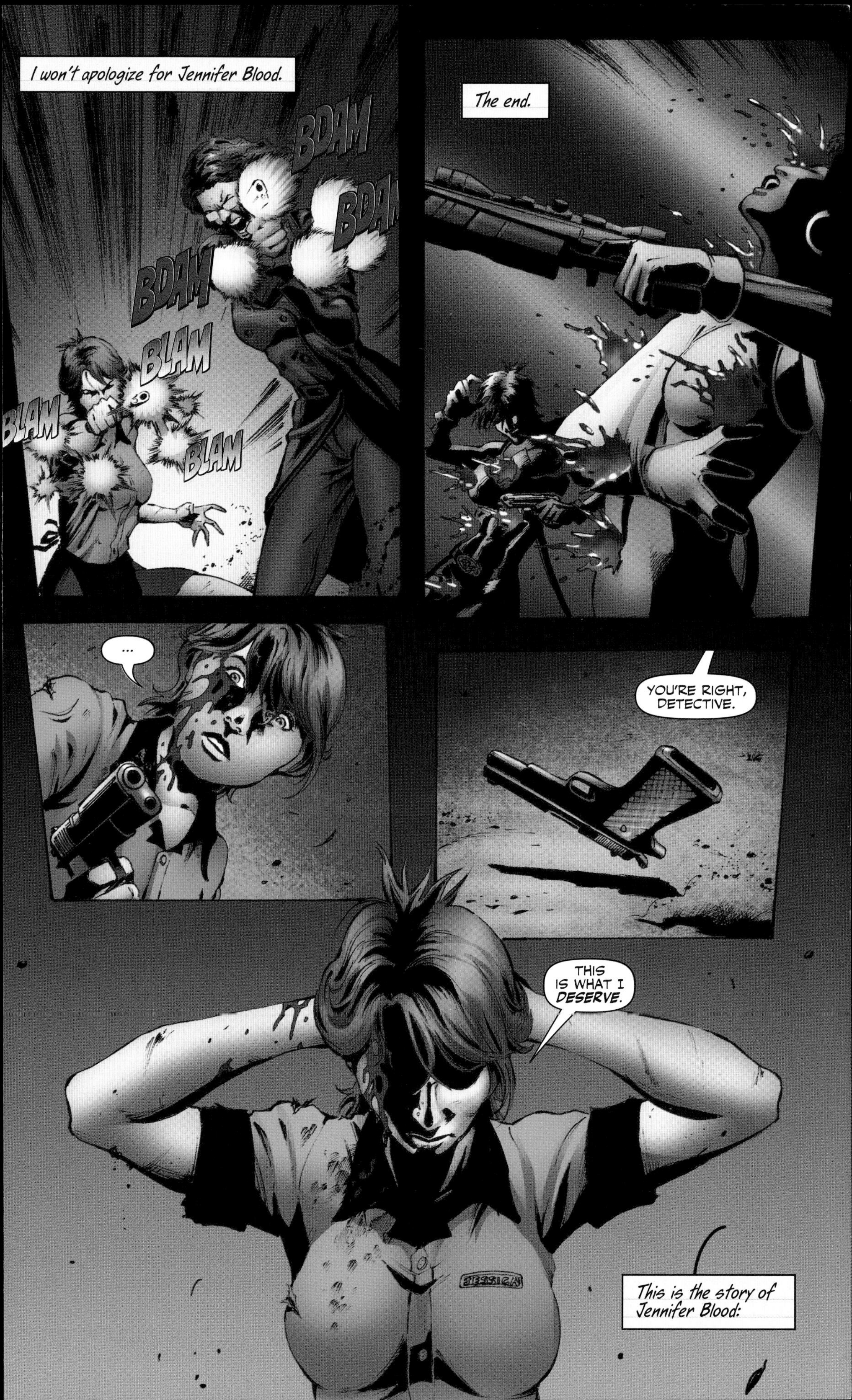
I won't apologize for Jennifer Blood.
BDAM
BDAM
BDAM
BLAM
BLAM
BLAM
The end.
...
YOU'RE RIGHT, DETECTIVE.
THIS IS WHAT I DESERVE.
This is the story of Jennifer Blood:

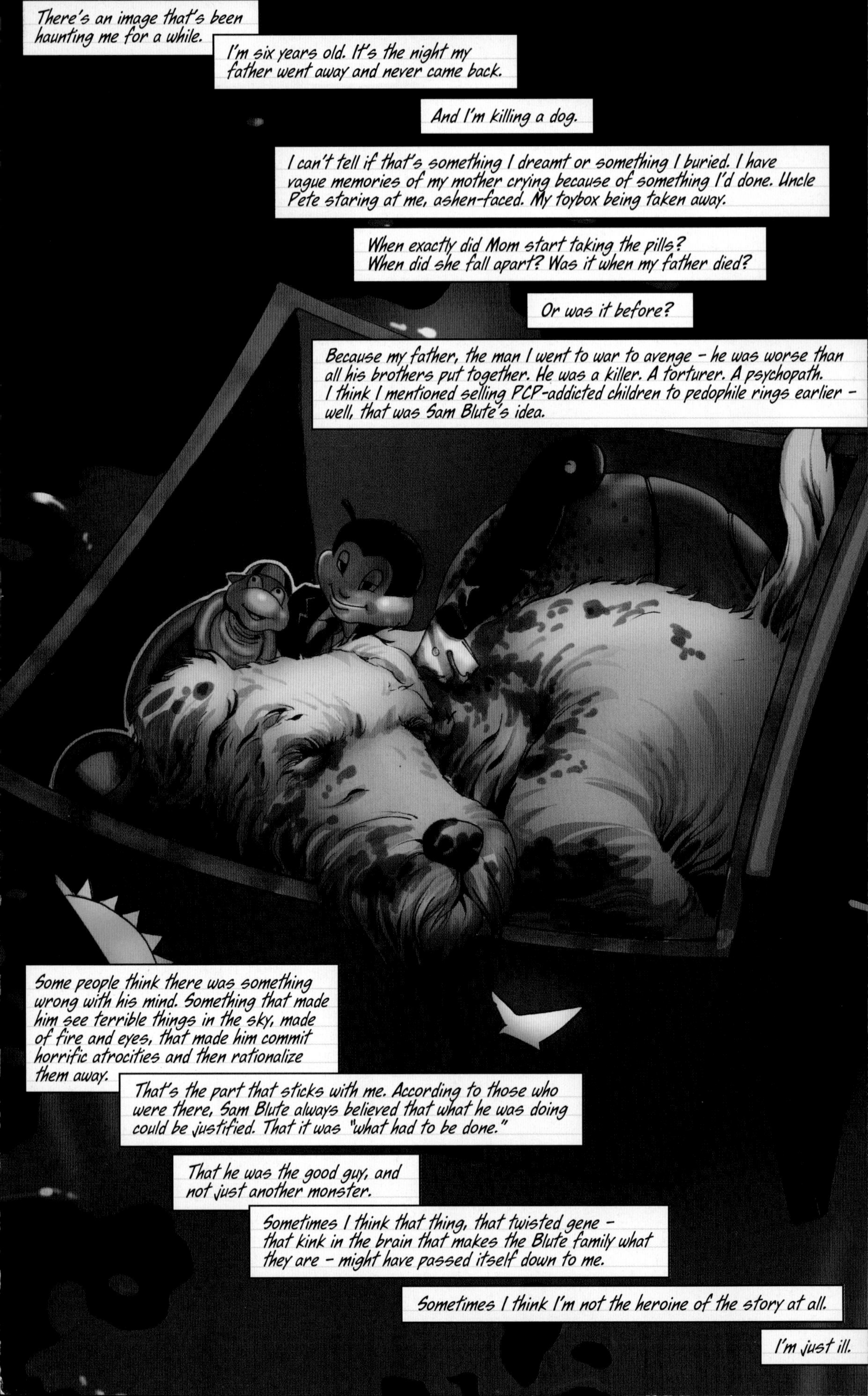
There's an image that's been haunting me for a while.
I'm six years old. It's the night my father went away and never came back.
And I'm killing a dog.
I can't tell if that's something I dreamt or something I buried. I have vague memories of my mother crying because of something I'd done. Uncle Pete staring at me, ashen-faced. My toybox being taken away.
When exactly did Mom start taking the pills? When did she fall apart? Was it when my father died?
Or was it before?
Because my father, the man I went to war to avenge – he was worse than all his brothers put together. He was a killer. A torturer. A psychopath. I think I mentioned selling PCP-addicted children to pedophile rings earlier – well, that was Sam Blute's idea.
Some people think there was something wrong with his mind. Something that made him see terrible things in the sky, made of fire and eyes, that made him commit horrific atrocities and then rationalize them away.
That's the part that sticks with me. According to those who were there, Sam Blute always believed that what he was doing could be justified. That it was "what had to be done."
That he was the good guy, and not just another monster.
Sometimes I think that thing, that twisted gene – that kink in the brain that makes the Blute family what they are – might have passed itself down to me.
Sometimes I think I'm not the heroine of the story at all.
I'm just ill.

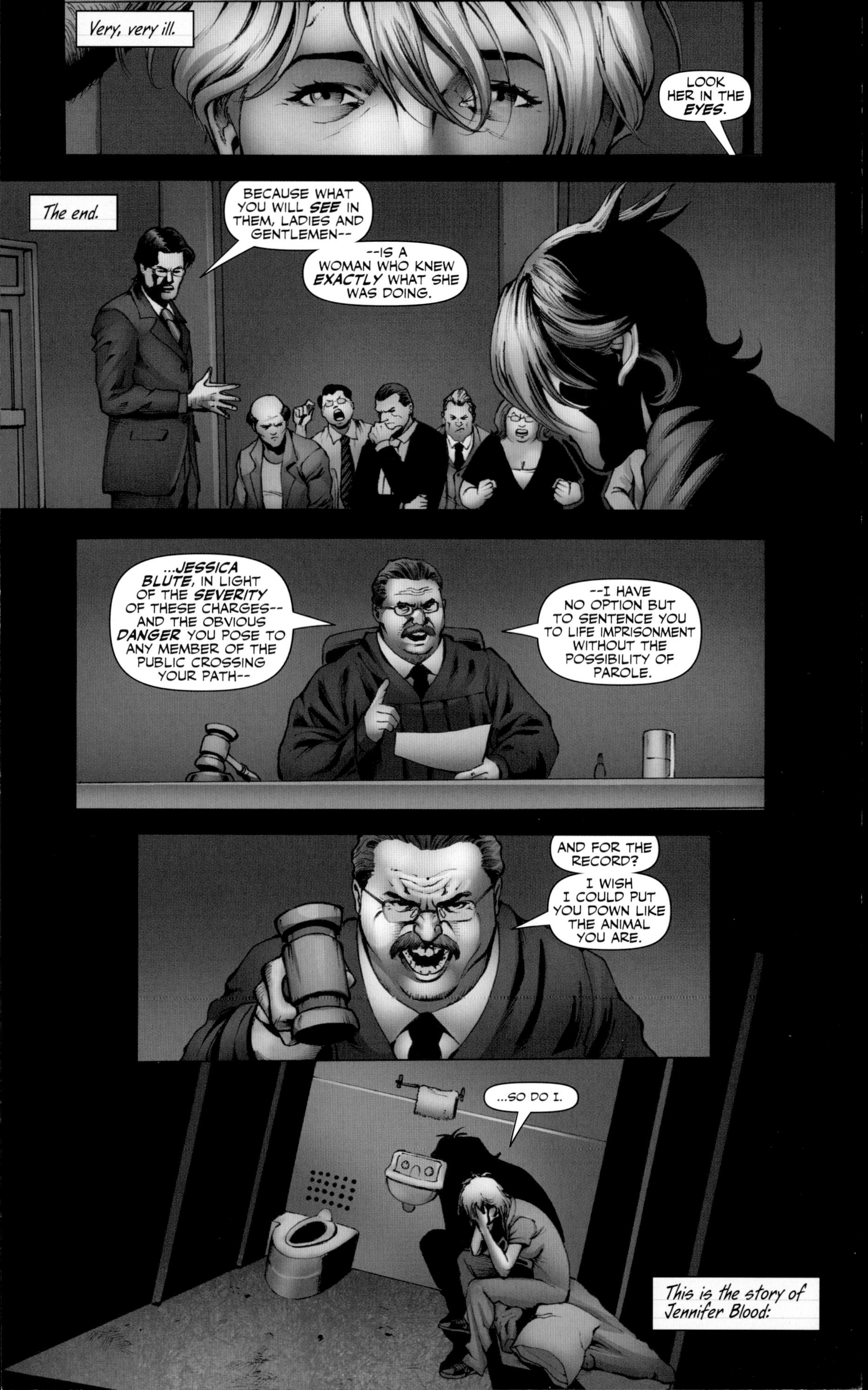
Very, very ill.
LOOK HER IN THE EYES.
The end.
BECAUSE WHAT YOU WILL SEE IN THEM, LADIES AND GENTLEMEN--
--IS A WOMAN WHO KNEW EXACTLY WHAT SHE WAS DOING.
...JESSICA BLÜTE, IN LIGHT OF THE SEVERITY OF THESE CHARGES-- AND THE OBVIOUS DANGER YOU POSE TO ANY MEMBER OF THE PUBLIC CROSSING YOUR PATH--
--I HAVE NO OPTION BUT TO SENTENCE YOU TO LIFE IMPRISONMENT WITHOUT THE POSSIBILITY OF PAROLE.
AND FOR THE RECORD?
I WISH I COULD PUT YOU DOWN LIKE THE ANIMAL YOU ARE.
...SO DO I.
This is the story of Jennifer Blood:

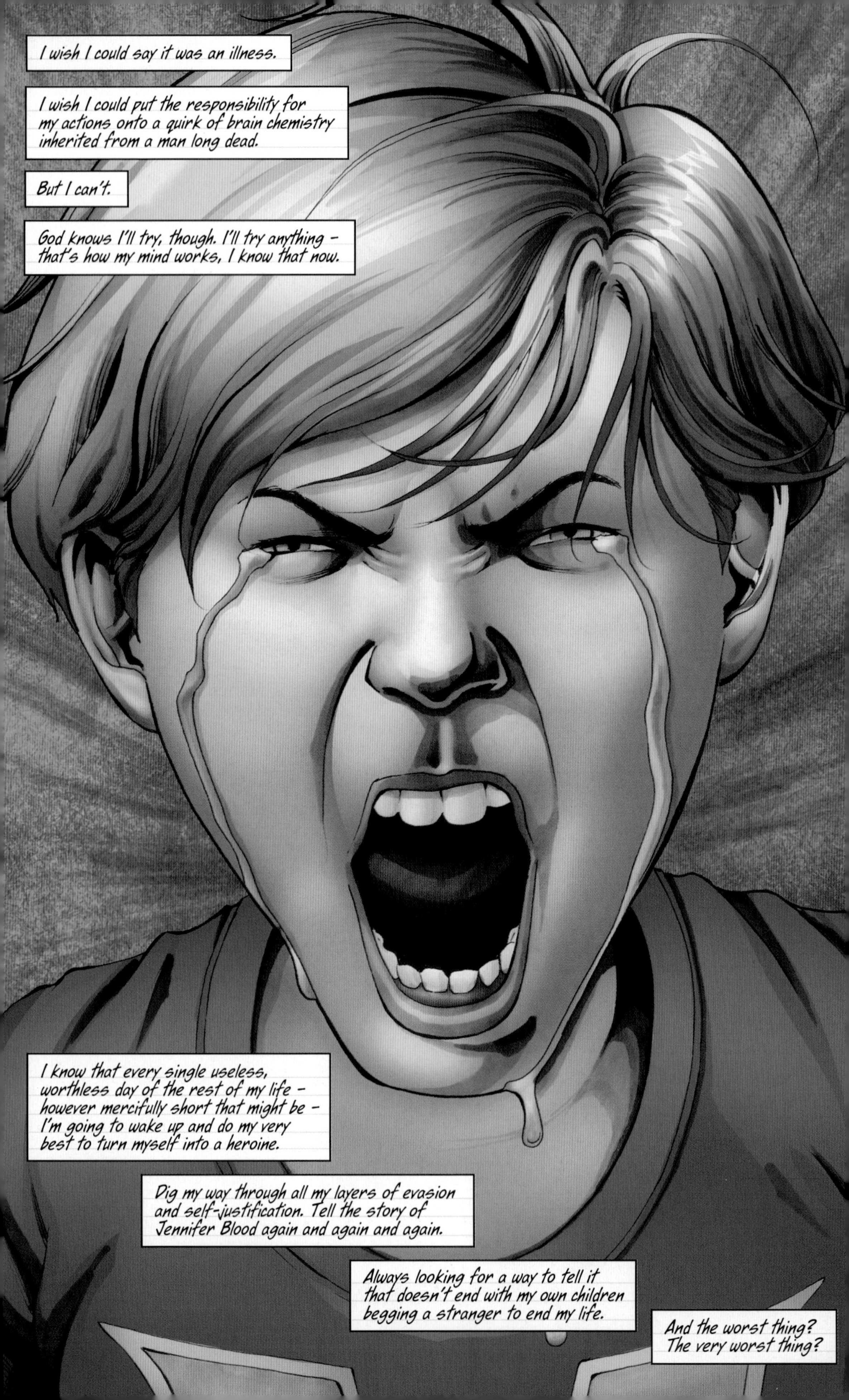

I wish I could say it was an illness.
I wish I could put the responsibility for my actions onto a quirk of brain chemistry inherited from a man long dead.
But I can't.
God knows I'll try, though. I'll try anything - that's how my mind works, I know that now.
I know that every single useless, worthless day of the rest of my life - however mercifully short that might be - I'm going to wake up and do my very best to turn myself into a heroine.
Dig my way through all my layers of evasion and self-justification. Tell the story of Jennifer Blood again and again and again.
Always looking for a way to tell it that doesn't end with my own children begging a stranger to end my life.
And the worst thing? The very worst thing?

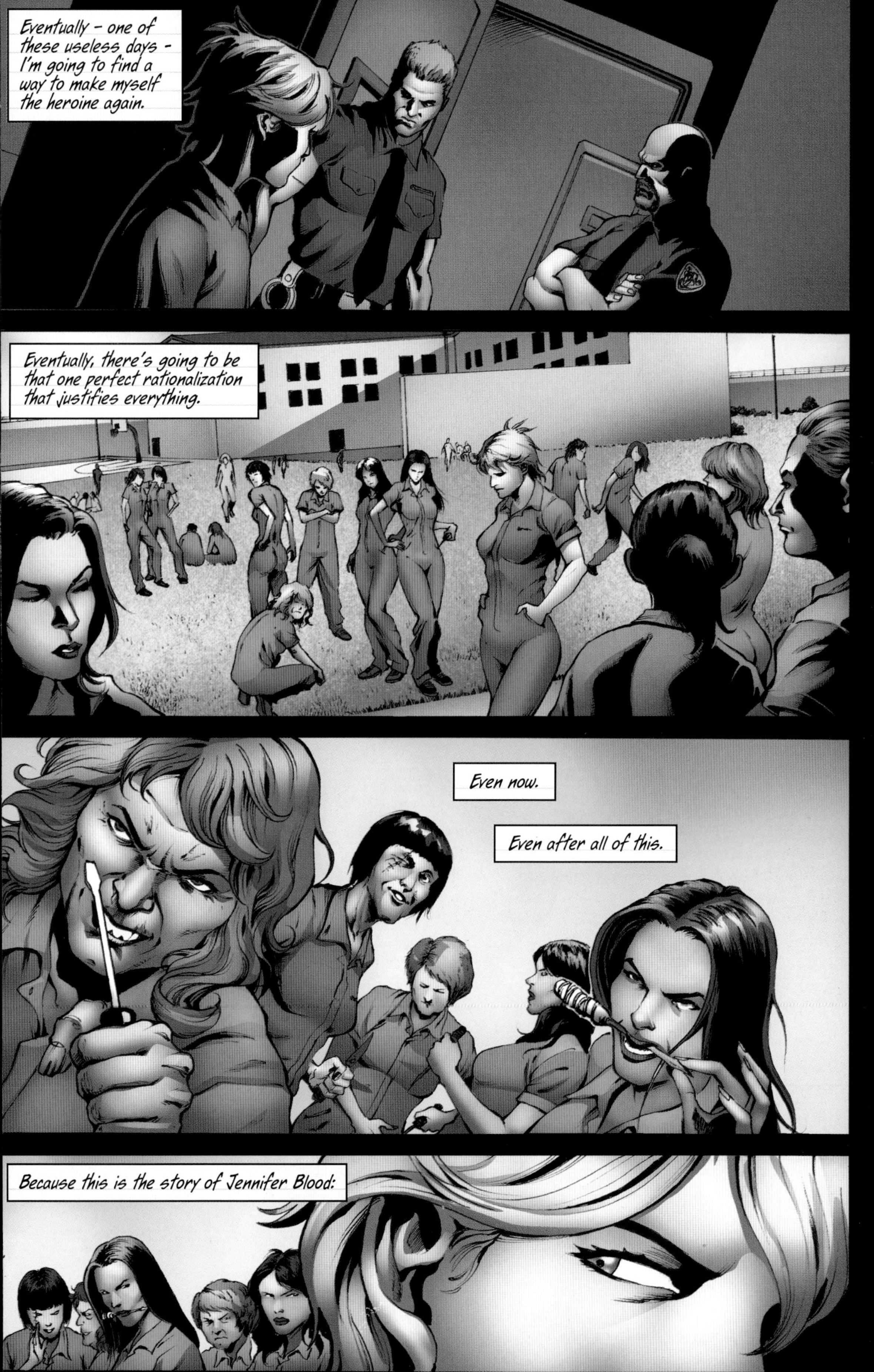
Eventually - one of these useless days - I'm going to find a way to make myself the heroine again.
Eventually, there's going to be that one perfect rationalization that justifies everything.
Even now.
Even after all of this.
Because this is the story of Jennifer Blood:

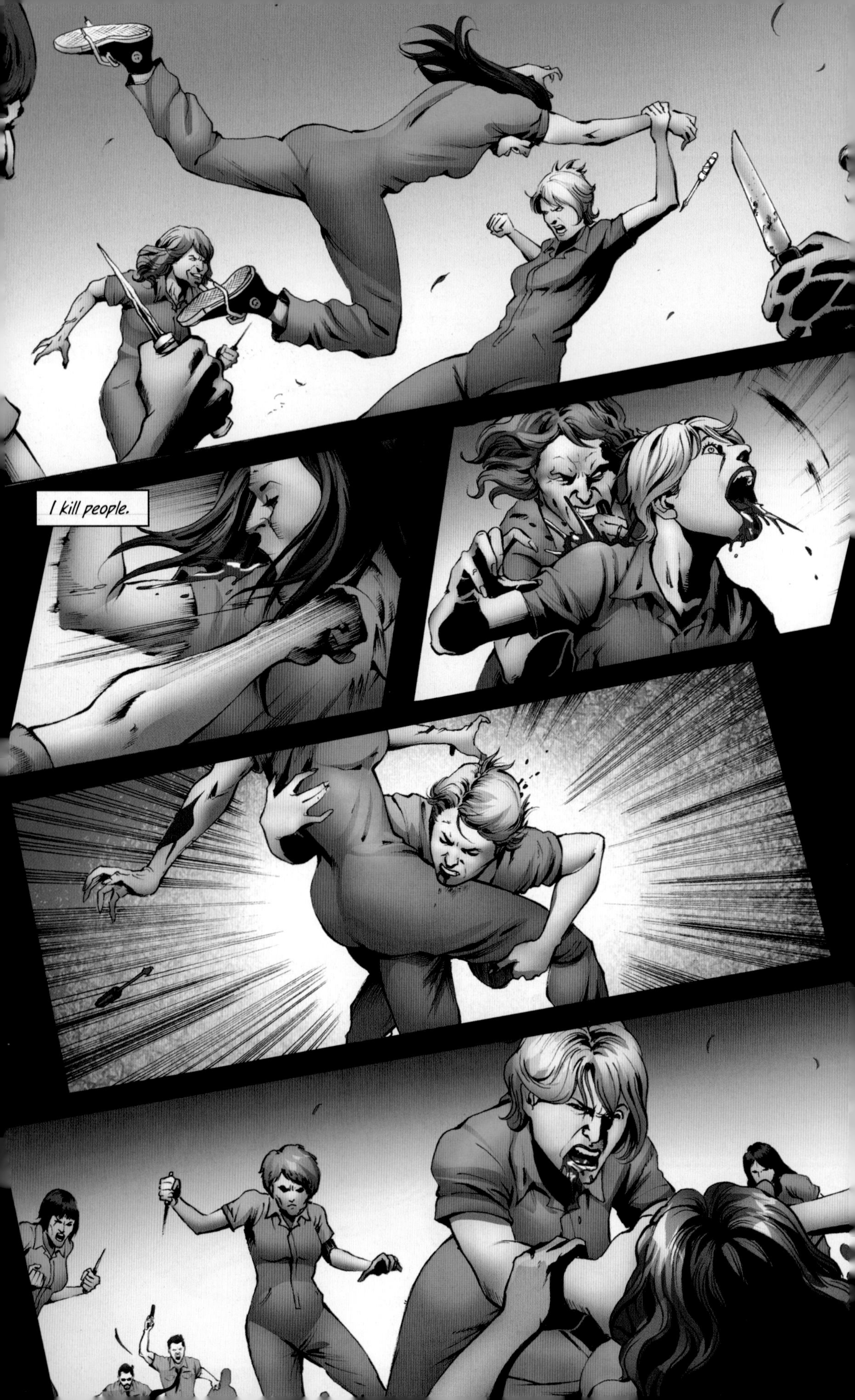
I kill people.

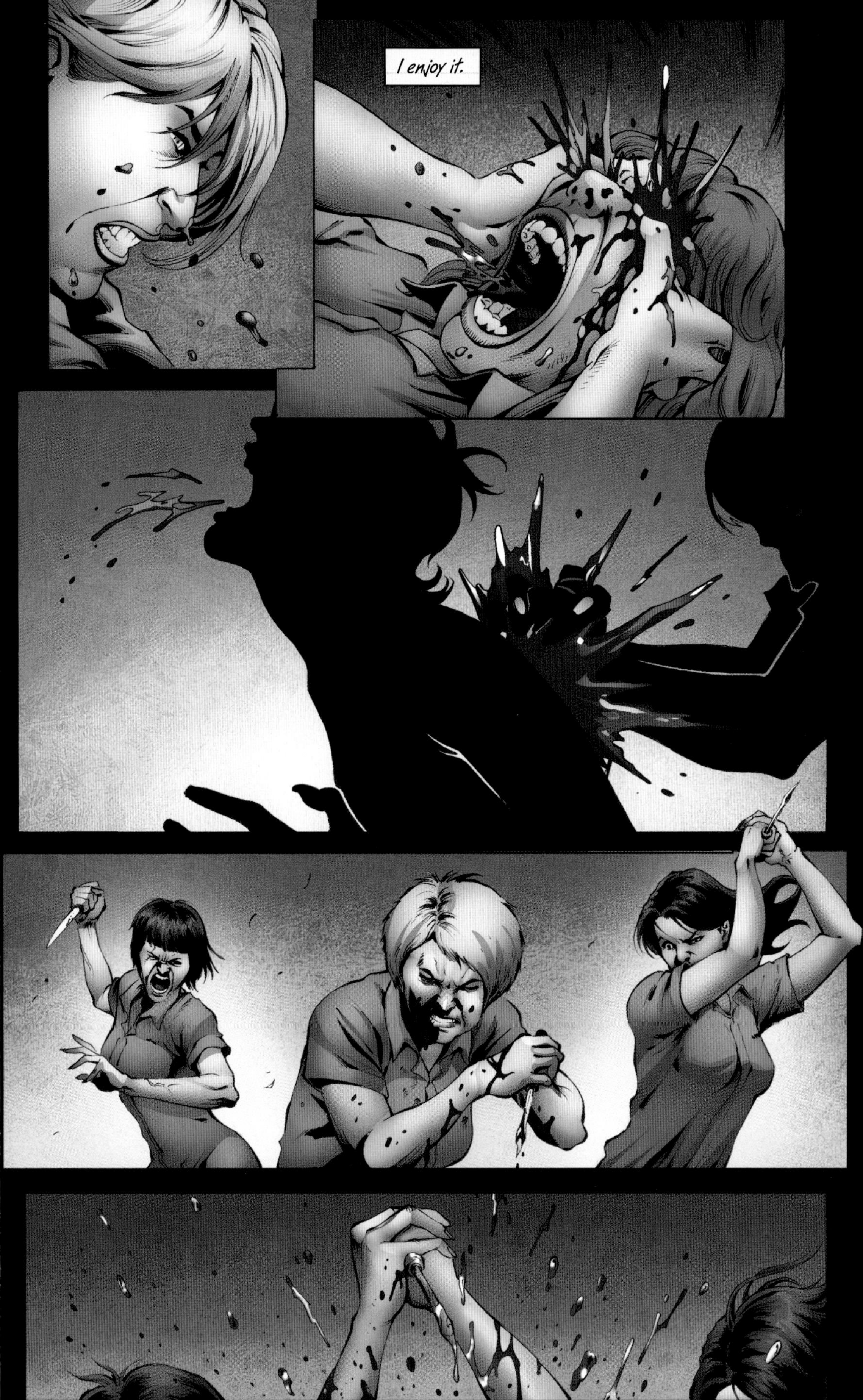
I enjoy it.

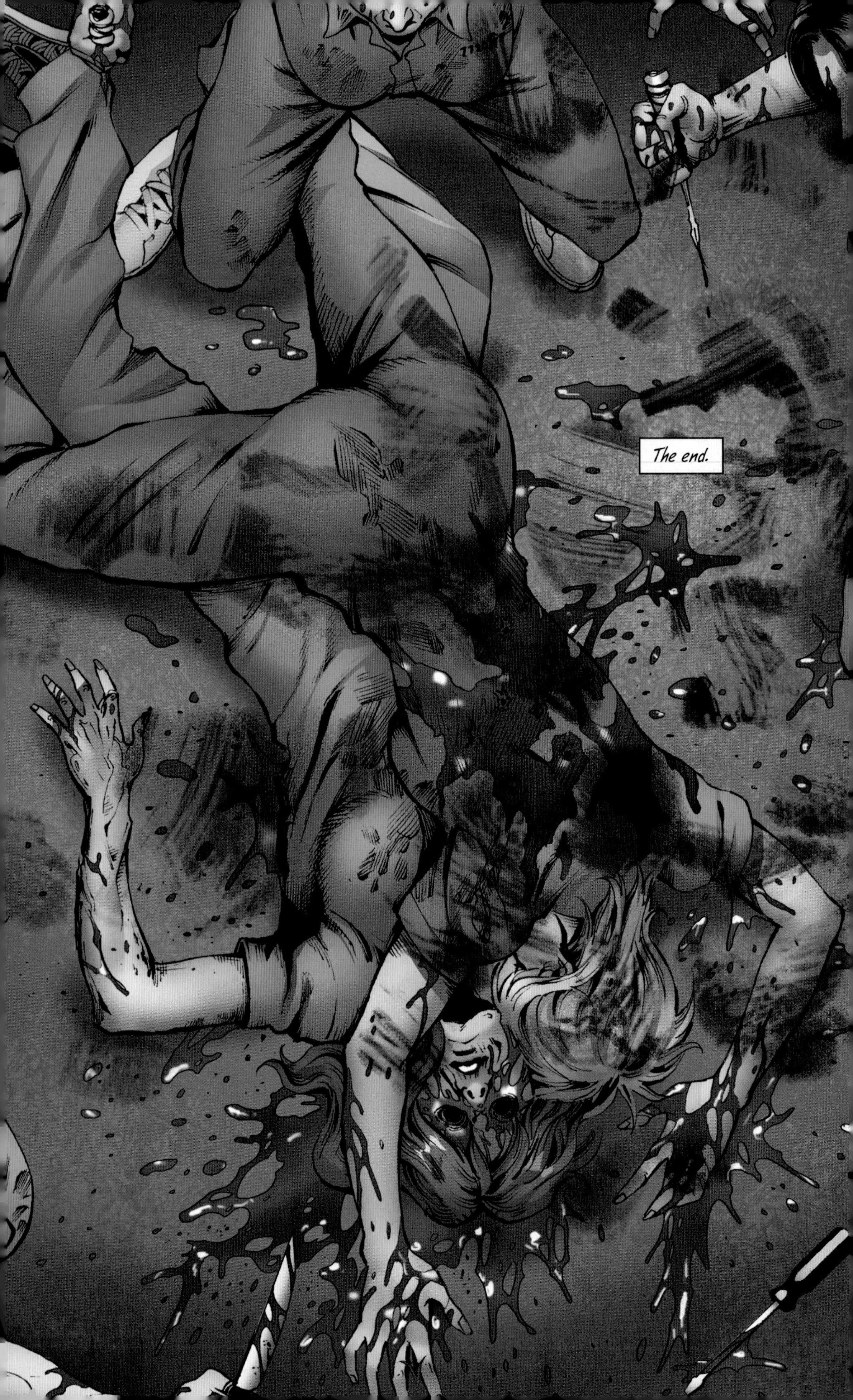
The end.

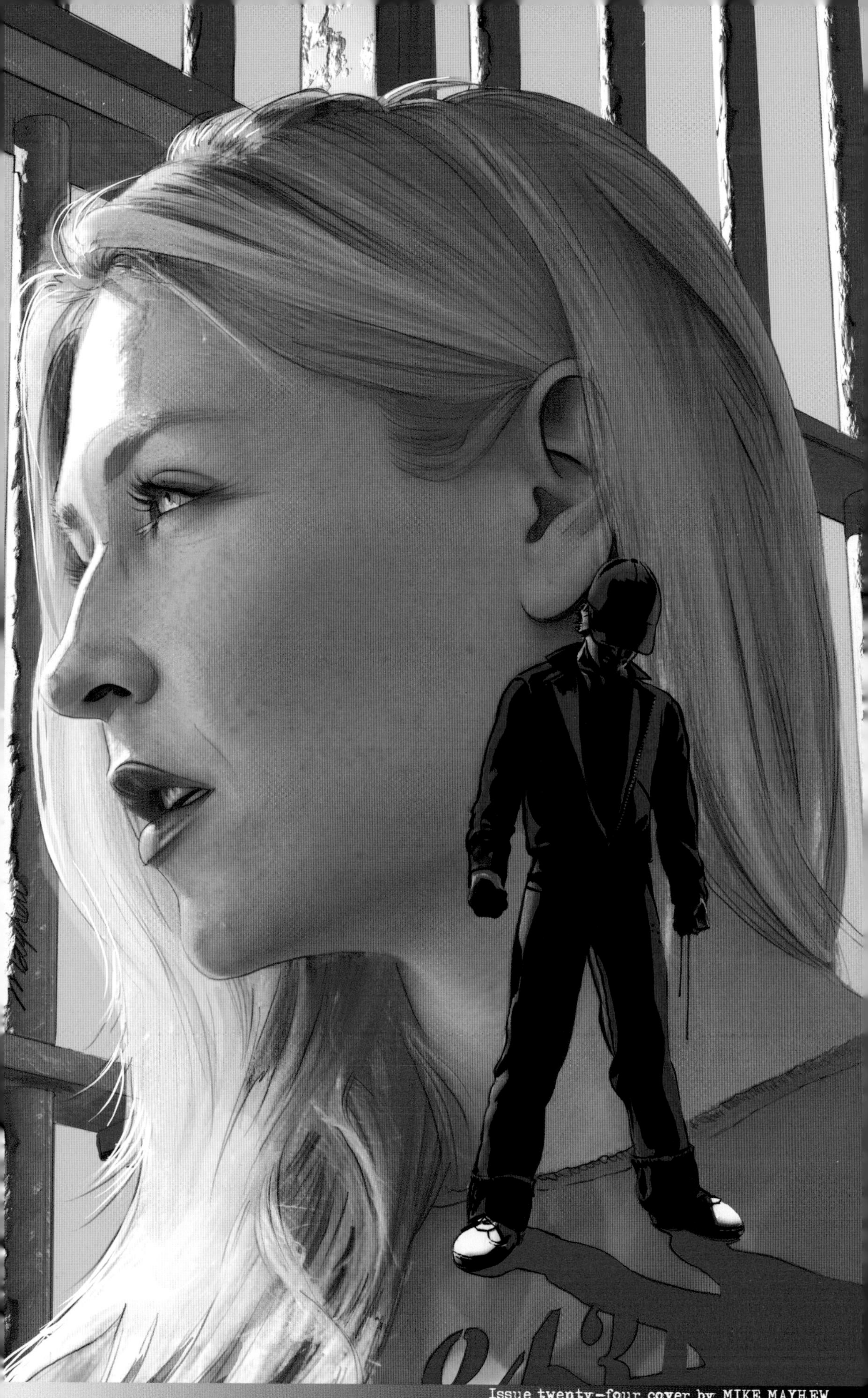

Issue twenty-four cover by MIKE MAYHEW

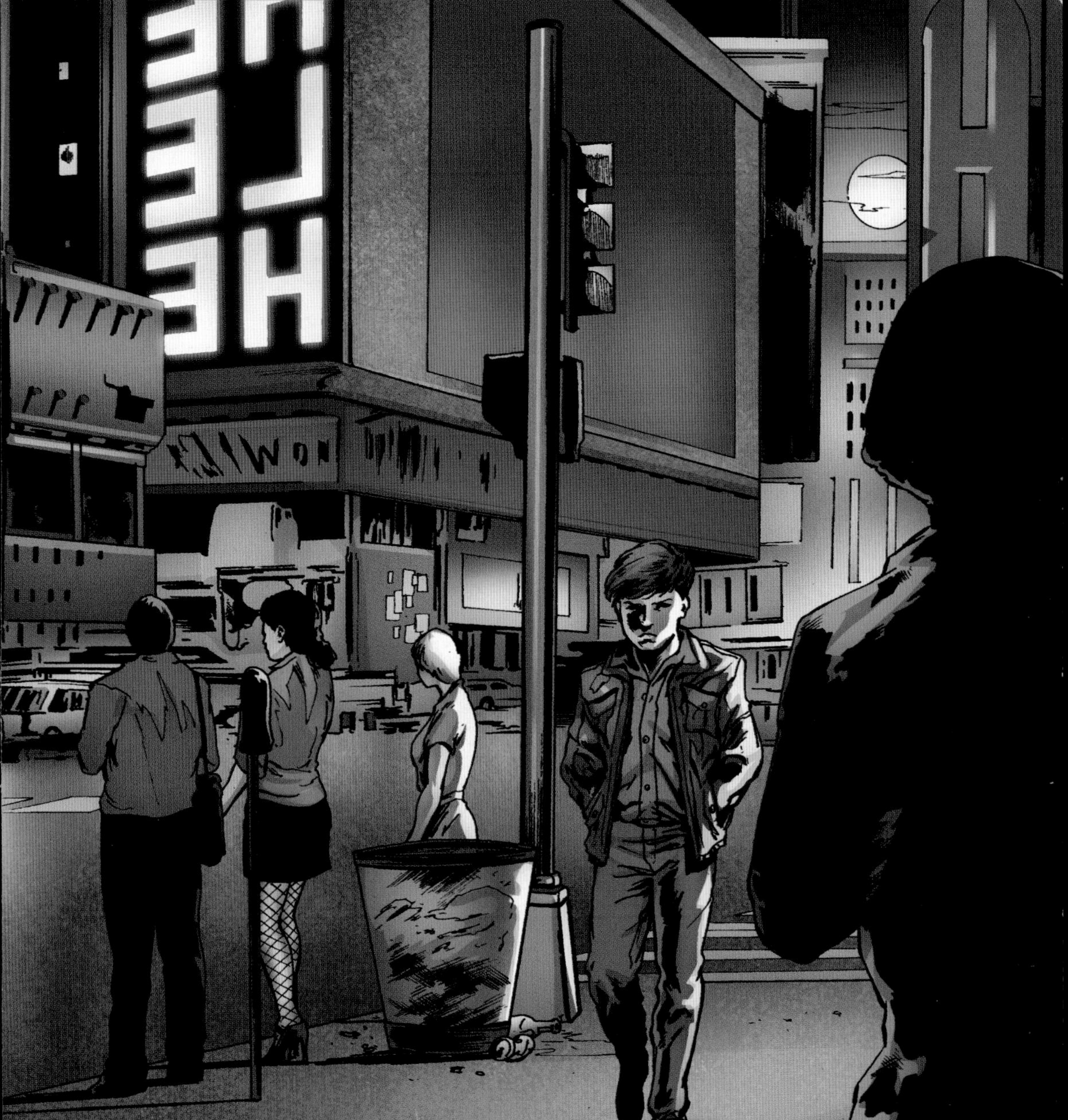

6/6/65

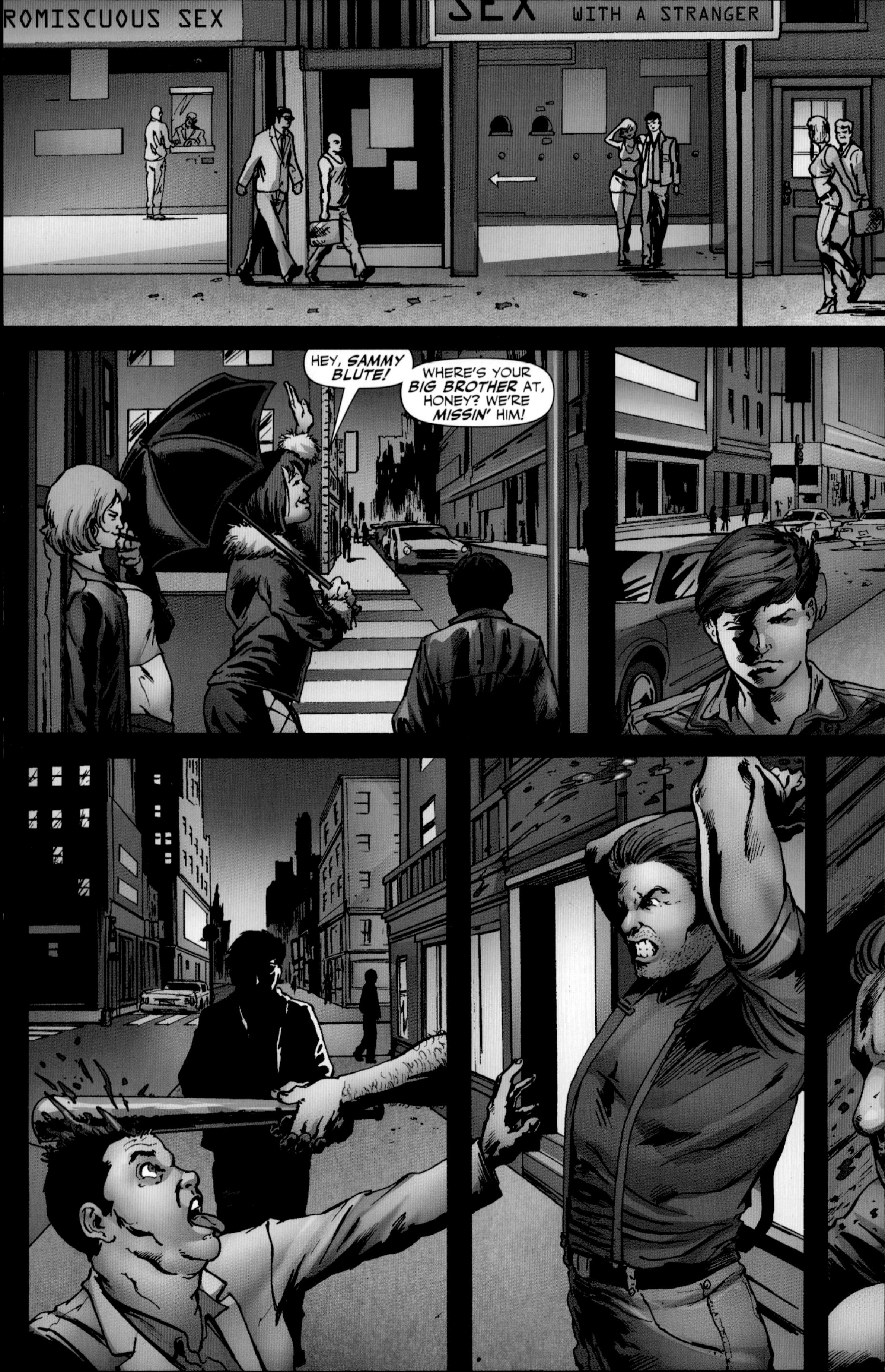
ROMISCUOUS SEX
SEX WITH A STRANGER
HEY, SAMMY BLUTE!
WHERE'S YOUR BIG BROTHER AT, HONEY? WE'RE MISSIN' HIM!

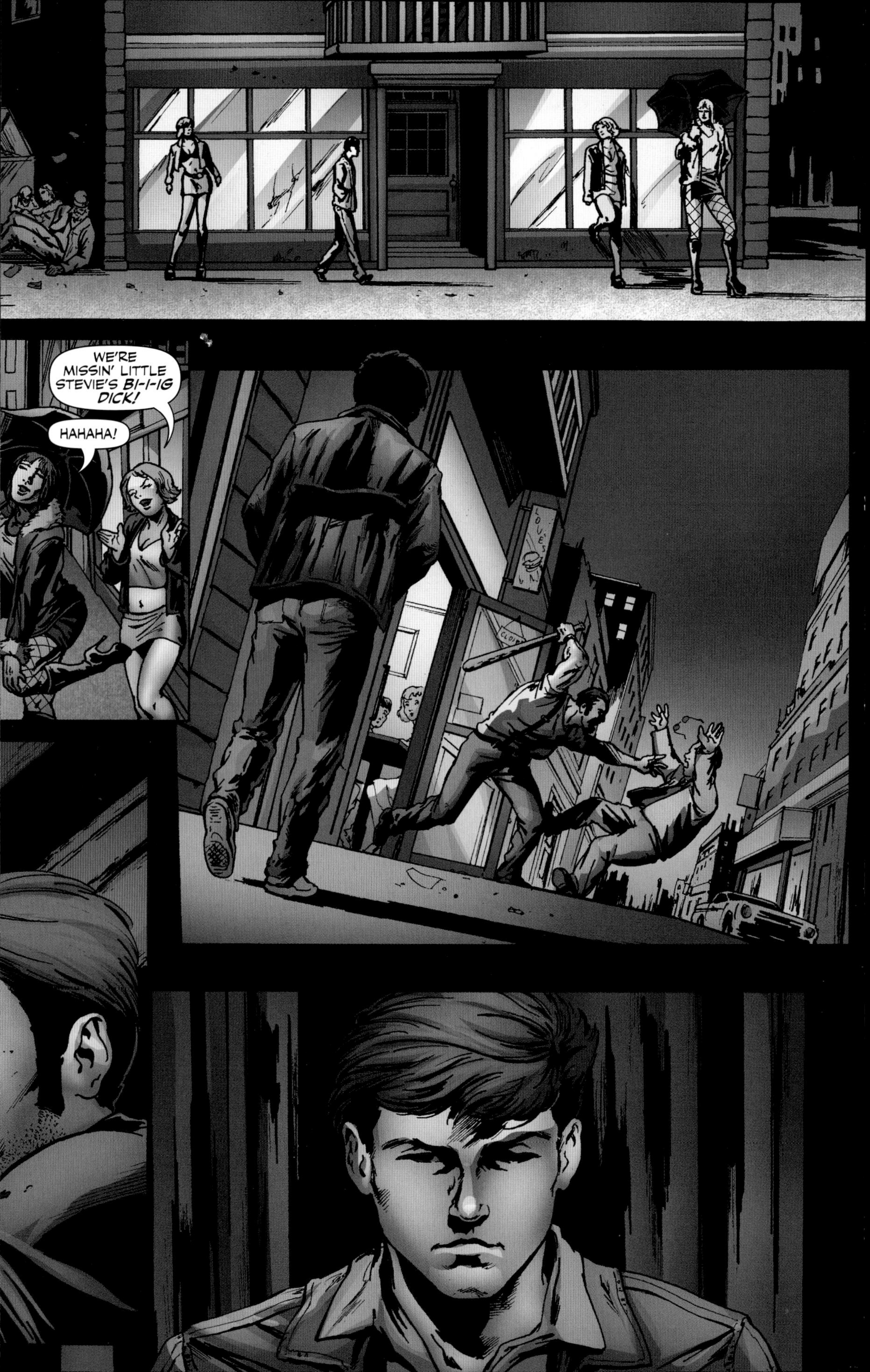
WE'RE MISSIN' LITTLE STEVIE'S BI-I-IG DICK!
HAHAHA!

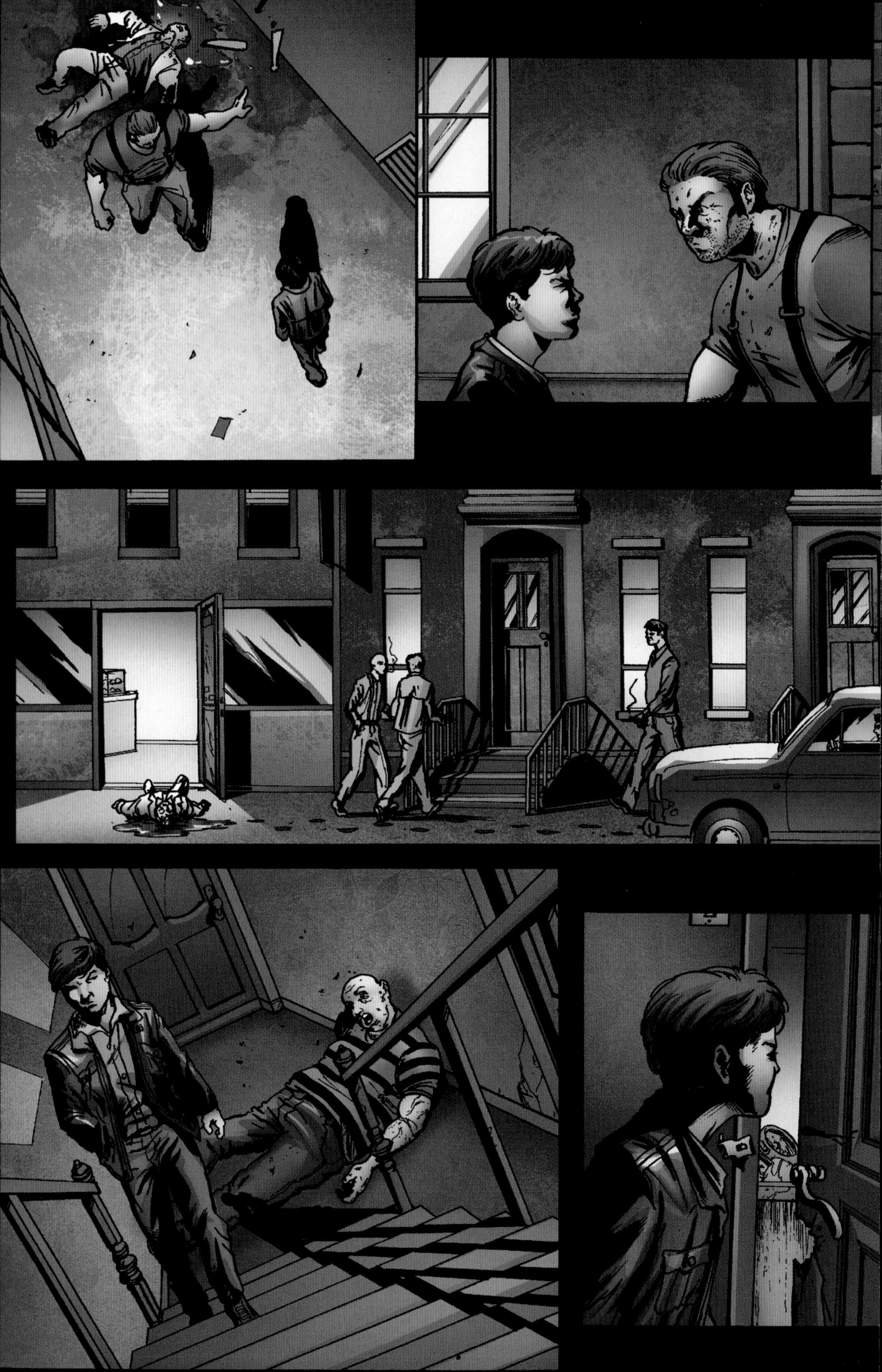

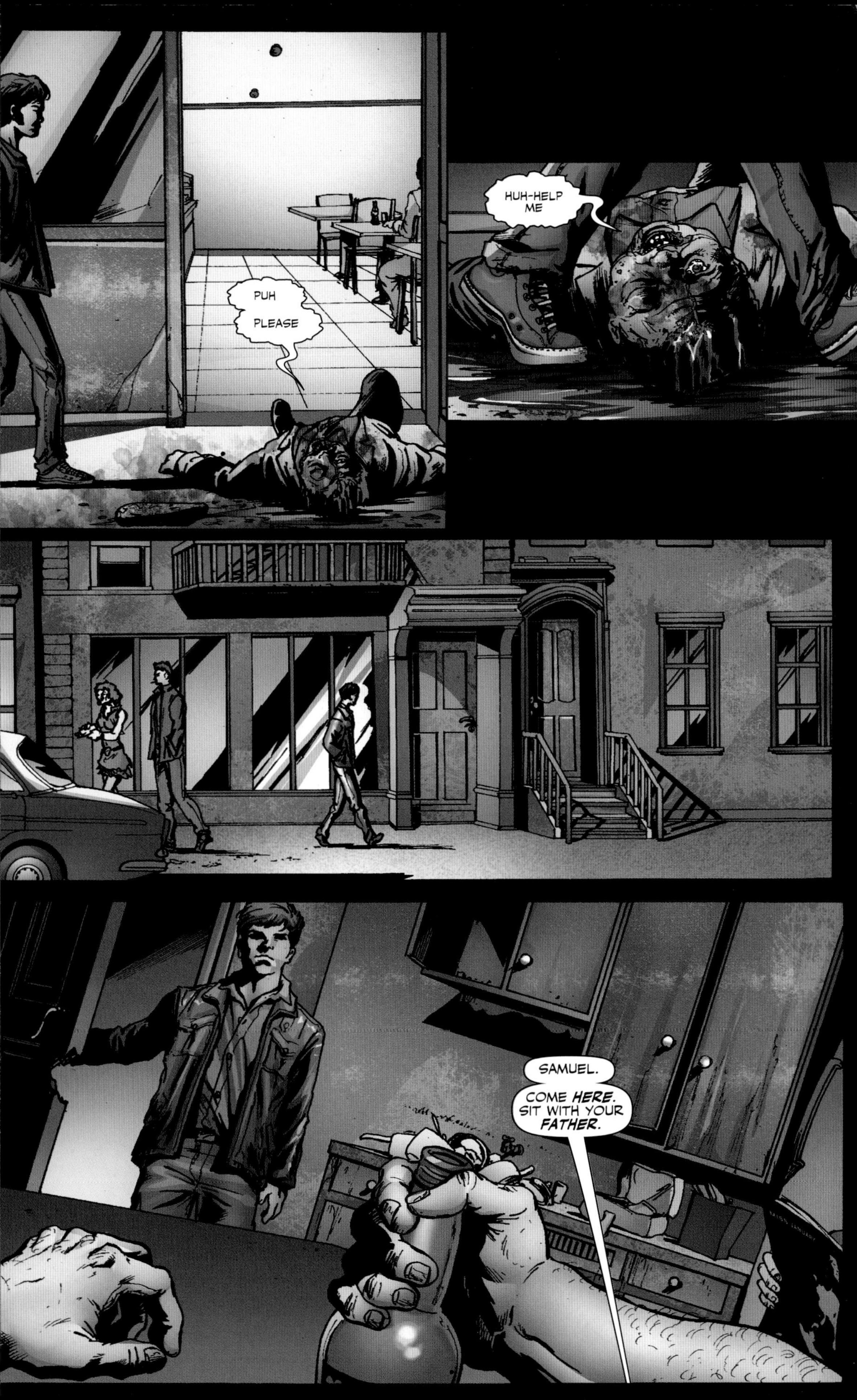
PUH
PLEASE
HUH-HELP ME
SAMUEL.
COME HERE. SIT WITH YOUR FATHER.

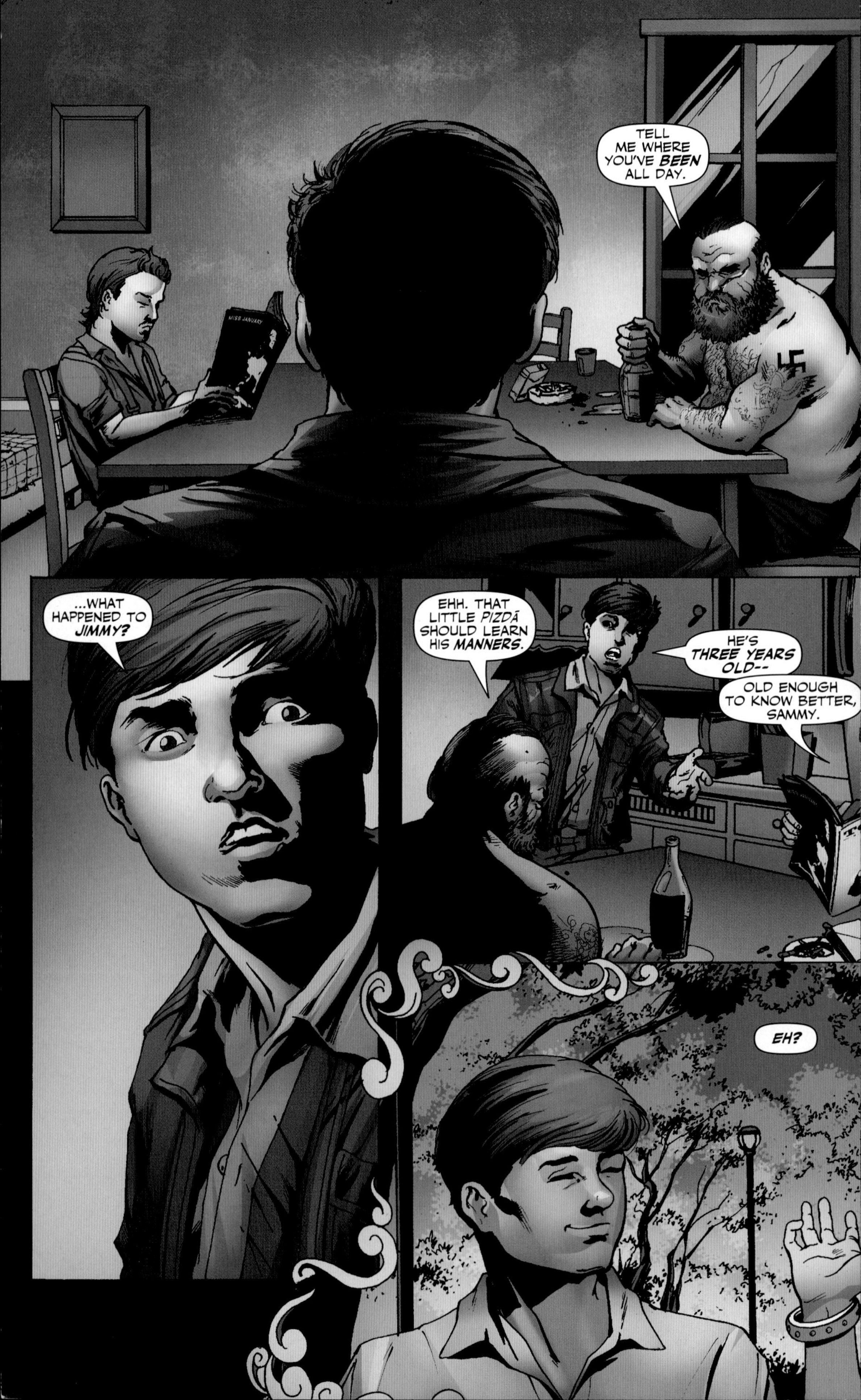
TELL ME WHERE YOU'VE BEEN ALL DAY.
MISS JANUARY
...WHAT HAPPENED TO JIMMY?
EHH. THAT LITTLE PIZDĂ SHOULD LEARN HIS MANNERS.
HE'S THREE YEARS OLD--
OLD ENOUGH TO KNOW BETTER, SAMMY.
EH?

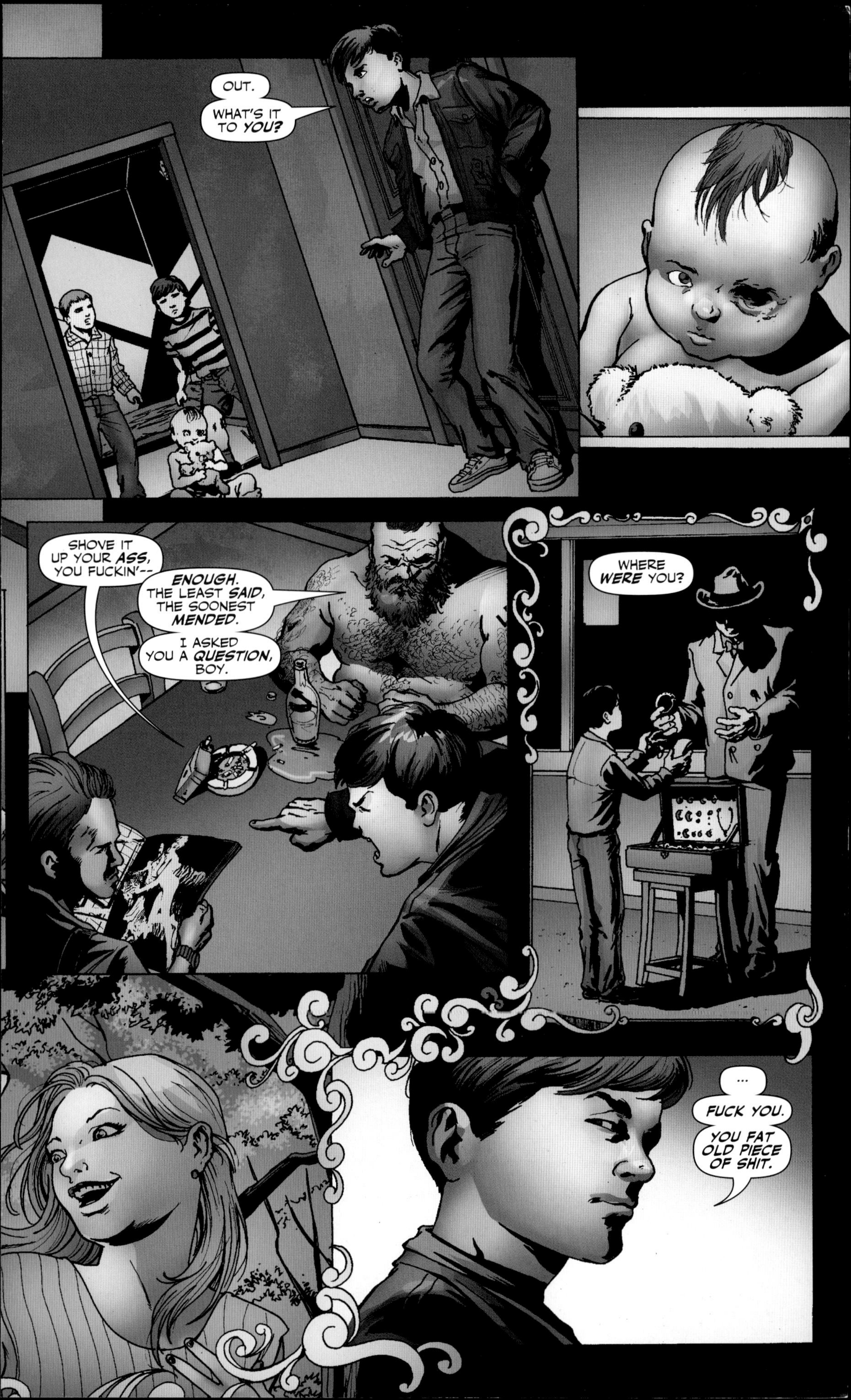
OUT.
WHAT'S IT TO YOU?
SHOVE IT UP YOUR ASS, YOU FUCKIN'--
ENOUGH. THE LEAST SAID, THE SOONEST MENDED.
I ASKED YOU A QUESTION, BOY.
WHERE WERE YOU?
...
FUCK YOU.
YOU FAT OLD PIECE OF SHIT.

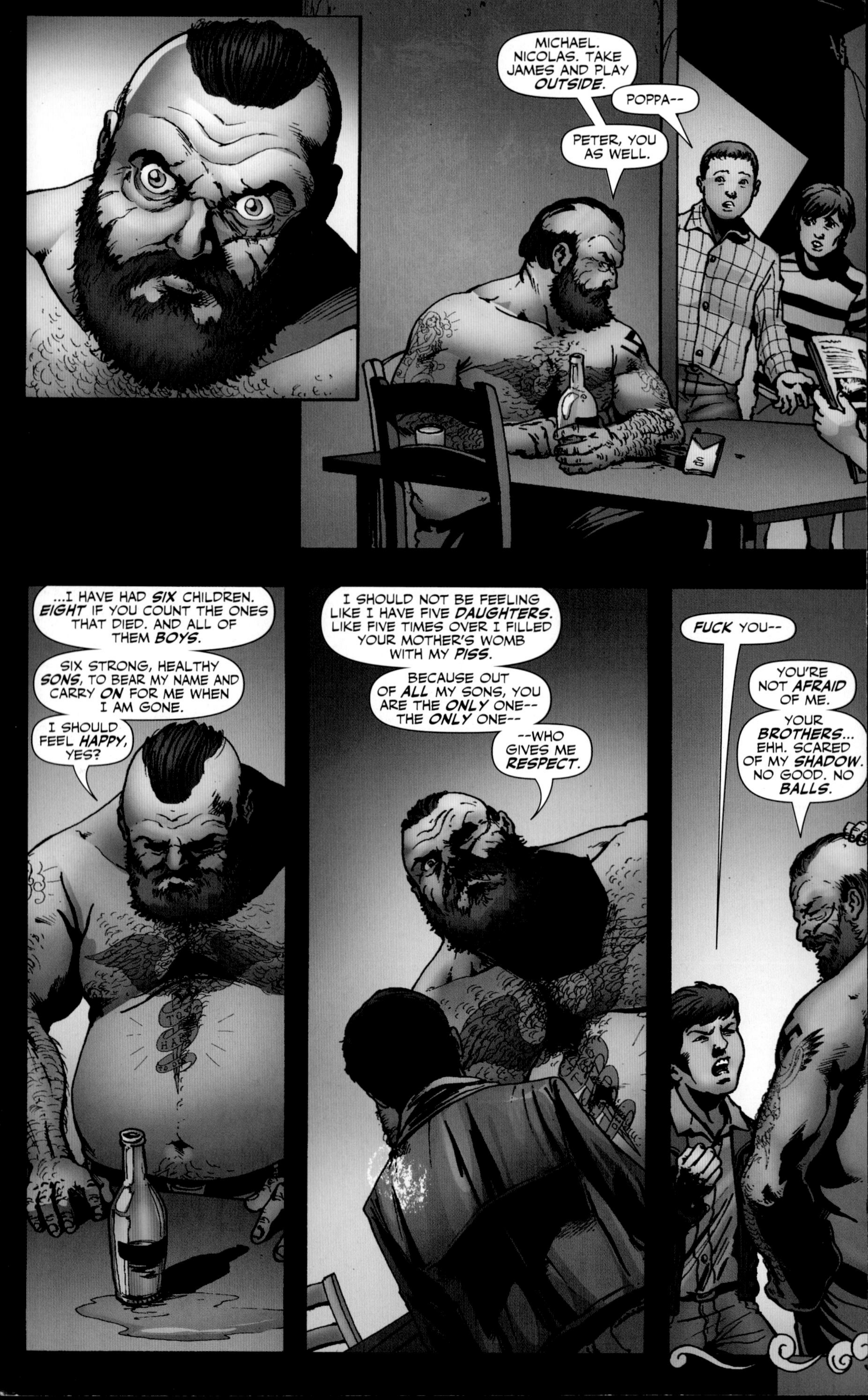
MICHAEL. NICOLAS. TAKE JAMES AND PLAY OUTSIDE.
POPPA--
PETER, YOU AS WELL.
...I HAVE HAD SIX CHILDREN. EIGHT IF YOU COUNT THE ONES THAT DIED. AND ALL OF THEM BOYS.
SIX STRONG, HEALTHY SONS, TO BEAR MY NAME AND CARRY ON FOR ME WHEN I AM GONE.
I SHOULD FEEL HAPPY, YES?
I SHOULD NOT BE FEELING LIKE I HAVE FIVE DAUGHTERS. LIKE FIVE TIMES OVER I FILLED YOUR MOTHER'S WOMB WITH MY PISS.
BECAUSE OUT OF ALL MY SONS, YOU ARE THE ONLY ONE-- THE ONLY ONE--
--WHO GIVES ME RESPECT.
FUCK YOU--
YOU'RE NOT AFRAID OF ME.
YOUR BROTHERS... EHH. SCARED OF MY SHADOW. NO GOOD. NO BALLS.

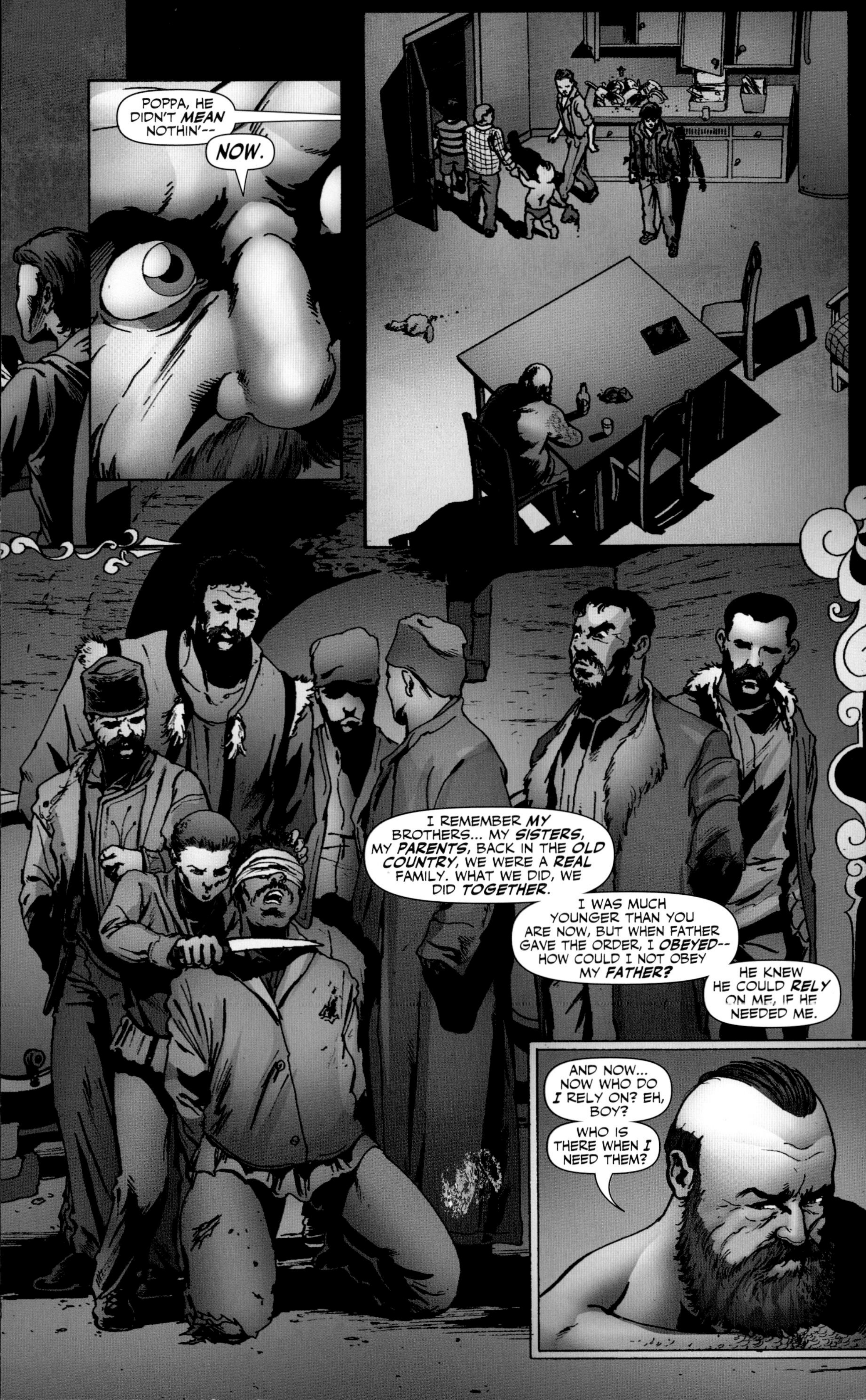

POPPA, HE DIDN'T *MEAN* NOTHIN'--
NOW.
I REMEMBER *MY* BROTHERS... MY *SISTERS*, MY *PARENTS*, BACK IN THE *OLD COUNTRY*, WE WERE A *REAL* FAMILY. WHAT WE DID, WE DID *TOGETHER*.
I WAS MUCH YOUNGER THAN YOU ARE NOW, BUT WHEN FATHER GAVE THE ORDER, I *OBEYED*-- HOW COULD I NOT OBEY MY *FATHER?*
HE KNEW HE COULD *RELY* ON ME, IF HE NEEDED ME.
AND NOW... NOW WHO DO *I* RELY ON? EH, BOY?
WHO IS THERE WHEN *I* NEED THEM?

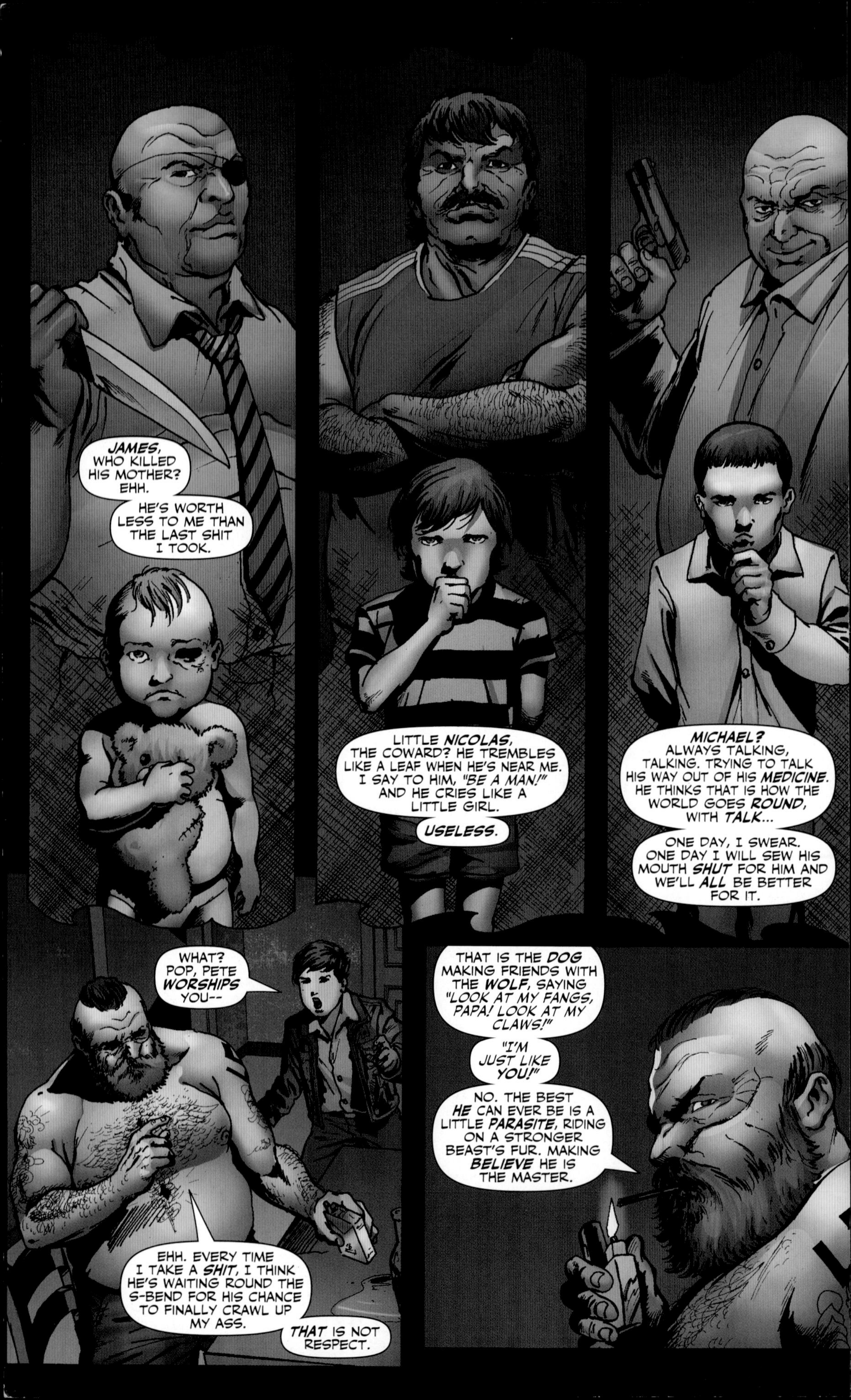
JAMES, WHO KILLED HIS MOTHER? EHH.
HE'S WORTH LESS TO ME THAN THE LAST SHIT I TOOK.
LITTLE NICOLAS, THE COWARD? HE TREMBLES LIKE A LEAF WHEN HE'S NEAR ME. I SAY TO HIM, "BE A MAN!" AND HE CRIES LIKE A LITTLE GIRL.
USELESS.
MICHAEL? ALWAYS TALKING, TALKING. TRYING TO TALK HIS WAY OUT OF HIS MEDICINE. HE THINKS THAT IS HOW THE WORLD GOES ROUND, WITH TALK...
ONE DAY, I SWEAR. ONE DAY I WILL SEW HIS MOUTH SHUT FOR HIM AND WE'LL ALL BE BETTER FOR IT.
WHAT? POP, PETE WORSHIPS YOU--
EHH. EVERY TIME I TAKE A SHIT, I THINK HE'S WAITING ROUND THE S-BEND FOR HIS CHANCE TO FINALLY CRAWL UP MY ASS.
THAT IS NOT RESPECT.
THAT IS THE DOG MAKING FRIENDS WITH THE WOLF, SAYING "LOOK AT MY FANGS, PAPA! LOOK AT MY CLAWS!"
"I'M JUST LIKE YOU!"
NO. THE BEST HE CAN EVER BE IS A LITTLE PARASITE, RIDING ON A STRONGER BEAST'S FUR. MAKING BELIEVE HE IS THE MASTER.

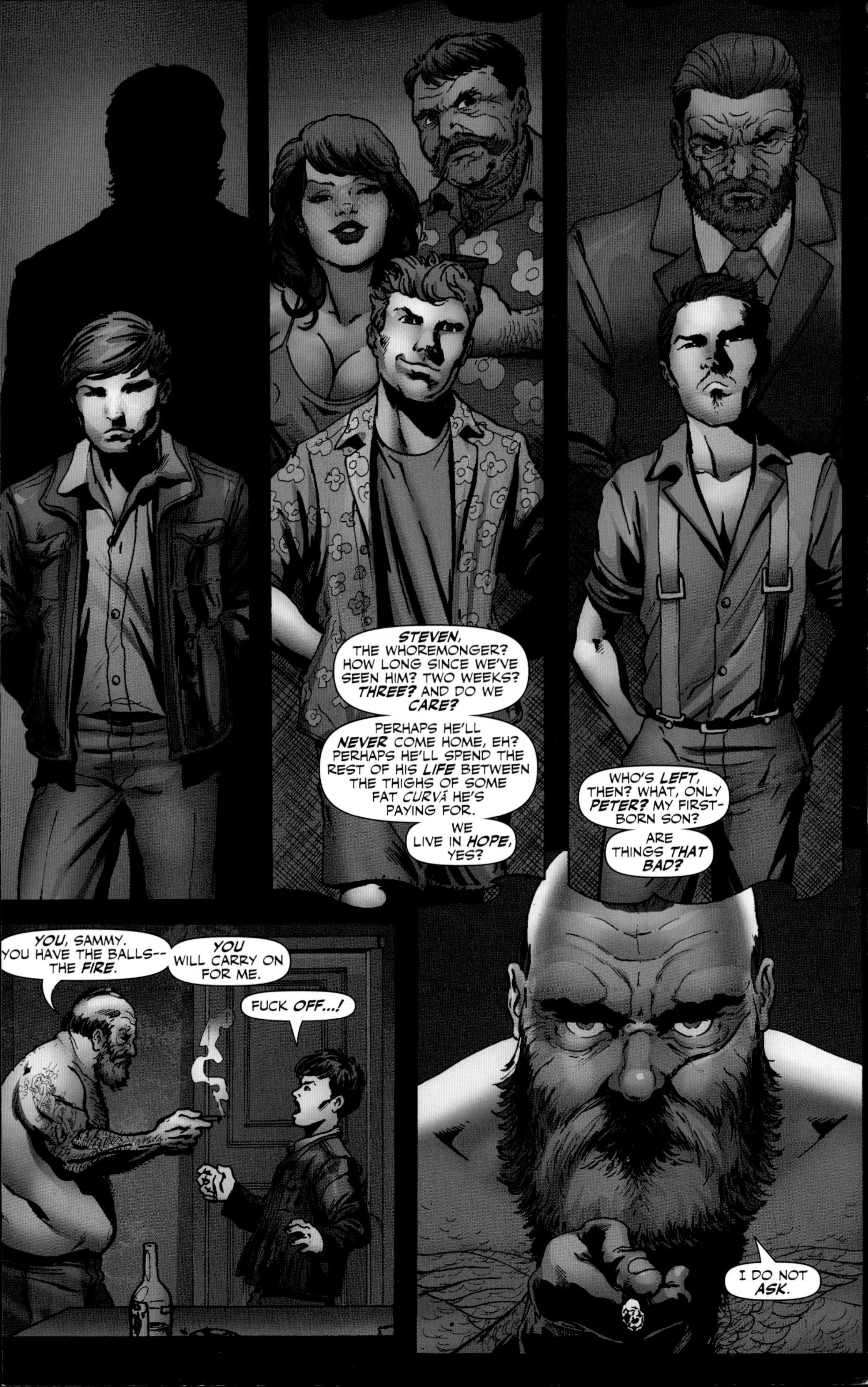
STEVEN, THE WHOREMONGER? HOW LONG SINCE WE'VE SEEN HIM? TWO WEEKS? THREE? AND DO WE CARE?
PERHAPS HE'LL NEVER COME HOME, EH? PERHAPS HE'LL SPEND THE REST OF HIS LIFE BETWEEN THE THIGHS OF SOME FAT CURVĂ HE'S PAYING FOR.
WE LIVE IN HOPE, YES?
WHO'S LEFT, THEN? WHAT, ONLY PETER? MY FIRST-BORN SON?
ARE THINGS THAT BAD?
YOU, SAMMY. YOU HAVE THE BALLS-- THE FIRE.
YOU WILL CARRY ON FOR ME.
FUCK OFF...!
I DO NOT ASK.

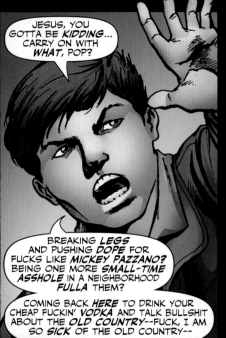

JESUS, YOU GOTTA BE *KIDDING...* CARRY ON WITH *WHAT*, POP?

BREAKING *LEGS* AND PUSHING *DOPE* FOR FUCKS LIKE *MICKEY PAZZANO?* BEING ONE MORE *SMALL-TIME ASSHOLE* IN A NEIGHBORHOOD *FULLA* THEM?

COMING BACK *HERE* TO DRINK YOUR CHEAP FUCKIN' *VODKA* AND TALK BULLSHIT ABOUT THE *OLD COUNTRY*--FUCK, I AM SO *SICK* OF THE OLD COUNTRY--

WHAT'S SO WRONG WITH THE OLD COUNTRY? IT'S WHERE YOU *CAME* FROM. THOSE WERE *GOOD DAYS*--

WHAT, WHEN YOU TOOK MONEY FROM THE FUCKIN' *NAZIS?*

WHY *NOT?* MONEY IS MONEY.

SO WHAT WILL YOU DO *INSTEAD?*

I DUNNO, SOMETHING-- SOMETHING *STRAIGHT*--LIKE, I DUNNO, WORK IN A *BANK*, OR SELL *FISH*, OR *SHOES*, OR-- OR *SOMETHING*--

WITH WHAT? NO SCHOOL WILL *HAVE* YOU ANYMORE. YOUR FATHER WORKS FOR A *MOBSTER*, YOUR *BROTHERS* ARE PETTY CRIMINALS.

WHO *HIRES* YOU, AT THIS BANK? *EH*, BOY? WHO'S GOING TO LOOK AT *YOU* AND SEE A *MAN?*

THIS *BLONDE* PIECE OF ASS YOU BUY *TRINKETS* FOR, MAYBE? YOUR *JENNIFER?*

HERE IS THE TRUTH, BOY.

EVERYTHING I HAVE *DONE*-- *EVERYTHING*--I HAVE DONE FOR MY *FAMILY*. FOR *YOU*.

AM I *CRUEL* TO YOU? *GOOD.* THE WORLD IS CRUEL. YOU MUST LEARN IT *NOW*.

WHEN I BLACK YOUR *EYES* AND BREAK YOUR *BONES*, I *PROMISE* YOU, THEY GROW BACK *STRONGER*.

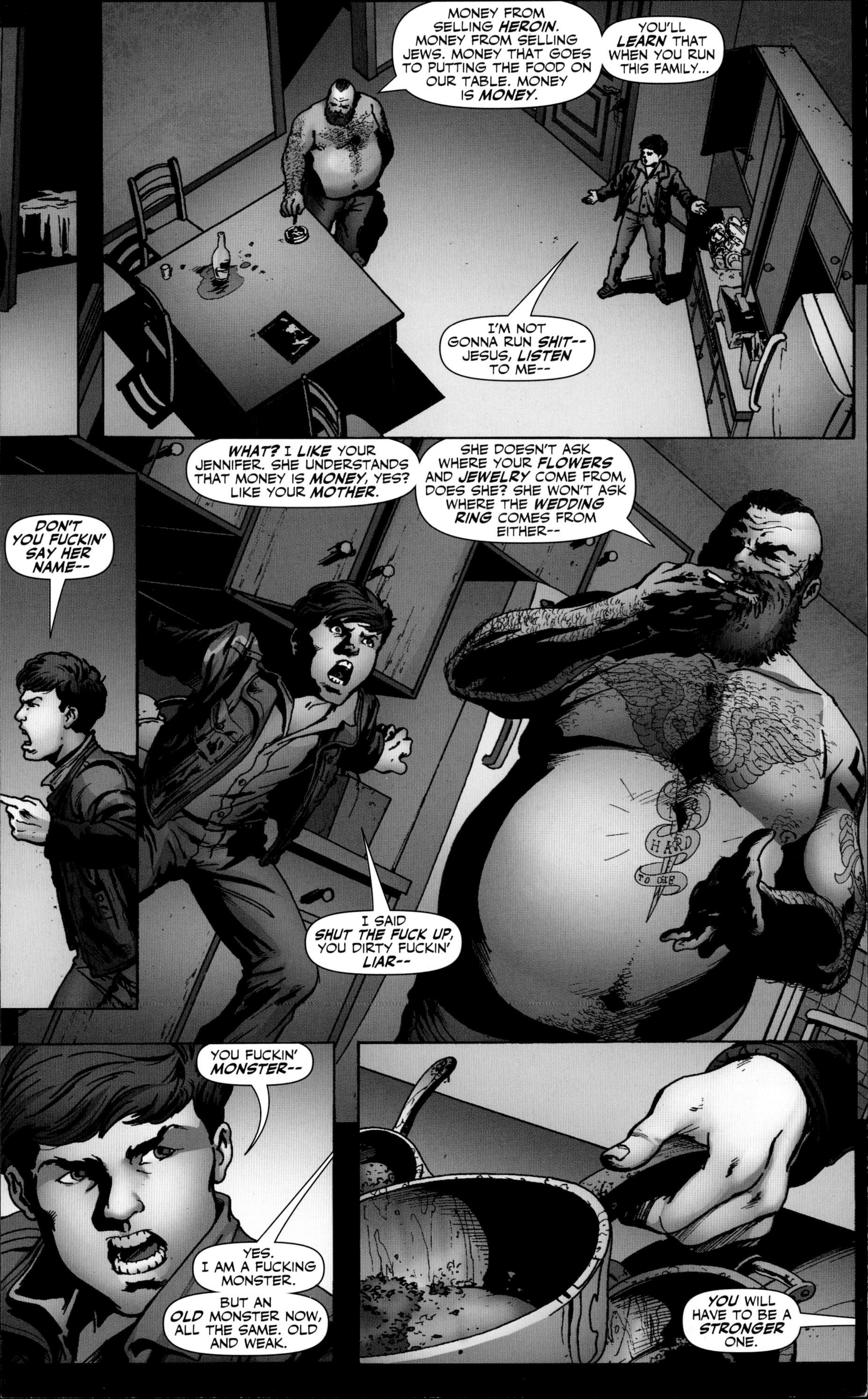
MONEY FROM SELLING HEROIN. MONEY FROM SELLING JEWS. MONEY THAT GOES TO PUTTING THE FOOD ON OUR TABLE. MONEY IS MONEY.
YOU'LL LEARN THAT WHEN YOU RUN THIS FAMILY...
I'M NOT GONNA RUN SHIT-- JESUS, LISTEN TO ME--
WHAT? I LIKE YOUR JENNIFER. SHE UNDERSTANDS THAT MONEY IS MONEY, YES? LIKE YOUR MOTHER.
SHE DOESN'T ASK WHERE YOUR FLOWERS AND JEWELRY COME FROM, DOES SHE? SHE WON'T ASK WHERE THE WEDDING RING COMES FROM EITHER--
DON'T YOU FUCKIN' SAY HER NAME--
I SAID SHUT THE FUCK UP, YOU DIRTY FUCKIN' LIAR--
HARD TO DIE
YOU FUCKIN' MONSTER--
YES. I AM A FUCKING MONSTER.
BUT AN OLD MONSTER NOW, ALL THE SAME. OLD AND WEAK.
YOU WILL HAVE TO BE A STRONGER ONE.

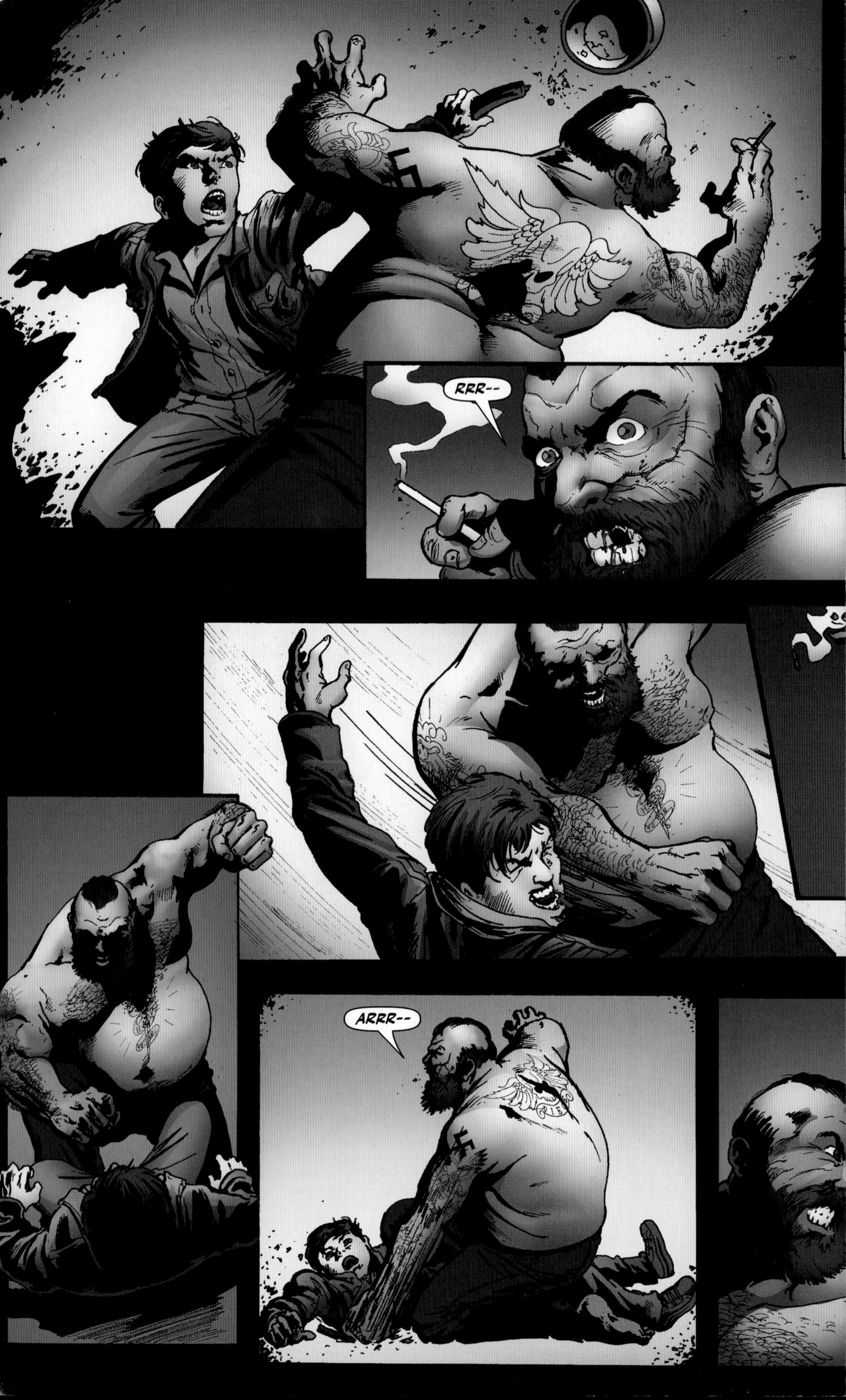
RRR--
ARRR--

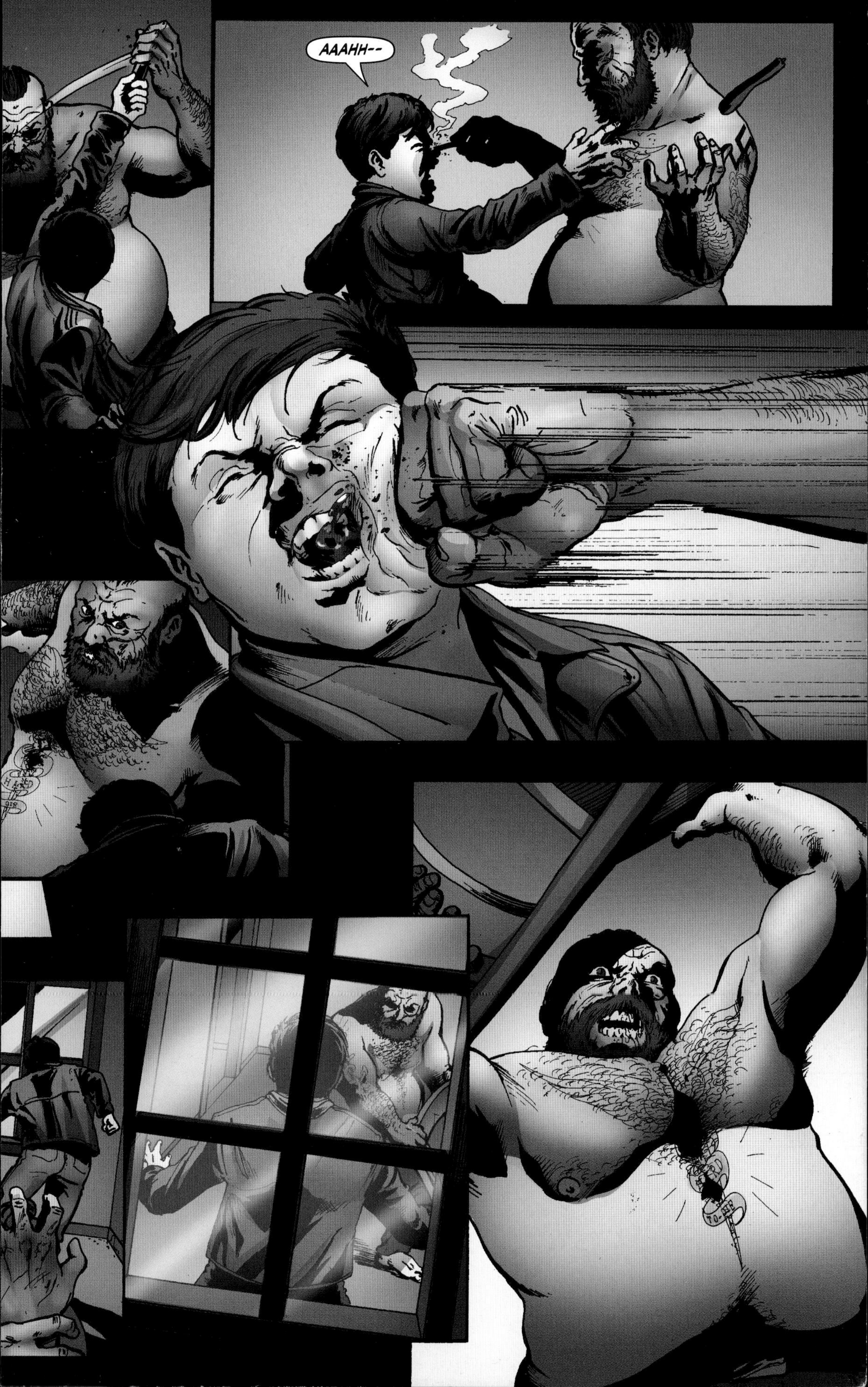
AAAHH--

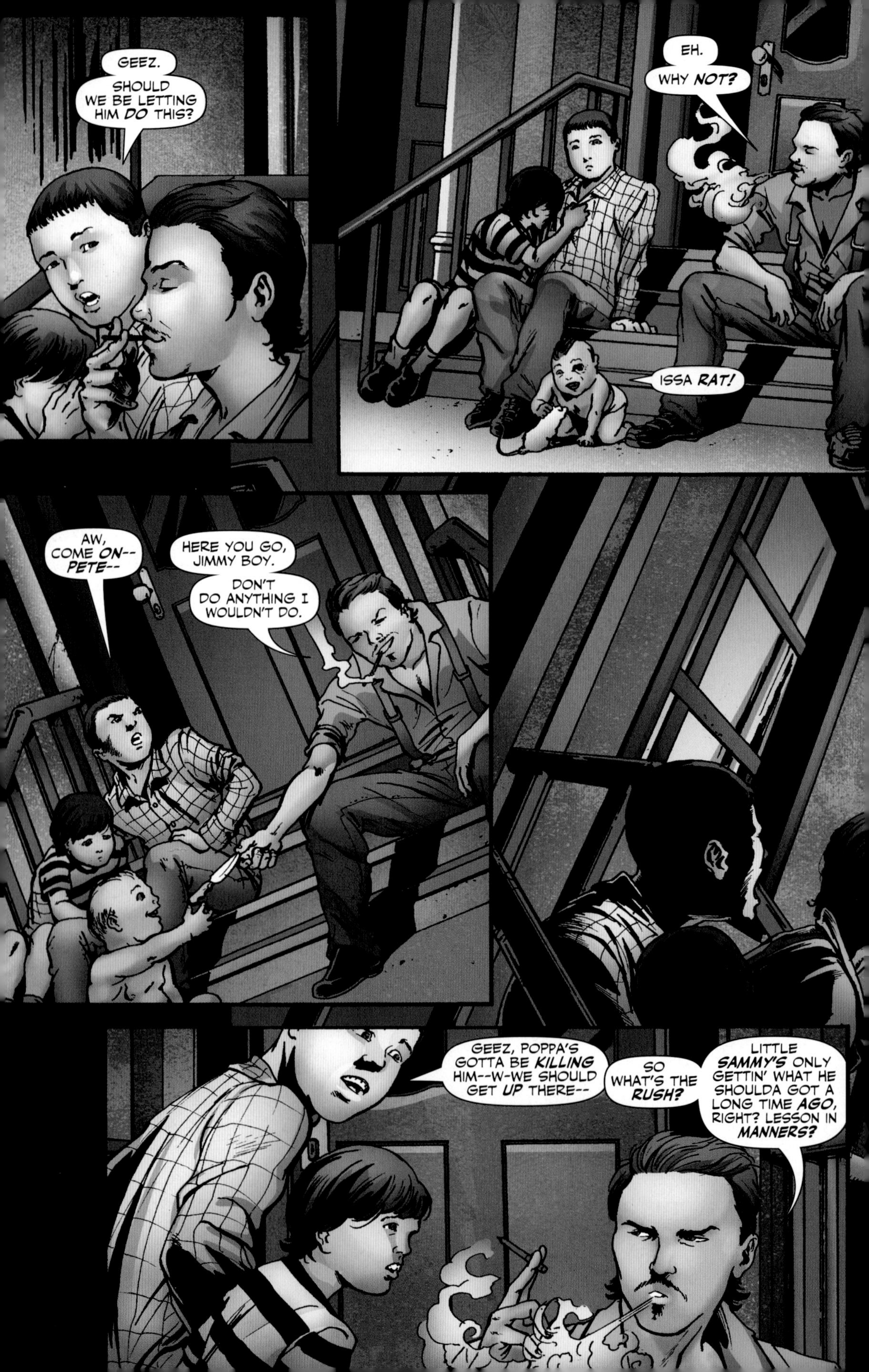
GEEZ.
SHOULD WE BE LETTING HIM DO THIS?
EH.
WHY NOT?
ISSA RAT!
AW, COME ON-- PETE--
HERE YOU GO, JIMMY BOY.
DON'T DO ANYTHING I WOULDN'T DO.
GEEZ, POPPA'S GOTTA BE KILLING HIM--W-WE SHOULD GET UP THERE--
SO WHAT'S THE RUSH?
LITTLE SAMMY'S ONLY GETTIN' WHAT HE SHOULDA GOT A LONG TIME AGO, RIGHT? LESSON IN MANNERS?

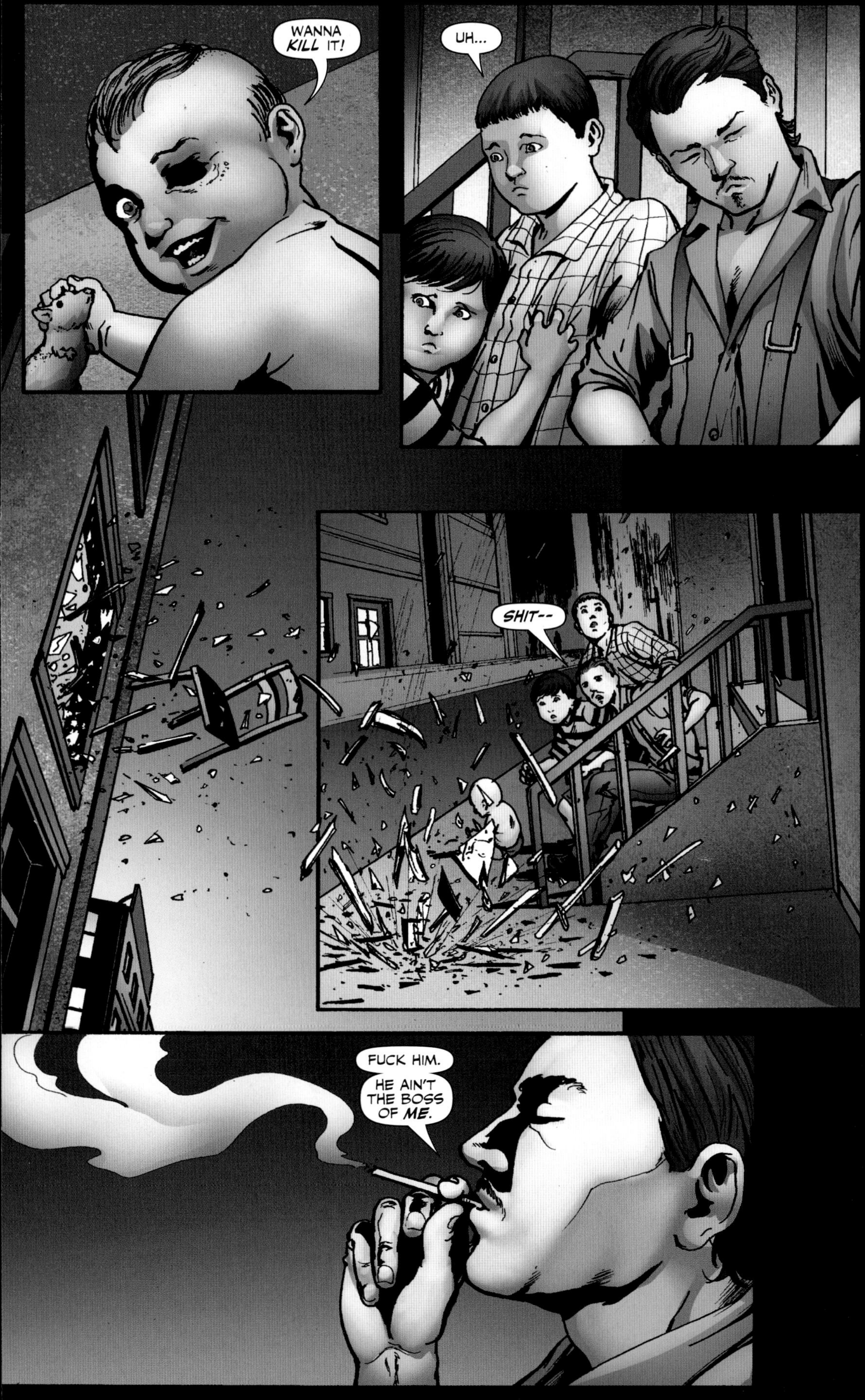
WANNA KILL IT!
UH...
SHIT--
FUCK HIM.
HE AIN'T THE BOSS OF ME.

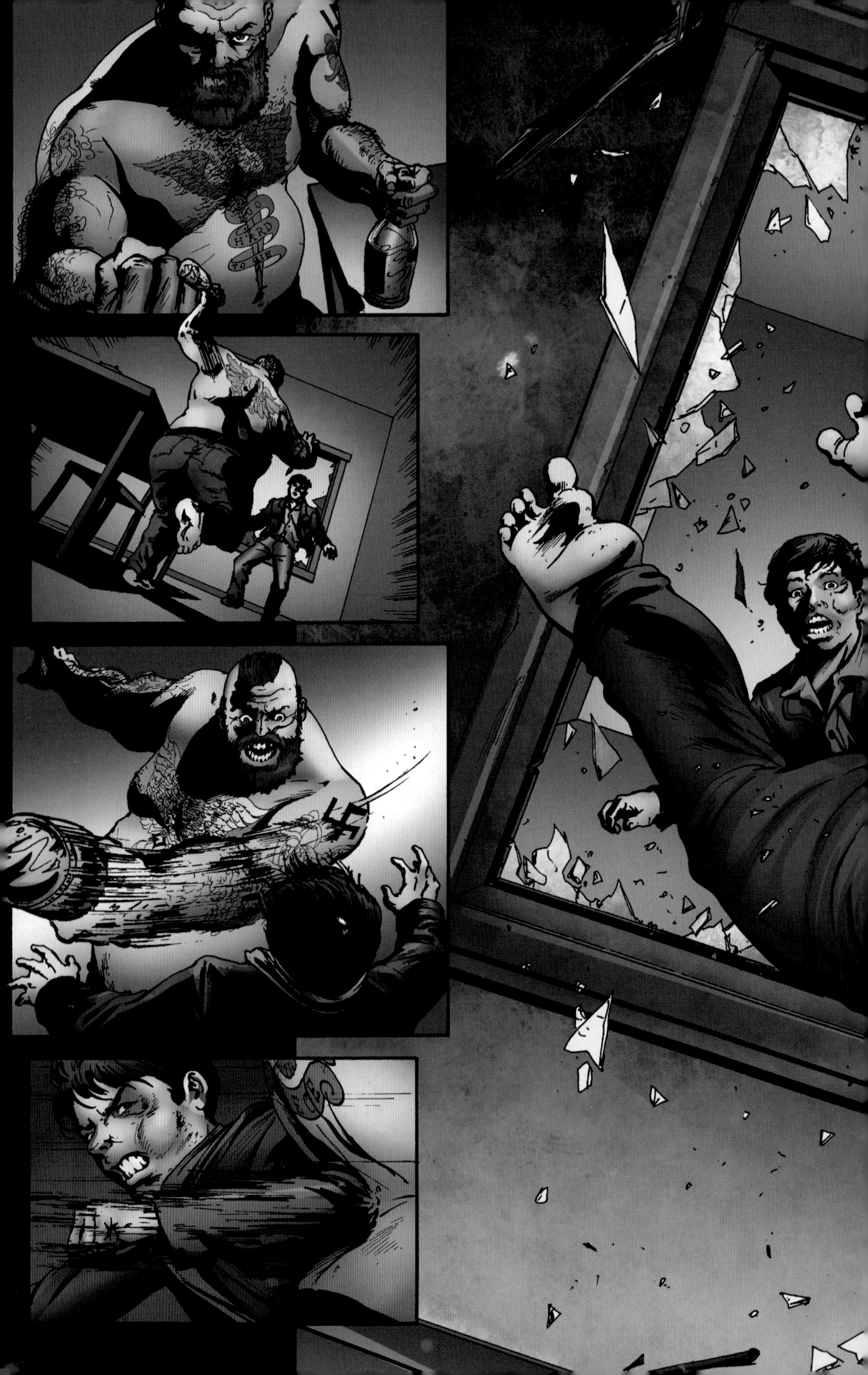
HARD
TO

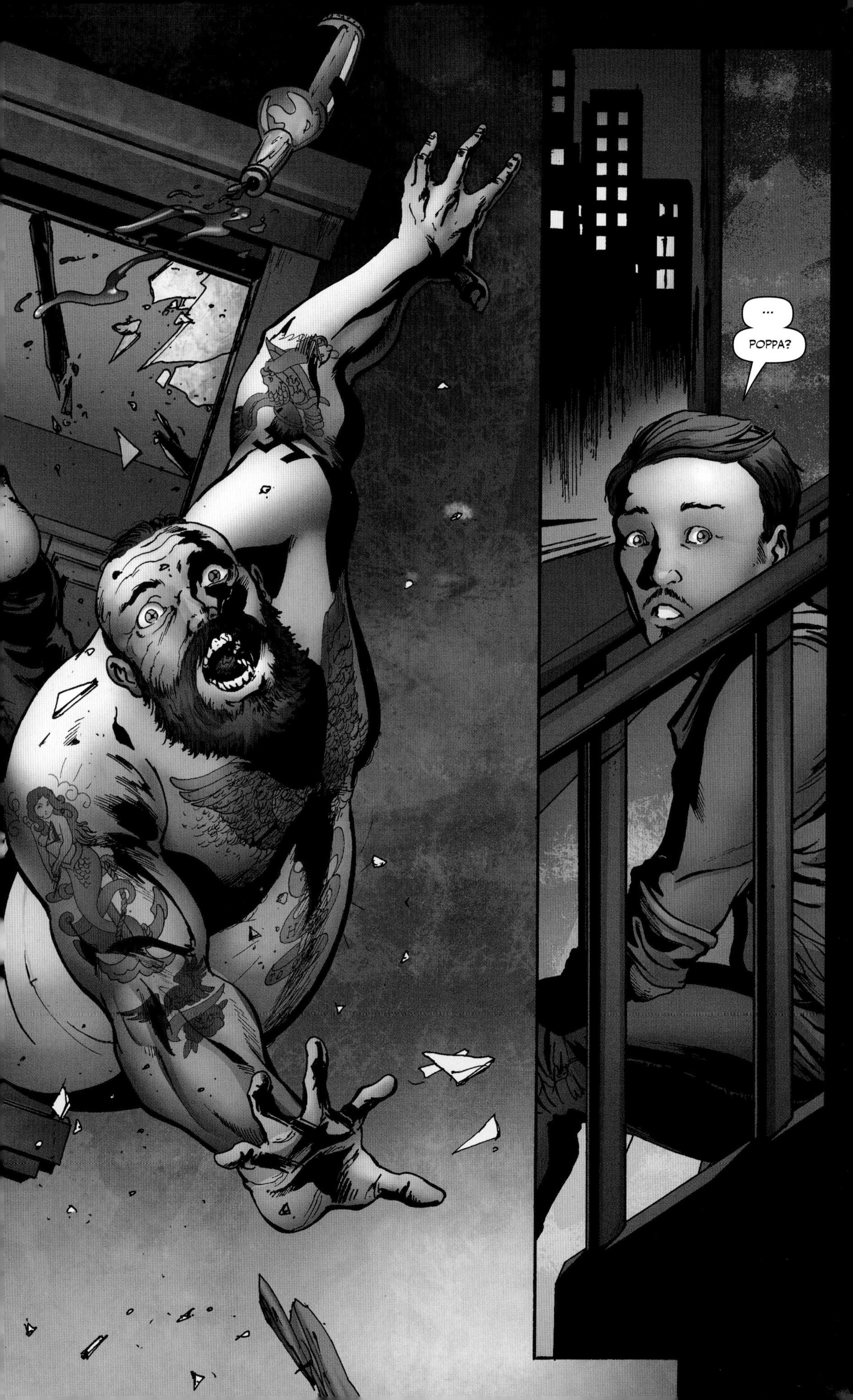
...
POPPA?

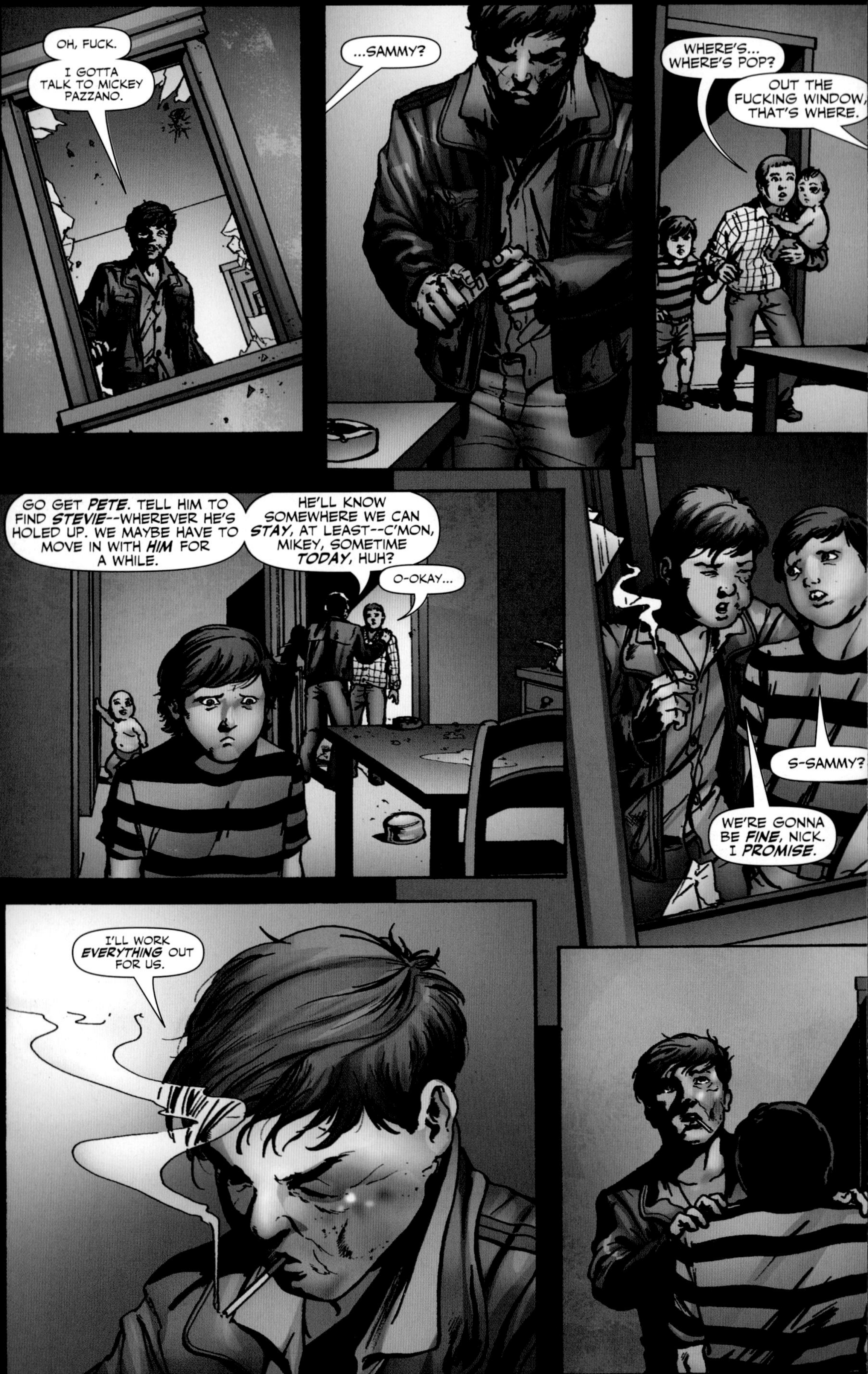
OH, FUCK.
I GOTTA TALK TO MICKEY PAZZANO.
...SAMMY?
WHERE'S... WHERE'S POP?
OUT THE FUCKING WINDOW, THAT'S WHERE.
GO GET PETE. TELL HIM TO FIND STEVIE--WHEREVER HE'S HOLED UP. WE MAYBE HAVE TO MOVE IN WITH HIM FOR A WHILE.
HE'LL KNOW SOMEWHERE WE CAN STAY, AT LEAST--C'MON, MIKEY, SOMETIME TODAY, HUH?
O-OKAY...
S-SAMMY?
WE'RE GONNA BE FINE, NICK. I PROMISE.
I'LL WORK EVERYTHING OUT FOR US.

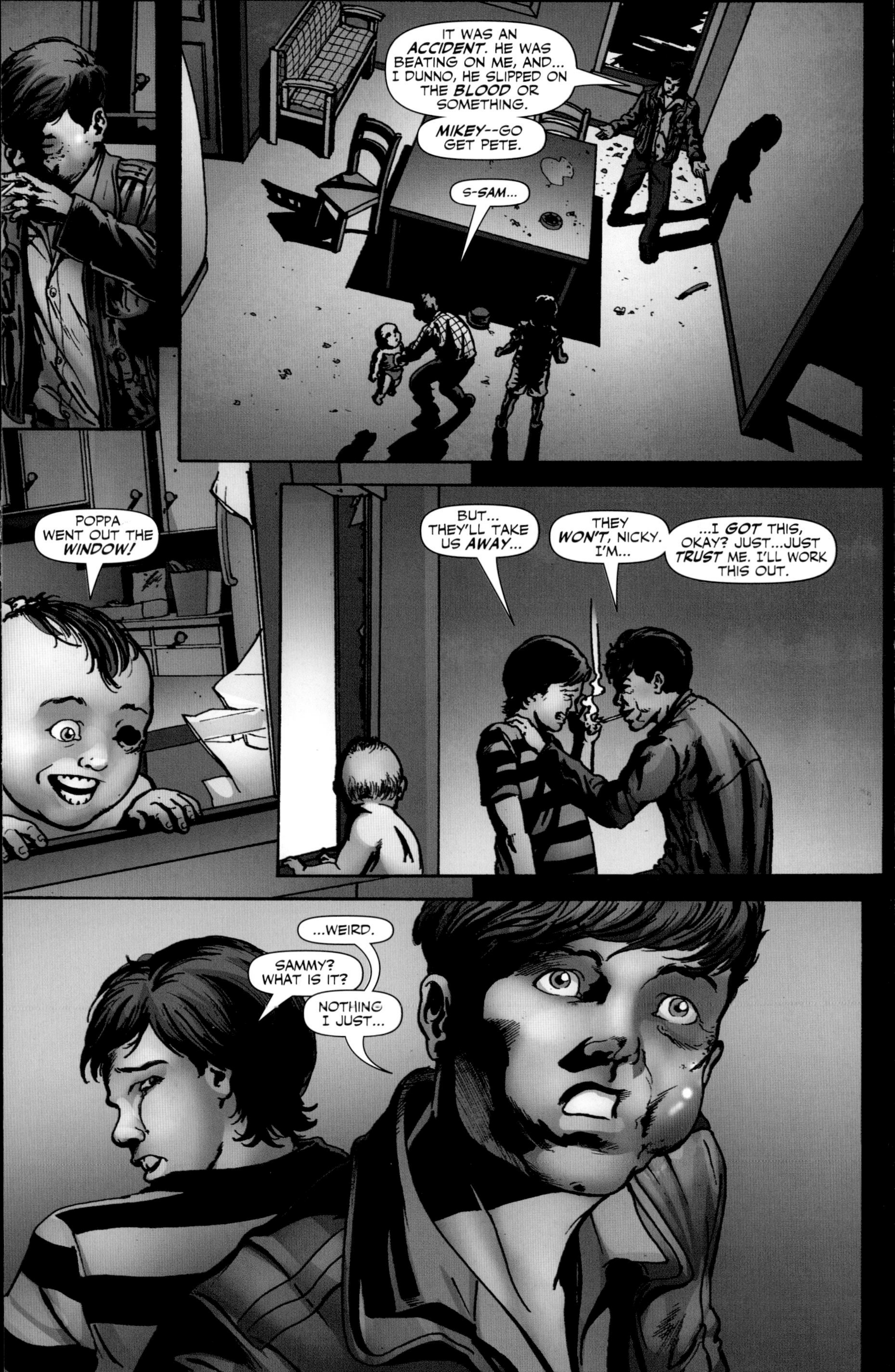
IT WAS AN ACCIDENT. HE WAS BEATING ON ME, AND... I DUNNO, HE SLIPPED ON THE BLOOD OR SOMETHING.
MIKEY--GO GET PETE.
S-SAM...
POPPA WENT OUT THE WINDOW!
BUT... THEY'LL TAKE US AWAY...
THEY WON'T, NICKY. I'M...
...I GOT THIS, OKAY? JUST...JUST TRUST ME. I'LL WORK THIS OUT.
...WEIRD.
SAMMY? WHAT IS IT?
NOTHING I JUST...

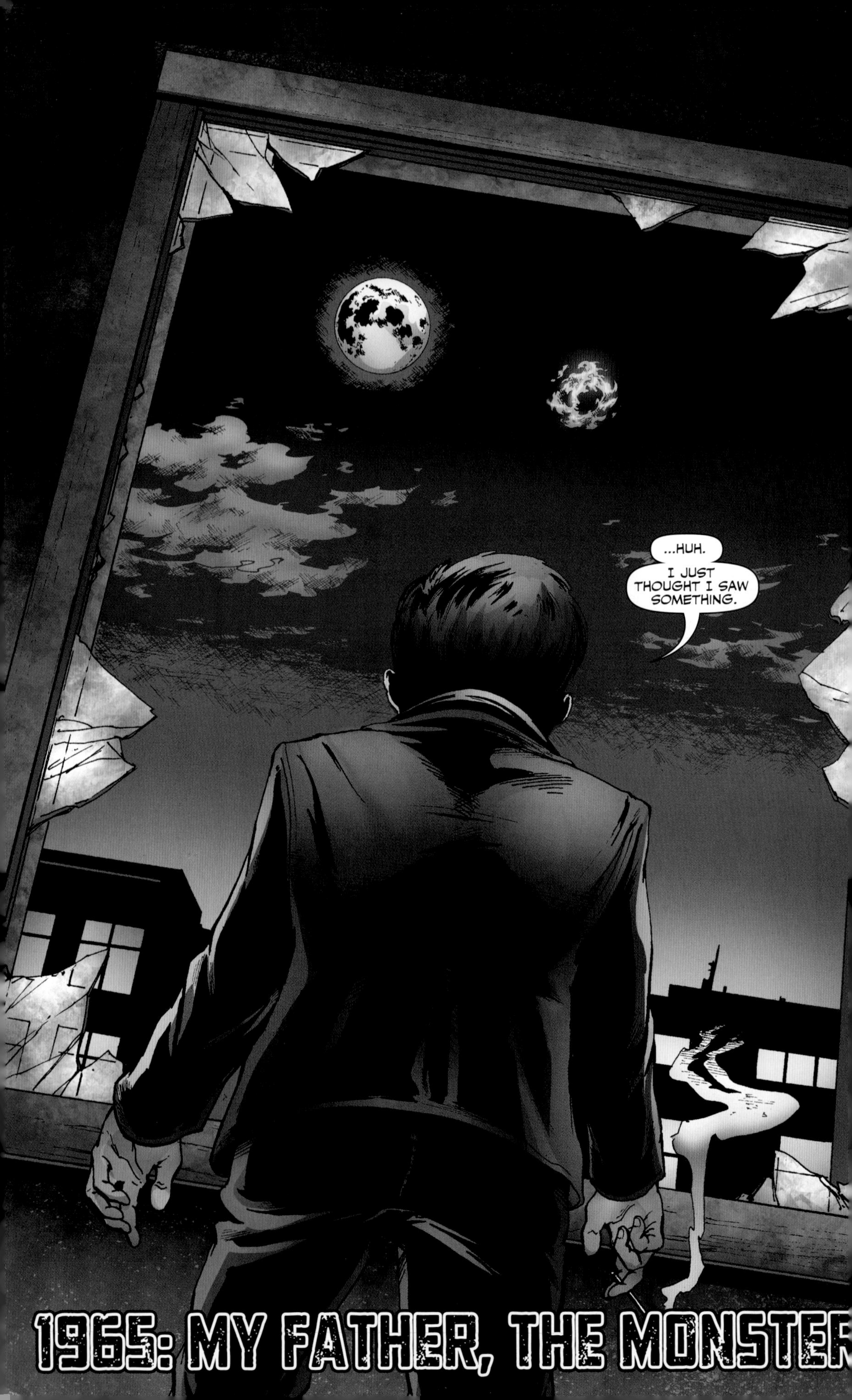
...HUH.
I JUST THOUGHT I SAW SOMETHING.
1965: MY FATHER, THE MONSTER

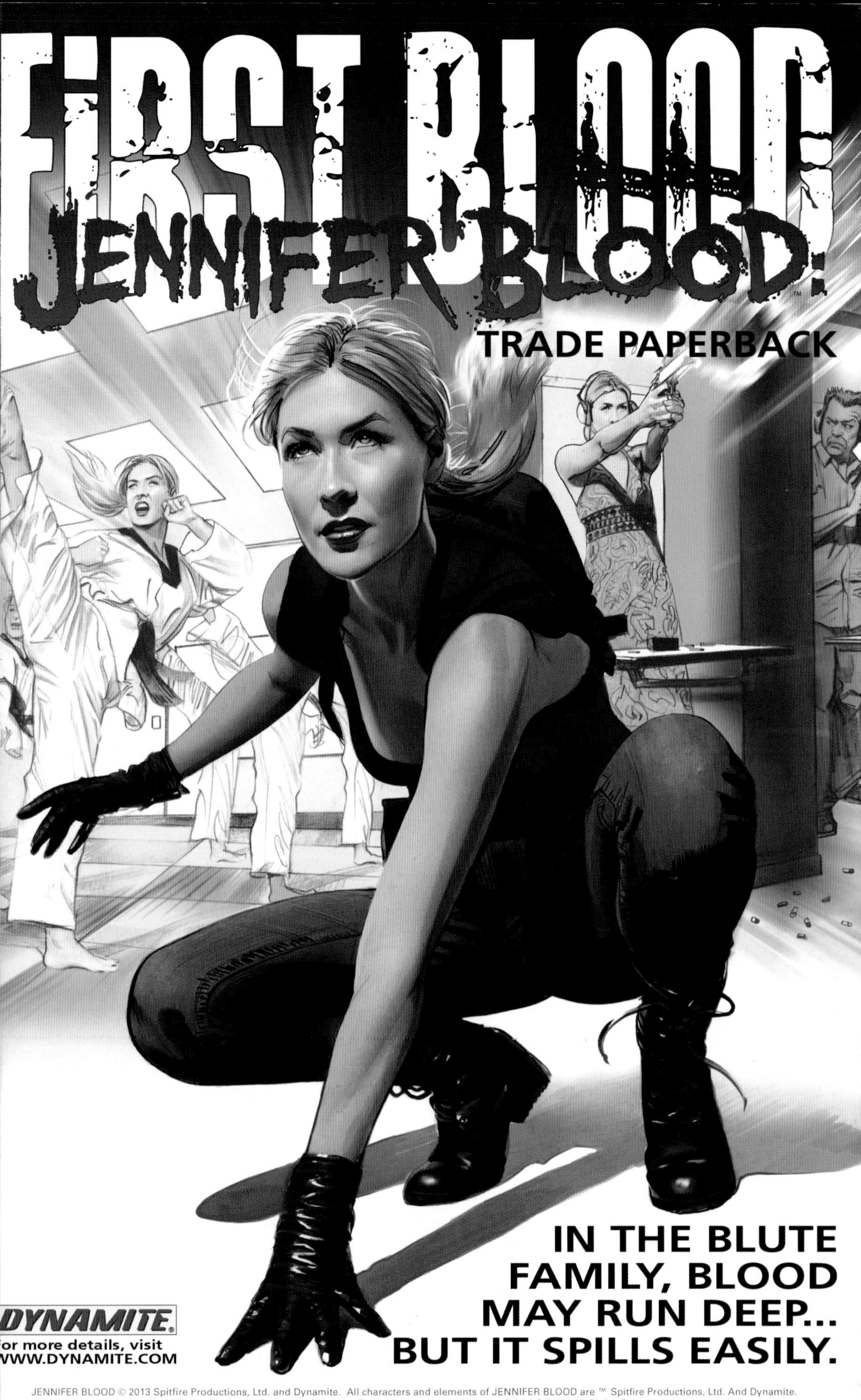
FIRST BLOOD
JENNIFER BLOOD:
TRADE PAPERBACK
IN THE BLUTE FAMILY, BLOOD MAY RUN DEEP... BUT IT SPILLS EASILY.
DYNAMITE
or more details, visit
WWW.DYNAMITE.COM

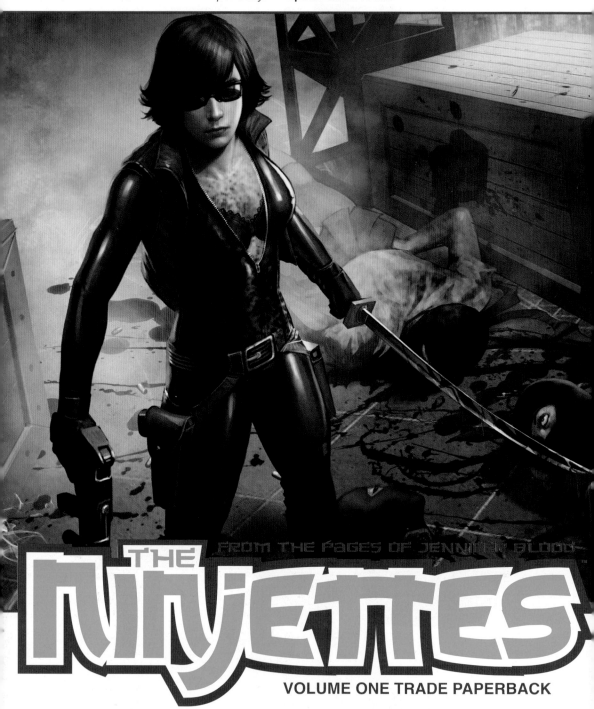

THE NINJETTES

FROM THE PAGES OF JENNIFER BLOOD

VOLUME ONE TRADE PAPERBACK

Tearing out of the pages of **GARTH ENNIS' JENNIFER BLOOD** comes **THE NINJETTES** – a searing four-color indictment of a society that turns blushing college girls into kill-hungry ninjas!

Collecting the complete, 6-issue mini series by **AL EWING** and **EMAN CASALLOS** along with all of the covers by Admira Wijaya, Johnny Desjardins & more, a writer's commentary for issue #1 by Al Ewing and sketches and designs by Eman Casallos!

DON'T MISS THESE GREAT COLLECTIONS FROM *NEW YORK TIMES* BEST-SELLING AUTHOR

GARTH ENNIS & DYNAMITE

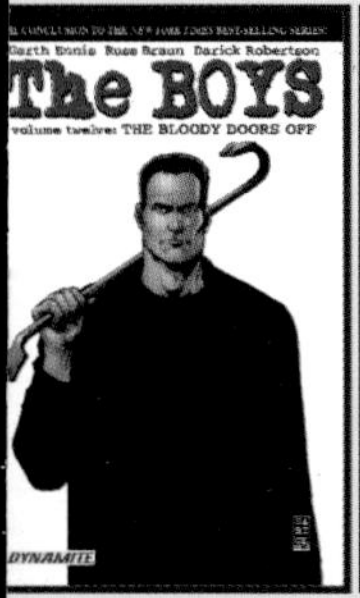
The BOYS
Garth Ennis Russ Braun Darick Robertson
volume twelve: THE BLOODY DOORS OFF
DYNAMITE
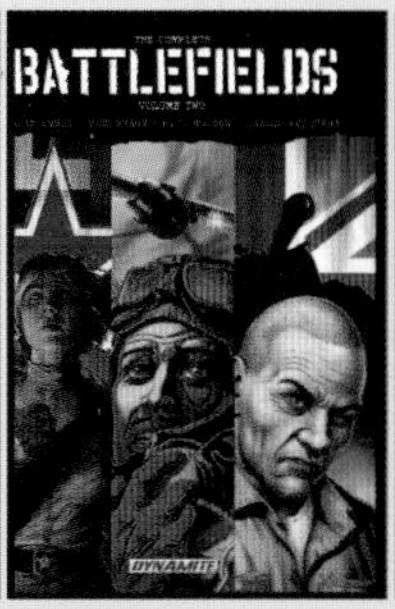
BATTLEFIELDS
DYNAMITE
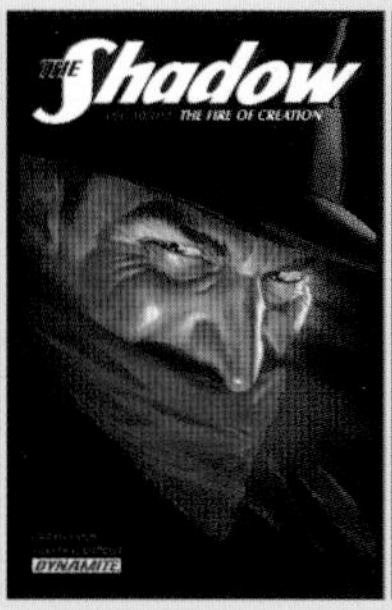
The Shadow
THE FIRE OF CREATION
DYNAMITE
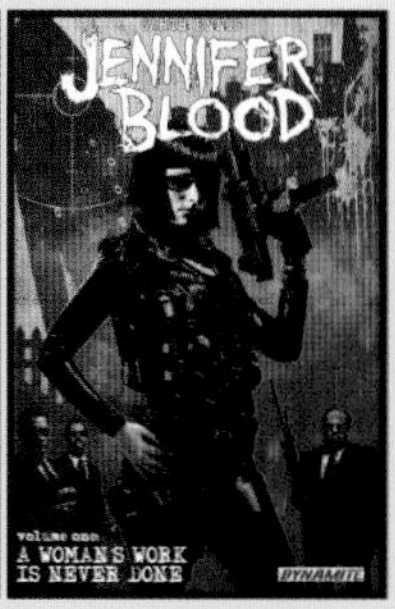
JENNIFER BLOOD
volume one
A WOMAN'S WORK IS NEVER DONE
DYNAMITE
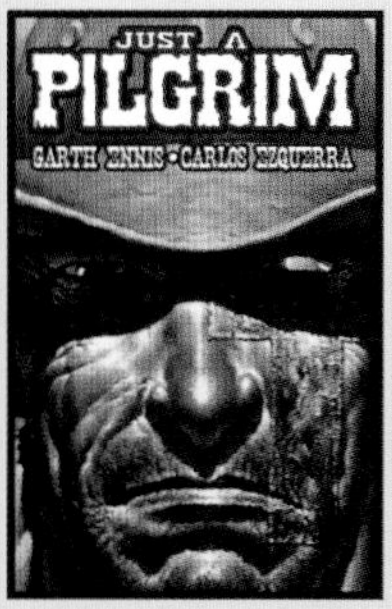
JUST A
PILGRIM
GARTH ENNIS • CARLOS EZQUERRA
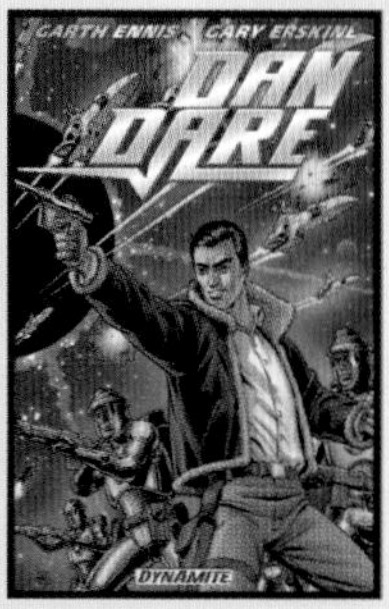
GARTH ENNIS GARY ERSKINE
DAN DARE
DYNAMITE

THE BOYS DEFINITIVE EDITION VOL. 1 HARDCOVER..........(SOLD OUT!)..........1933305800
- Collects issues 1-14 of the hit series by Ennis and Robertson

THE BOYS DEFINITIVE EDITION VOL. 2 HARDCOVER..........1606900730
- Collects issues 15-30 of the hit series by Ennis and Robertson

THE BOYS DEFINITIVE EDITION VOL. 3 HARDCOVER..........1606901656
- Collects issues 31-38 plus the 6-issue Herogasm mini-series

THE BOYS DEFINITIVE EDITION VOL. 4 HARDCOVER..........1606903403
- Collects issues 39-47 plus the 6-issue Highland Laddie mini-series

THE BOYS VOL. 1: THE NAME OF THE GAME..........1933305738
- Collects issues 1-6 by Ennis & Robertson

THE BOYS VOL. 2: GET SOME..........1933305681
- Collects issues 7-14 by Ennis, Robertson and Snejbjerg

THE BOYS VOL. 3: GOOD FOR THE SOUL..........1933305924
- Collects issues 15-22 by Ennis & Robertson

THE BOYS VOL. 4: WE GOTTA GO NOW..........1606900358
- Collects issues 23-30 by Ennis, Robertson and Higgins

THE BOYS VOL. 5: HEROGASM..........160690082X
- Collects issues 1-6 of the hit mini-series by Ennis and McCrea

THE BOYS VOL. 6: THE SELF-PRESERVATION SOCIETY..........1606901257
- Collects issues 31-38 by Ennis, Robertson and Ezquerra

THE BOYS VOL. 7: THE INNOCENTS..........1606901508
- Collects issues 39-47 by Ennis, Robertson, Braun & McCrea

THE BOYS VOL. 8: HIGHLAND LADDIE..........1606902075
- Collects issues 1-6 by Ennis & McCrea

THE BOYS VOL. 9: THE BIG RIDE..........1606902202
- Collects issues 48-59 by Ennis, Braun & McCrea

THE BOYS VOL. 10: BUTCHER, BAKER, CANDLESTICKMAKER..........1606902644
- Collects issues 1-6 of the hit mini series by Ennis and Robertson

THE BOYS VOL. 11: OVER THE HILL WITH THE SWORDS OF A THOUSAND MEN..........1606903411
- Collects issues 60-65 by Ennis, Braun & McCrea

THE BOYS VOL. 12: THE BLOODY DOORS OFF..........160690373X
- Collects issues 66-72 by Ennis, Braun & Robertson

THE COMPLETE BATTLEFIELDS VOL. 1 TRADE PAPERBACK..........1606902555
- Collects the first 3 Battlefields mini-series by Ennis, Braun, Snejbjerg and Ezquerra

THE COMPLETE BATTLEFIELDS VOL. 2 HARDCOVER..........1606902229
- Collects the final 3 Battlefields mini-series by Ennis, Braun, Holden and Ezquerra

BATTLEFIELDS VOL. 1: THE NIGHT WITCHES..........1606900285
- Collects issues 1-3 by Ennis and Braun

BATTLEFIELDS VOL. 2: DEAR BILLY..........1606900579
- Collects issues 1-3 by Ennis and Snejbjerg

BATTLEFIELDS VOL. 3: THE TANKIES..........1606900757
- Collects issues 1-3 by Ennis and Ezquerra

BATTLEFIELDS VOL. 4: HAPPY VALLEY..........1606901281
- Collects issues 1-3 by Ennis and Holden

BATTLEFIELDS VOL. 5: THE FIREFLY AND HIS MAJESTY..........1606901451
- Collects issues 4-6 by Ennis and Ezquerra

BATTLEFIELDS VOL. 6: MOTHERLAND..........1606902210
- Collects issues 7-9 by Ennis and Braun

DAN DARE OMNIBUS TRADE PAPERBACK..........1606900404
- Collects issues 1-7 by Ennis and Erskine

JENNIFER BLOOD VOL. 1: A WOMAN'S WORK IS NEVER DONE..........160690261X
- Collecting issues 1-6 by Ennis, Batista, Marz and Baal

THE COMPLETE JUST A PILGRIM TRADE PAPERBACK..........1606900072
- Collects both mini-series by Ennis and Ezquerra together for the first time

SEVEN BROTHERS OMNIBUS VOL. 1..........160690258X
- Collects both mini series by Ennis, Raab, Kang and more

THE SHADOW VOL. 1: THE FIRE OF CREATION..........1606903616
- Collects issues 1-6 by Ennis and Campbell

DYNAMITE.COM | **FOLLOW US ON TWITTER: #DYNAMITECOMICS** | **LIKE US ON FACEBOOK: /DYNAMITECOMICS**

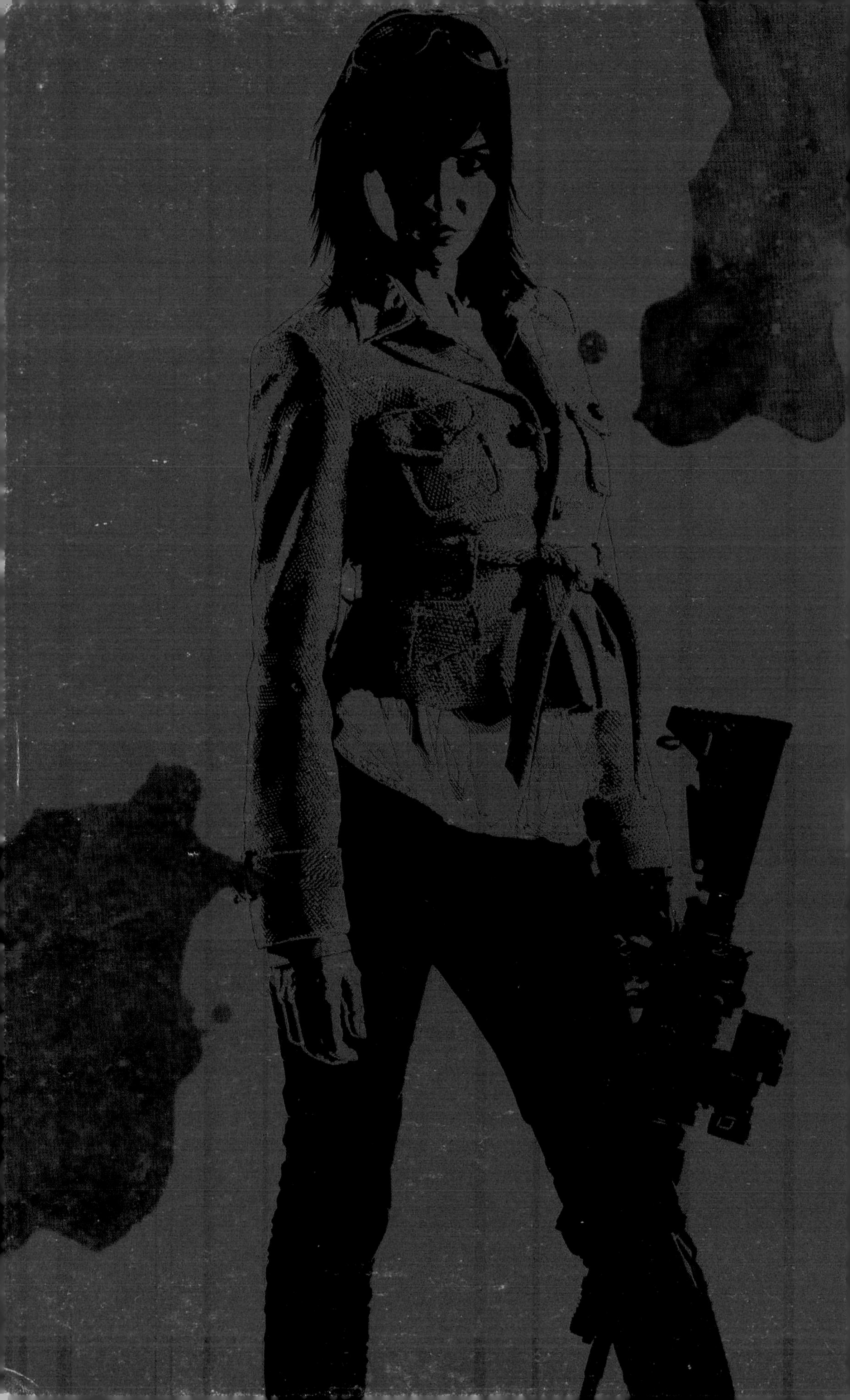